[kra_]
[koa_]

[dawn_of_x]

X-MEN BY JONATHAN HICKMAN VOL. 1. Contains material originally published in magazine form as X-MEN (2019) #1-6 and INCOMING (2019) #1. First printing 2020. ISBN 978-1-302-91981-8. Published by MARVEL WORLDWIDE, INC., a subsidiary of MARVEL ENTERTAINMENT, LLC. OFFICE OF PUBLICATION: 1290 Avenue of the Americas, New York, NY 10104. © 2020 MARVEL No similarity between any of the names, characters, persons, and/or institutions in this magazine with those of any living or dead person or institution is intended, and any such similarity which may exist is purely coincidental. **Printed in the U.S.A.** KEVIN FEIGE, Chief Creative Officer; DAN BUCKLEY, President, Marvel Entertainment; JOHN NEE, Publisher; JOE QUESADA, EVP & Creative Director; TOM BREVOORT, SVP of Publishing; DAVID BOGART, Associate Publisher & SVP of Talent Affairs; Publishing & Partnership; DAVID GABRIEL, VP of Print & Digital Publishing; JEFF YOUNGQUIST, VP of Production & Special Projects; DAN CARR, Executive Director of Publishing Technology; ALEX MORALES, Director of Publishing Operations; DAN EDINGTON, Managing Editor; SUSAN CRESPI, Production Manager; STAN LEE, Chairman Emeritus. For information regarding advertising in Marvel Comics or on Marvel.com, please contact Vit DeBellis, Custom Solutions & Integrated Advertising Manager, at vdebellis@marvel.com. For Marvel subscription inquiries, please call 888-511-5480. **Manufactured between 2/14/2020 and 3/17/2020 by LSC COMMUNICATIONS INC., KENDALLVILLE, IN, USA.**

10 9 8 7 6 5 4 3 2 1

Vol. 1

Writer: Jonathan Hickman
Pencilers: Leinil Francis Yu (#1-4), R.B. Silva (#5, *Incoming*) & Matteo Buffagni (#6)
Inkers   Gerry Alanguilan (#1-4), Leinil Francis Yu (#3-4), R.B. Silva (#5, *Incoming*) & Matteo Buffagni (#6)
Color Artists: Sunny Gho (#1-4, #6), Rain Beredo (#3) & Marte Gracia (#5, *Incoming*)
Letterer: VC's Clayton Cowles
Cover Art: Leinil Francis Yu & Sunny Gho

Head of X: Jonathan Hickman
Design: Tom Muller
Assistant Editor: Annalise Bissa
Editor: Jordan D. White

X-Men created by   Stan Lee & Jack Kirby

Collection Editor: Jennifer Grünwald
Assistant Managing Editor: Maia Loy
Assistant Managing Editor: Lisa Montalbano
Editor, Special Projects: Mark D. Beazley
VP Production & Special Projects: Jeff Youngquist
SVP Print, Sales & Marketing: David Gabriel
Editor in Chief: C.B. Cebulski

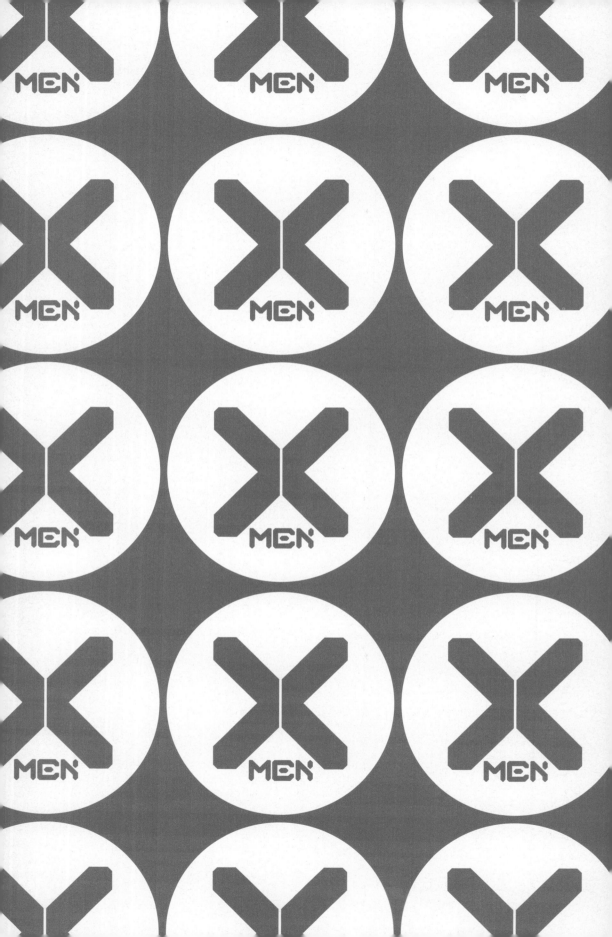

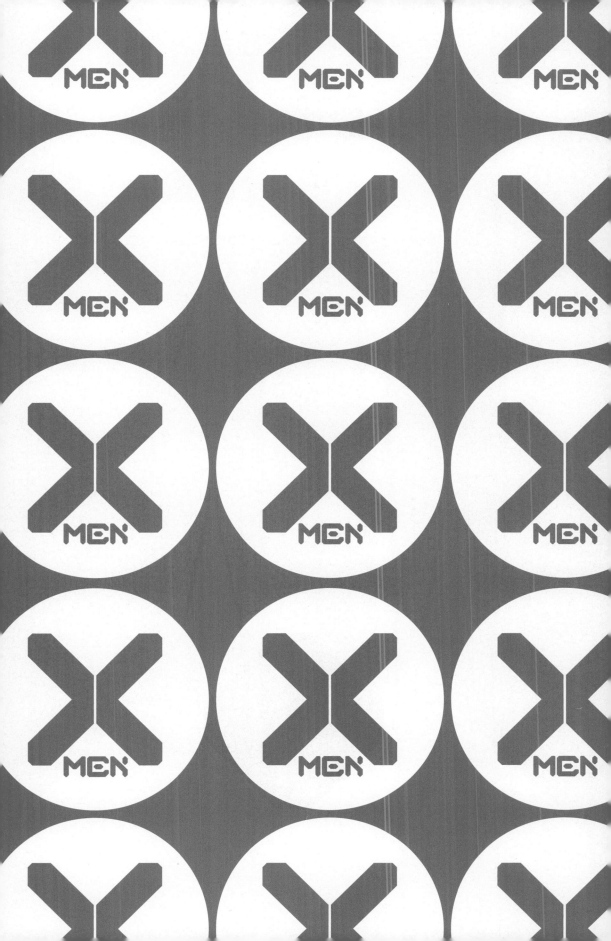

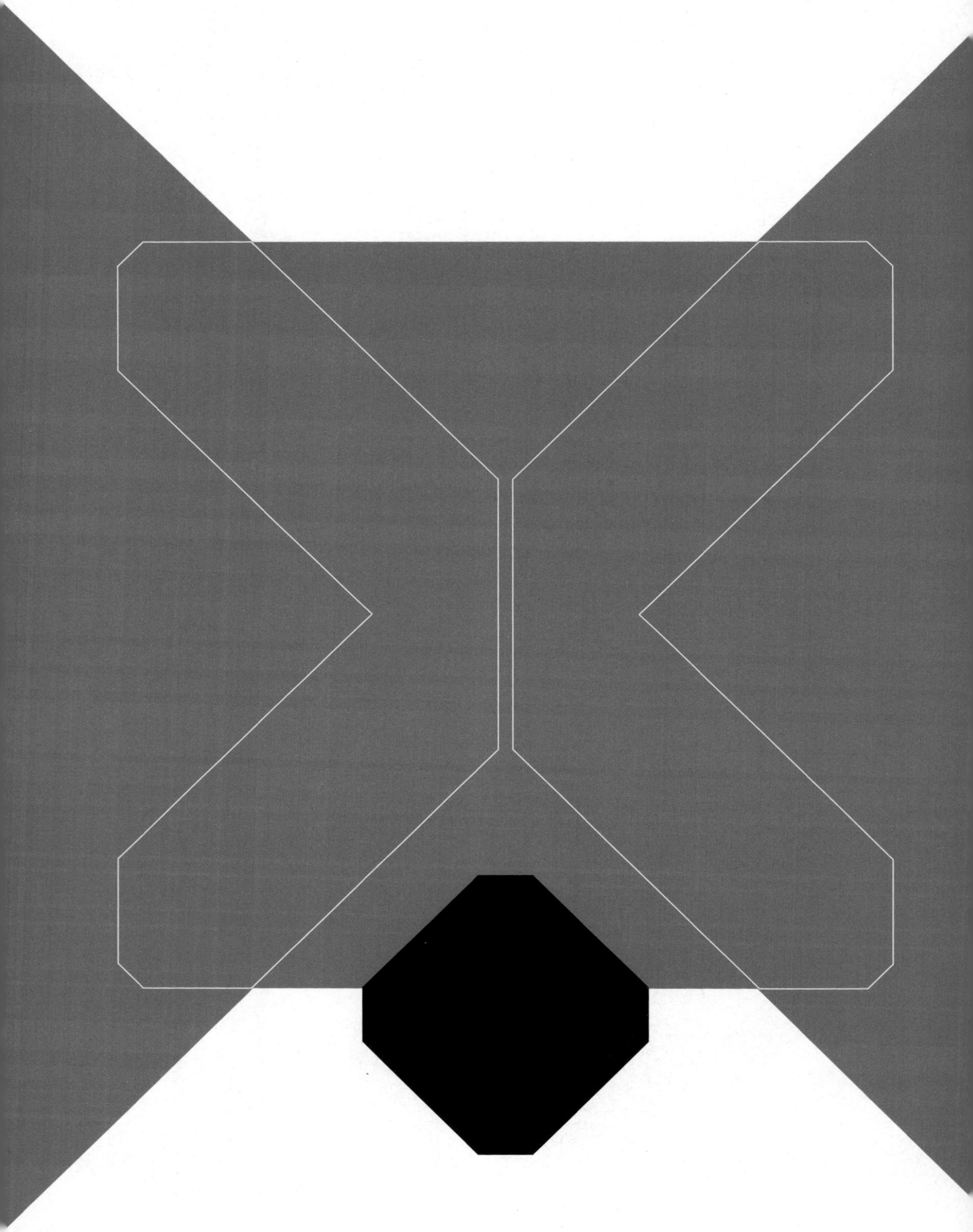

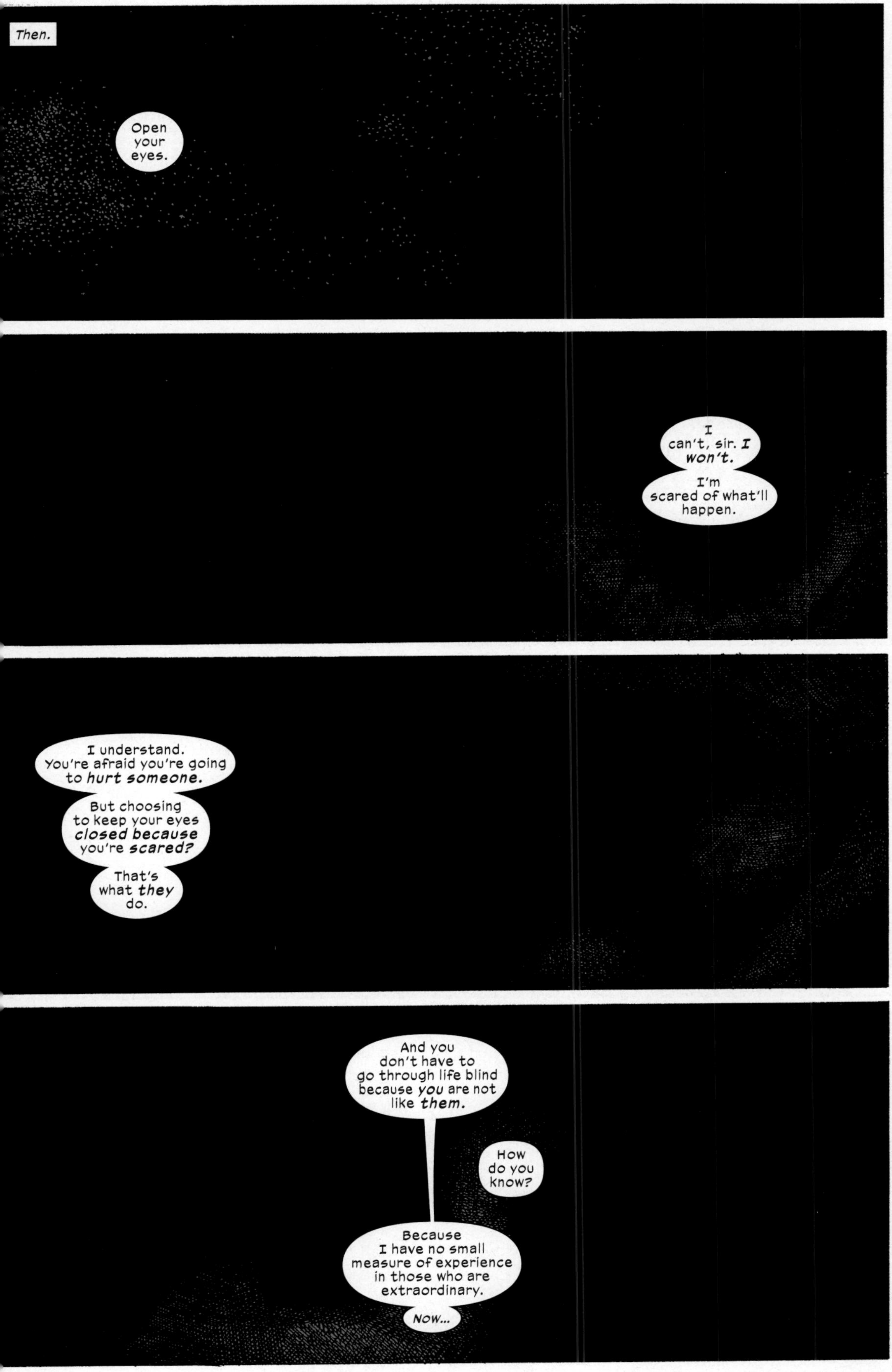
Then.
Open your eyes.
I can't, sir. I won't.
I'm scared of what'll happen.
I understand. You're afraid you're going to hurt someone.
But choosing to keep your eyes closed because you're scared?
That's what they do.
And you don't have to go through life blind because you are not like them.
How do you know?
Because I have no small measure of experience in those who are extraordinary.
Now...

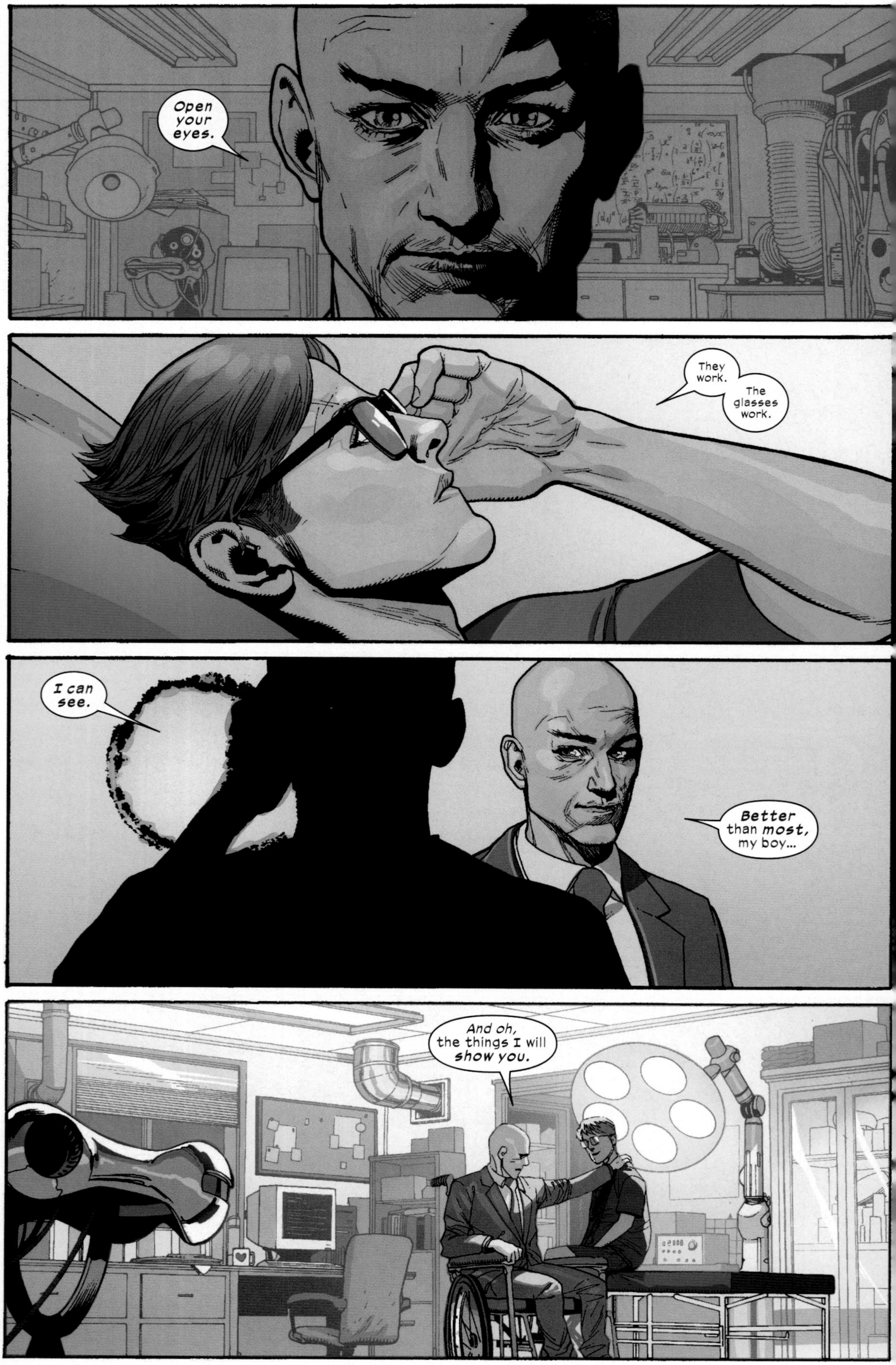
Open your eyes.
They work.
The glasses work.
I can see.
Better than most, my boy...
And oh, the things I will show you.

[kra_[0.1]
[koa_[0.1]

[kra_[0.X]
[koa_[0.X]

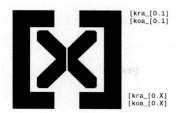

IT'S A BRAVE NEW WORLD

Mutants around the world are flocking to the island-nation of Krakoa for safety, security and to be part of the first mutant society.

Standing between that sacred land and the human world are the heroes of mutantdom, the X-MEN.

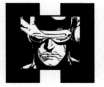

Cyclops

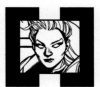

Storm

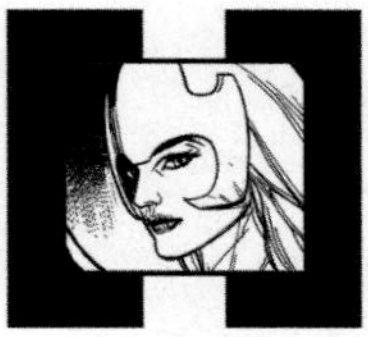

Polaris

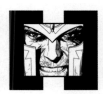

Magneto

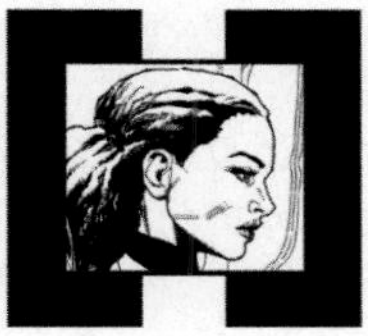

Dr. Reyes

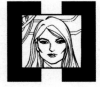

Jean Grey

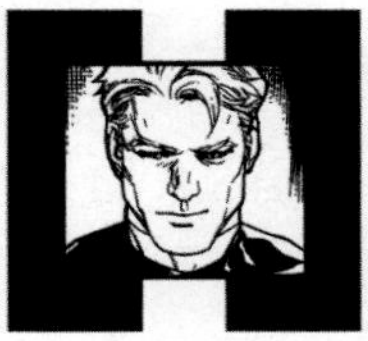

Havok

Vulcan

Wolverine

Cable

Prestige

Corsair

[kra_[0.1]...]
[koa_[0.1]...]

[A._New_World]

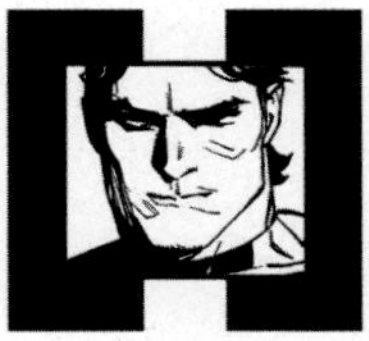

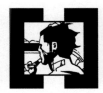

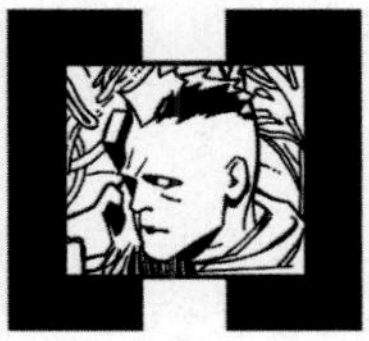

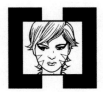

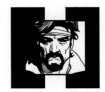

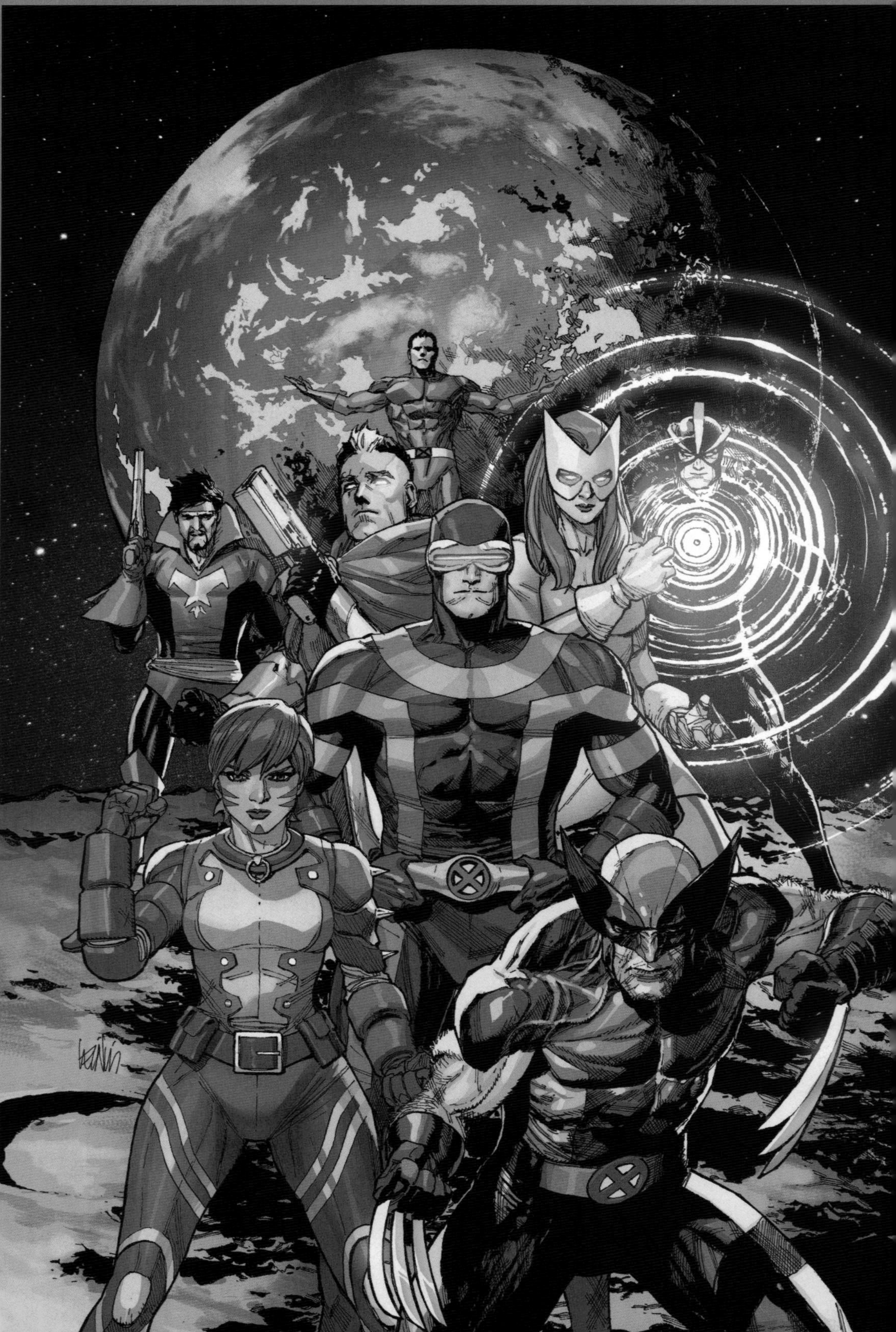

Pax Krakoa

1

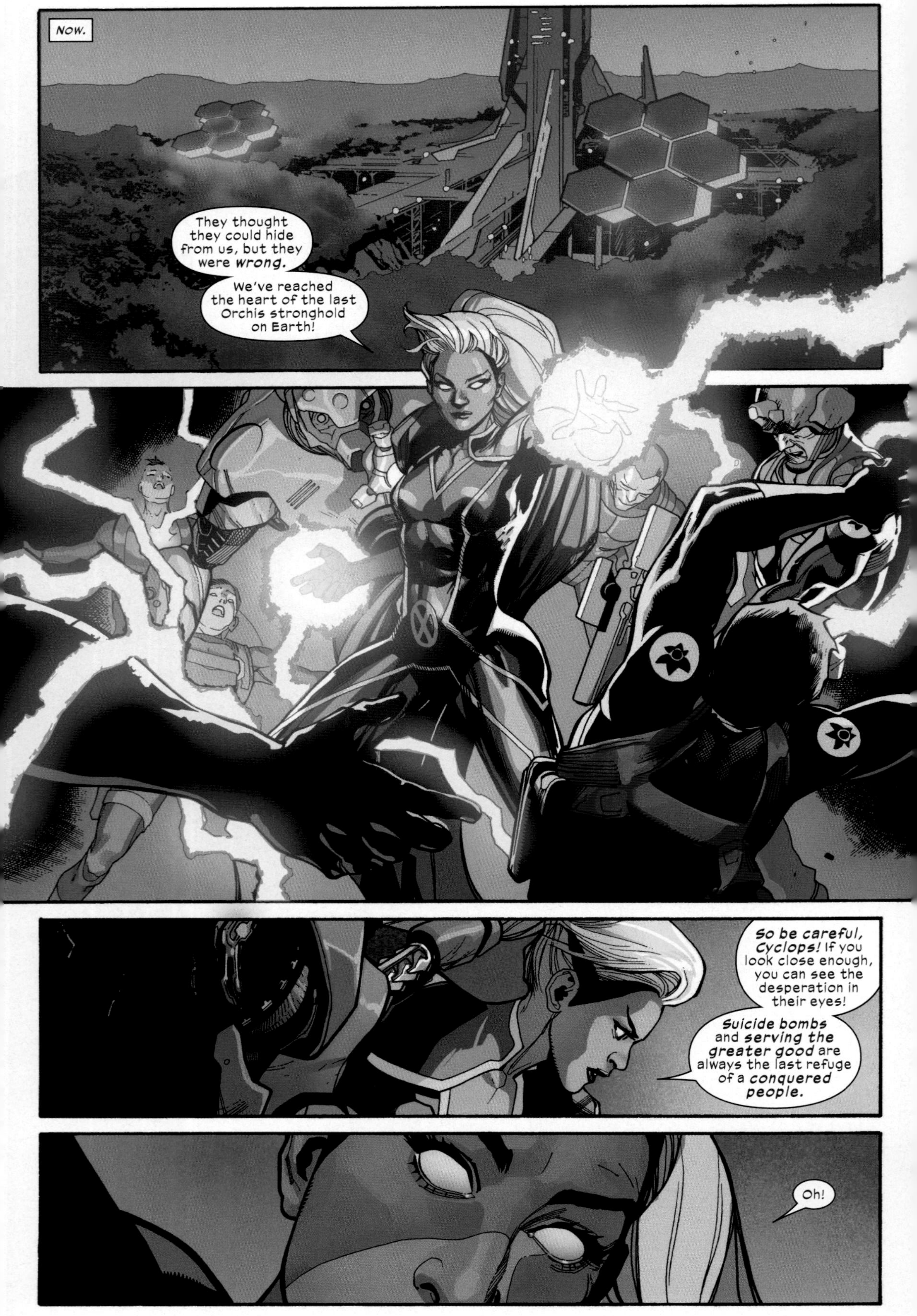
NOW.
They thought they could hide from us, but they were *wrong.*
We've reached the heart of the last Orchis stronghold on Earth!
So be careful, Cyclops! If you look close enough, you can see the desperation in their eyes!
Suicide bombs and *serving the greater good* are always the last refuge of a *conquered people.*
Oh!

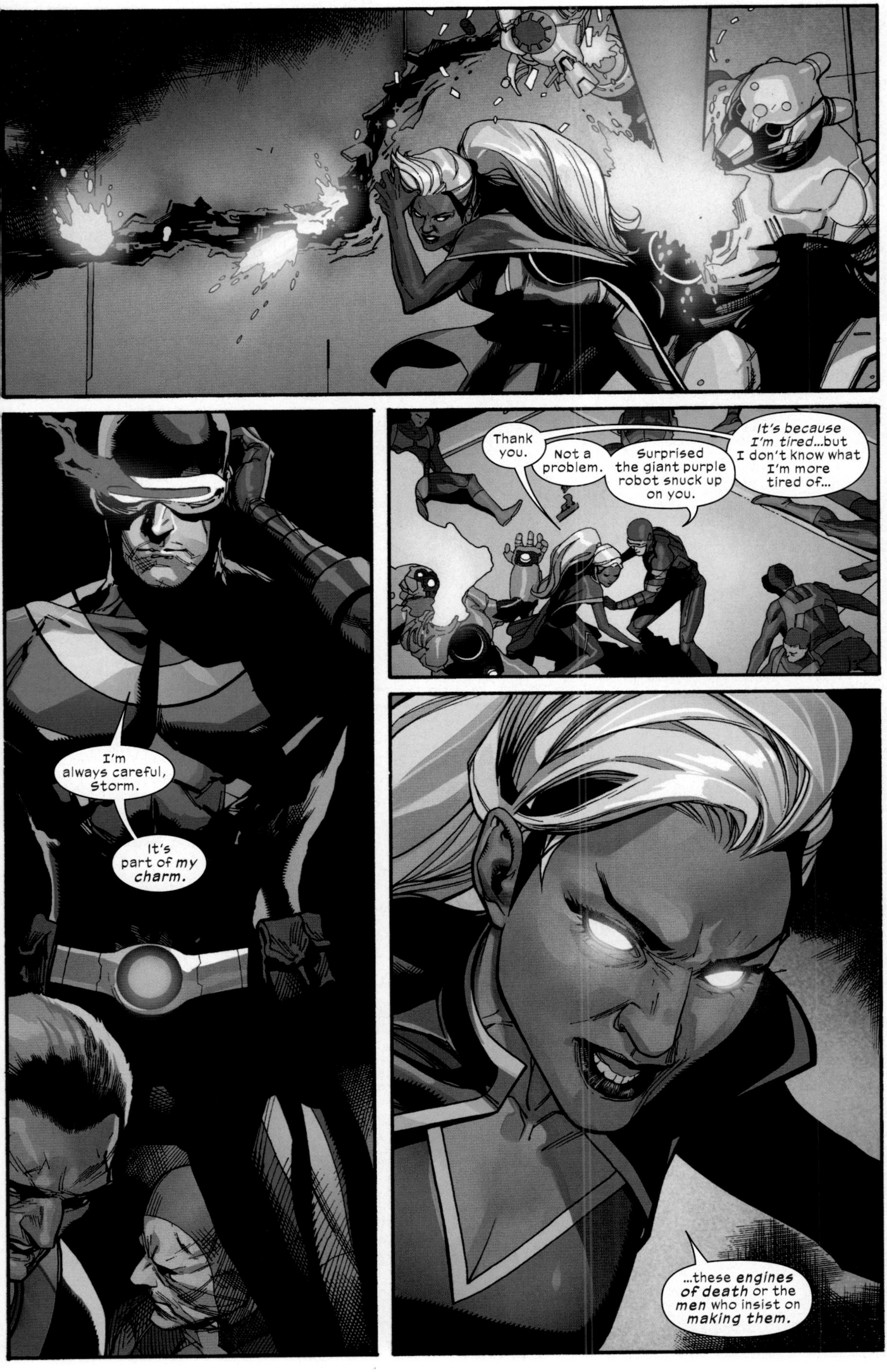

Thank you.
Not a problem.
Surprised the giant purple robot snuck up on you.
I'm always careful, Storm.
It's part of my *charm.*
It's because I'm tired...but I don't know what I'm more tired of...
...these *engines of death* or the *men* who insist on *making them.*

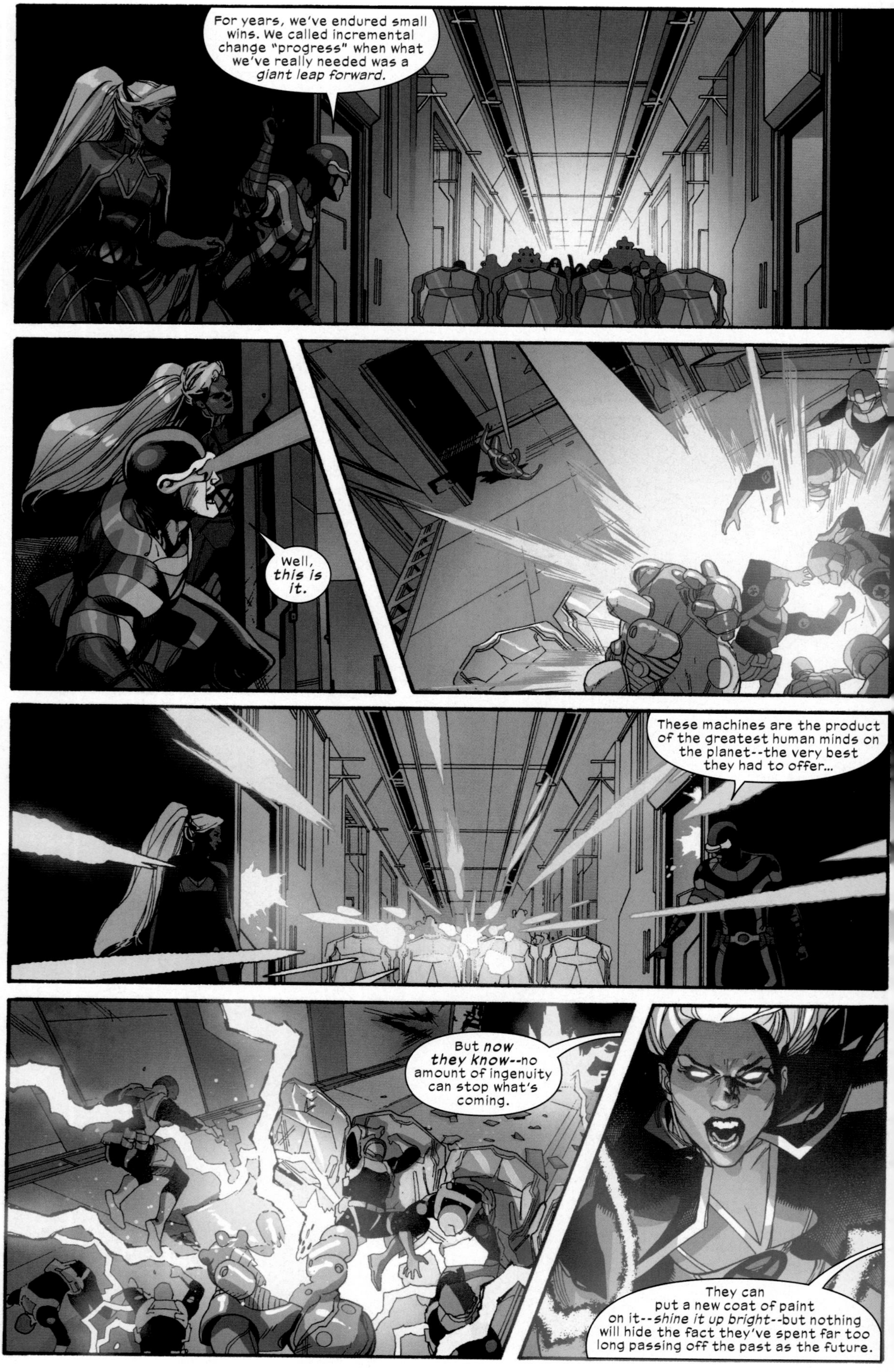
For years, we've endured small wins. We called incremental change "progress" when what we've really needed was a *giant leap forward.*
Well, *this is it.*
These machines are the product of the greatest human minds on the planet--the very best they had to offer...
But *now they know*--no amount of ingenuity can stop what's coming.
They can put a new coat of paint on it--*shine it up bright*--but nothing will hide the fact they've spent far too long passing off the past as the future.

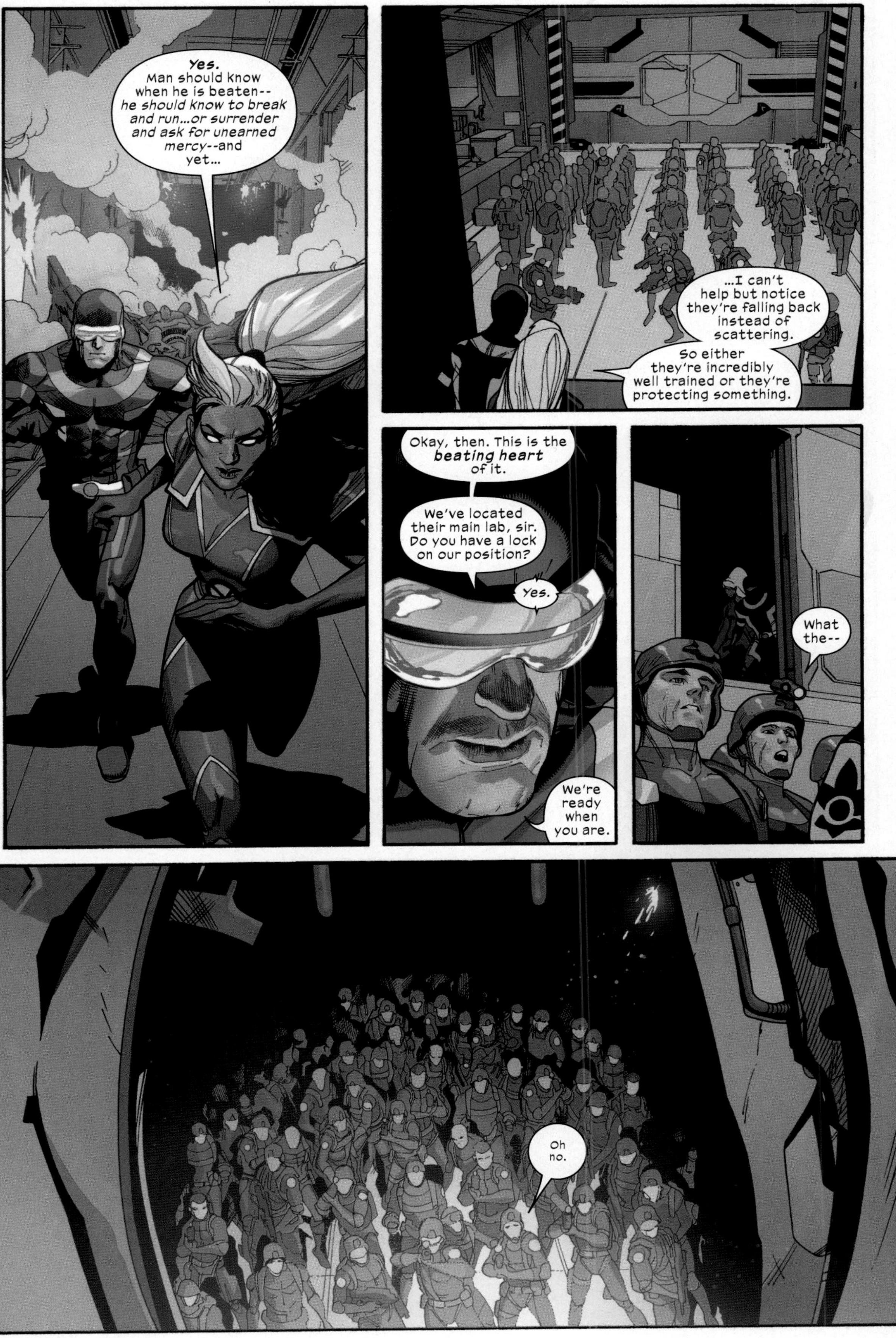
Yes. Man should know when he is beaten--he should know to break and run...or surrender and ask for unearned mercy--and yet...
...I can't help but notice they're falling back instead of scattering.
So either they're incredibly well trained or they're protecting something.
Okay, then. This is the beating heart of it.
We've located their main lab, sir. Do you have a lock on our position?
Yes.
We're ready when you are.
What the--
Oh no.

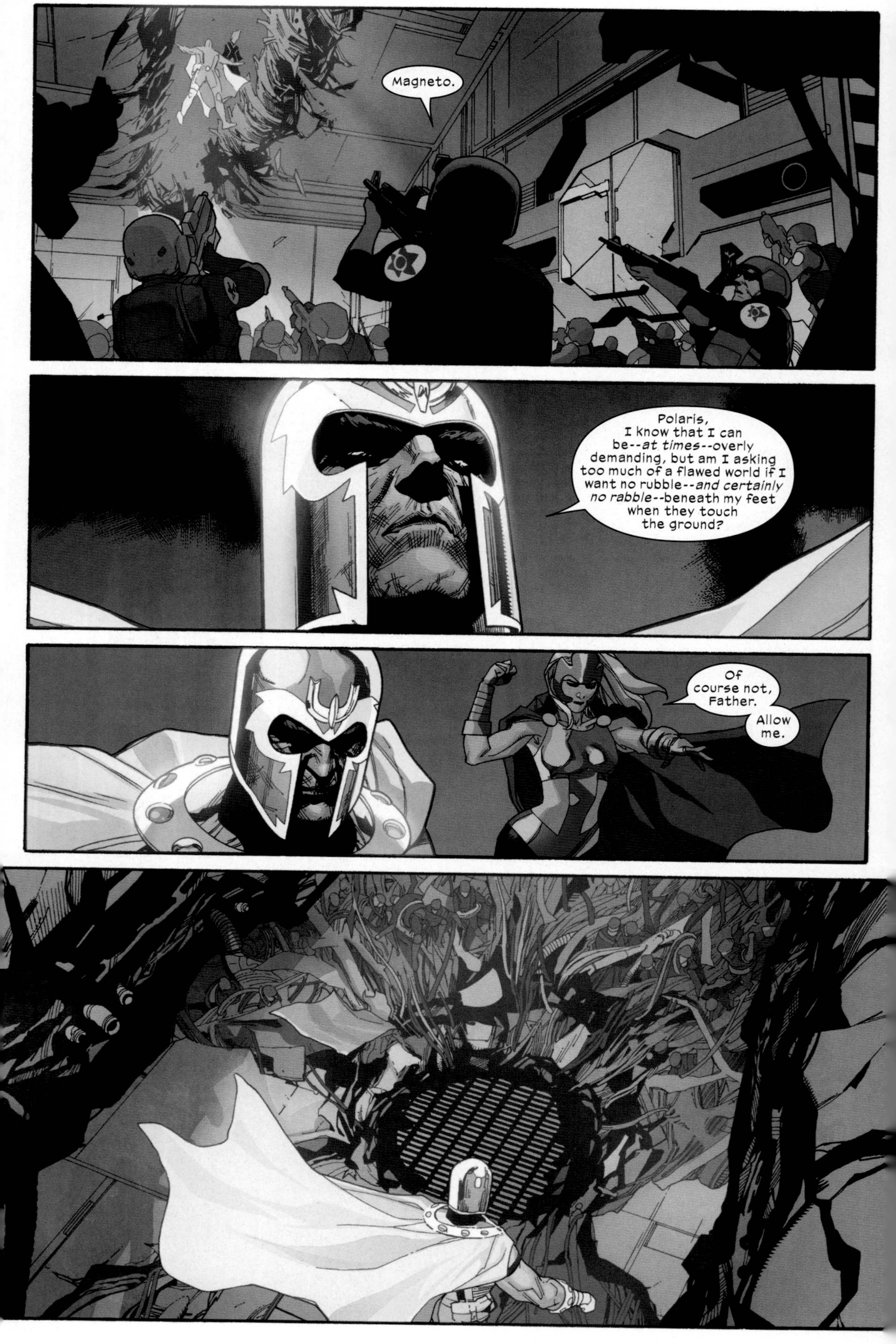
Magneto.
Polaris, I know that I can be--*at times*--overly demanding, but am I asking too much of a flawed world if I want no rubble--*and certainly no rabble*--beneath my feet when they touch the ground?
Of course not, Father.
Allow me.

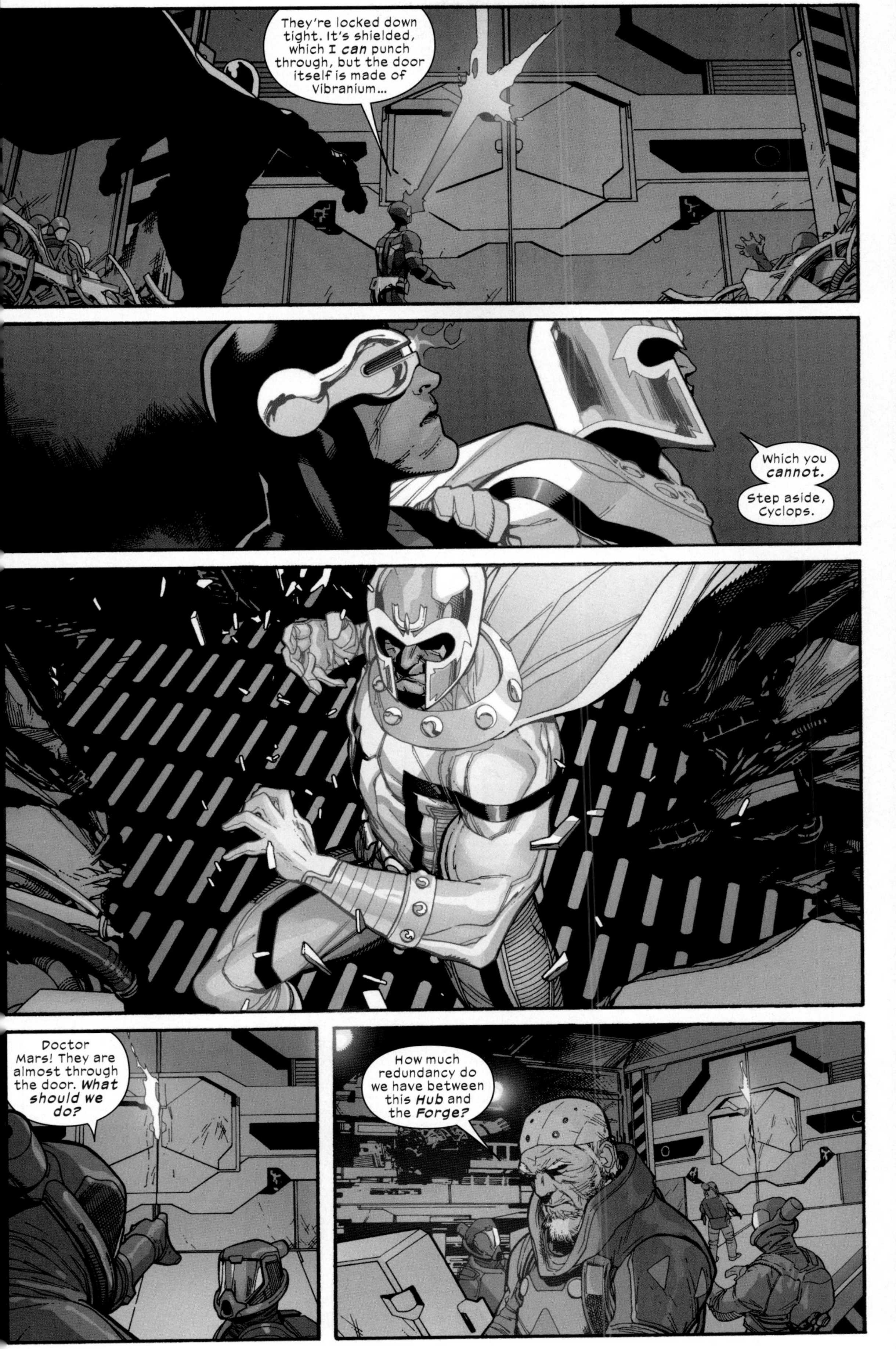
They're locked down tight. It's shielded, which I *can* punch through, but the door itself is made of Vibranium...
Which you *cannot.*
Step aside, Cyclops.
Doctor Mars! They are almost through the door. *What should we do?*
How much redundancy do we have between this *Hub* and the *Forge?*

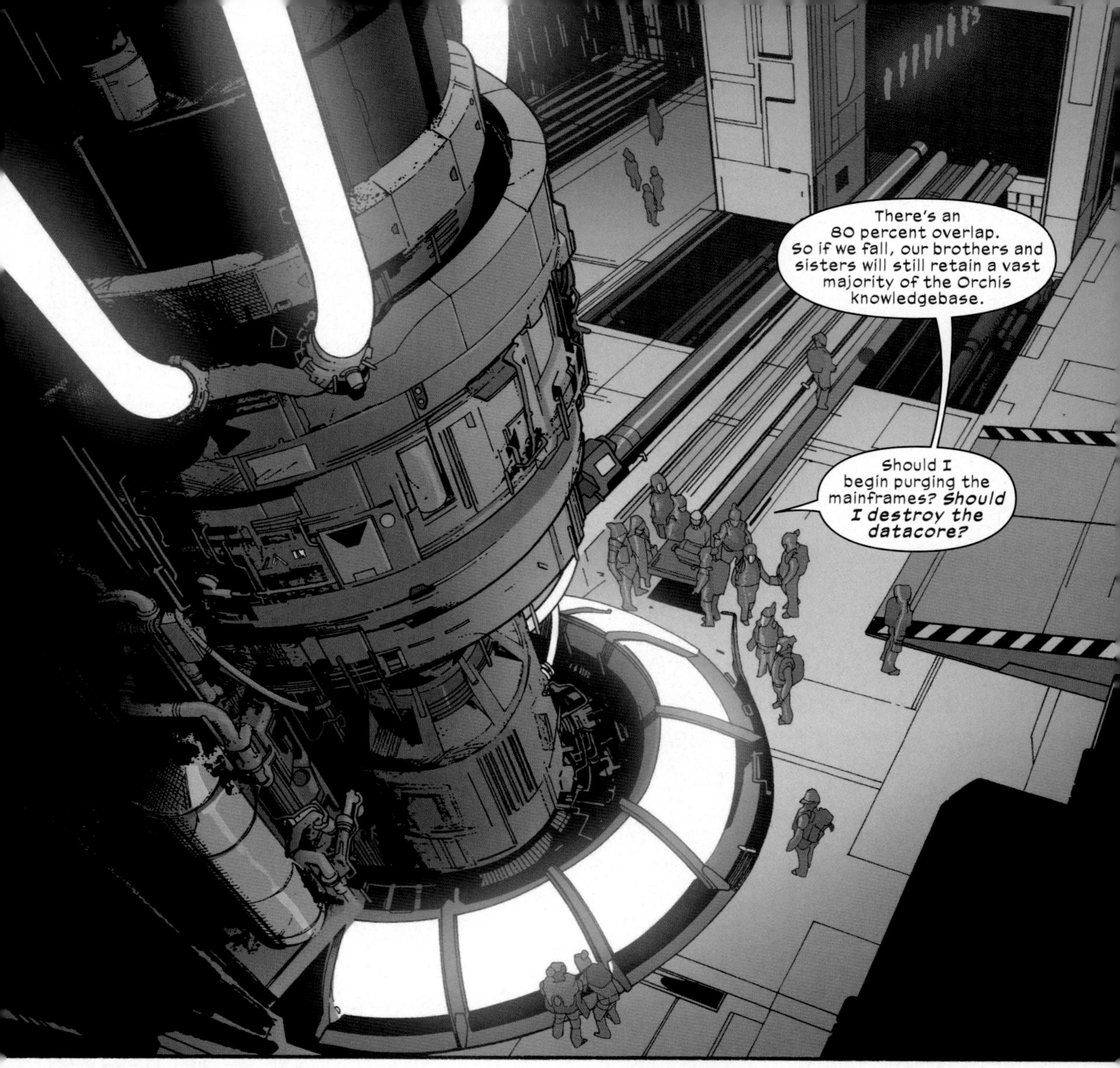
There's an 80 percent overlap. So if we fall, our brothers and sisters will still retain a vast majority of the Orchis knowledgebase.
Should I begin purging the mainframes? *Should I destroy the datacore?*

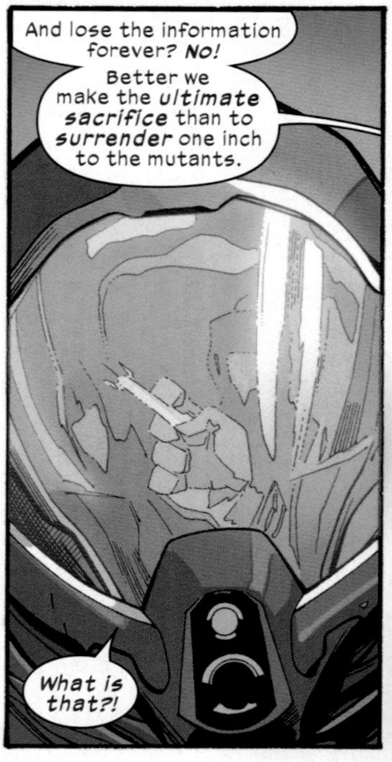
And lose the information forever? *No!*
Better we make the *ultimate sacrifice* than to *surrender* one inch to the mutants.
What is that?!

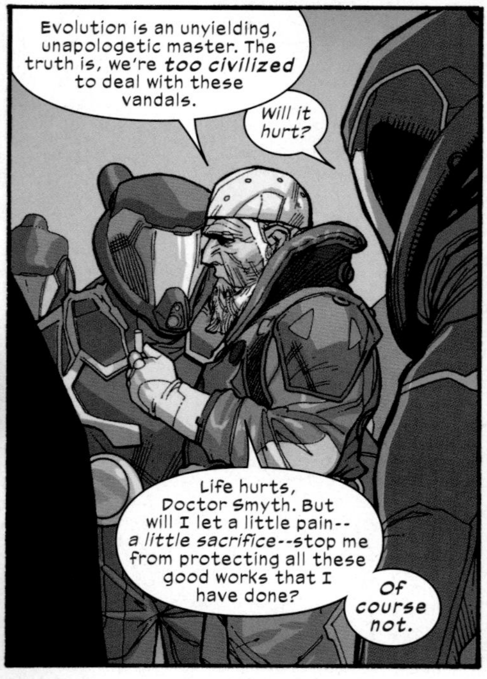
Evolution is an unyielding, unapologetic master. The truth is, we're *too civilized* to deal with these vandals.
Will it hurt?
Life hurts, Doctor Smyth. But will I let a little pain-- a *little sacrifice*--stop me from protecting all these good works that I have done?
Of course not.

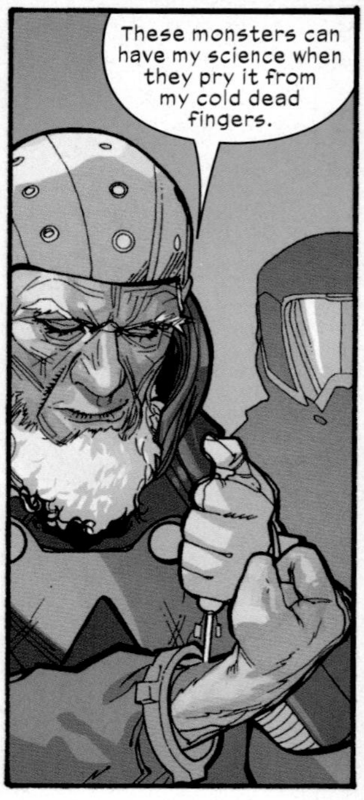
These monsters can have my science when they pry it from my cold dead fingers.

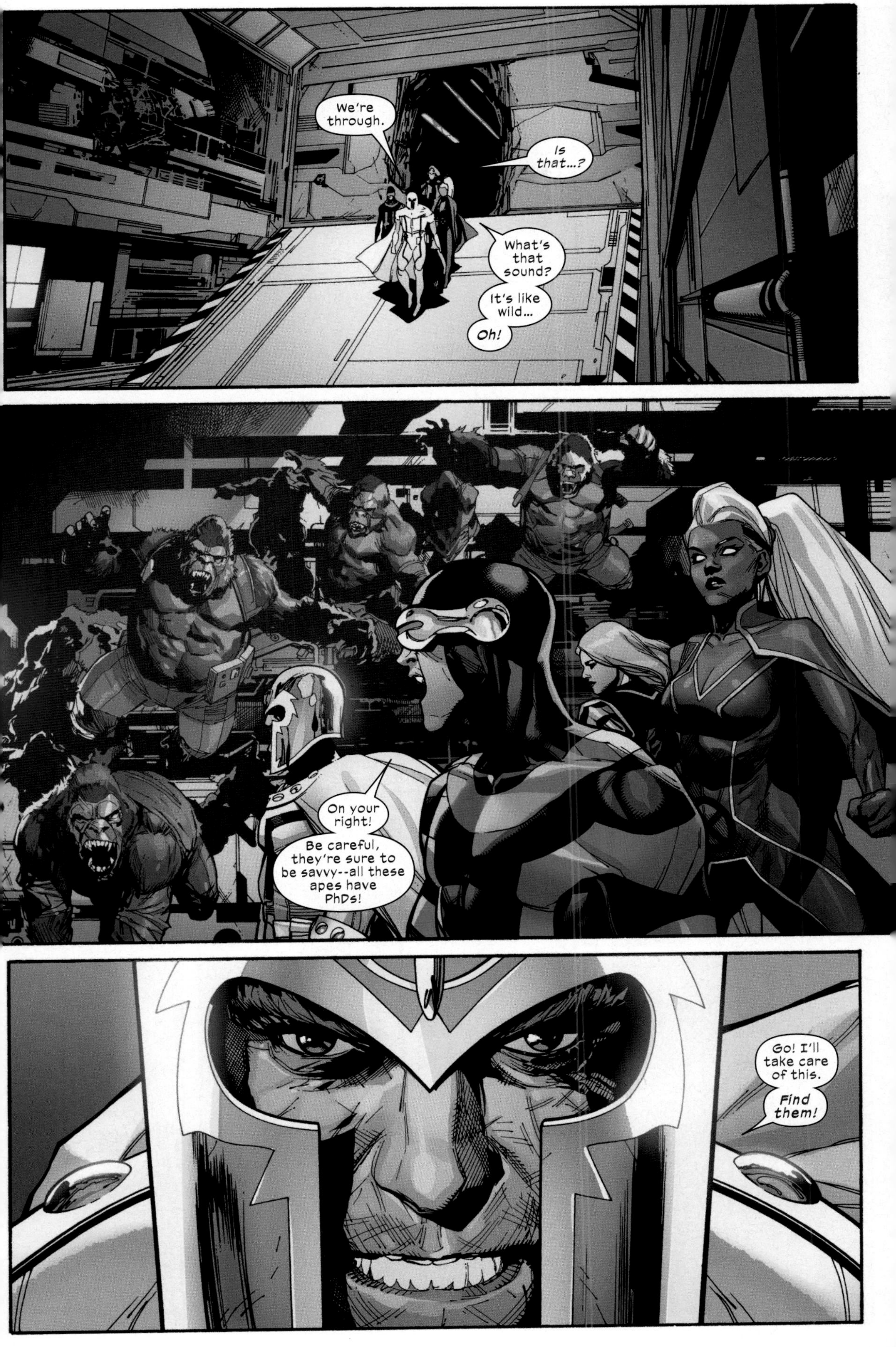
We're through.
Is that...?
What's that sound?
It's like wild...
Oh!
On your right!
Be careful, they're sure to be savvy--all these apes have PhDs!
Go! I'll take care of this.
Find them!

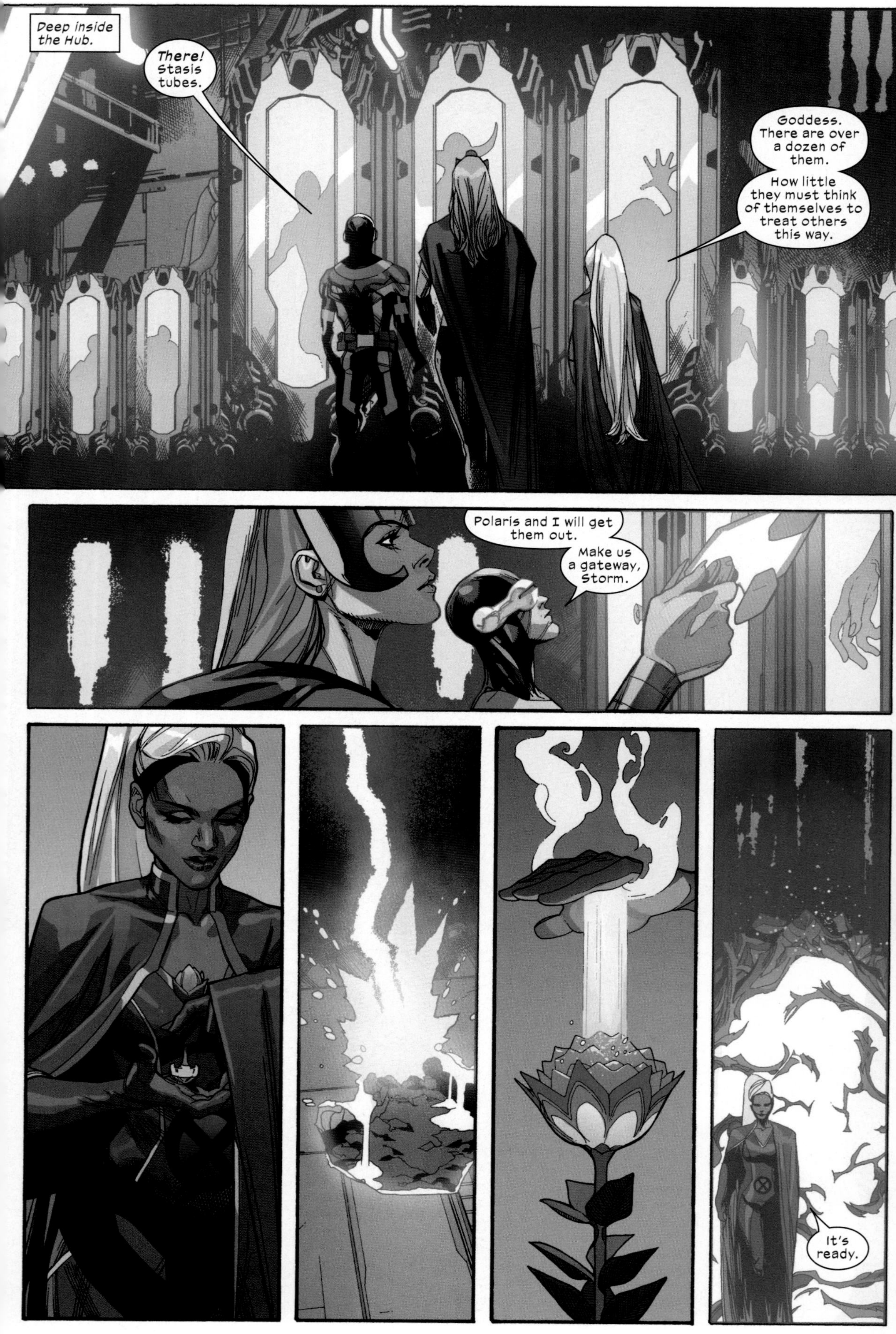
Deep inside the Hub.
There! Stasis tubes.
Goddess. There are over a dozen of them.
How little they must think of themselves to treat others this way.
Polaris and I will get them out.
Make us a gateway, Storm.
It's ready.

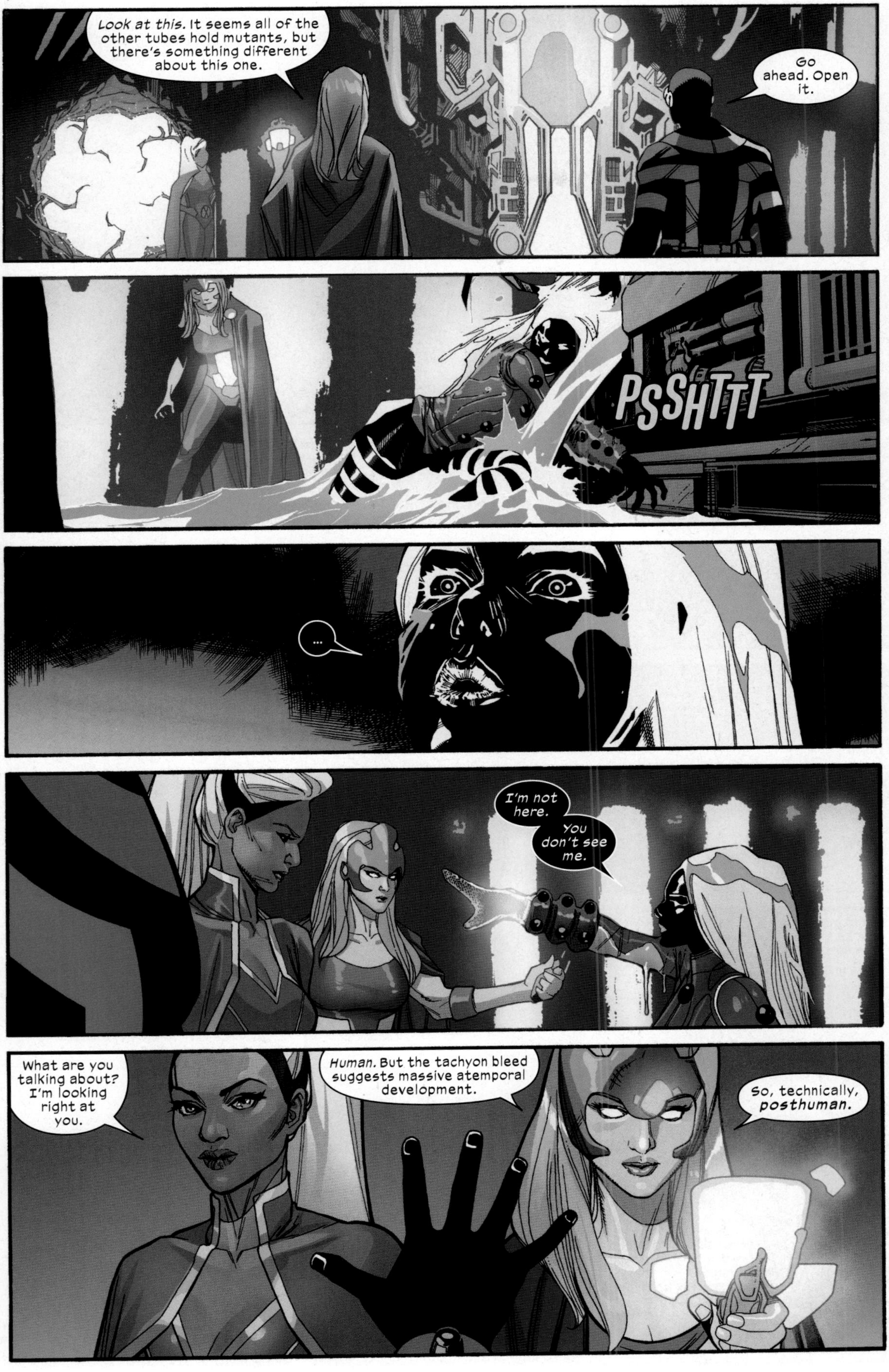

Look at this. It seems all of the other tubes hold mutants, but there's something different about this one.
Go ahead. Open it.
PSSHTTT
...
I'm not here.
You don't see me.
What are you talking about? I'm looking right at you.
Human. But the tachyon bleed suggests massive atemporal development.
So, technically, *posthuman.*

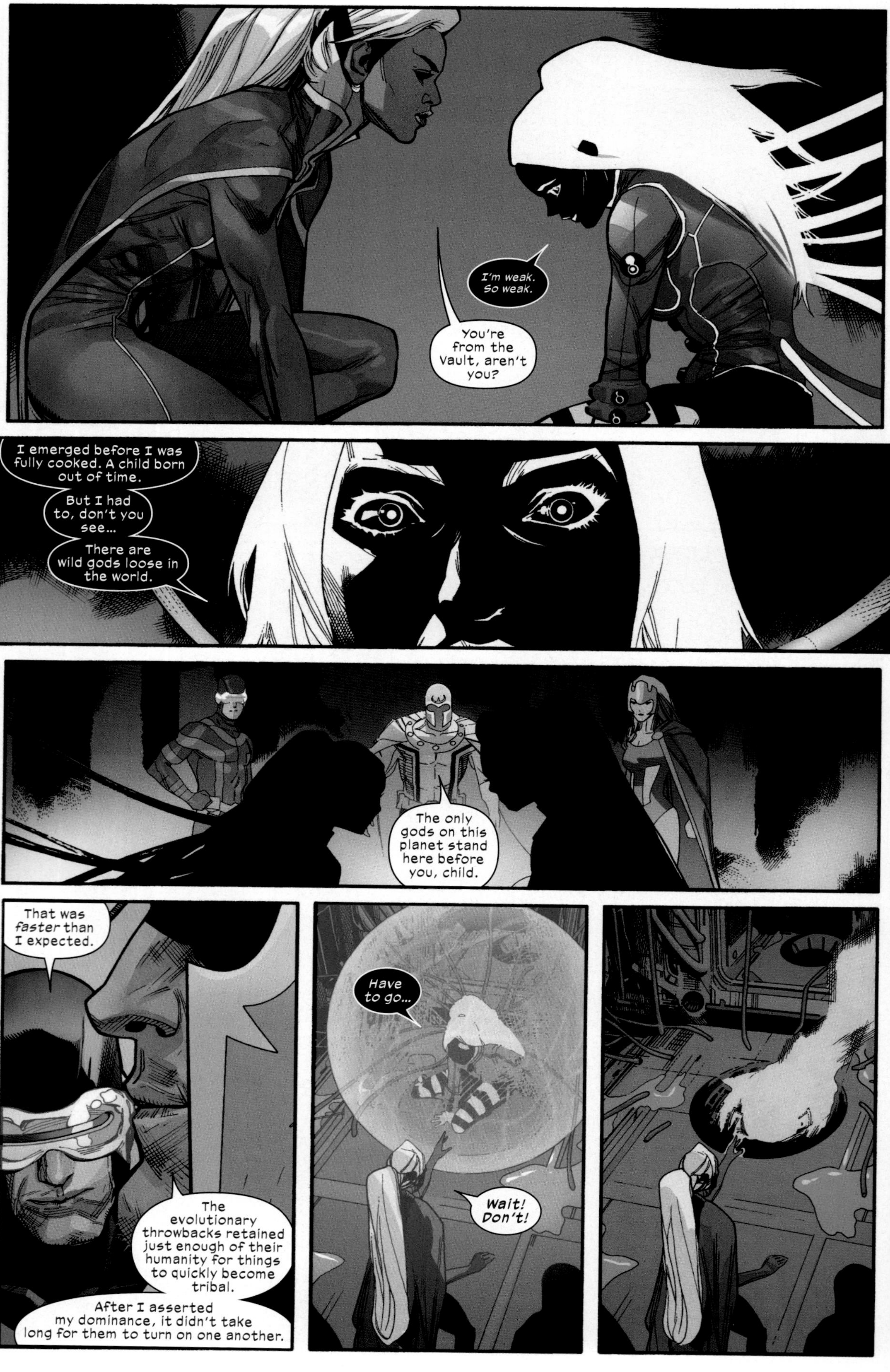

I'm weak. So weak.
You're from the Vault, aren't you?
I emerged before I was fully cooked. A child born out of time.
But I had to, don't you see...
There are wild gods loose in the world.
The only gods on this planet stand here before you, child.
That was *faster* than I expected.
The evolutionary throwbacks retained just enough of their humanity for things to quickly become tribal.
After I asserted my dominance, it didn't take long for them to turn on one another.
Have to go...
Wait! Don't!

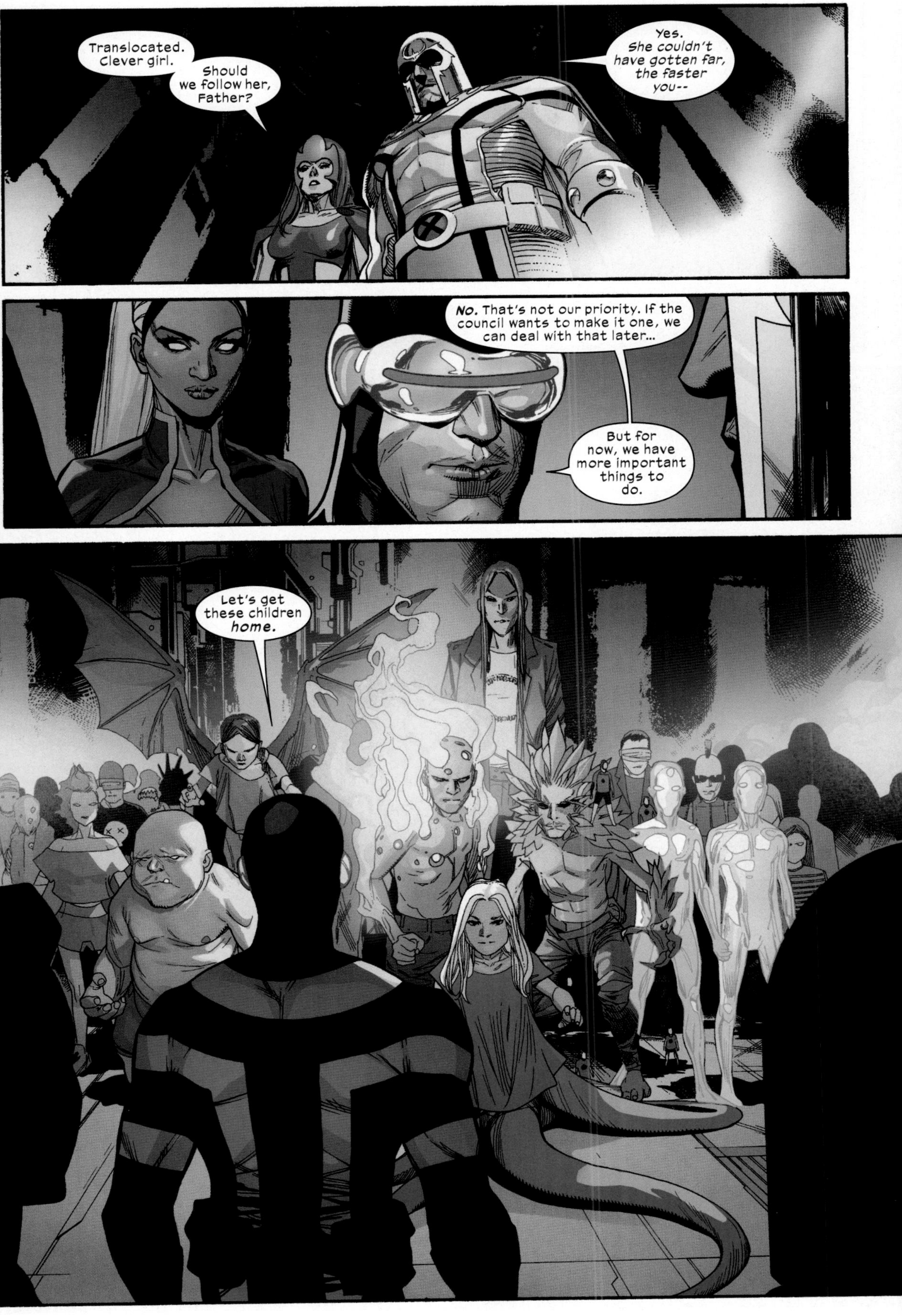
Translocated. Clever girl.
Should we follow her, Father?
Yes. She couldn't have gotten far, the faster you--
No. That's not our priority. If the council wants to make it one, we can deal with that later...
But for now, we have more important things to do.
Let's get these children home.

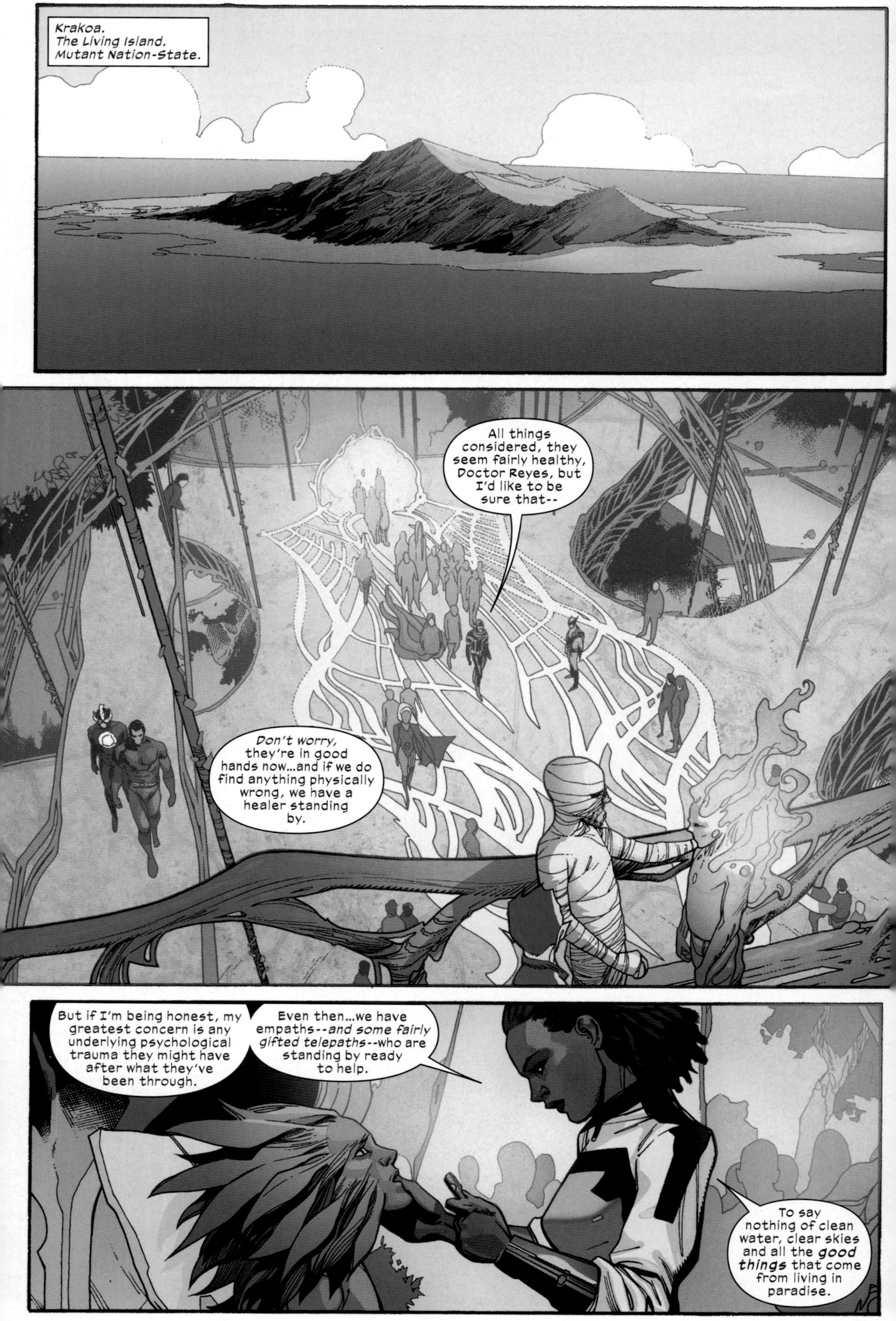
Krakoa.
The Living Island.
Mutant Nation-State.
All things considered, they seem fairly healthy, Doctor Reyes, but I'd like to be sure that--
Don't worry, they're in good hands now...and if we do find anything physically wrong, we have a healer standing by.
But if I'm being honest, my greatest concern is any underlying psychological trauma they might have after what they've been through.
Even then...we have empaths--*and some fairly gifted telepaths*--who are standing by ready to help.
To say nothing of clean water, clear skies and all the ***good things*** that come from living in paradise.

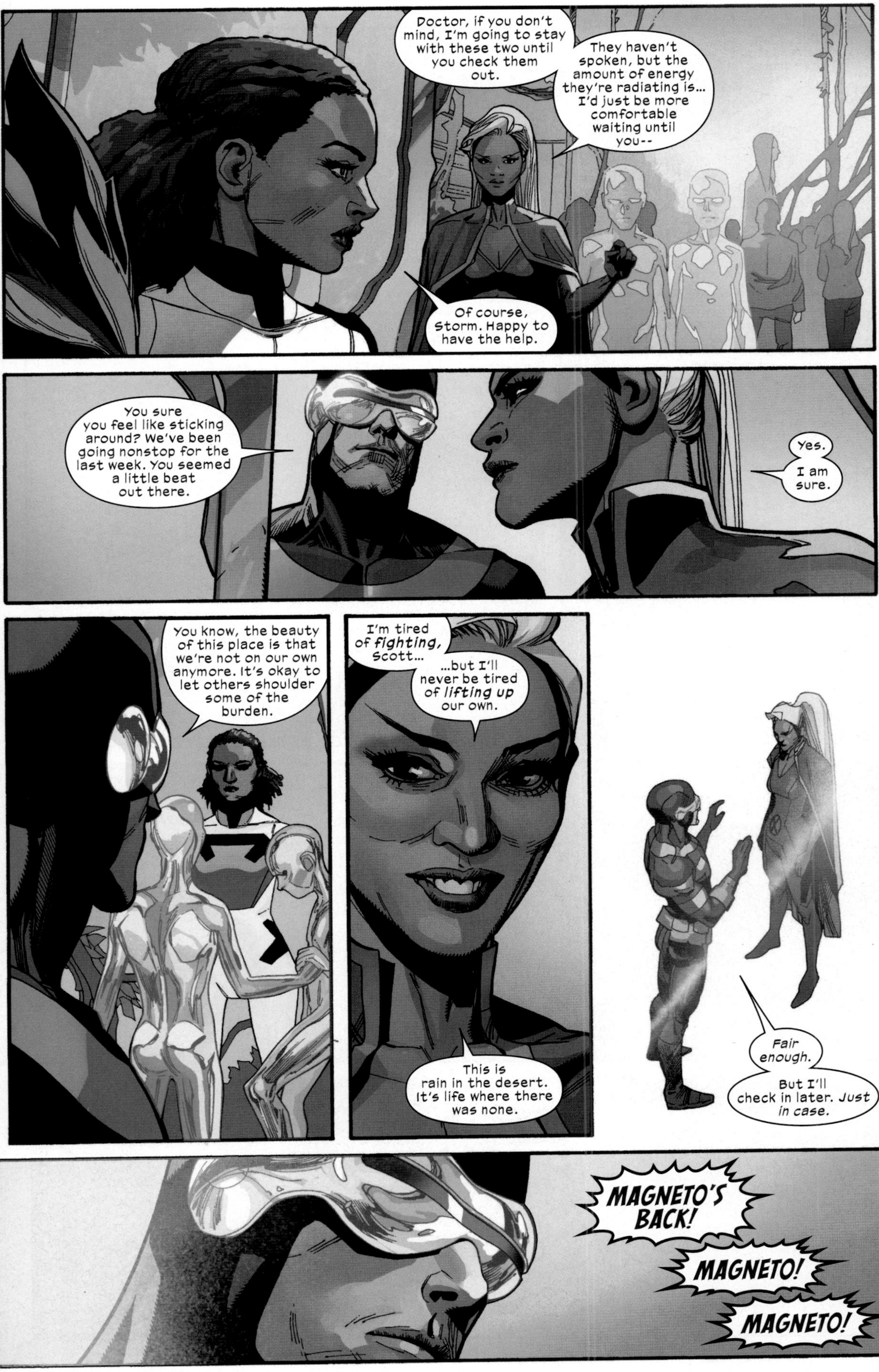

Doctor, if you don't mind, I'm going to stay with these two until you check them out.
They haven't spoken, but the amount of energy they're radiating is... I'd just be more comfortable waiting until you--
Of course, Storm. Happy to have the help.
You sure you feel like sticking around? We've been going nonstop for the last week. You seemed a little beat out there.
Yes.
I am sure.
You know, the beauty of this place is that we're not on our own anymore. It's okay to let others shoulder some of the burden.
I'm tired of *fighting,* Scott...
...but I'll never be tired of *lifting up* our own.
This is rain in the desert. It's life where there was none.
Fair enough.
But I'll check in later. *Just in case.*
MAGNETO'S BACK!
MAGNETO!
MAGNETO!

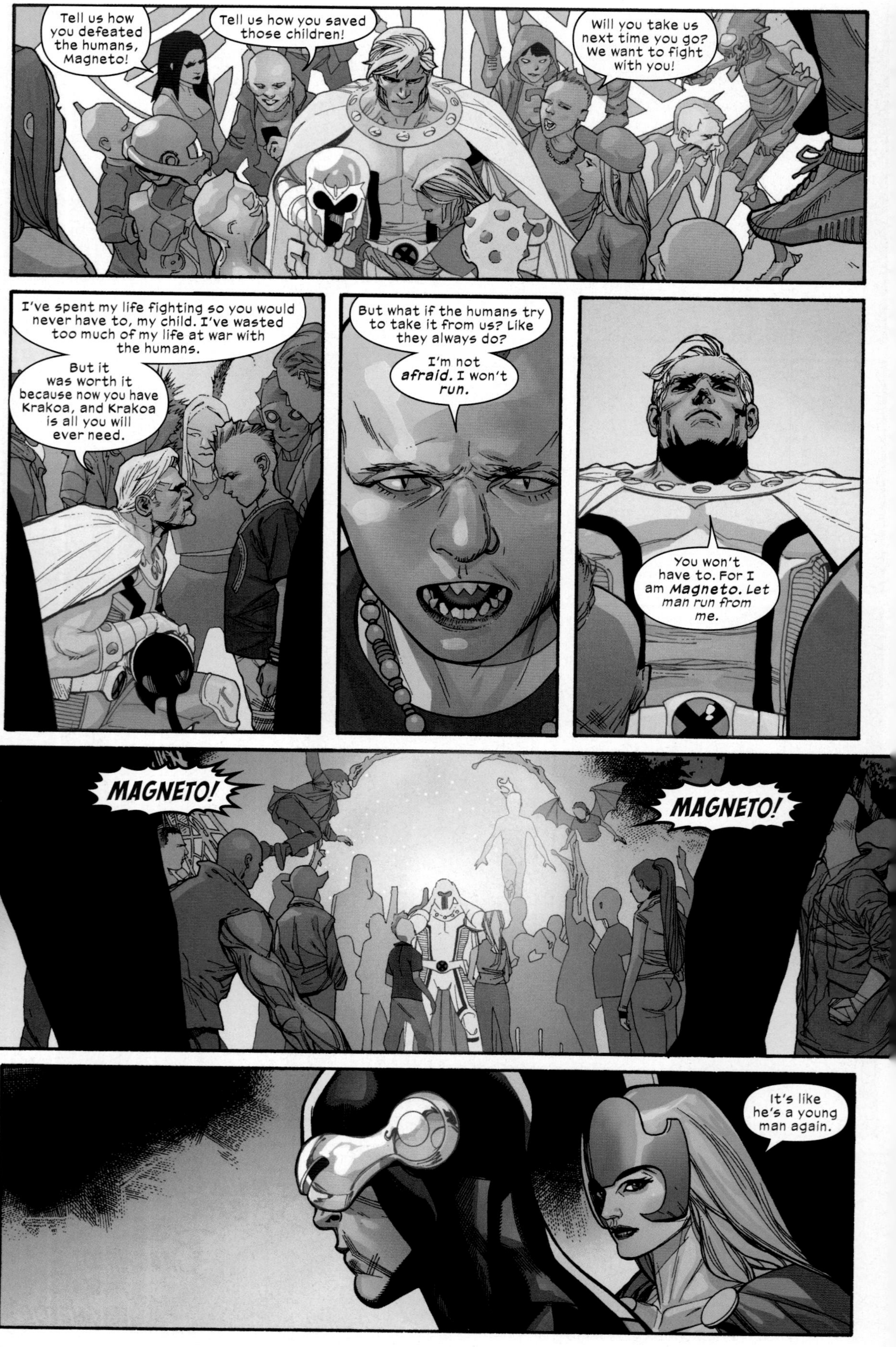
Tell us how you defeated the humans, Magneto!
Tell us how you saved those children!
Will you take us next time you go? We want to fight with you!
I've spent my life fighting so you would never have to, my child. I've wasted too much of my life at war with the humans.
But it was worth it because now you have Krakoa, and Krakoa is all you will ever need.
But what if the humans try to take it from us? Like they always do?
I'm not *afraid.* I won't *run.*
You won't have to. For I am *Magneto.* Let man run from me.
MAGNETO!
MAGNETO!
It's like he's a young man again.

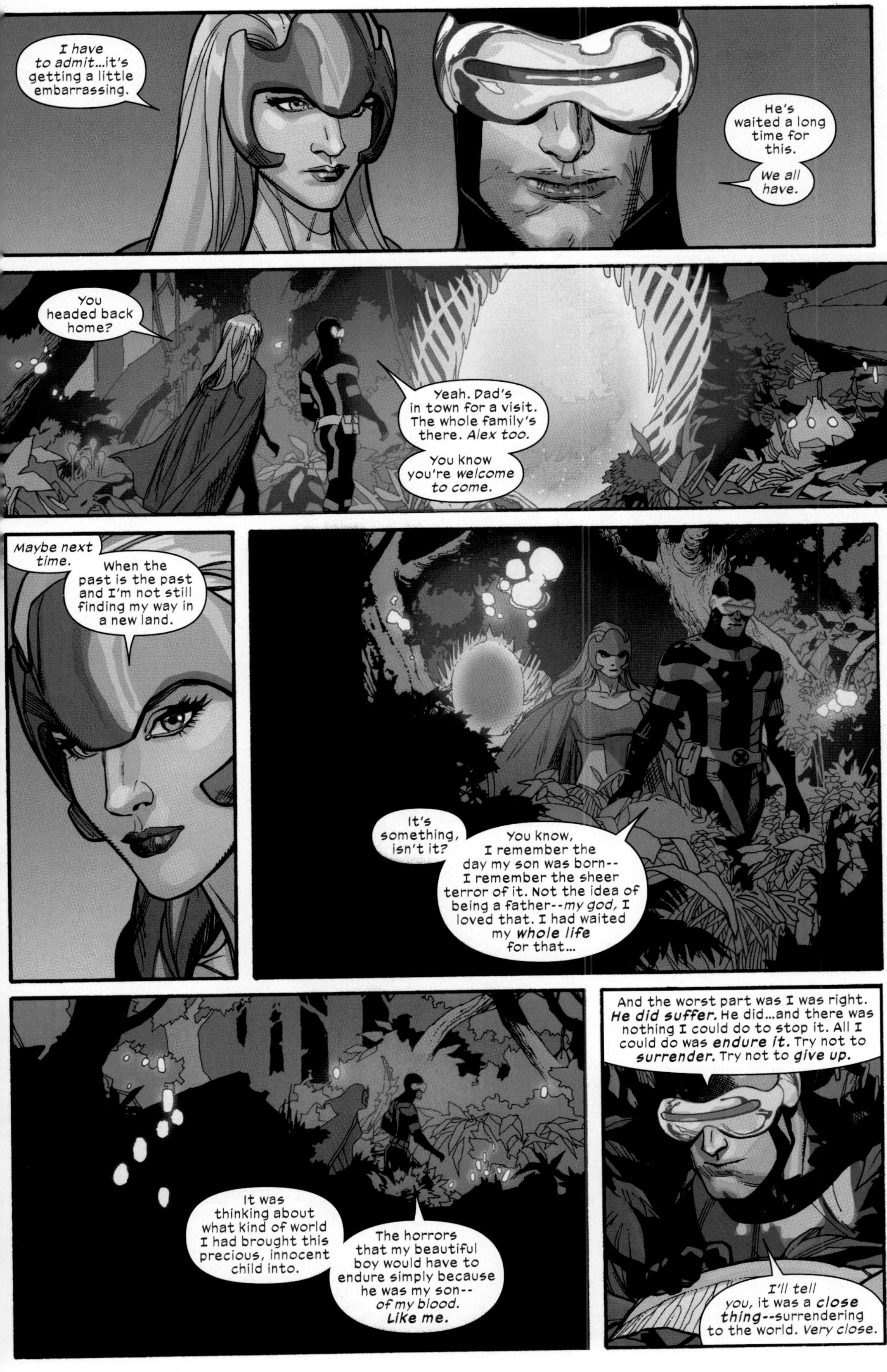

I have to admit...it's getting a little embarrassing.
He's waited a long time for this.
We all have.
You headed back home?
Yeah. Dad's in town for a visit. The whole family's there. Alex too.
You know you're welcome to come.
Maybe next time.
When the past is the past and I'm not still finding my way in a new land.
It's something, isn't it?
You know, I remember the day my son was born-- I remember the sheer terror of it. Not the idea of being a father--my god, I loved that. I had waited my whole life for that...
It was thinking about what kind of world I had brought this precious, innocent child into.
The horrors that my beautiful boy would have to endure simply because he was my son-- of my blood. Like me.
And the worst part was I was right. He did suffer. He did...and there was nothing I could do to stop it. All I could do was endure it. Try not to surrender. Try not to give up.
I'll tell you, it was a close thing--surrendering to the world. Very close.

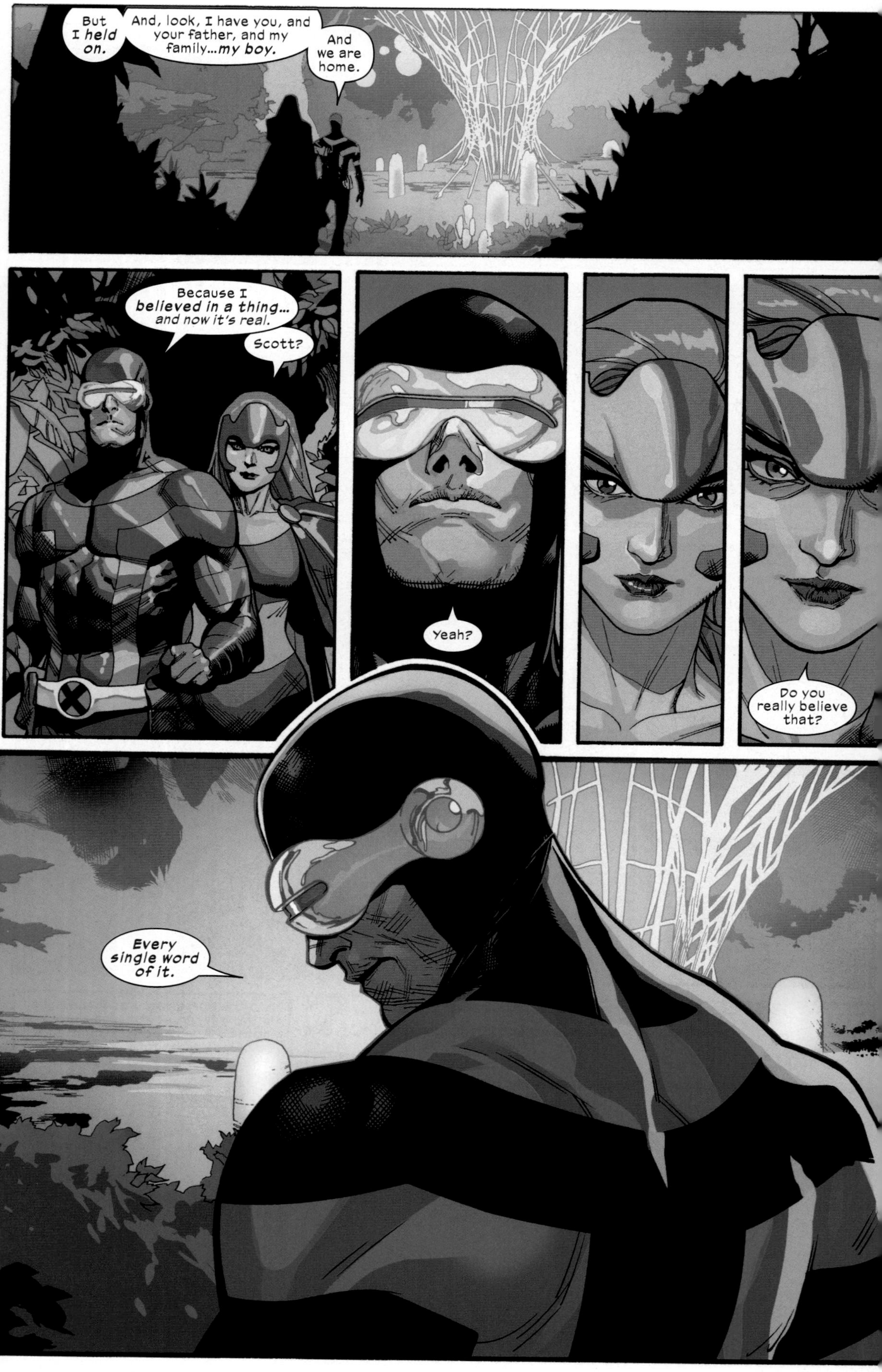
But I *held on.*
And, look, I have you, and your father, and my family...*my boy.*
And we are home.
Because I *believed in a thing...* and now it's real.
Scott?
Yeah?
Do you really believe that?
Every single word of it.

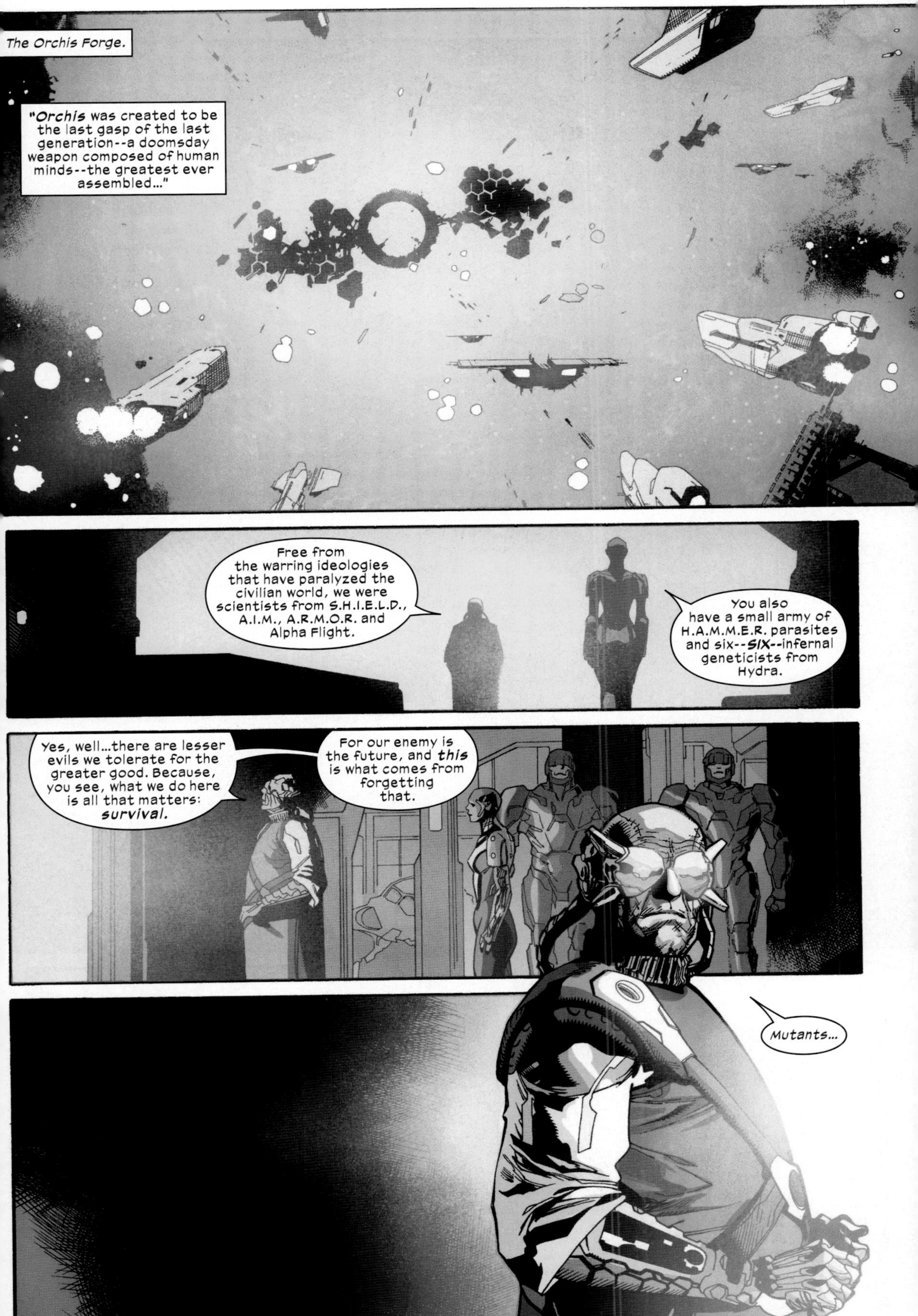

The Orchis Forge.
"Orchis was created to be the last gasp of the last generation--a doomsday weapon composed of human minds--the greatest ever assembled..."
Free from the warring ideologies that have paralyzed the civilian world, we were scientists from S.H.I.E.L.D., A.I.M., A.R.M.O.R. and Alpha Flight.
You also have a small army of H.A.M.M.E.R. parasites and six--SIX--infernal geneticists from Hydra.
Yes, well...there are lesser evils we tolerate for the greater good. Because, you see, what we do here is all that matters: survival.
For our enemy is the future, and this is what comes from forgetting that.
Mutants...

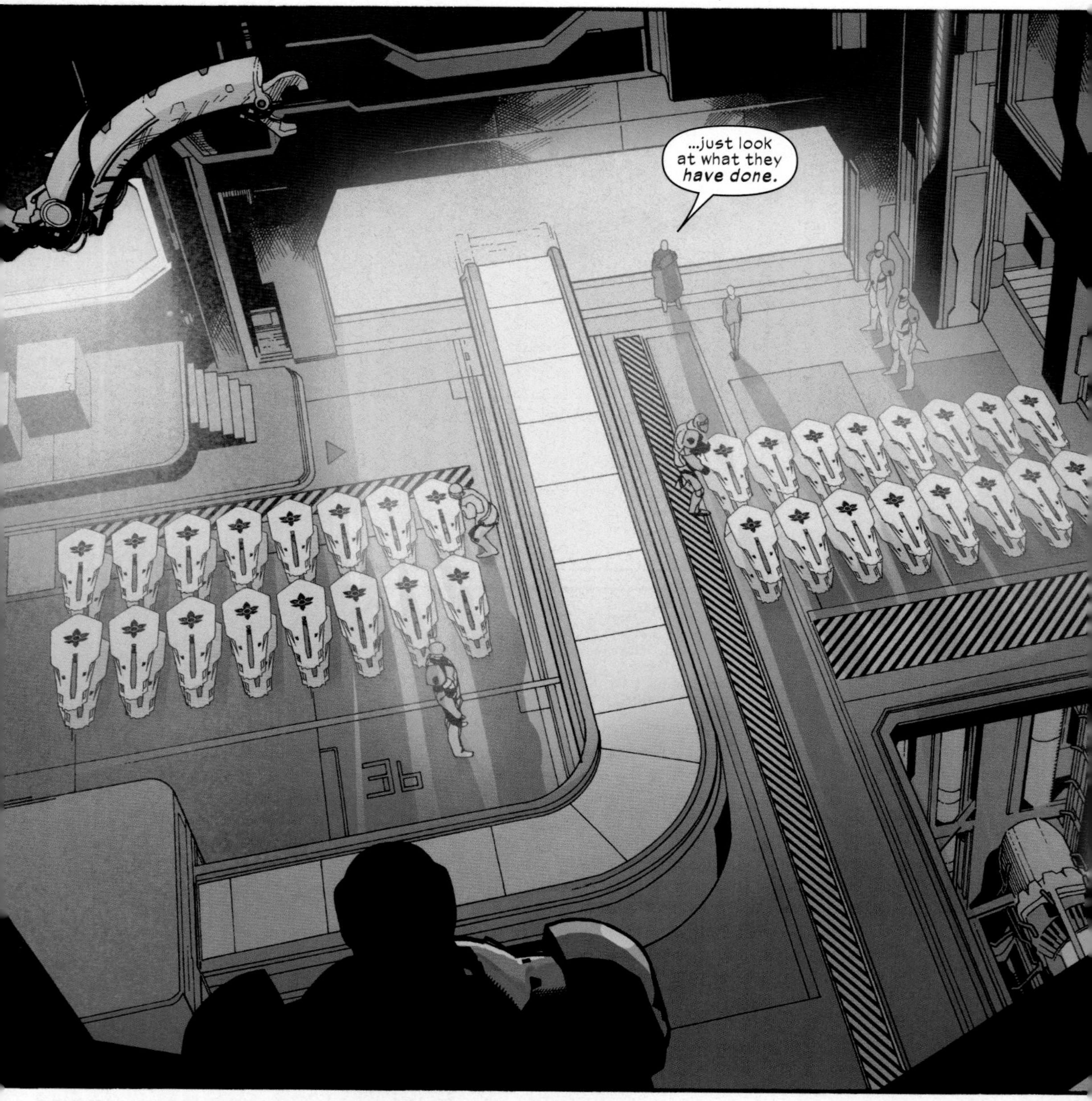
...just look at what they *have done.*

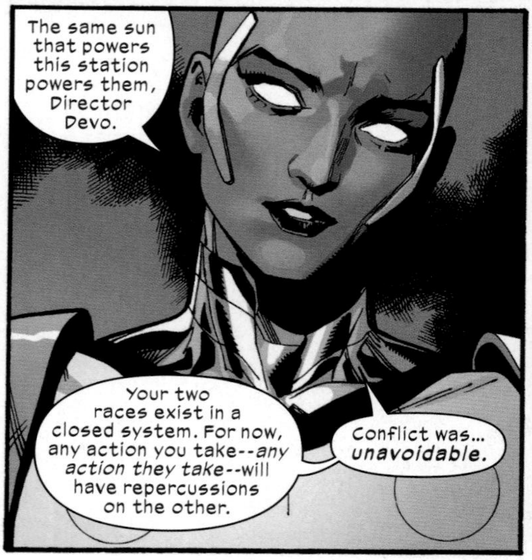
The same sun that powers this station powers them, Director Devo.
Your two races exist in a closed system. For now, any action you take--*any action they take*--will have repercussions on the other.
Conflict was... *unavoidable.*

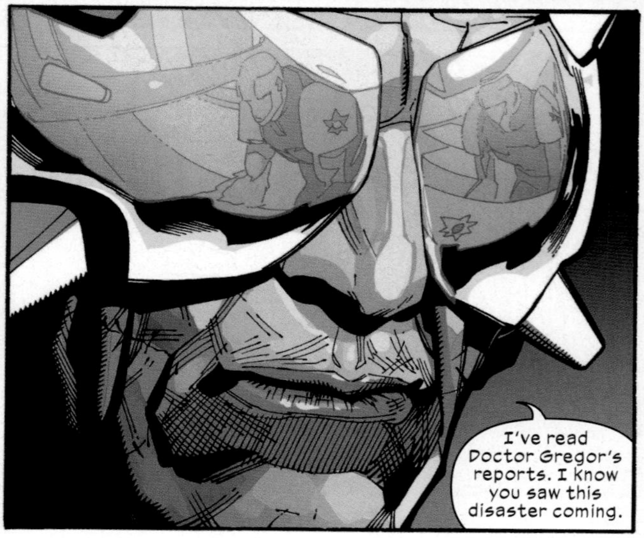
I've read Doctor Gregor's reports. I know you saw this disaster coming.

Oh, the signs were there for anyone to see.

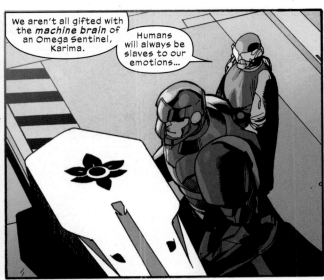

We aren't all gifted with the *machine brain* of an Omega Sentinel, Karima.

Humans will always be slaves to our emotions...

...and in that spirit, we built the Forge as a last hope for humanity.

A great refuge in case evolution saw fit to leave mankind behind.

It's one thing to shake your fist at God, Director...

...but it's something else altogether to call down the thunder.

Putting 93 million miles between you and the Earth was a *human deterrent*--not a *mutant one.*

And placing a Mother Mold in orbit around the sun was always going to spark a response.

Doctor Gregor was--

The blame is *mine,* not *hers.*

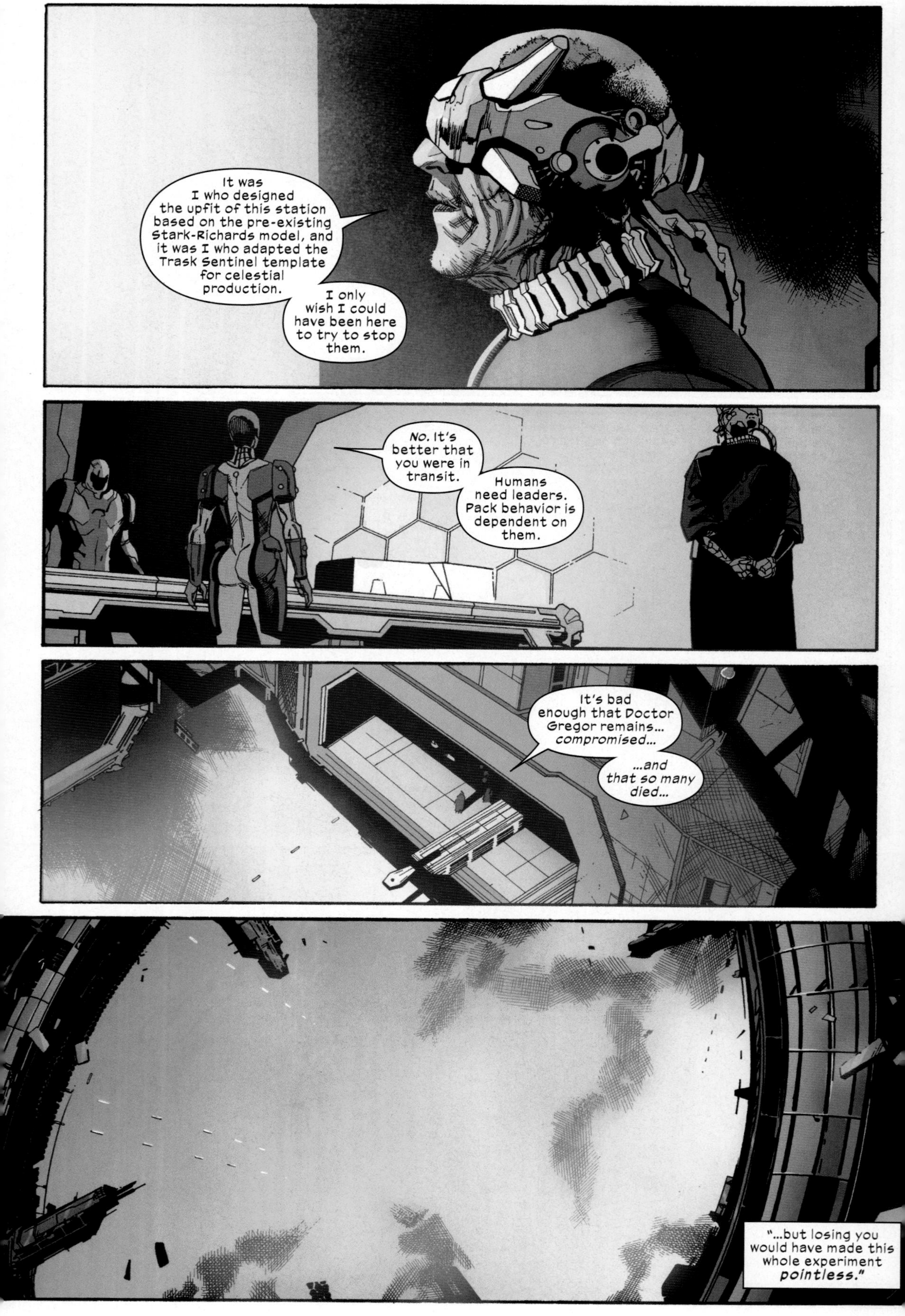
It was I who designed the upfit of this station based on the pre-existing Stark-Richards model, and it was I who adapted the Trask Sentinel template for celestial production.
I only wish I could have been here to try to stop them.
No. It's better that you were in transit.
Humans need leaders. Pack behavior is dependent on them.
It's bad enough that Doctor Gregor remains... *compromised...*
...and that so many died...
"...but losing you would have made this whole experiment *pointless.*"

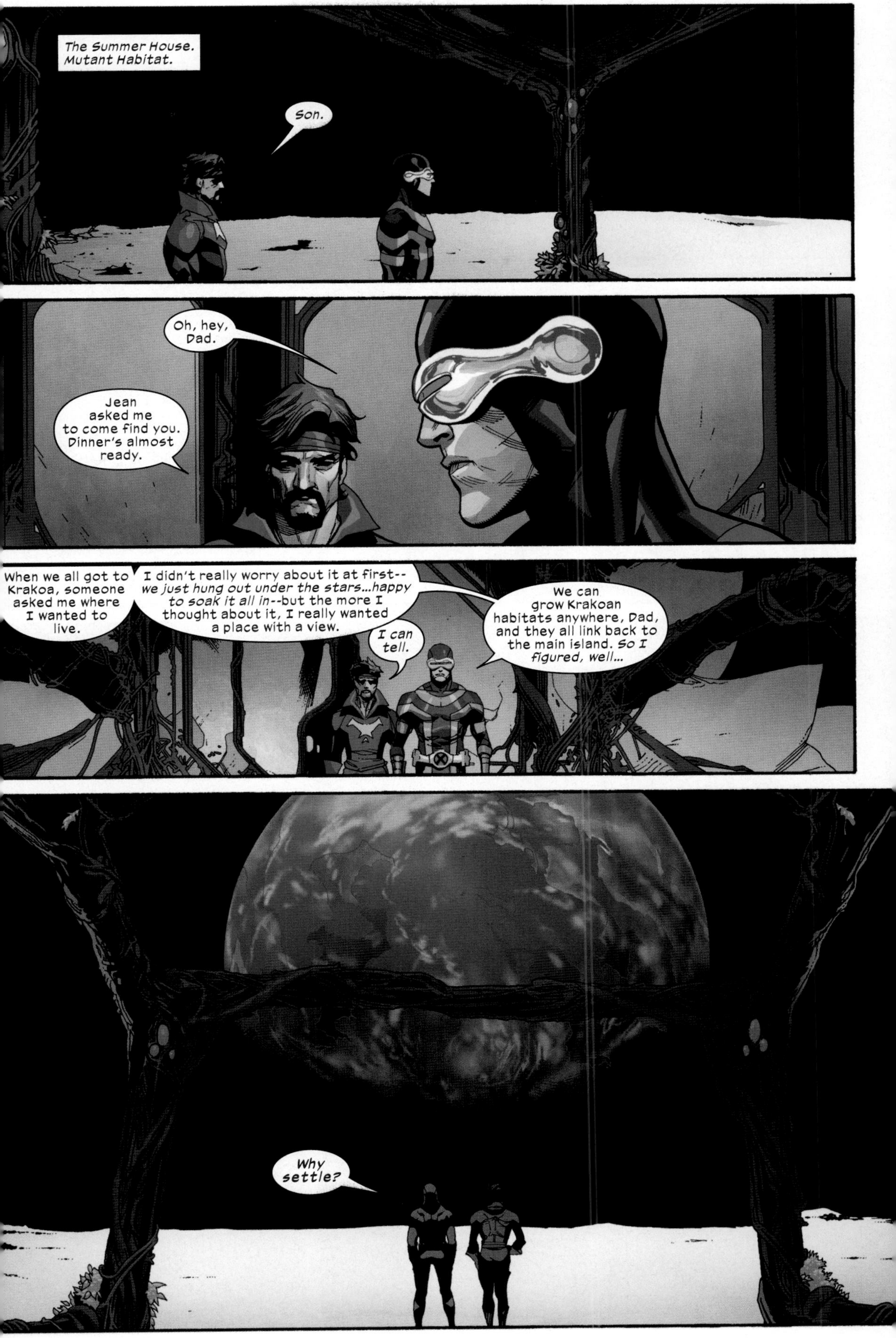
The Summer House. Mutant Habitat.
Son.
Oh, hey, Dad.
Jean asked me to come find you. Dinner's almost ready.
When we all got to Krakoa, someone asked me where I wanted to live.
I didn't really worry about it at first--we just hung out under the stars...happy to soak it all in--but the more I thought about it, I really wanted a place with a view.
I can tell.
We can grow Krakoan habitats anywhere, Dad, and they all link back to the main island. So I figured, well...
Why settle?

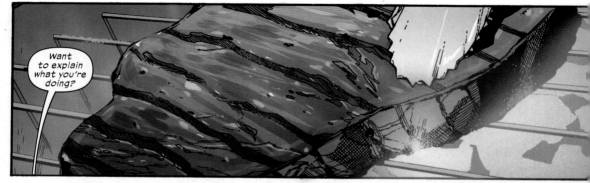

Want to explain what you're doing?

Inside this device an *inferno* burns.

That fire matches the one *inside* of me.

Do you *see?* I was born for such things, and I will not stop until these all-consuming flames have--

Yeah, you're not listening...

I want my steak *rare.*

You put the meat on the fire and expect, *what*, the *fire* not to *be* fire?

I'm going to fight you.

Peace, warrior. Because you are *valiant* and have earned my *respect...*

...I will give you your steak *rare.*

Thank you.

WOOOSH

Medium rare.

You sonofa--

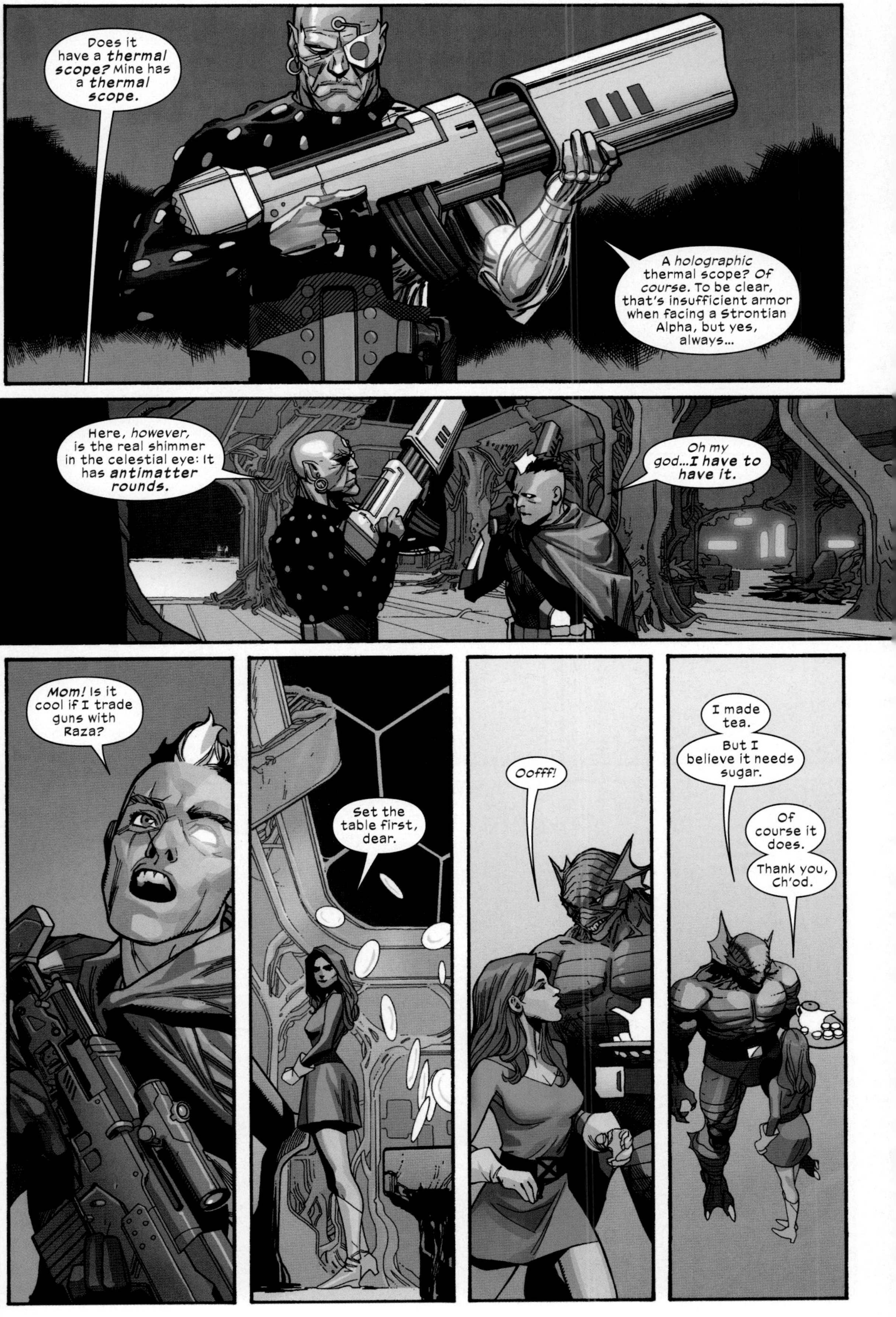
Does it have a *thermal scope?* Mine has a ***thermal scope.***
A *holographic* thermal scope? *Of course.* To be clear, that's insufficient armor when facing a Strontian Alpha, but yes, always...
Here, *however,* is the real shimmer in the celestial eye: It has ***antimatter rounds.***
*Oh my god...****I have to have it.***
Mom! Is it cool if I trade guns with Raza?
Set the table first, dear.
Oofff!
I made tea.
But I believe it needs sugar.
Of course it does.
Thank you, Ch'od.

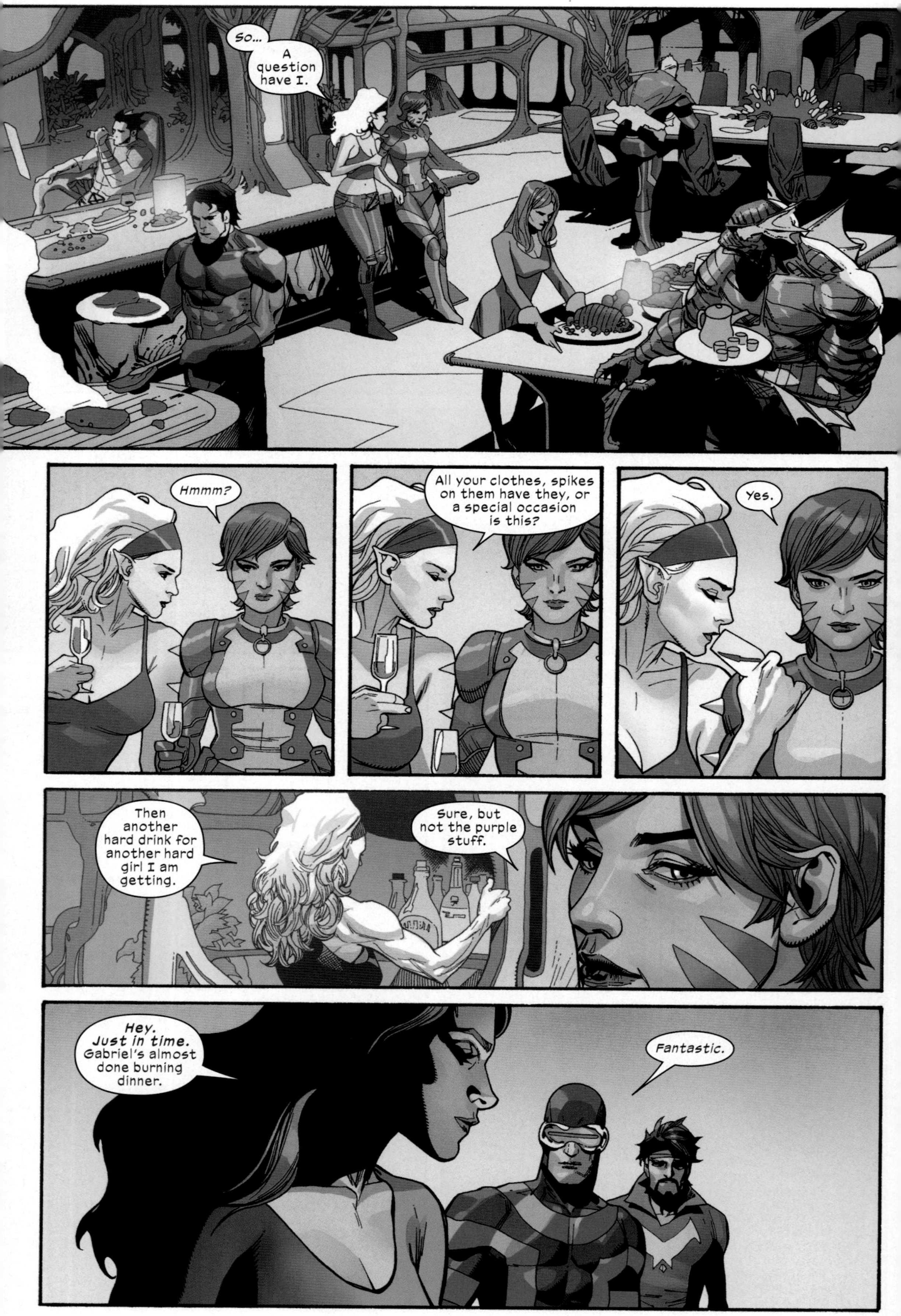
So...
A question have I.
Hmmm?
All your clothes, spikes on them have they, or a special occasion is this?
Yes.
Then another hard drink for another hard girl I am getting.
Sure, but not the purple stuff.
Hey. Just in time. Gabriel's almost done burning dinner.
Fantastic.

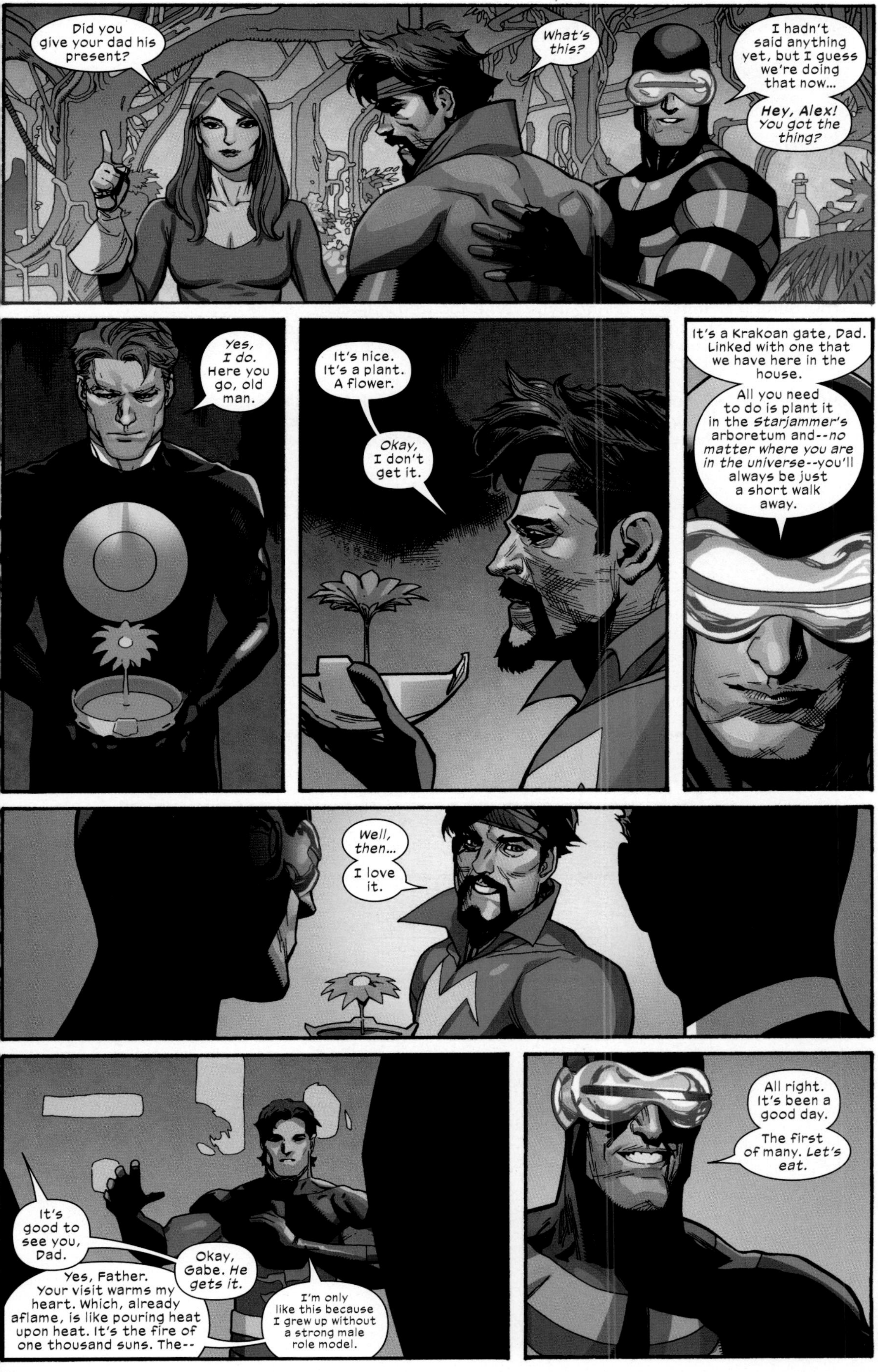

Did you give your dad his present?
What's this?
I hadn't said anything yet, but I guess we're doing that now...
Hey, Alex! You got the thing?
Yes, I do. Here you go, old man.
It's nice. It's a plant. A flower.
Okay, I don't get it.
It's a Krakoan gate, Dad. Linked with one that we have here in the house.
All you need to do is plant it in the Starjammer's arboretum and--no matter where you are in the universe--you'll always be just a short walk away.
Well, then...
I love it.
It's good to see you, Dad.
Yes, Father. Your visit warms my heart. Which, already aflame, is like pouring heat upon heat. It's the fire of one thousand suns. The--
Okay, Gabe. He gets it.
I'm only like this because I grew up without a strong male role model.
All right. It's been a good day.
The first of many. Let's eat.

SUMMER HOUSE

THE BLUE AREA OF THE MOON

The Summer House is a Krakoan biome located adjacent to the Blue Area of the moon. Occupied by the Summers clan and other mutant allies, the base also serves as a departure point for first response / first strike capabilities.

NOTE: While all mutants are technically welcome, Vulcan has been bringing home quite a few acquaintances from the Krakoan mainland who have stretched the acceptable bounds of decorum.

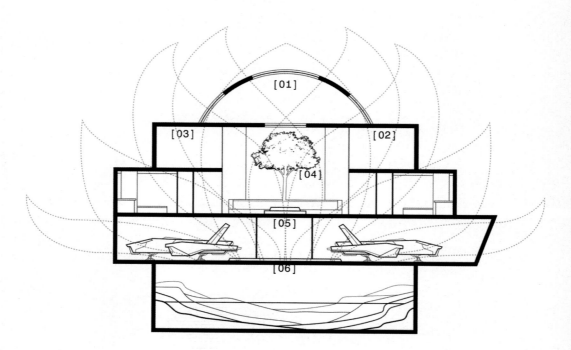

ELEVATION

```
[01]..................................................Observation
[02]..................................................Tactical ops
[03]..................................................Gymnasium
[04]..................Central living / dining / sleeping area
[05]..................................Hangar / turnabout
[06]..................Sublunar biome / pool / gateway access
```

SUMMER HOUSE

[14]
[13]
[15]
[16]
[11]
[17]
[12]
[18]
[10]
[09]
[08]
[07]

FLOOR PLAN

[07]..Kitchen
[08]...Dining
[09].......................................Living area

[10]....................................Cyclops' Room
[11]..................................Wolverine's Room
[12].......................................Jean's Room

[13]....................................Vulcan's Room
[14].....................................Havok's Room
[15]..Empty

[16].....................................Cable's Room
[17]..Empty
[18]....................................Rachel's Room

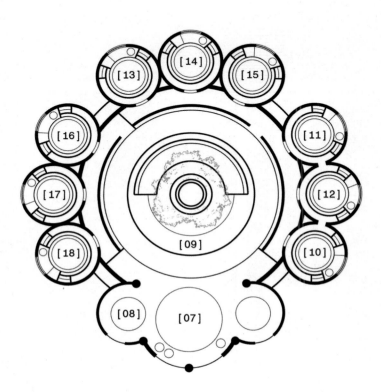

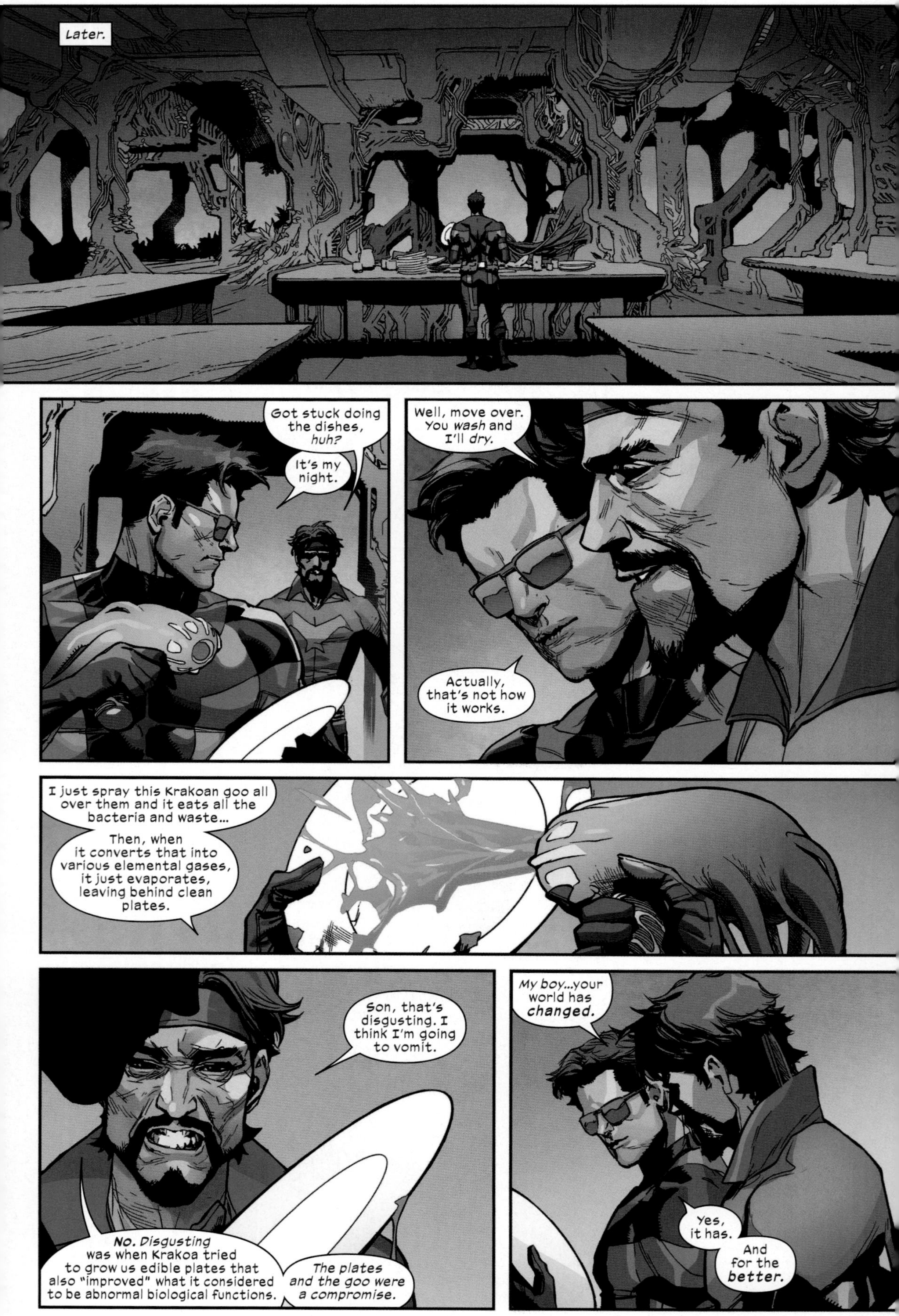
Later.
Got stuck doing the dishes, *huh?*
It's my night.
Well, move over. You *wash* and I'll *dry.*
Actually, that's not how it works.
I just spray this Krakoan goo all over them and it eats all the bacteria and waste...
Then, when it converts that into various elemental gases, it just evaporates, leaving behind clean plates.
Son, that's disgusting. I think I'm going to vomit.
No. *Disgusting* was when Krakoa tried to grow us edible plates that also "improved" what it considered to be abnormal biological functions.
The plates and the goo were a compromise.
My boy...your world has ***changed.***
Yes, it has.
And for the ***better.***

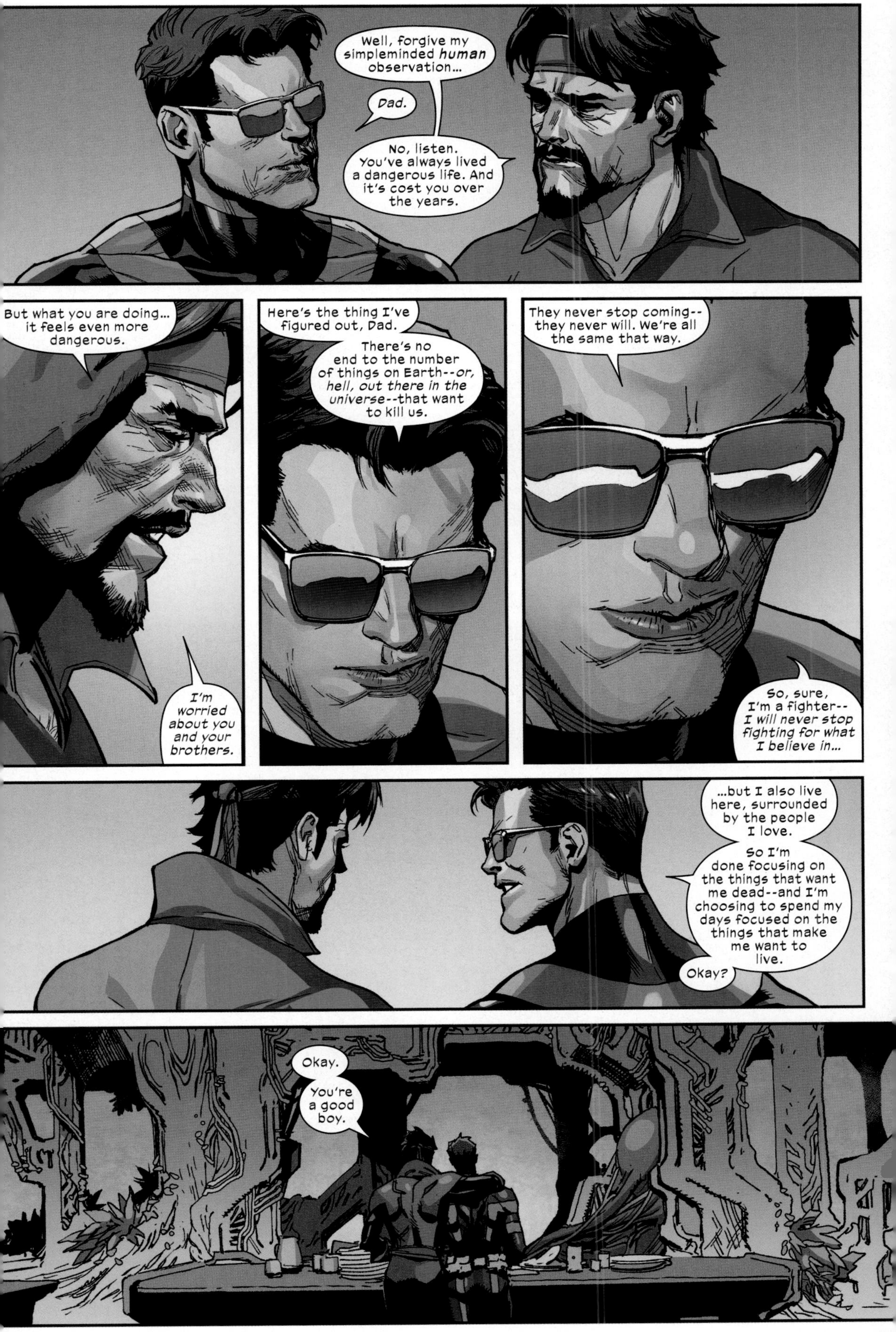
Well, forgive my simpleminded *human* observation...
Dad.
No, listen. You've always lived a dangerous life. And it's cost you over the years.
But what you are doing... it feels even more dangerous.
I'm worried about you and your brothers.
Here's the thing I've figured out, Dad.
There's no end to the number of things on Earth--*or, hell, out there in the universe*--that want to kill us.
They never stop coming--they never will. We're all the same that way.
So, sure, I'm a fighter--*I will never stop fighting for what I believe in...*
...but I also live here, surrounded by the people I love.
So I'm done focusing on the things that want me dead--and I'm choosing to spend my days focused on the things that make me want to live.
Okay?
Okay.
You're a good boy.

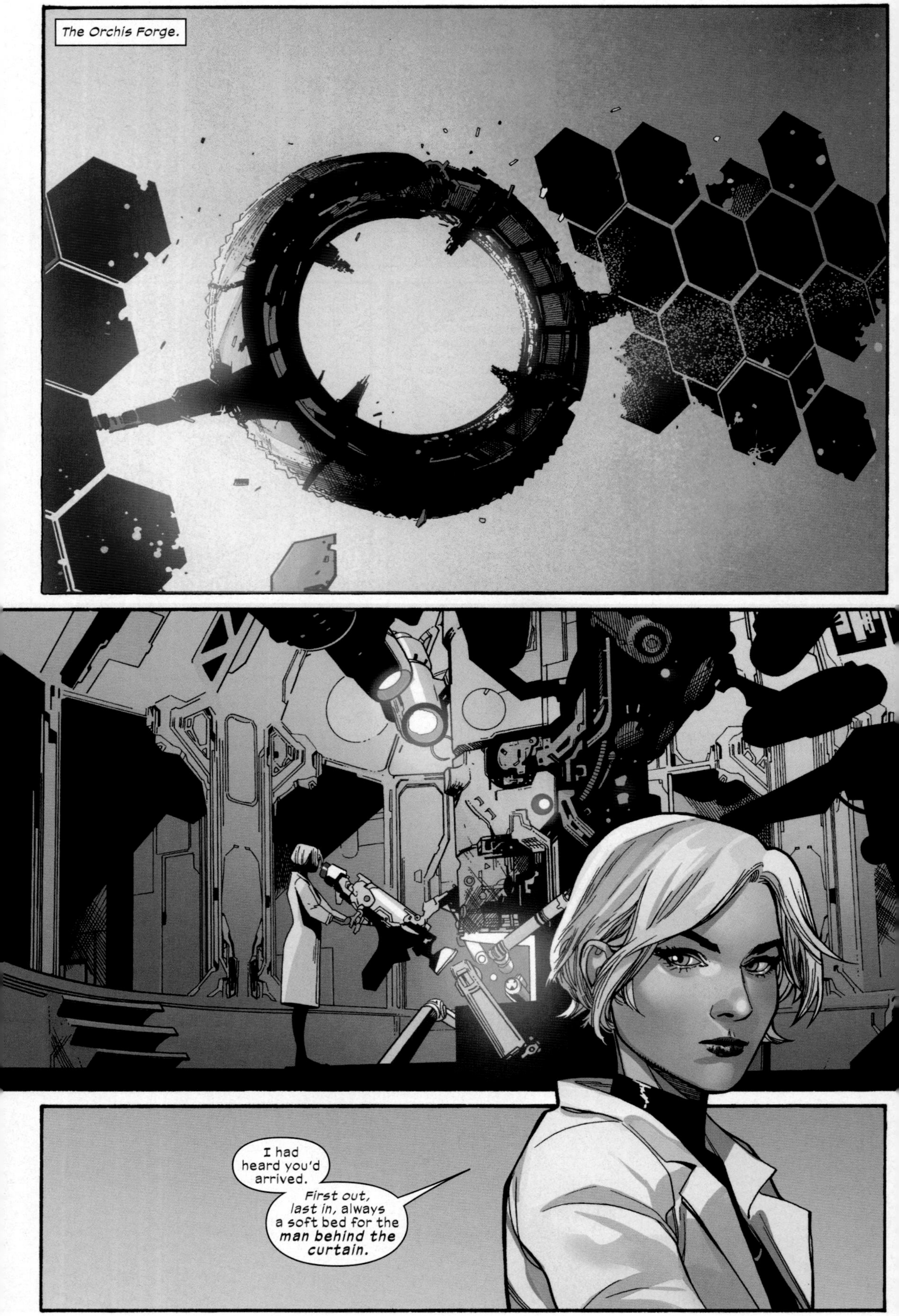
The Orchis Forge.
I had heard you'd arrived.
First out, last in, always a soft bed for the man behind the curtain.

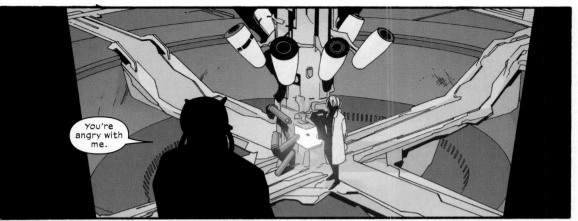

You're angry with me.

You think I shouldn't be angry? At you? At them?

If you want to use that rage for whatever it gets you, *Doctor Gregor*, that's fine...

So long as you don't get lost along the way or lose sight of where we are headed.

It's true. I was born blind, but through science I can see the world in infrared, ultraviolet and a hundred ways beyond that.

There's not much that slips past my observation... especially not when I'm looking closely.

I did not see you earlier at the funeral...

Lose sight?

You should have been there. We were *burying* your *husband*.

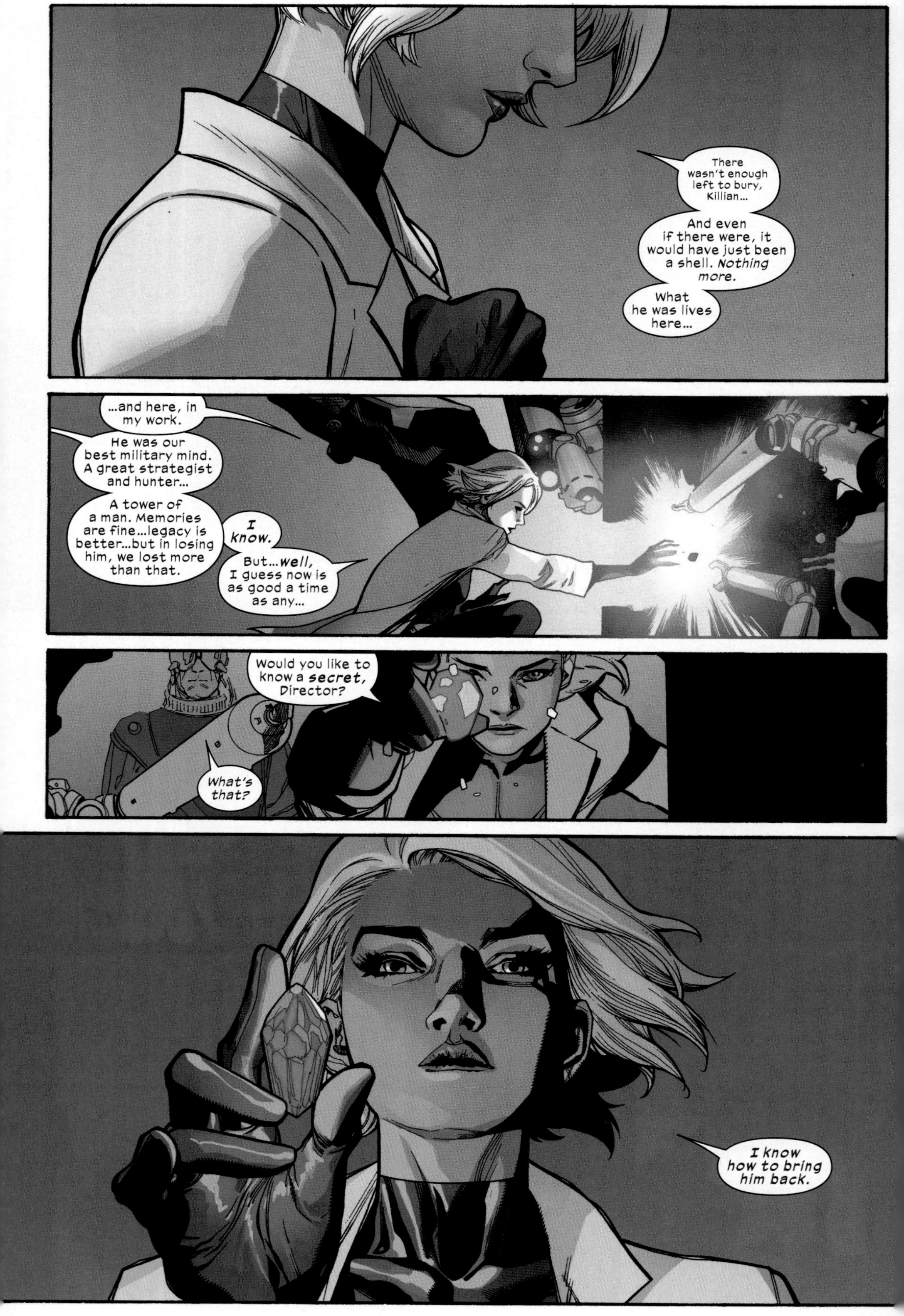
There wasn't enough left to bury, Killian...
And even if there were, it would have just been a shell. *Nothing more.*
What he was lives here...
...and here, in my work.
He was our best military mind. A great strategist and hunter...
A tower of a man. Memories are fine...legacy is better...but in losing him, we lost more than that.
I know.
But...*well,* I guess now is as good a time as any...
Would you like to know a *secret,* Director?
What's that?
I know how to bring him back.

[dawn_of_x]

[kra_]
[koa_]

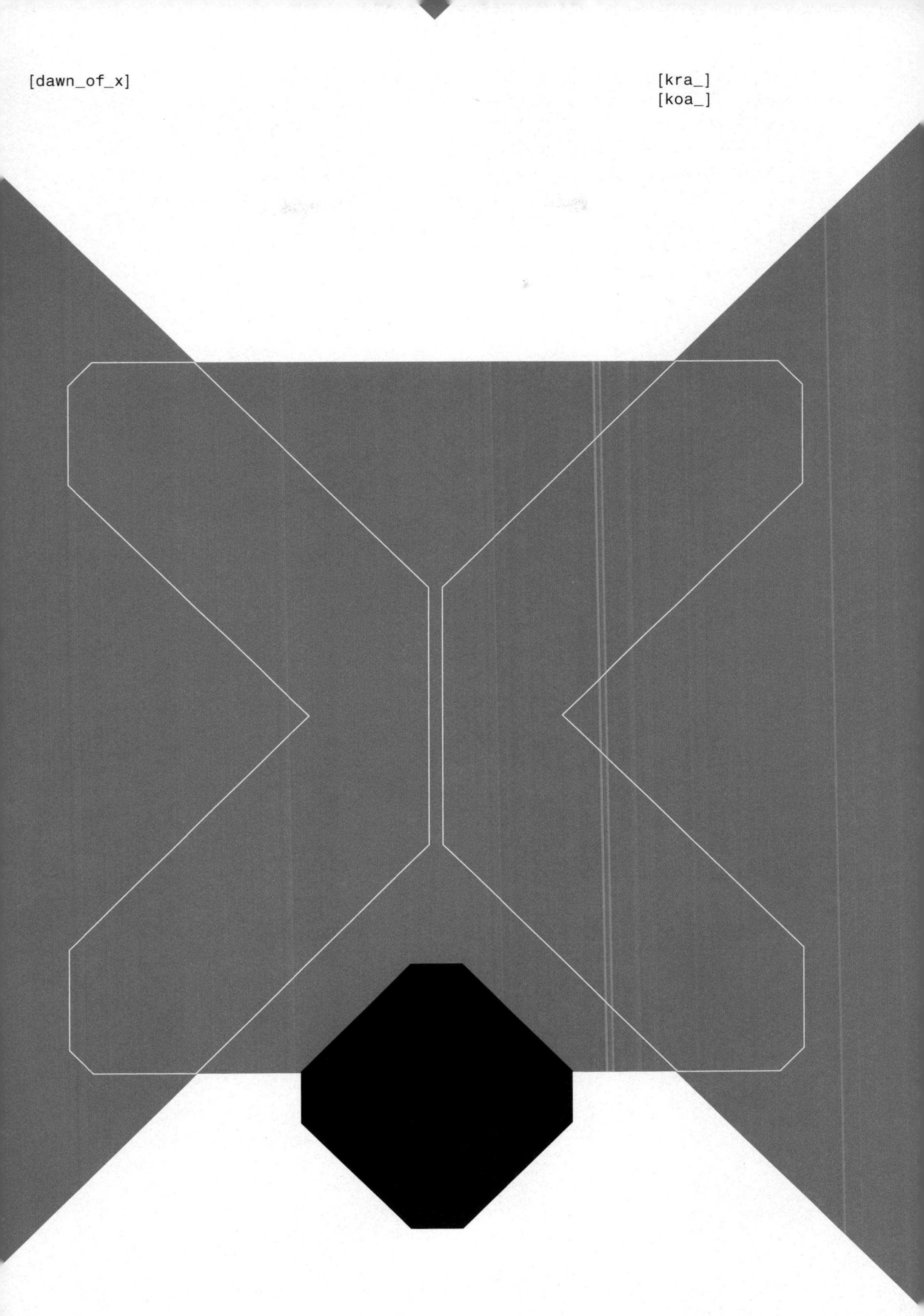

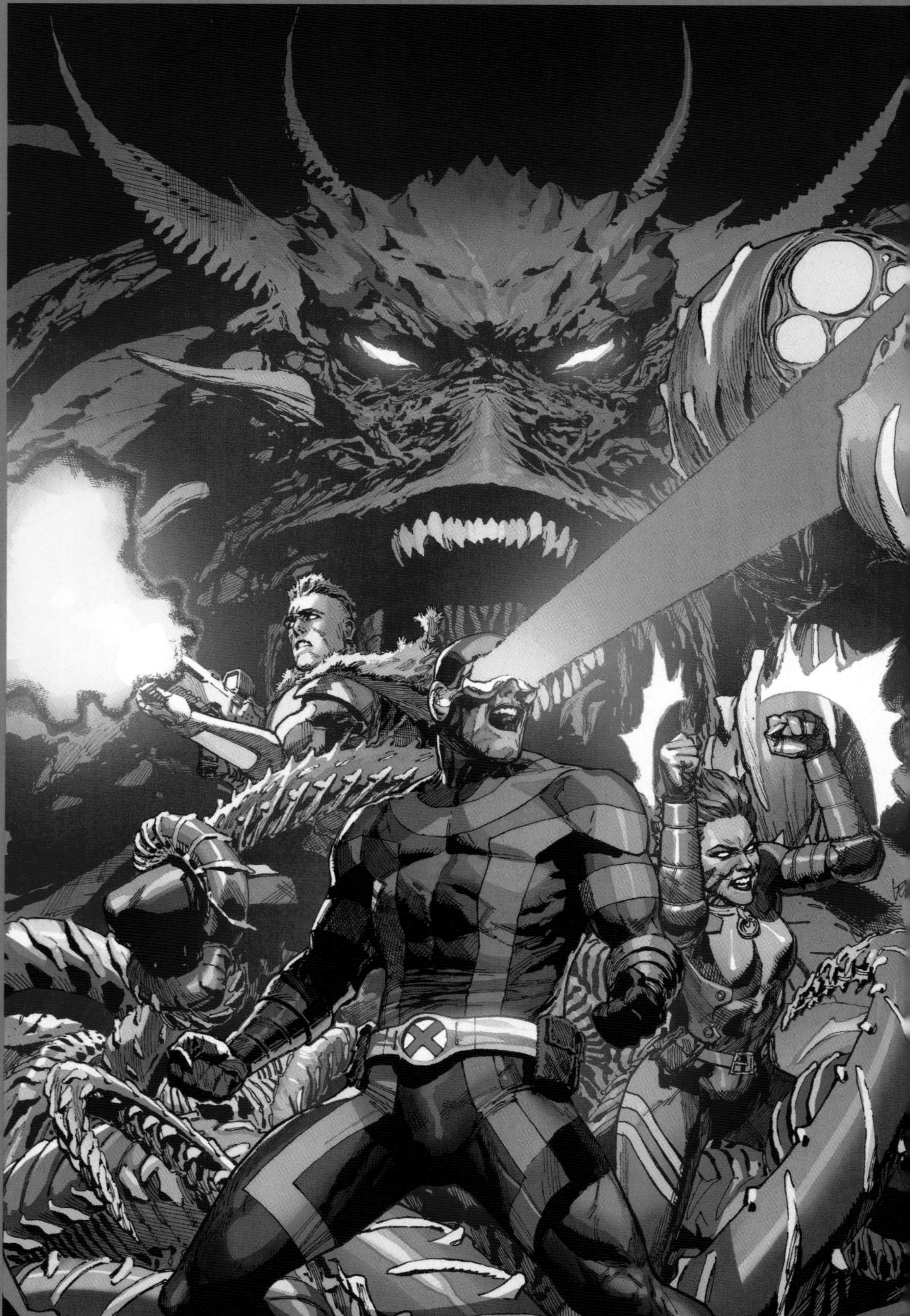

Summoner

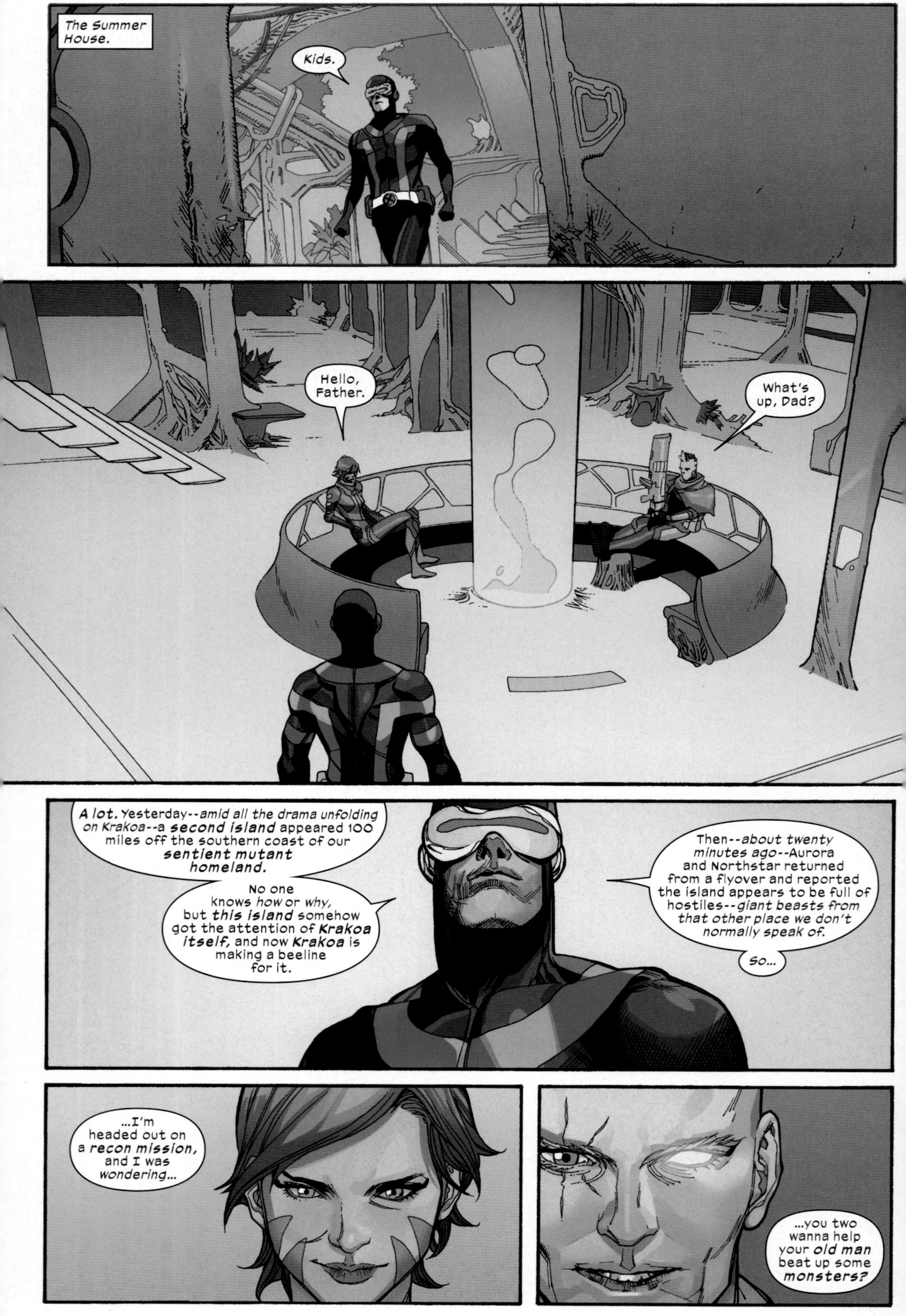
The Summer House.
Kids.
Hello, Father.
What's up, Dad?
A lot. Yesterday--amid all the drama unfolding on Krakoa--a second island appeared 100 miles off the southern coast of our sentient mutant homeland.
No one knows how or why, but this island somehow got the attention of Krakoa itself, and now Krakoa is making a beeline for it.
Then--about twenty minutes ago--Aurora and Northstar returned from a flyover and reported the island appears to be full of hostiles--giant beasts from that other place we don't normally speak of.
So...
...I'm headed out on a recon mission, and I was wondering...
...you two wanna help your old man beat up some monsters?

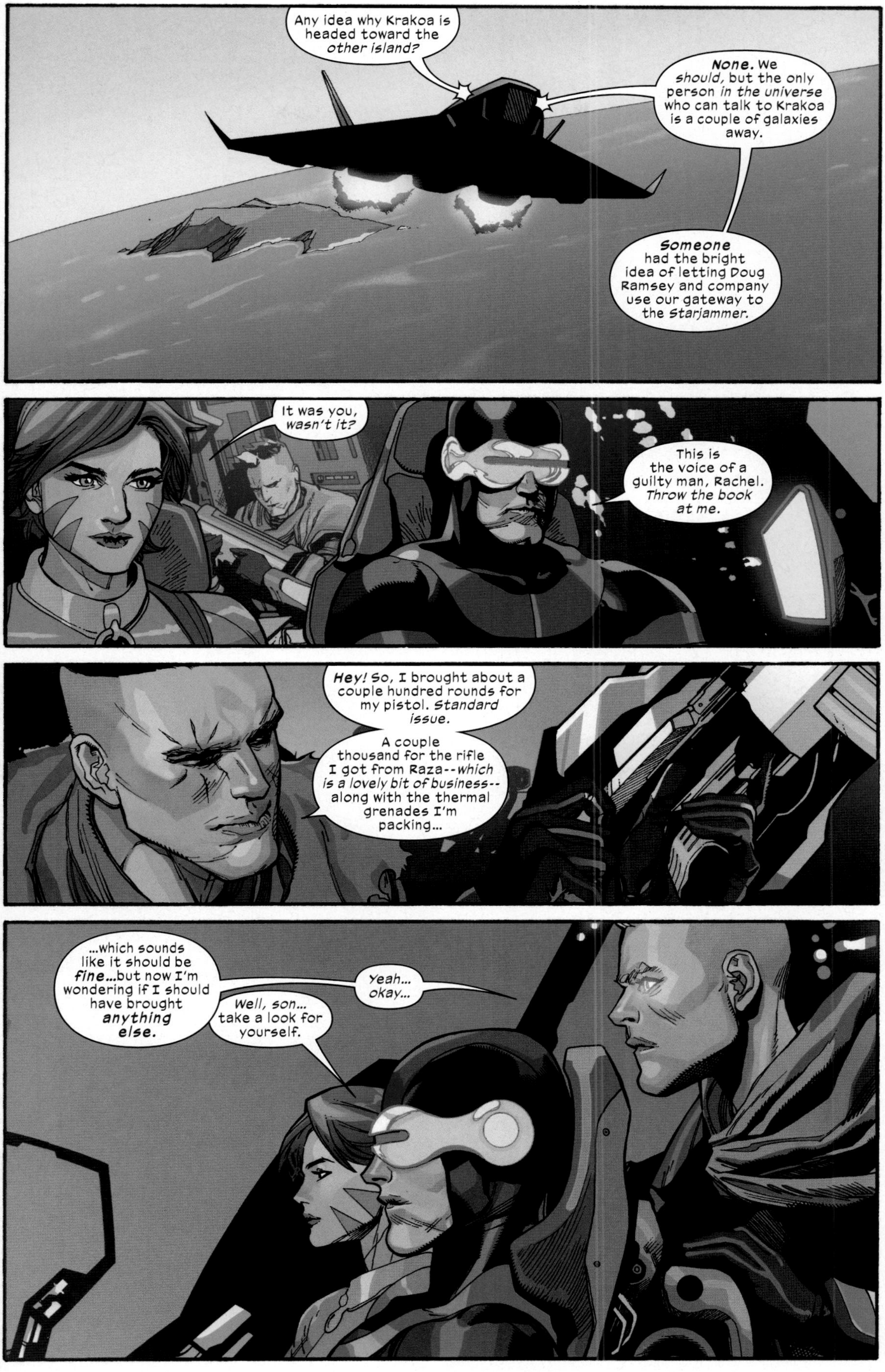
Any idea why Krakoa is headed toward the *other island?*
None. We *should,* but the only person *in the universe* who can talk to Krakoa is a couple of galaxies away.
Someone had the bright idea of letting Doug Ramsey and company use our gateway to the *Starjammer.*
It was you, *wasn't it?*
This is the voice of a guilty man, Rachel. *Throw the book at me.*
Hey! So, I brought about a couple hundred rounds for my pistol. *Standard issue.*
A couple thousand for the rifle I got from Raza--*which is a lovely bit of business*--along with the thermal grenades I'm packing...
...which sounds like it should be ***fine...*** but now I'm wondering if I should have brought ***anything else.***
Yeah... okay...
Well, son... take a look for yourself.

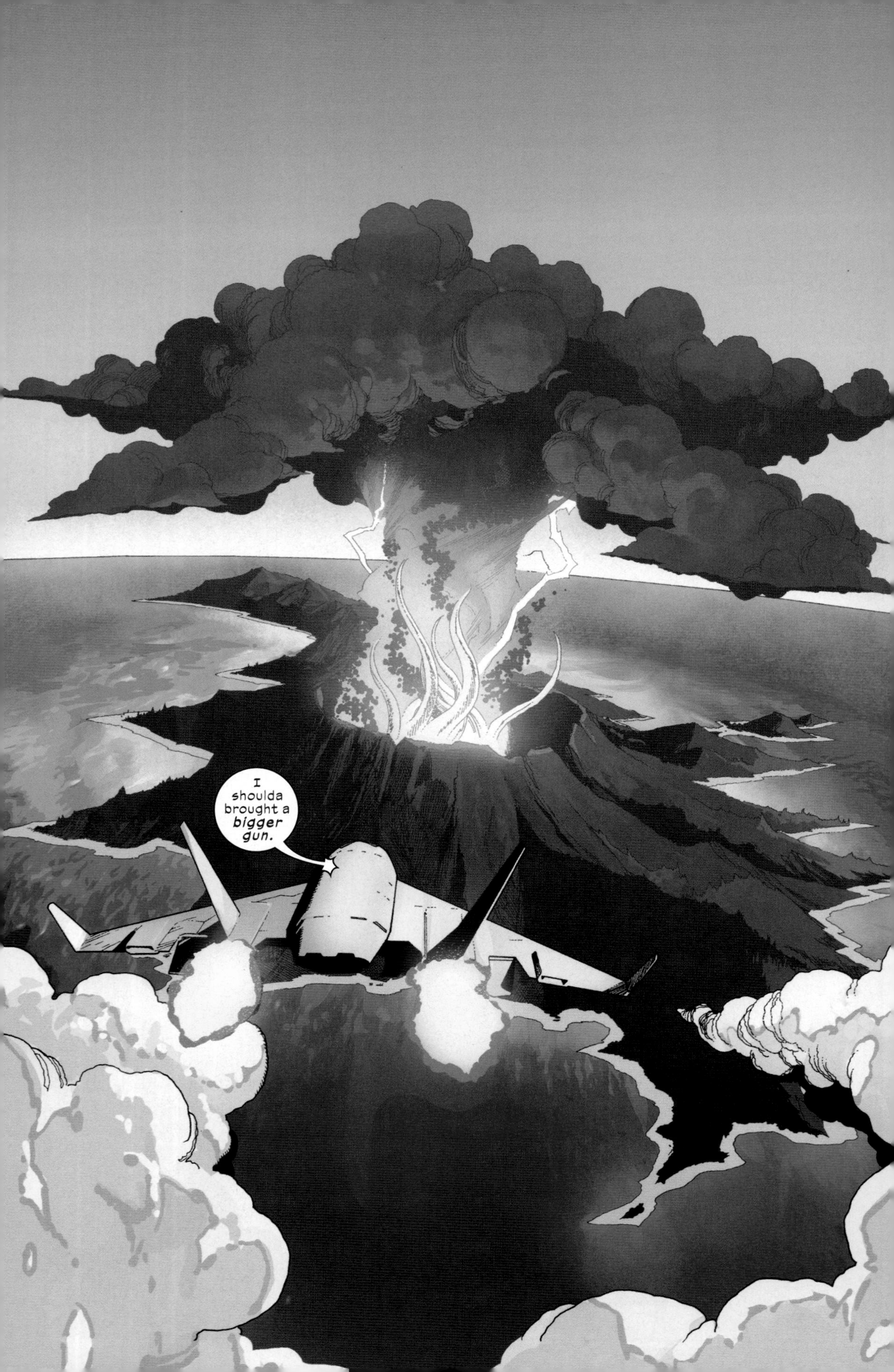
I shoulda brought a *bigger gun.*

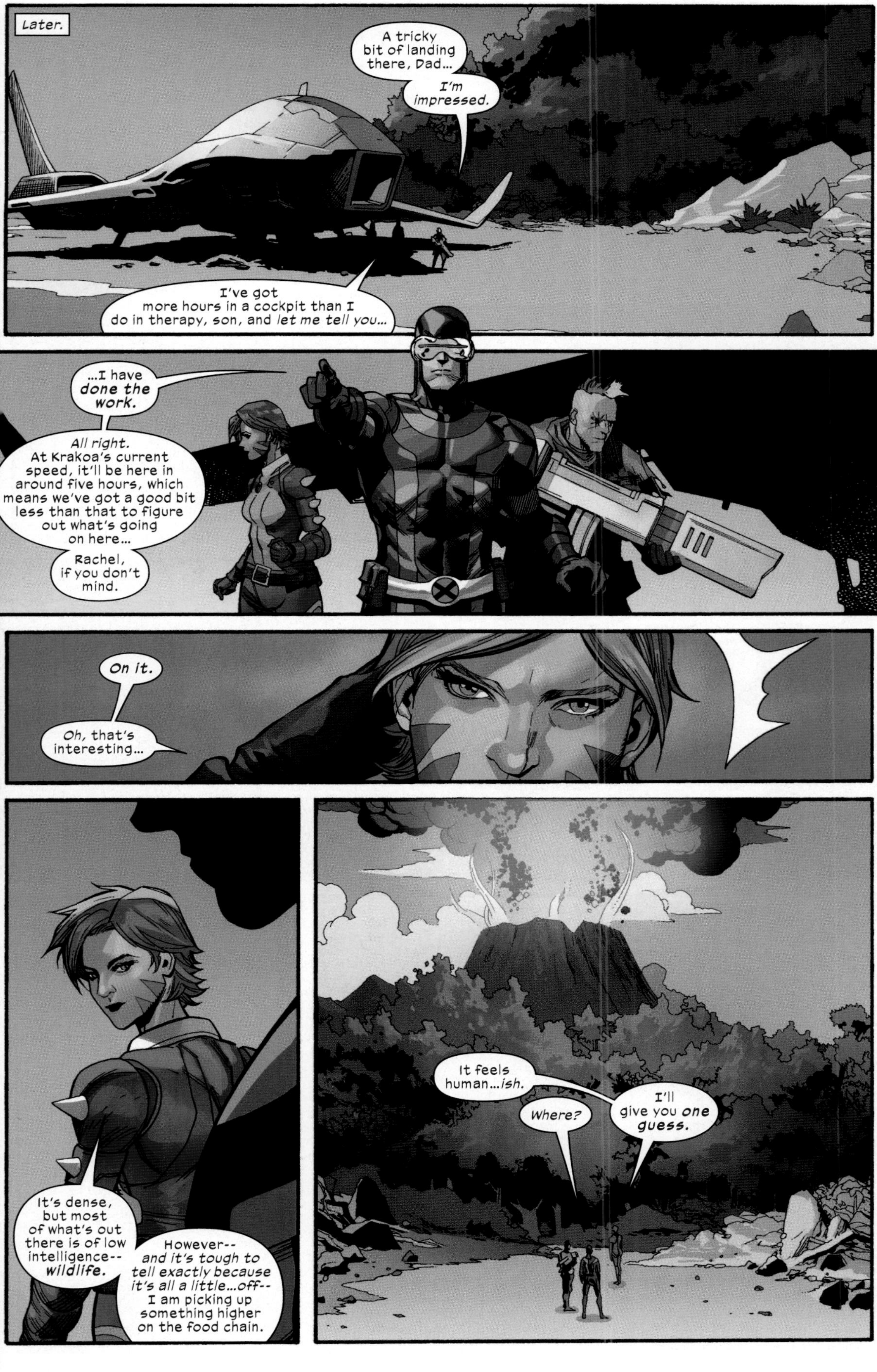
Later.
A tricky bit of landing there, Dad...
I'm impressed.
I've got more hours in a cockpit than I do in therapy, son, and let me tell you...
...I have done the work.
All right. At Krakoa's current speed, it'll be here in around five hours, which means we've got a good bit less than that to figure out what's going on here...
Rachel, if you don't mind.
On it.
Oh, that's interesting...
It's dense, but most of what's out there is of low intelligence-- wildlife.
However-- and it's tough to tell exactly because it's all a little...off-- I am picking up something higher on the food chain.
It feels human...ish.
Where?
I'll give you one guess.

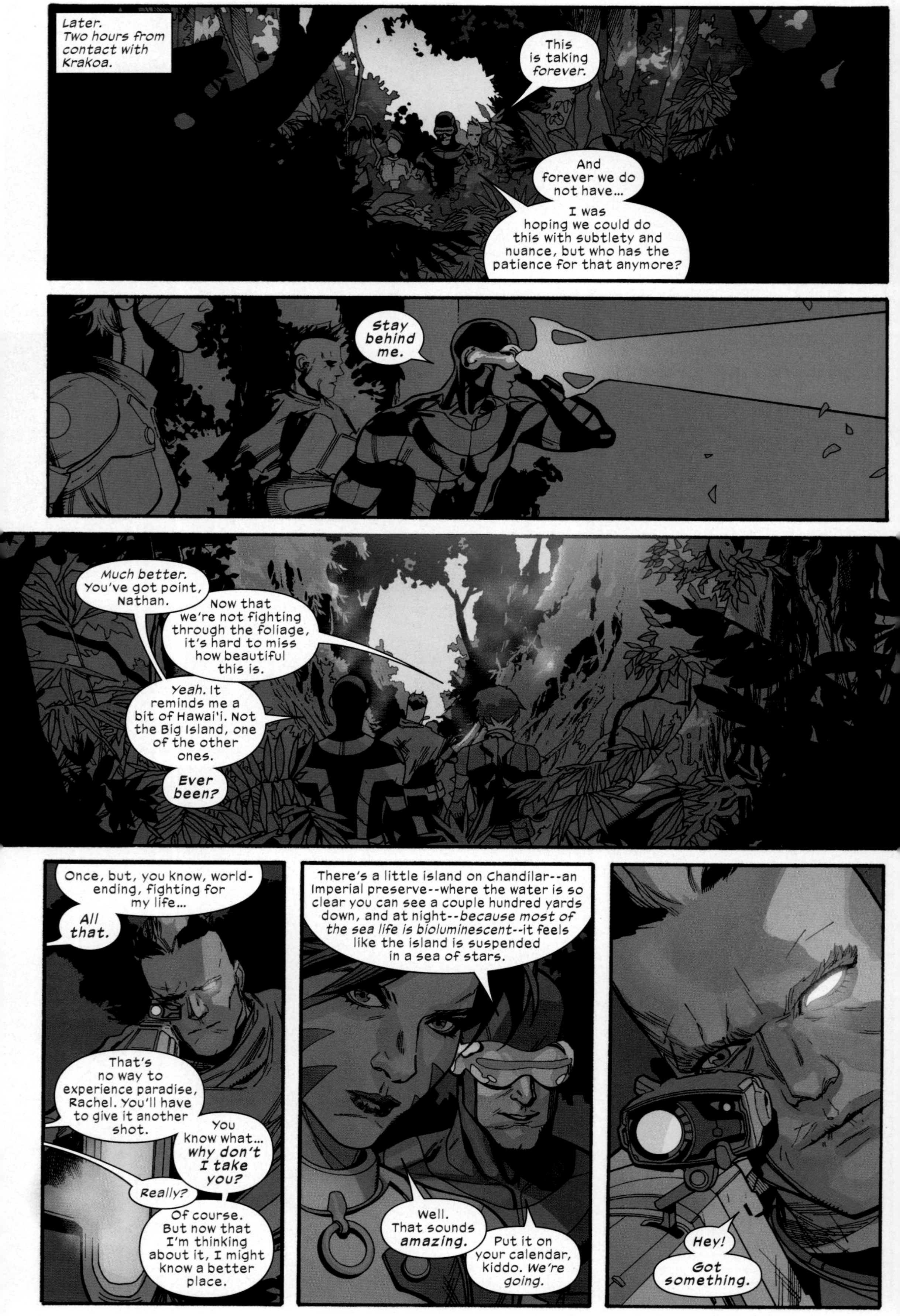

Later. Two hours from contact with Krakoa.
This is taking *forever.*
And forever we do not have...
I was hoping we could do this with subtlety and nuance, but who has the patience for that anymore?
Stay behind me.
Much better. You've got point, Nathan.
Now that we're not fighting through the foliage, it's hard to miss how beautiful this is.
Yeah. It reminds me a bit of Hawai'i. Not the Big Island, one of the other ones.
Ever been?
Once, but, you know, world-ending, fighting for my life...
All that.
There's a little island on Chandilar--an Imperial preserve--where the water is so clear you can see a couple hundred yards down, and at night--*because most of the sea life is bioluminescent*--it feels like the island is suspended in a sea of stars.
Hey! Got something.
That's no way to experience paradise, Rachel. You'll have to give it another shot.
You know what... ***why don't I take you?***
Really?
Of course. But now that I'm thinking about it, I might know a better place.
Well. That sounds ***amazing.***
Put it on your calendar, kiddo. *We're going.*

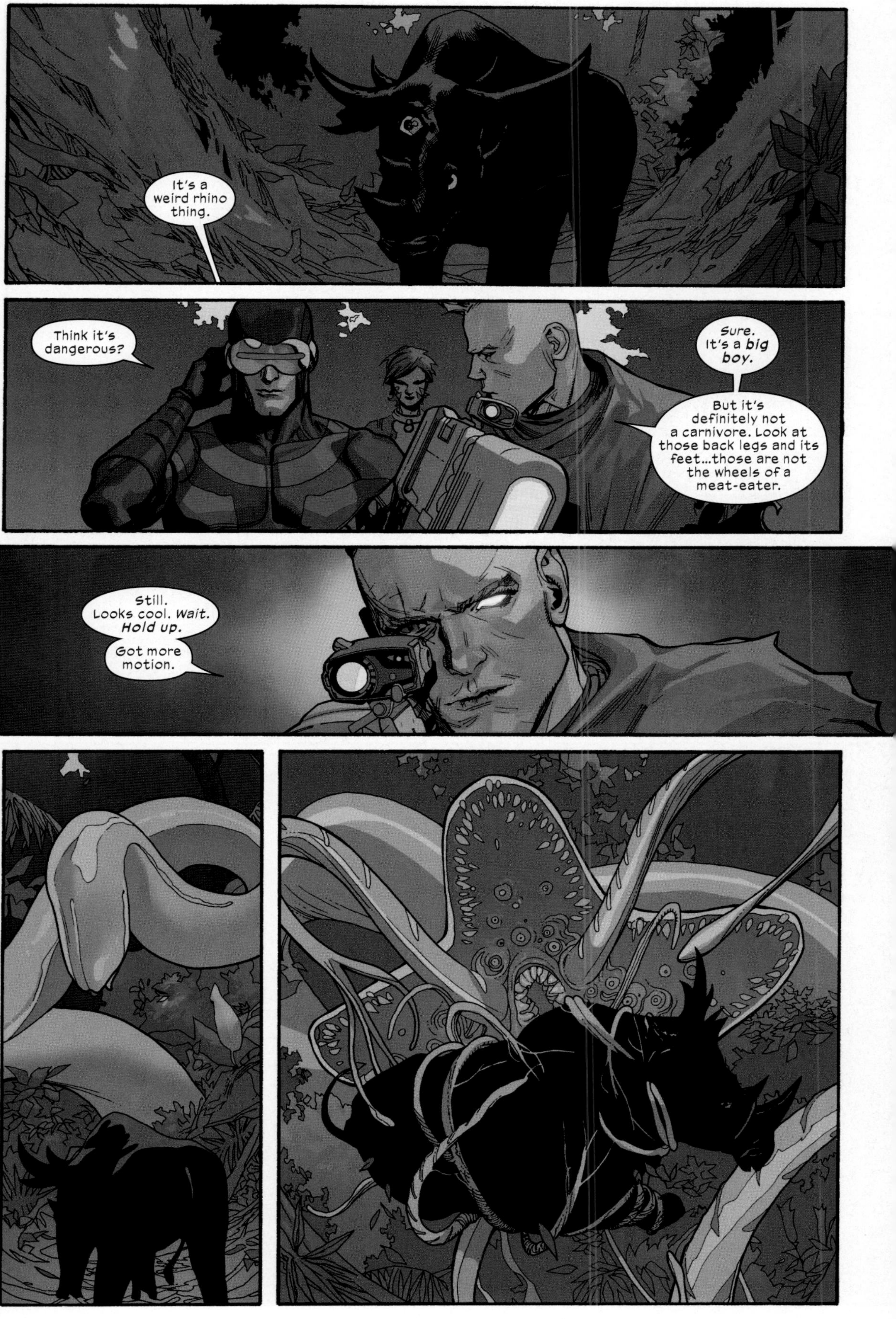
It's a weird rhino thing.
Think it's dangerous?
Sure. It's a *big boy.*
But it's definitely not a carnivore. Look at those back legs and its feet...those are not the wheels of a meat-eater.
Still. Looks cool. *Wait.* ***Hold up.***
Got more motion.

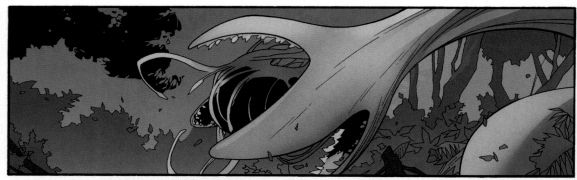

Damn.

Gross.

Okay...now *that's* a meat-eater.

Yes, it is.

Father? Should we...

I don't think we're gonna have a *choice...*

FIRE!

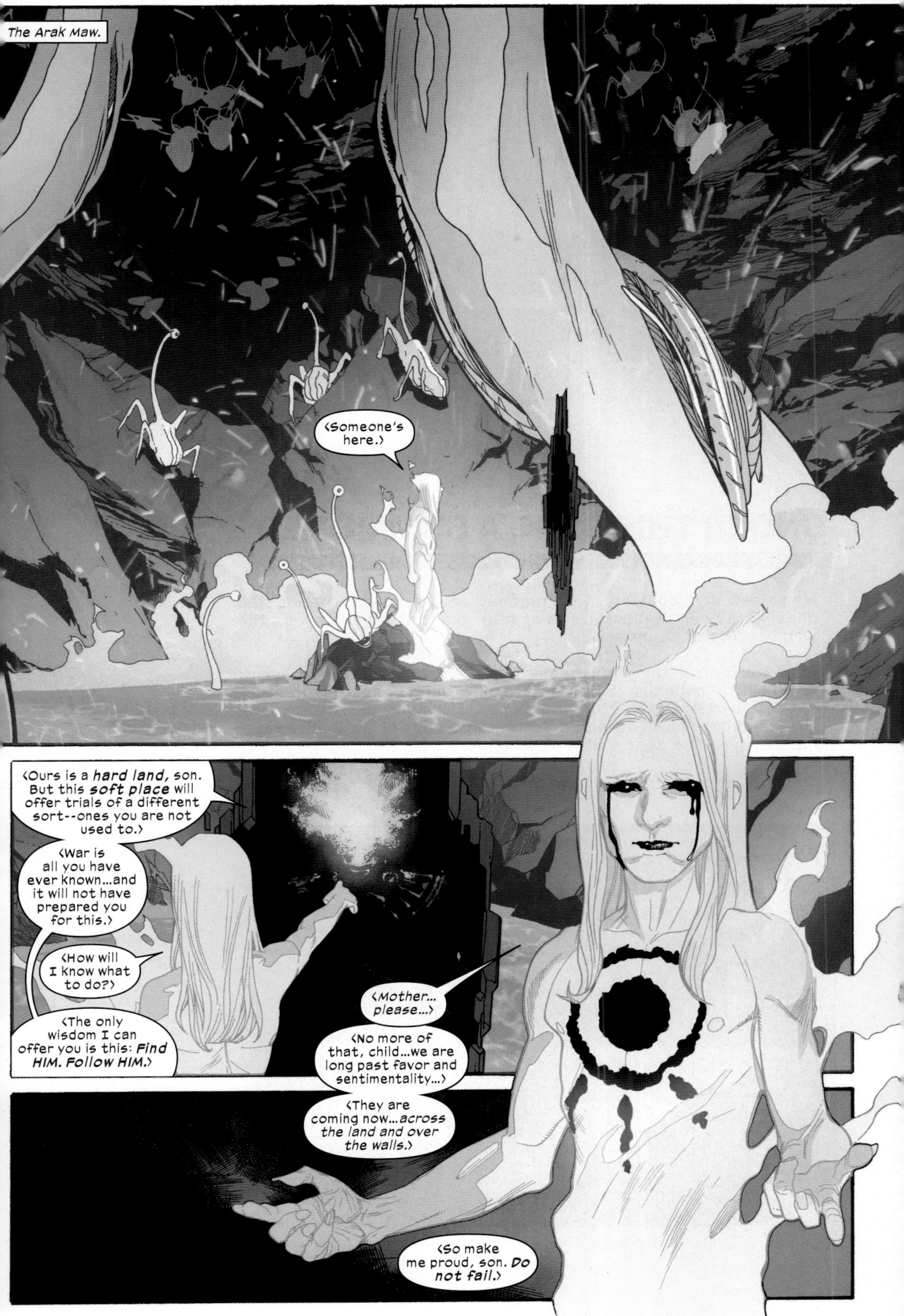
The Arak Maw.
‹Someone's here.›
‹Ours is a hard land, son. But this soft place will offer trials of a different sort--ones you are not used to.›
‹War is all you have ever known...and it will not have prepared you for this.›
‹How will I know what to do?›
‹The only wisdom I can offer you is this: Find HIM. Follow HIM.›
‹Mother... please...›
‹No more of that, child...we are long past favor and sentimentality...›
‹They are coming now...across the land and over the walls.›
‹So make me proud, son. Do not fail.›

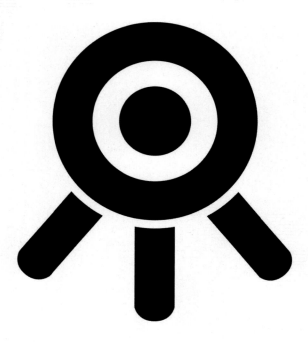

UNDER THIS SIGN, A SUMMONER

Nameless and ageless, a Summoner of Arakko can bridge the chasm between the lost island of Arakko and the land beyond the wild borders of Otherworld.

Able to control the dark beasts that serve the adversaries of Arakko, for millennia Summoners have served as the greatest deterrent to Arakko's eternal enemies. However, in recent years, their numbers have dwindled as the high cost of an endless war has resulted in a dearth of replacements.

Time continues to grow short for Arakko.

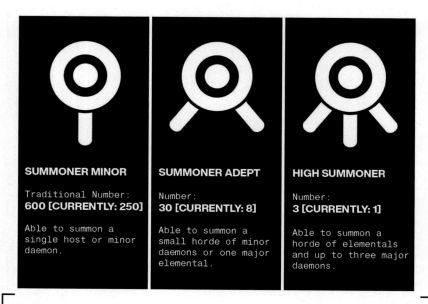

SUMMONER MINOR

Traditional Number:
600 [CURRENTLY: 250]

Able to summon a single host or minor daemon.

SUMMONER ADEPT

Number:
30 [CURRENTLY: 8]

Able to summon a small horde of minor daemons or one major elemental.

HIGH SUMMONER

Number:
3 [CURRENTLY: 1]

Able to summon a horde of elementals and up to three major daemons.

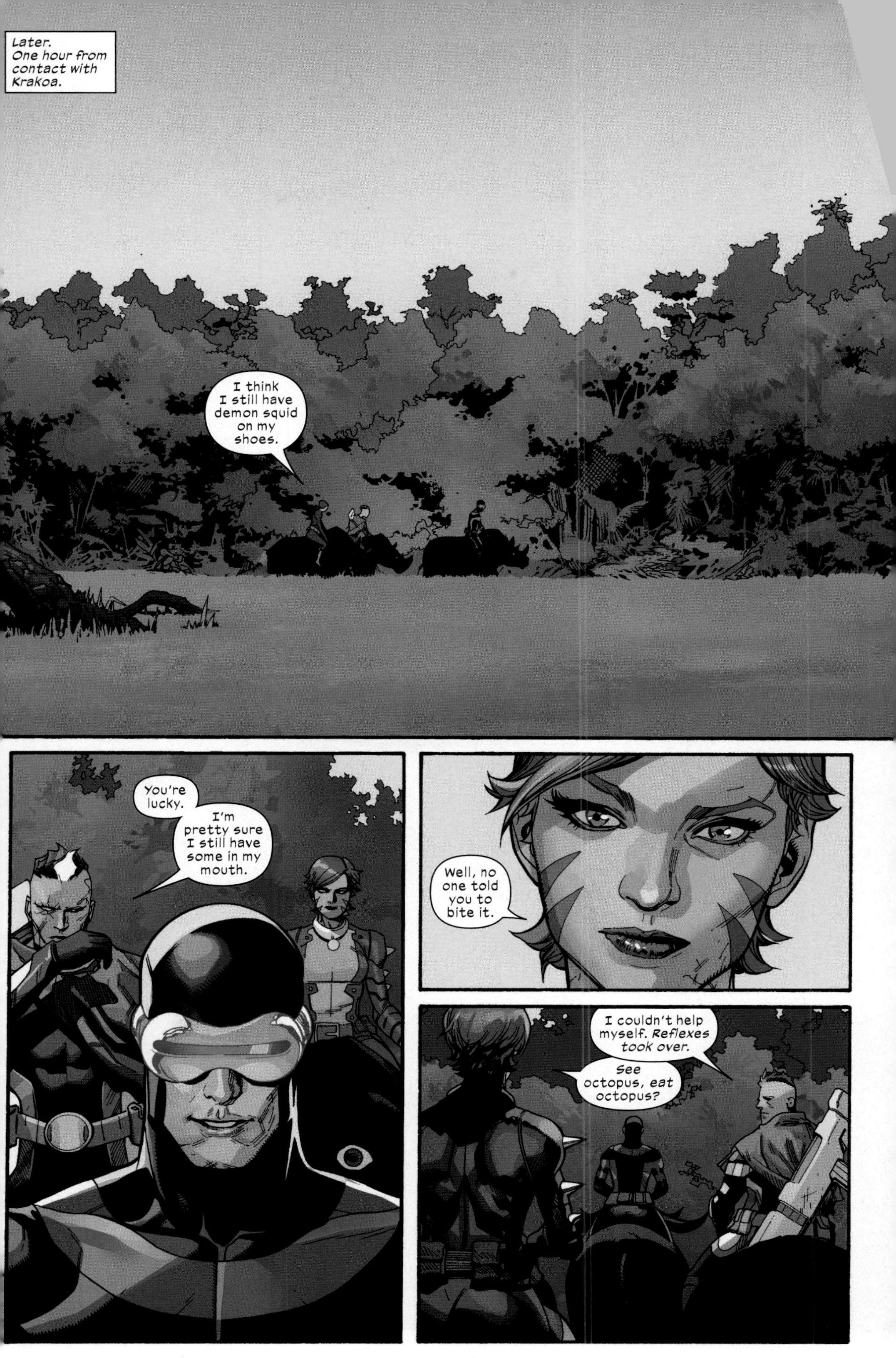
Later. One hour from contact with Krakoa.
I think I still have demon squid on my shoes.
You're lucky.
I'm pretty sure I still have some in my mouth.
Well, no one told you to bite it.
I couldn't help myself. *Reflexes* took over.
See octopus, eat octopus?

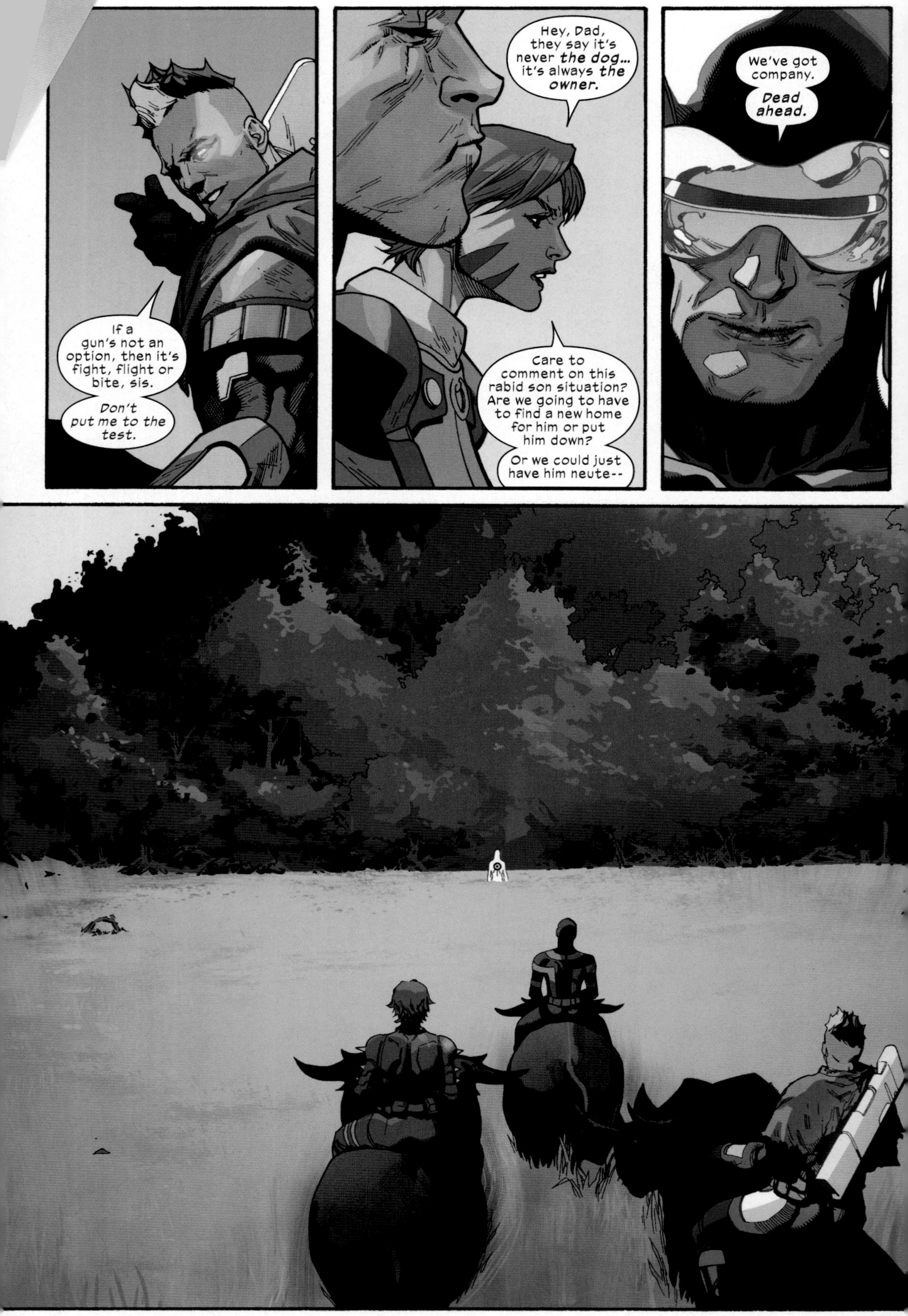

If a gun's not an option, then it's fight, flight or bite, sis.
Don't put me to the test.
Hey, Dad, they say it's never ***the dog...*** it's always ***the owner.***
Care to comment on this rabid son situation? Are we going to have to find a new home for him or put him down?
Or we could just have him neute--
We've got company.
Dead ahead.

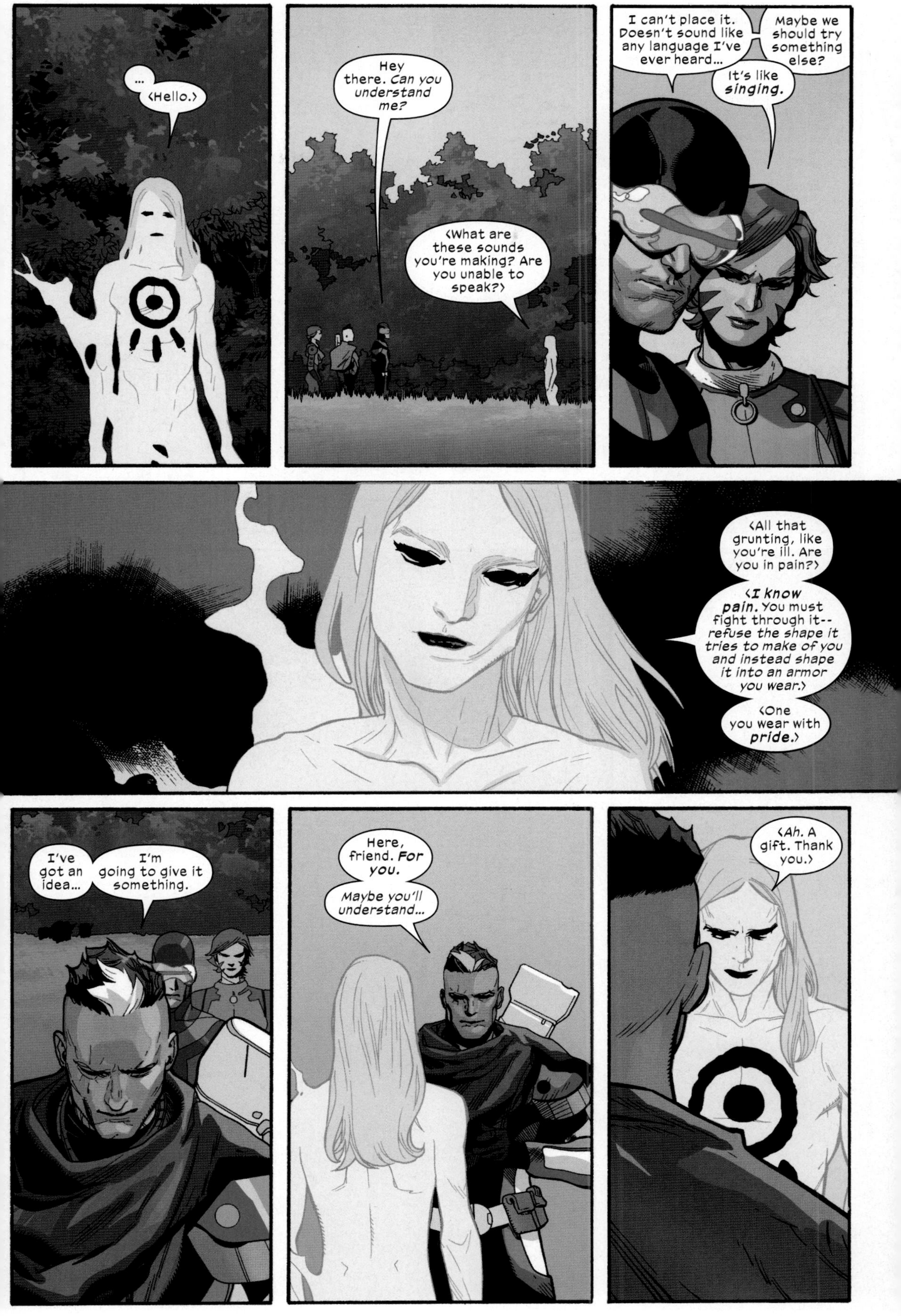

...
‹Hello.›
Hey there. Can you understand me?
‹What are these sounds you're making? Are you unable to speak?›
I can't place it. Doesn't sound like any language I've ever heard...
Maybe we should try something else?
It's like singing.
‹All that grunting, like you're ill. Are you in pain?›
‹I know pain. You must fight through it--refuse the shape it tries to make of you and instead shape it into an armor you wear.›
‹One you wear with pride.›
I've got an idea...
I'm going to give it something.
Here, friend. For you.
Maybe you'll understand...
‹Ah. A gift. Thank you.›

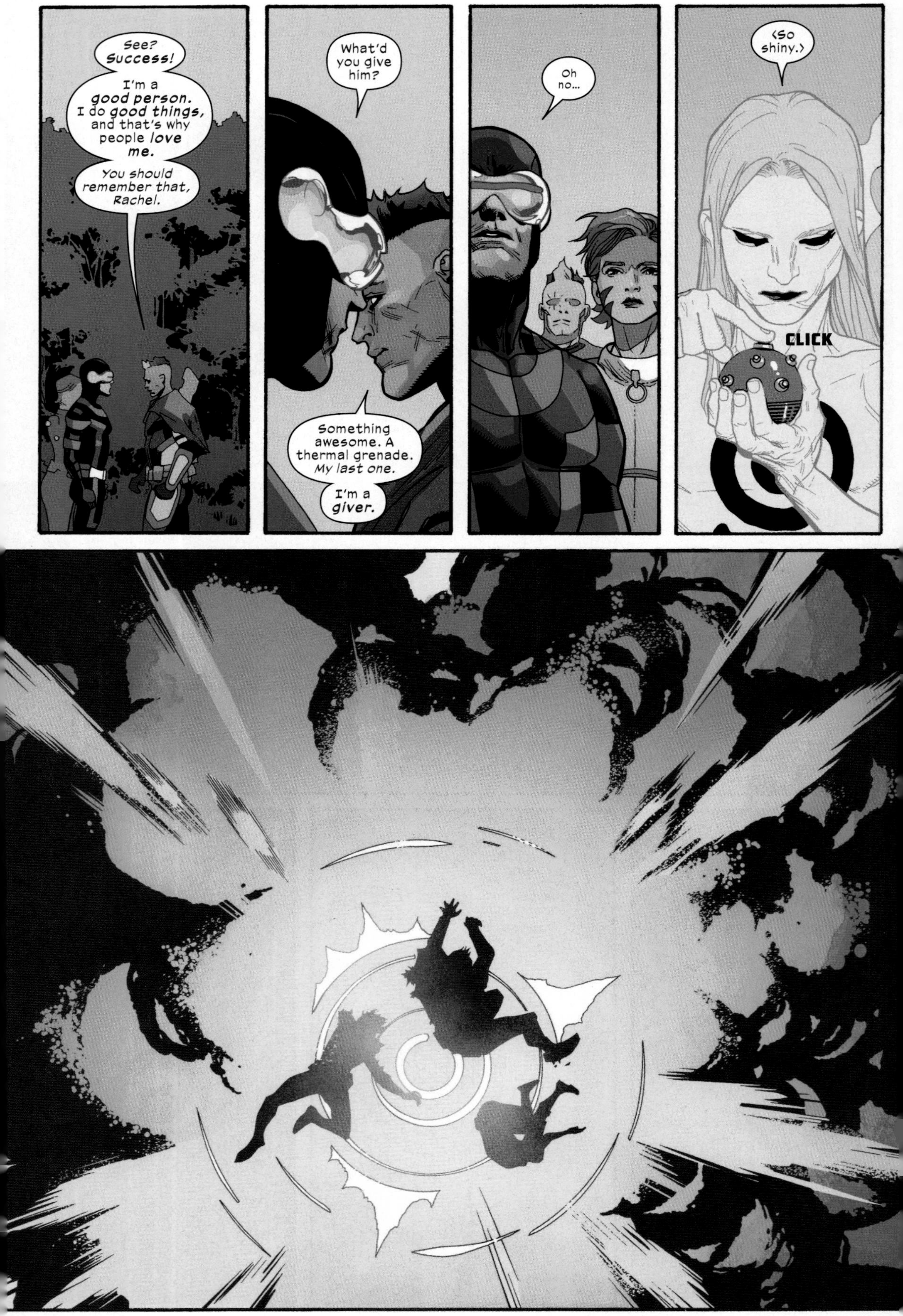
See? Success!
I'm a good person. I do good things, and that's why people love me.
You should remember that, Rachel.
What'd you give him?
Something awesome. A thermal grenade. My last one.
I'm a giver.
Oh no...
‹So shiny.›
CLICK

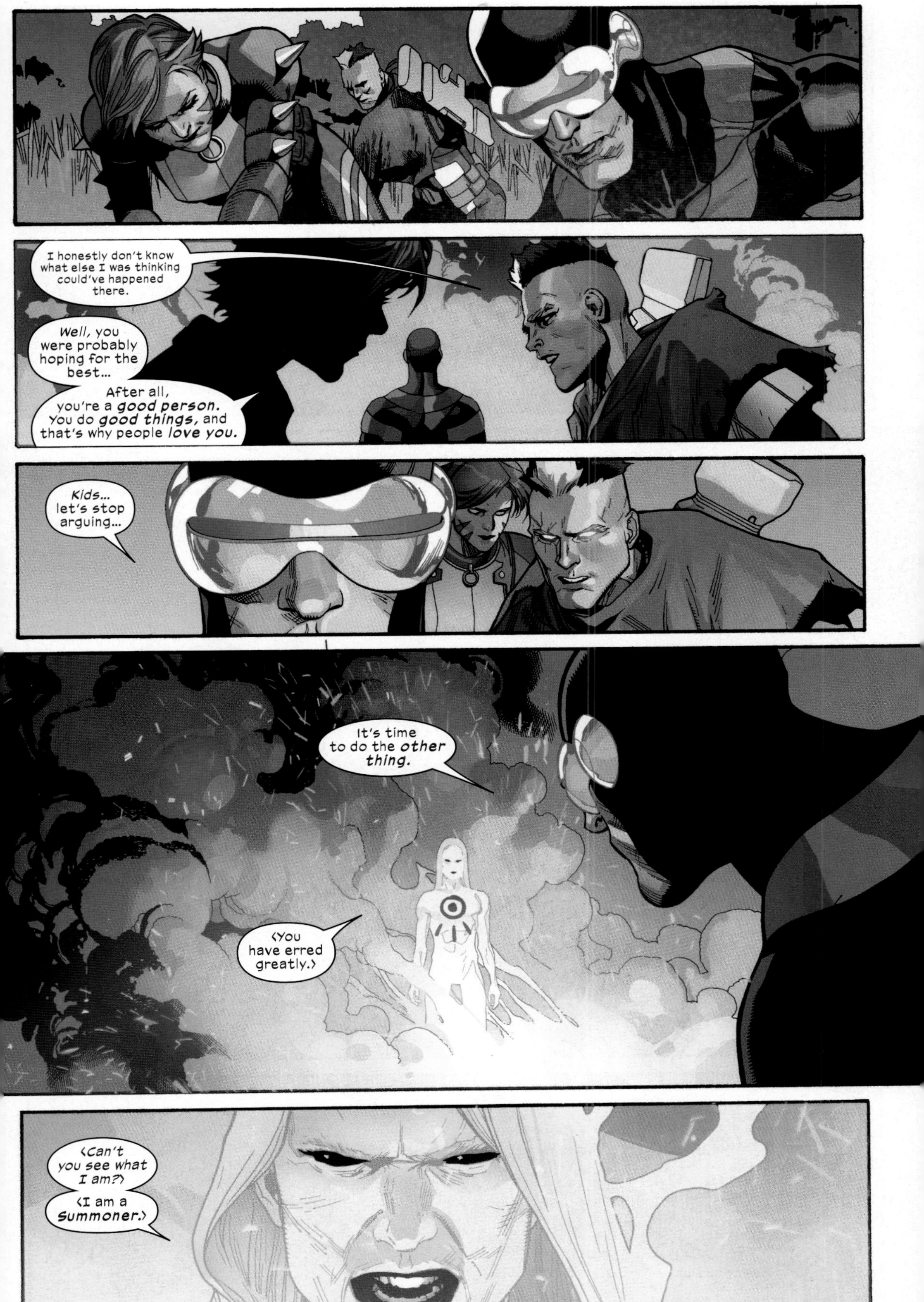
I honestly don't know what else I was thinking could've happened there.
Well, you were probably hoping for the best...
After all, you're a good person. You do good things, and that's why people love you.
Kids... let's stop arguing...
It's time to do the other thing.
‹You have erred greatly.›
‹Can't you see what I am?›
‹I am a Summoner.›

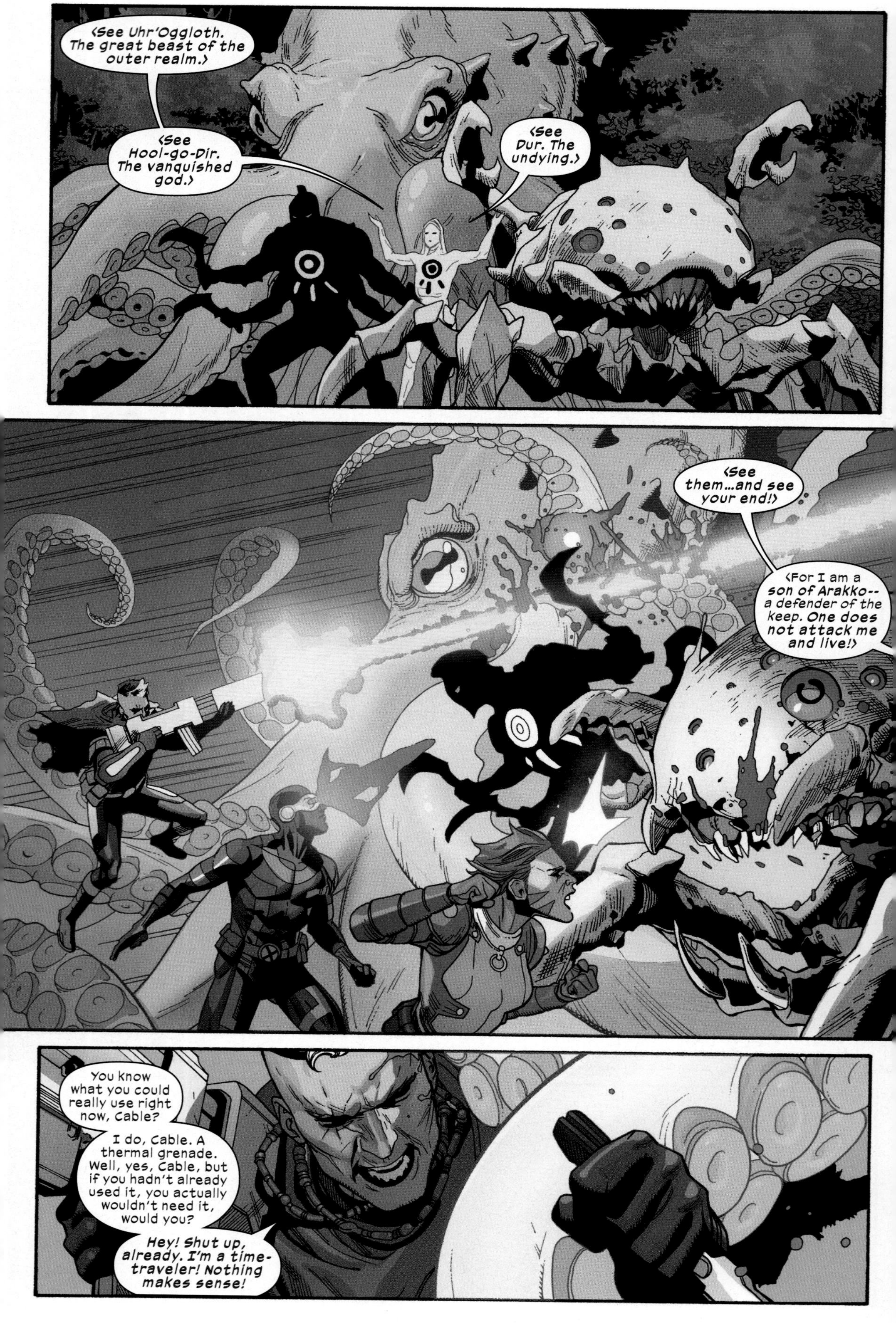
‹See Uhr'Oggloth. The great beast of the outer realm.›
‹See Hool-go-Dir. The vanquished god.›
‹See Dur. The undying.›
‹See them...and see your end!›
‹For I am a son of Arakko--a defender of the keep. One does not attack me and live!›
You know what you could really use right now, Cable?
I do, Cable. A thermal grenade.
Well, yes, Cable, but if you hadn't already used it, you actually wouldn't need it, would you?
Hey! Shut up, already. I'm a time-traveler! Nothing makes sense!

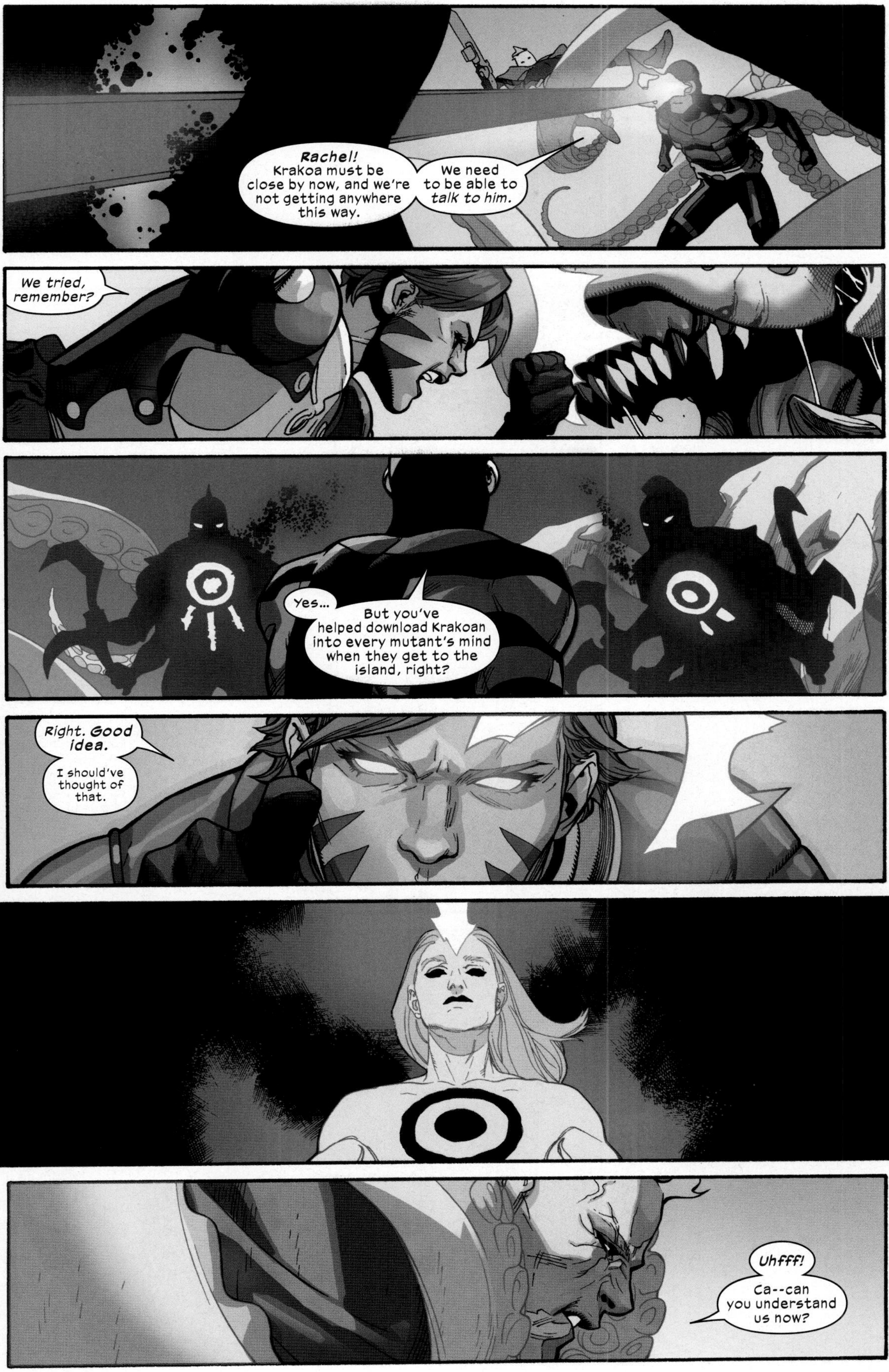
Rachel! Krakoa must be close by now, and we're not getting anywhere this way.
We need to be able to talk to him.
We tried, remember?
Yes...
But you've helped download Krakoan into every mutant's mind when they get to the island, right?
Right. Good idea.
I should've thought of that.
Uhfff!
Ca--can you understand us now?

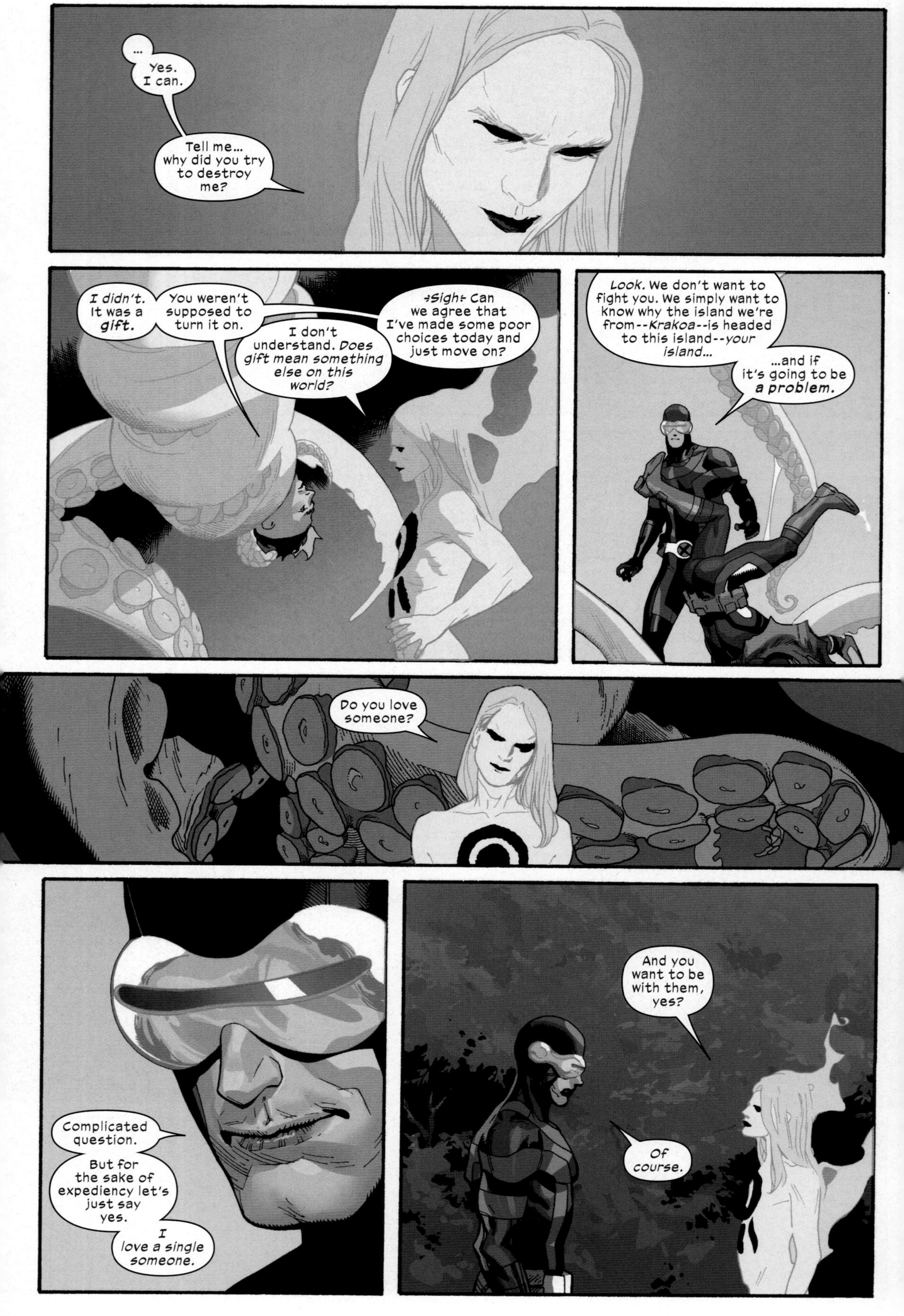
...
Yes. I can.
Tell me... why did you try to destroy me?
I didn't. It was a *gift.*
You weren't supposed to turn it on.
I don't understand. *Does gift mean something else on this world?*
-Sigh- Can we agree that I've made some poor choices today and just move on?
Look. We don't want to fight you. We simply want to know why the island we're from--*Krakoa*--is headed to this island--*your island...*
...and if it's going to be ***a problem.***
Do you love someone?
Complicated question.
But for the sake of expediency let's just say yes.
I love a single someone.
And you want to be with them, yes?
Of course.

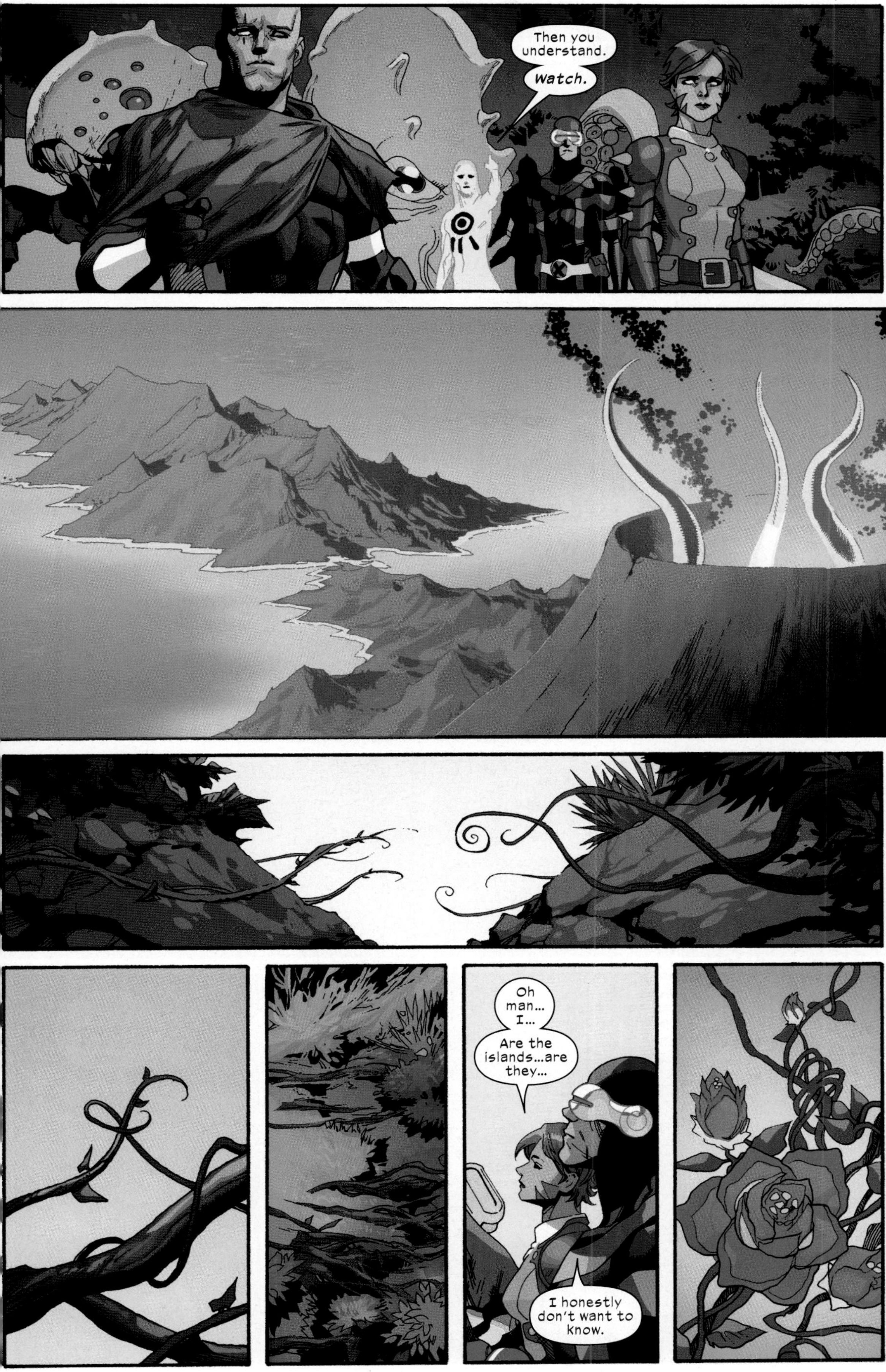
Then you understand.
Watch.
Oh man... I...
Are the islands...are they...
I honestly don't want to know.

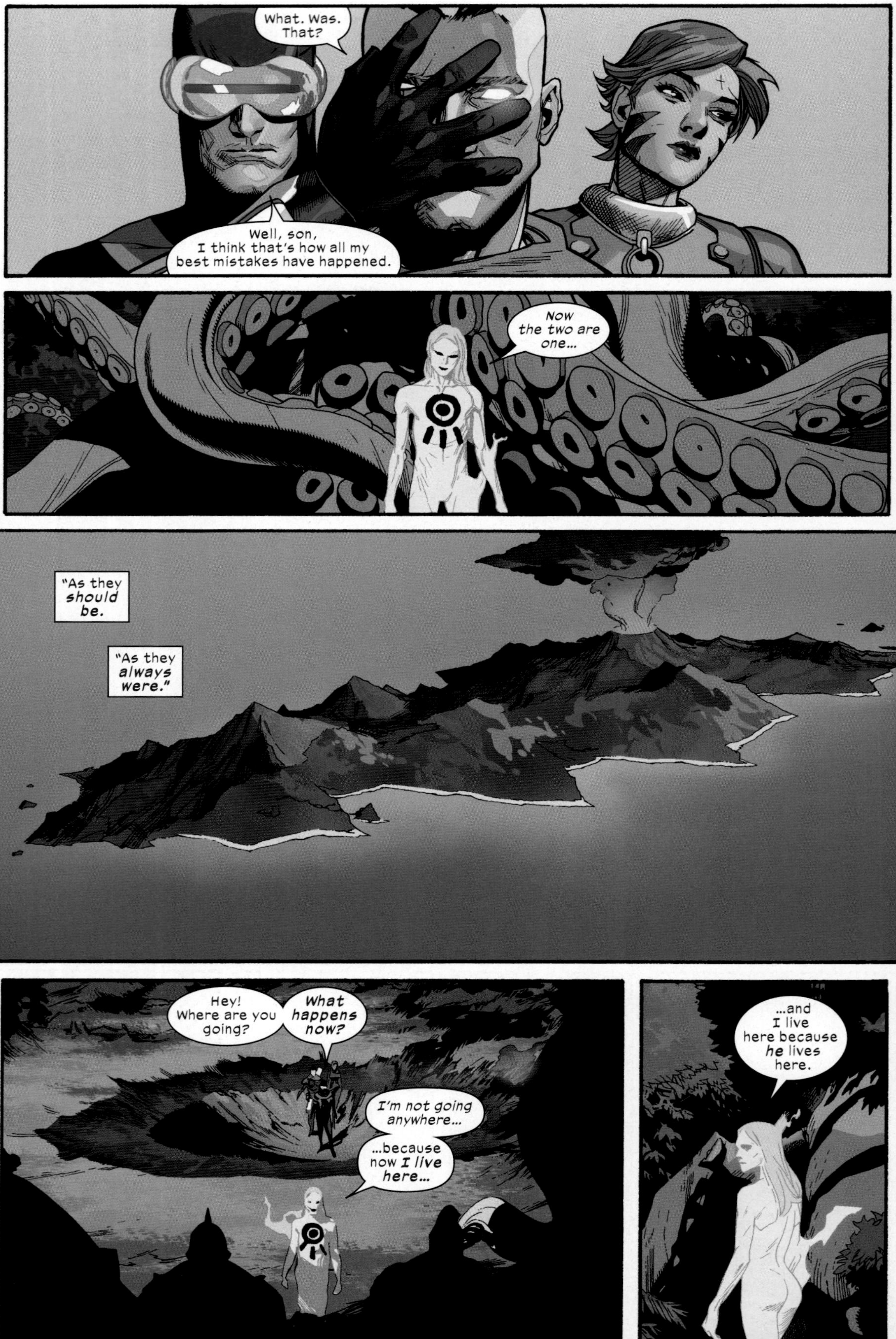
What. Was. That?
Well, son, I think that's how all my best mistakes have happened.
Now the two are one...
"As they should be.
"As they always were."
Hey! Where are you going?
What happens now?
I'm not going anywhere...
...because now I live here...
...and I live here because he lives here.

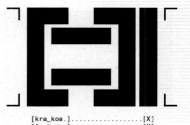

_ KRAKOA [+ARAK CORAL]

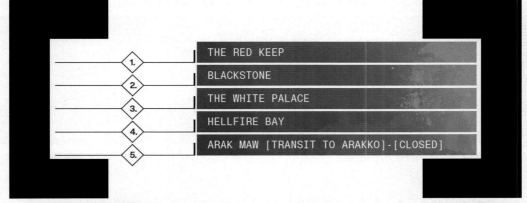

1.	THE RED KEEP
2.	BLACKSTONE
3.	THE WHITE PALACE
4.	HELLFIRE BAY
5.	ARAK MAW [TRANSIT TO ARAKKO]-[CLOSED]

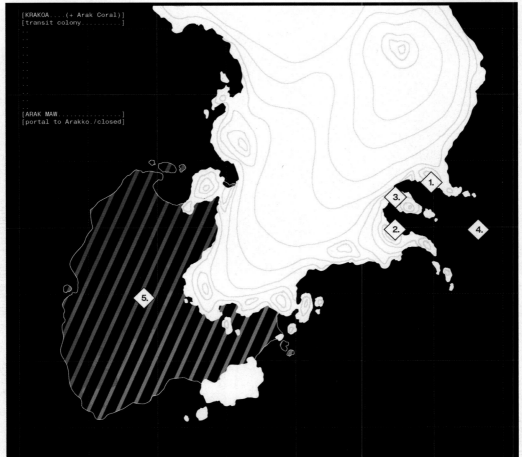

[KRAKOA....(+ Arak Coral)]
[transit colony..........]
..
..
..
..
..
..
..
..
..
[ARAK MAW...............]
[portal to Arakko./closed]

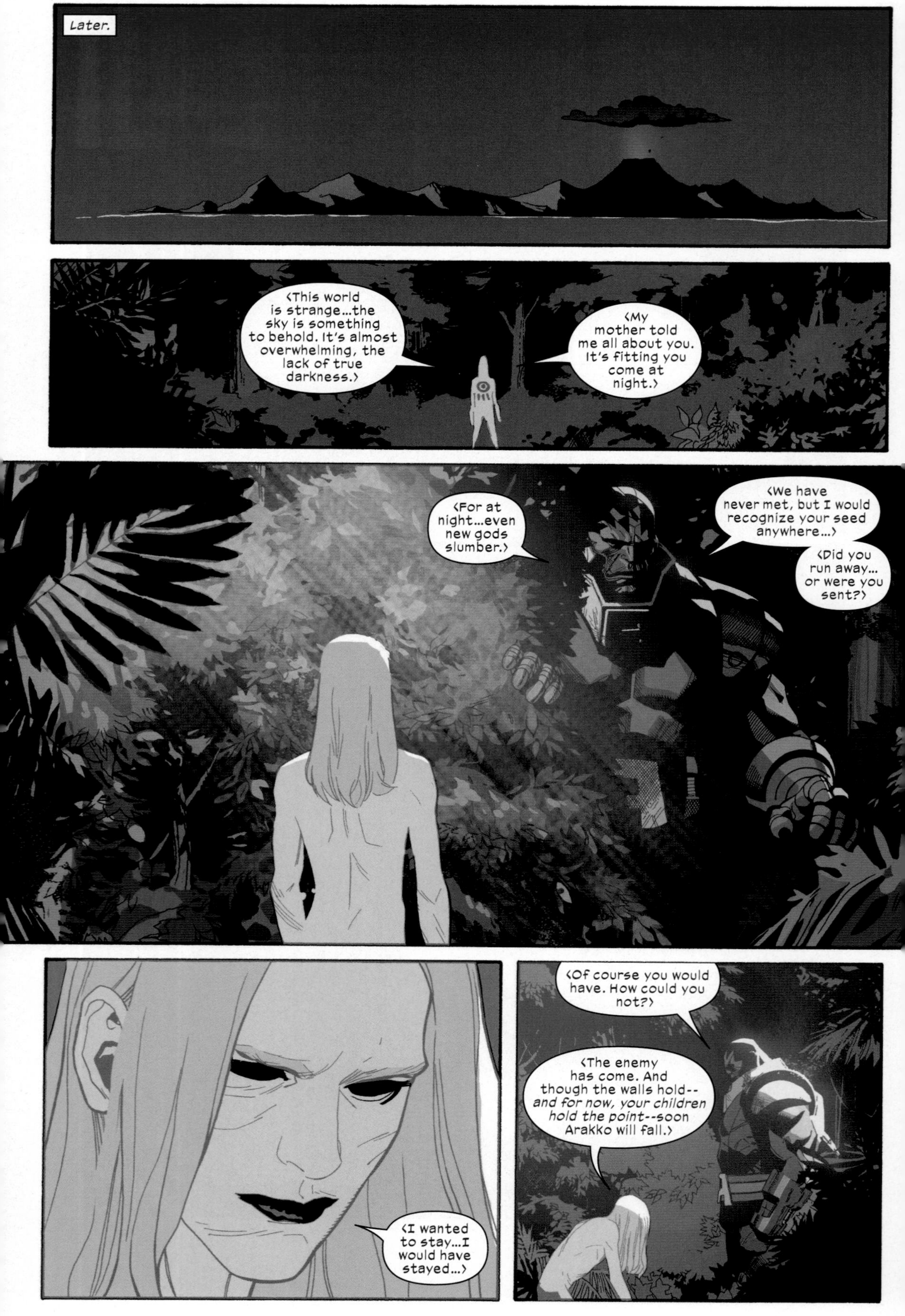
Later.
‹This world is strange...the sky is something to behold. It's almost overwhelming, the lack of true darkness.›
‹My mother told me all about you. It's fitting you come at night.›
‹For at night...even new gods slumber.›
‹We have never met, but I would recognize your seed anywhere...›
‹Did you run away... or were you sent?›
‹I wanted to stay...I would have stayed...›
‹Of course you would have. How could you not?›
‹The enemy has come. And though the walls hold--*and for now, your children hold the point*--soon Arakko will fall.›

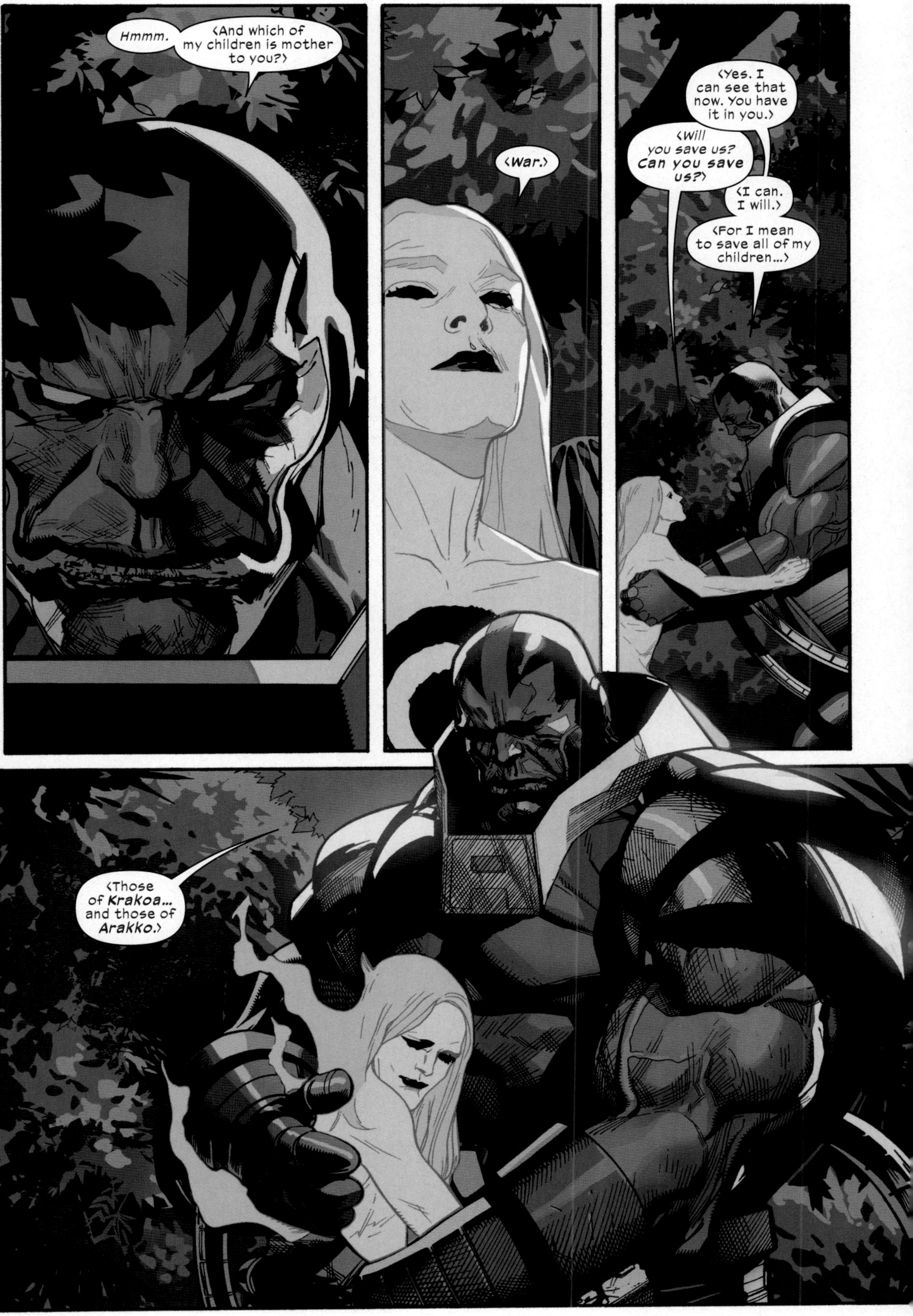
Hmmm.
‹And which of my children is mother to you?›
‹War.›
‹Yes. I can see that now. You have it in you.›
‹Will you save us? **Can you save us?**›
‹I can. I will.›
‹For I mean to save all of my children...›
‹Those of **Krakoa...** and those of **Arakko.**›

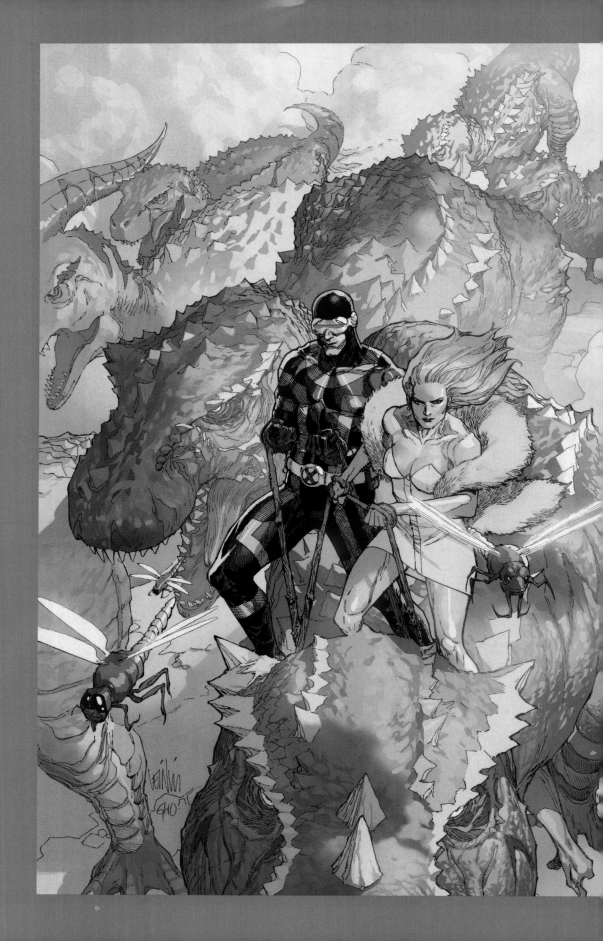

Hordeculture

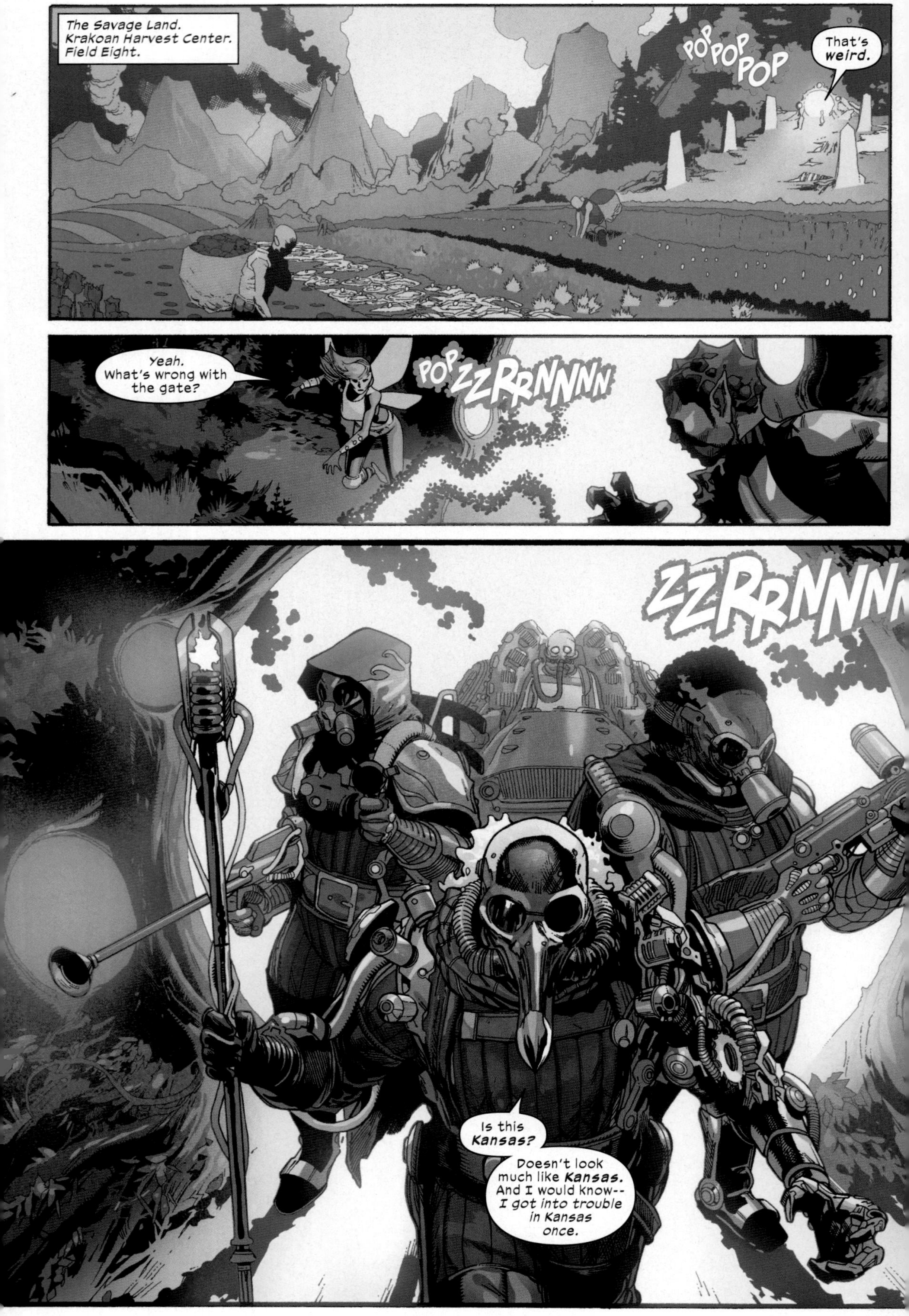
The Savage Land.
Krakoan Harvest Center.
Field Eight.
POP POP POP POP
That's weird.
Yeah. What's wrong with the gate?
POP ZZRRNNNN
ZZRRNNNN
Is this Kansas?
Doesn't look much like Kansas. And I would know-- I got into trouble in Kansas once.

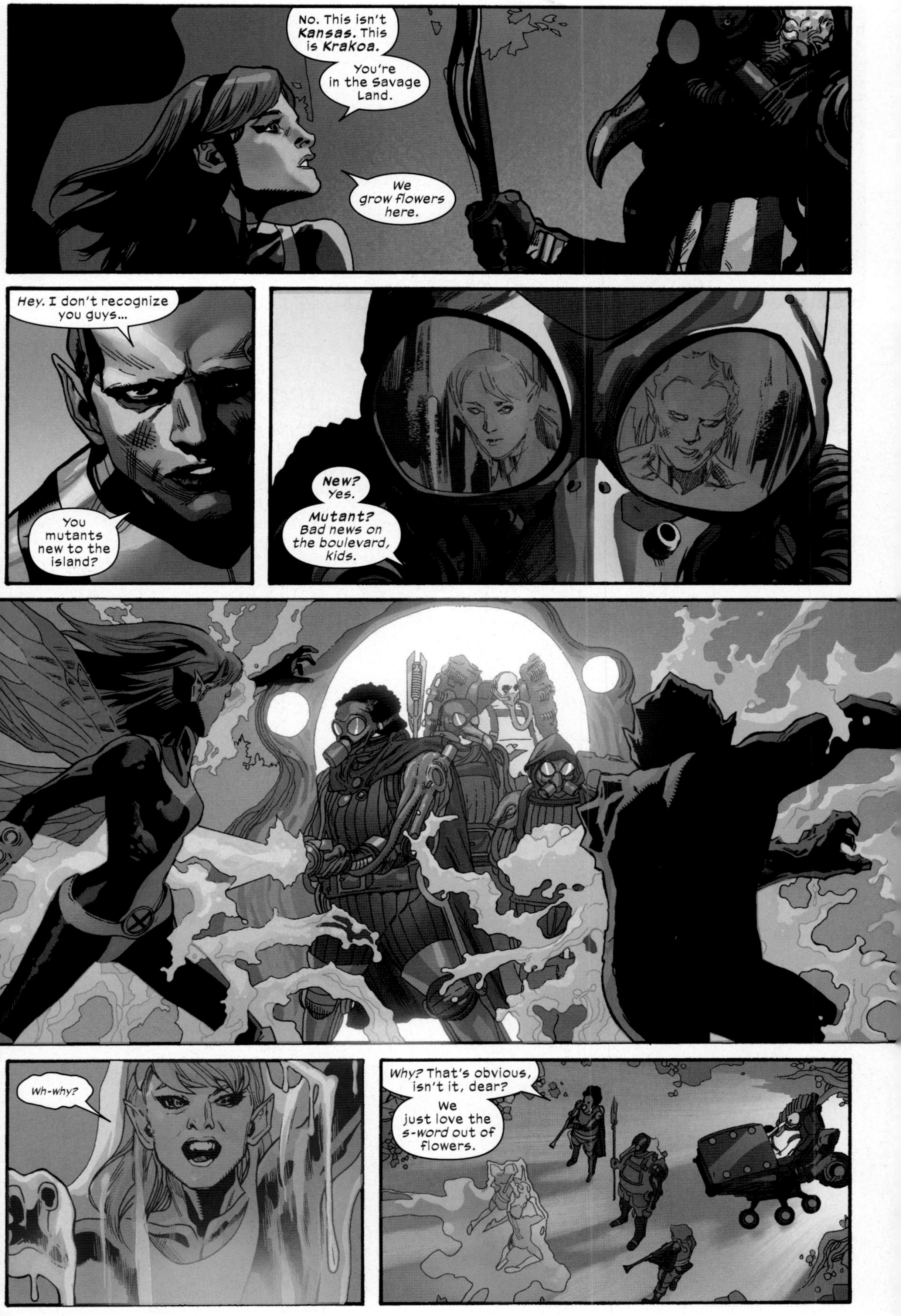
No. This isn't Kansas. This is Krakoa.
You're in the Savage Land.
We grow flowers here.
Hey. I don't recognize you guys...
You mutants new to the island?
New? Yes.
Mutant? Bad news on the boulevard, kids.
Wh-why?
Why? That's obvious, isn't it, dear?
We just love the s-word out of flowers.

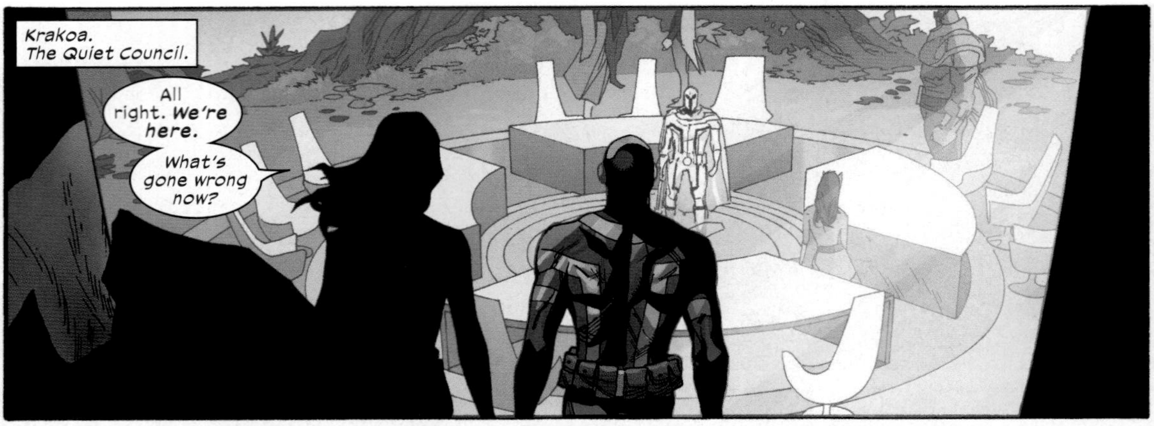
Krakoa.
The Quiet Council.
All right. We're here.
What's gone wrong now?

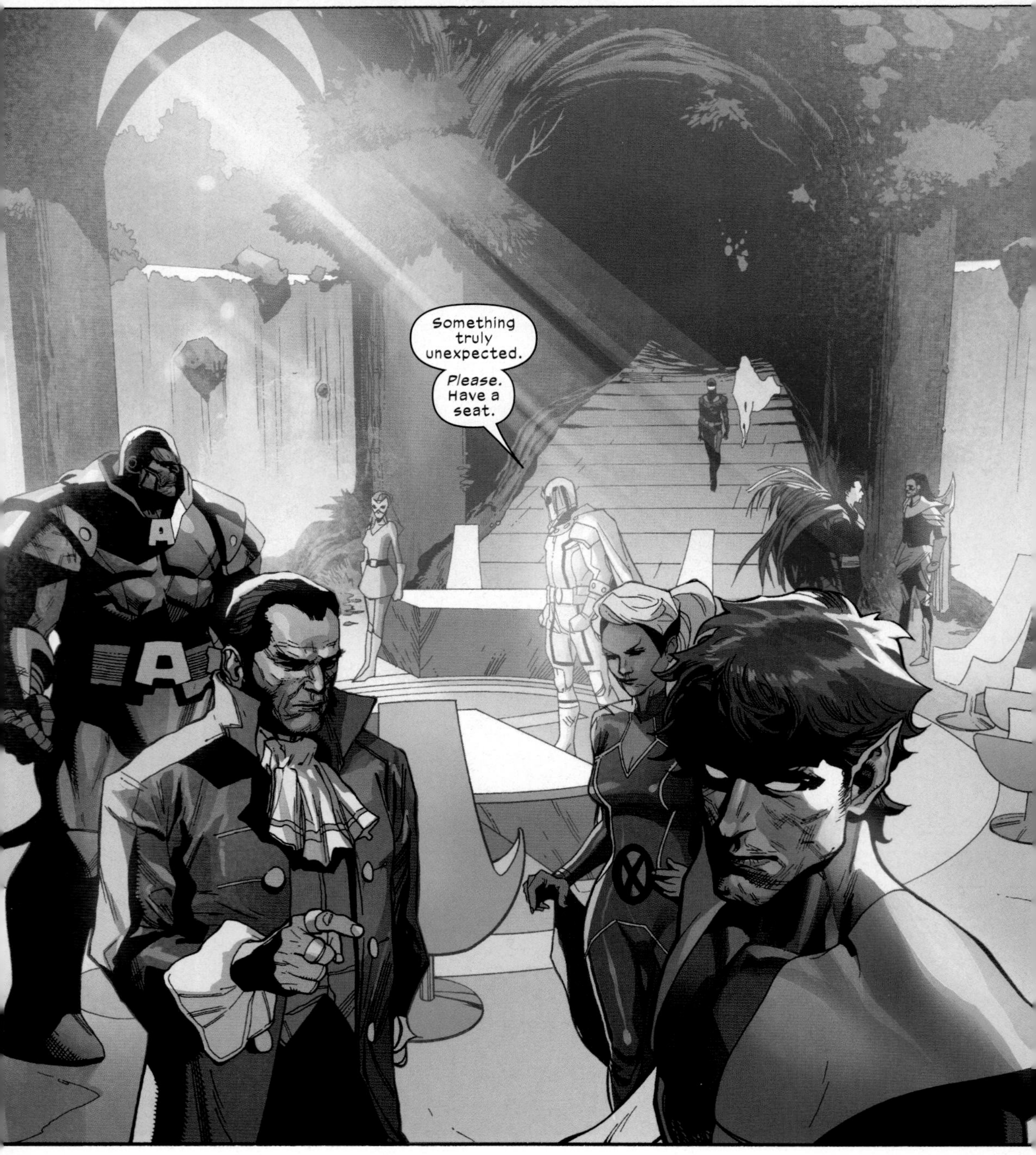
Something truly unexpected.
Please. Have a seat.

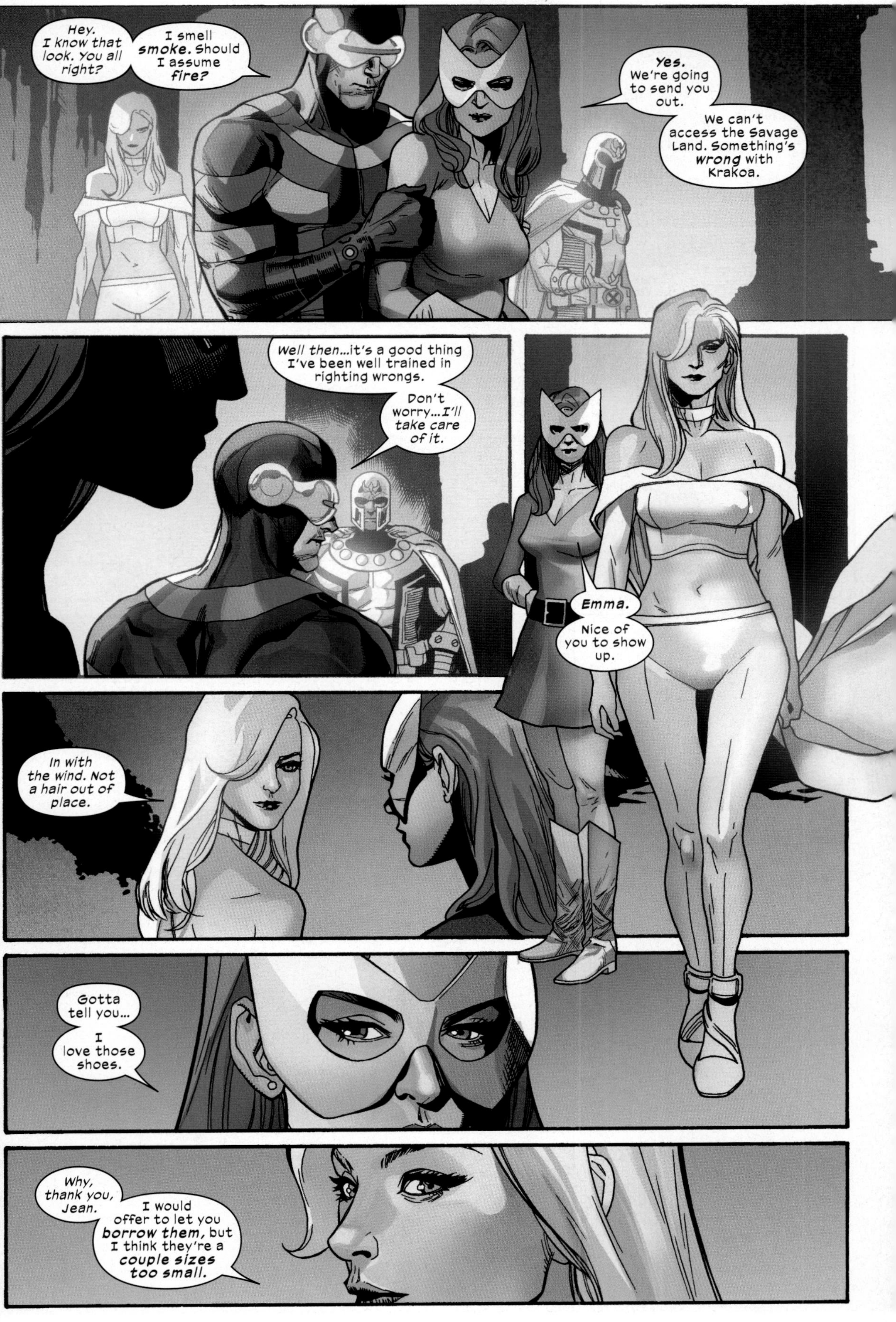
Hey. I know that look. You all right?
I smell smoke. Should I assume fire?
Yes. We're going to send you out.
We can't access the Savage Land. Something's wrong with Krakoa.
Well then...it's a good thing I've been well trained in righting wrongs.
Don't worry...I'll take care of it.
Emma.
Nice of you to show up.
In with the wind. Not a hair out of place.
Gotta tell you...
I love those shoes.
Why, thank you, Jean.
I would offer to let you borrow them, but I think they're a couple sizes too small.

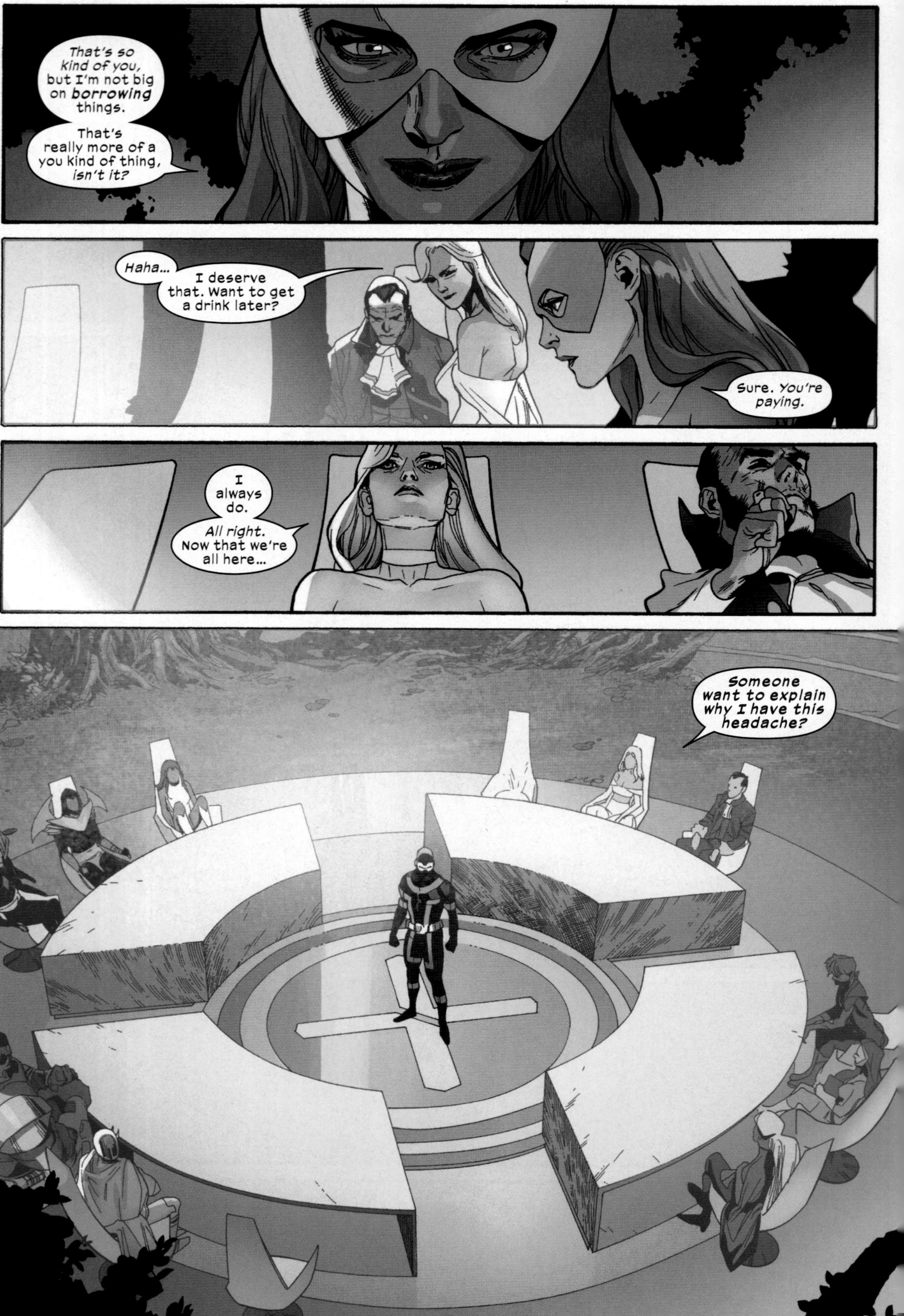

That's so kind of you, but I'm not big on borrowing things.
That's really more of a you kind of thing, isn't it?
Haha... I deserve that. Want to get a drink later?
Sure. You're paying.
I always do.
All right. Now that we're all here...
Someone want to explain why I have this headache?

[00.Krakoa.........X]
[00................0]

KRAKOA IS SCREAMING

SAVAGE LAND GATEWAY NONRESPONSIVE

[Krakoa].............[EAT]
[......].............[NUL]

The [suspected] forced seizure of a Krakoan gate has caused Krakoa itself incredible discomfort -- this has resulted in several unexpected, abnormal island disturbances:

- Krakoan wildlife has gotten more aggressive. After a period of over a month with no reported incidences with the island's wildlife, there have been six in the last hour.
- Undetectable to most mutants, Black Tom Cassidy has noted a decrease in island mass. Beast has confirmed this and noted a decrease of .0001 percent, or roughly 158 square feet.
- Finally, all telepaths within the localized manifestation of the island are currently experiencing an increased level of psychic assault/consumption.*

An action team has been tasked with discovering what has happened to the gate and, if possible, re-establishing its connection to Krakoa.

FEED THE ISLAND

*As most know, Krakoa "feeds" on the psychic energy of mutants. When the island is at maximum growth [not the contracted, pre-nation state, "winter" version], Krakoa needs to consume two mutants a year to maintain a stable environment. However, the current population of Krakoa means that only a minimal amount of psychic energy is needed from each citizen to maintain the health of the island -- something each mutant is happy to give.

There are aggressive protocols in place to ensure that Krakoa is not exceeding its minimal psychic draw. Two mutants who share similar limitations as the island [mutants who feed on mutants], Selene and Emplate, have been tasked to observe the levels of psychic depletion among the island's mutant population. [Similar protocols are used for the two of them as well.]

[SELENE]................[EAT]
[MPLATE]................[ALL]

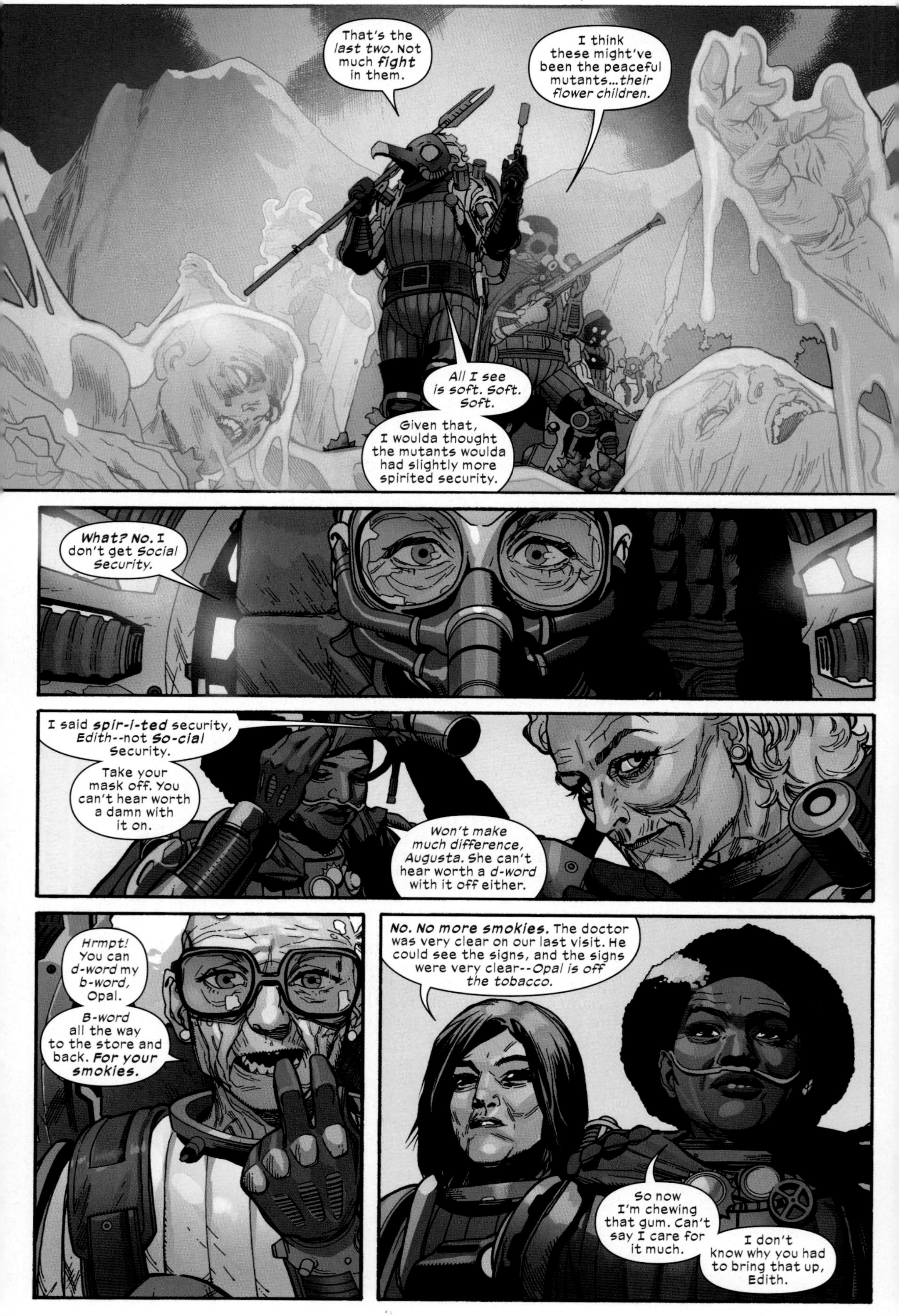

That's the last two. Not much fight in them.
I think these might've been the peaceful mutants...their flower children.
All I see is soft. Soft. Soft.
Given that, I woulda thought the mutants woulda had slightly more spirited security.
What? No. I don't get Social Security.
I said spir-i-ted security, Edith--not So-cial Security.
Take your mask off. You can't hear worth a damn with it on.
Won't make much difference, Augusta. She can't hear worth a d-word with it off either.
Hrmpt! You can d-word my b-word, Opal.
B-word all the way to the store and back. For your smokies.
No. No more smokies. The doctor was very clear on our last visit. He could see the signs, and the signs were very clear--Opal is off the tobacco.
So now I'm chewing that gum. Can't say I care for it much.
I don't know why you had to bring that up, Edith.

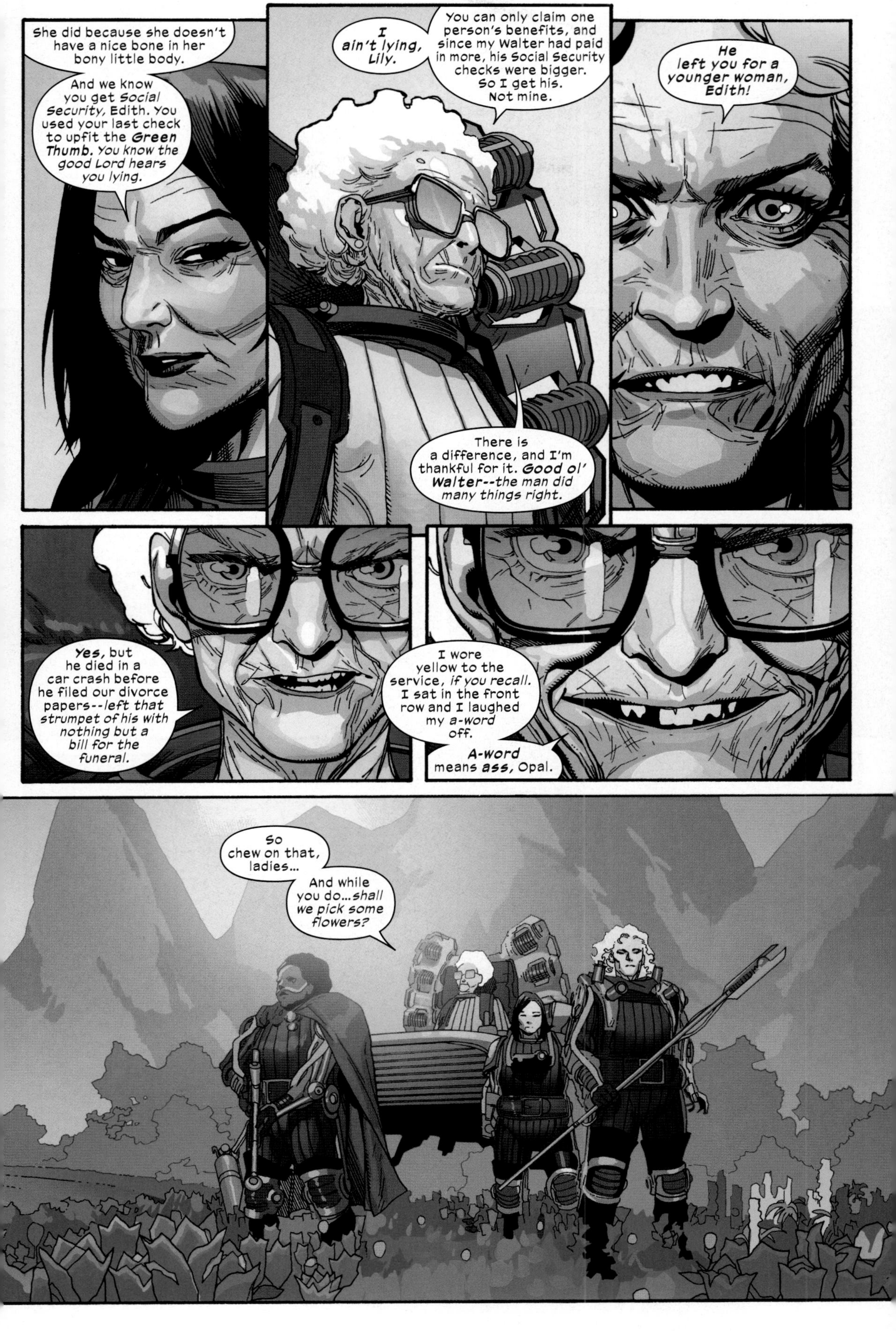

She did because she doesn't have a nice bone in her bony little body.
And we know you get *Social Security*, Edith. You used your last check to upfit the ***Green Thumb***. *You know the good Lord hears you lying.*
I ain't lying, Lily.
You can only claim one person's benefits, and since my Walter had paid in more, his Social Security checks were bigger. So I get his. Not mine.
He left you for a younger woman, Edith!
There is a difference, and I'm thankful for it. ***Good ol' Walter****--the man did many things right.*
Yes, but he died in a car crash before he filed our divorce papers--*left that strumpet of his with nothing but a bill for the funeral.*
I wore yellow to the service, *if you recall.* I sat in the front row and I laughed my *a-word* off.
A-word means ***ass,*** Opal.
So chew on that, ladies...
And while you do...*shall we pick some flowers?*

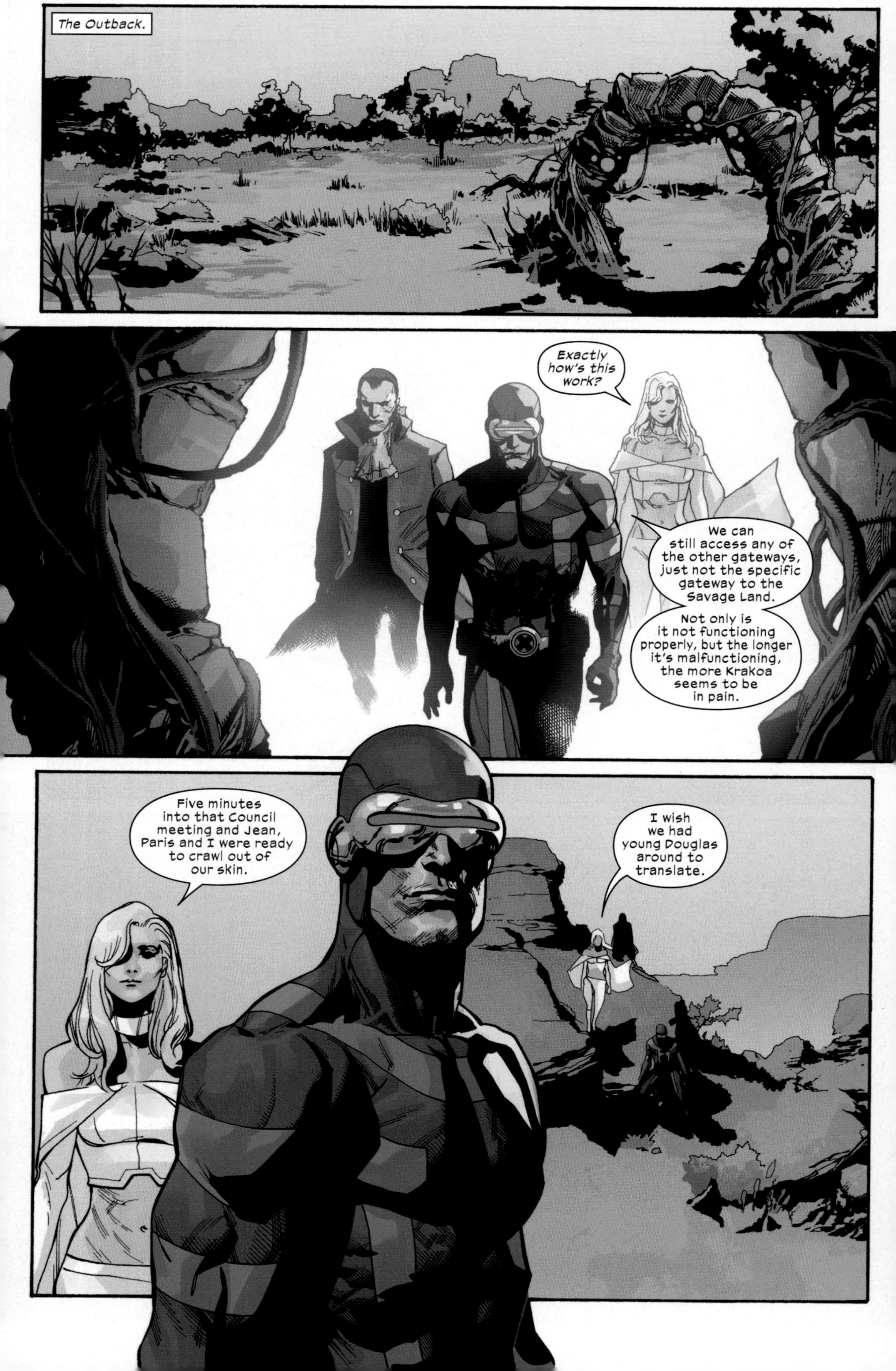
The Outback.
Exactly how's this work?
We can still access any of the other gateways, just not the specific gateway to the Savage Land.
Not only is it not functioning properly, but the longer it's malfunctioning, the more Krakoa seems to be in pain.
Five minutes into that Council meeting and Jean, Paris and I were ready to crawl out of our skin.
I wish we had young Douglas around to translate.

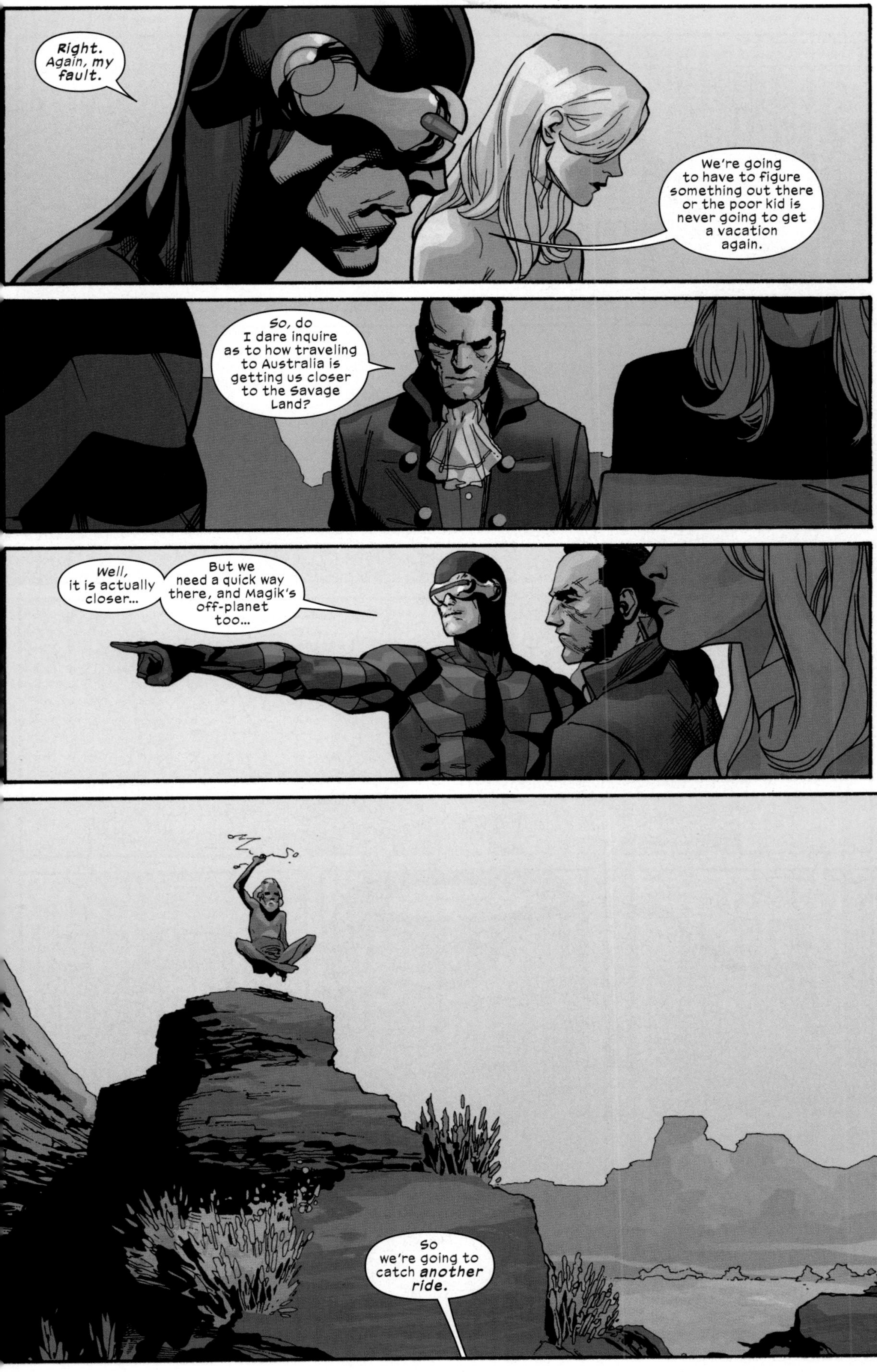
Right. Again, my fault.
We're going to have to figure something out there or the poor kid is never going to get a vacation again.
So, do I dare inquire as to how traveling to Australia is getting us closer to the Savage Land?
Well, it is actually closer...
But we need a quick way there, and Magik's off-planet too...
So we're going to catch another ride.

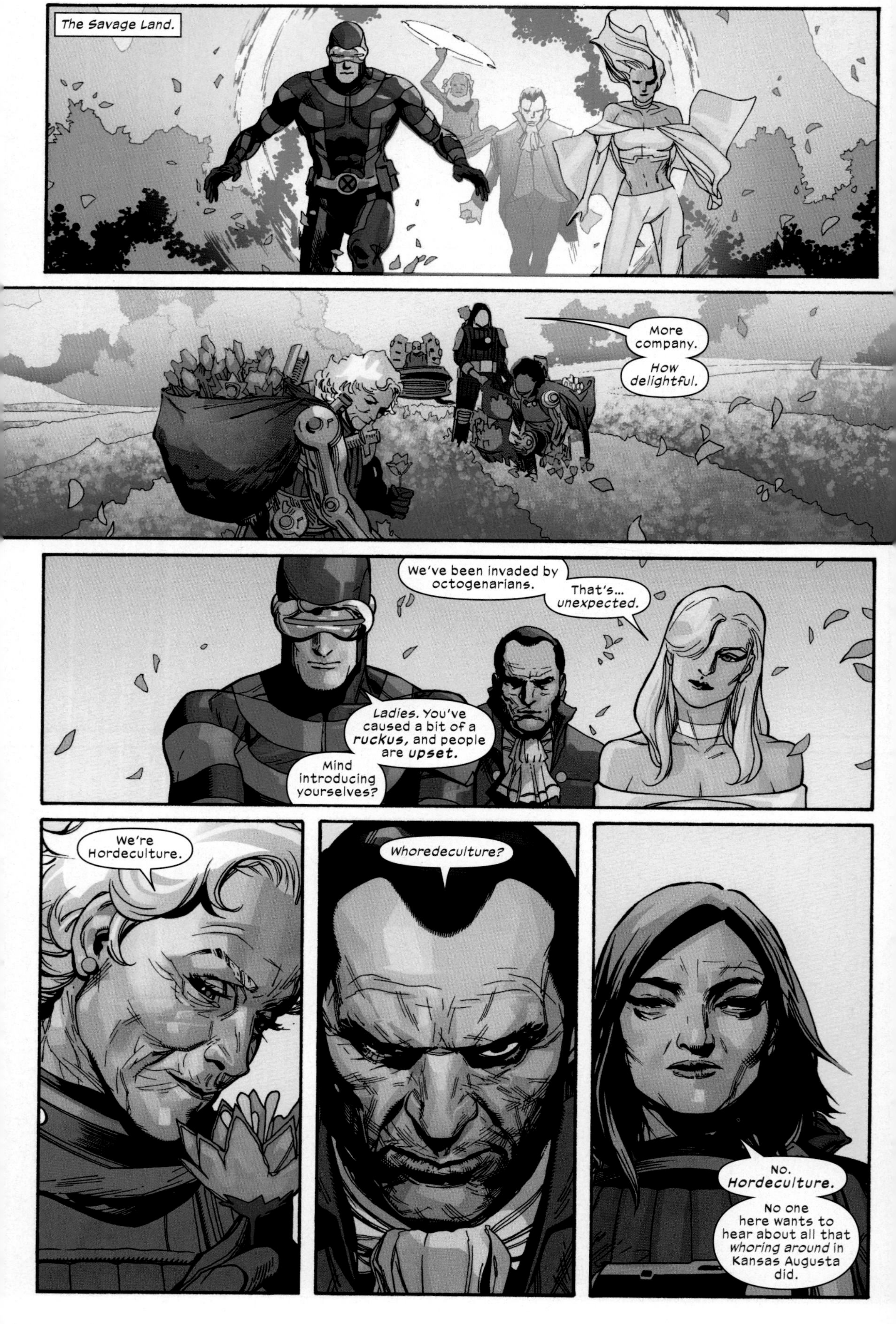

The Savage Land.
More company.
How delightful.
We've been invaded by octogenarians.
That's... *unexpected.*
Ladies. You've caused a bit of a ***ruckus,*** and people are ***upset.***
Mind introducing yourselves?
We're Hordeculture.
Whoredeculture?
No. ***Hordeculture.***
No one here wants to hear about all that *whoring around* in Kansas Augusta did.

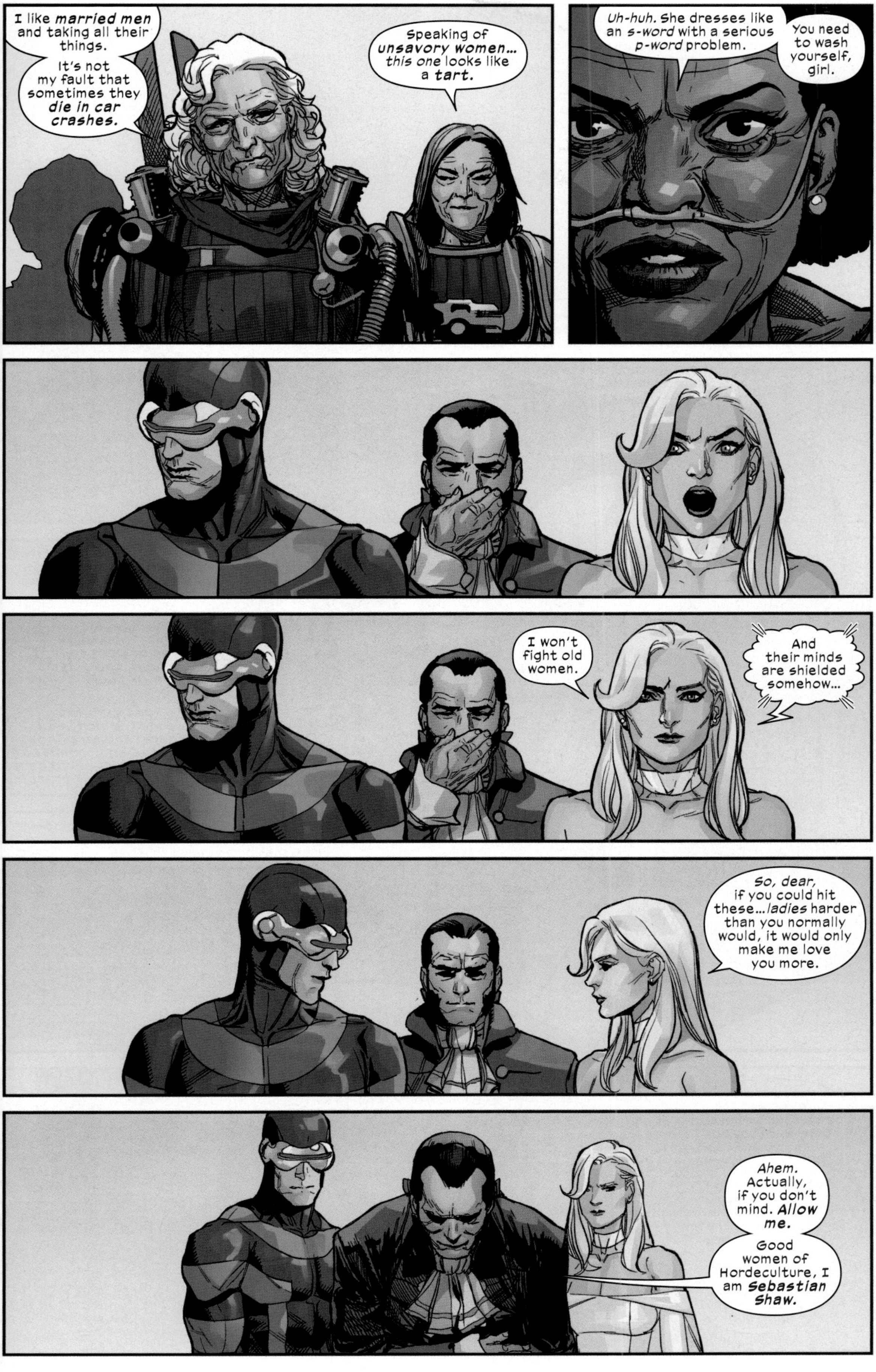
I like married men and taking all their things.
It's not my fault that sometimes they die in car crashes.
Speaking of unsavory women... this one looks like a tart.
Uh-huh. She dresses like an s-word with a serious p-word problem.
You need to wash yourself, girl.
I won't fight old women.
And their minds are shielded somehow...
So, dear, if you could hit these...ladies harder than you normally would, it would only make me love you more.
Ahem. Actually, if you don't mind. Allow me.
Good women of Hordeculture, I am Sebastian Shaw.

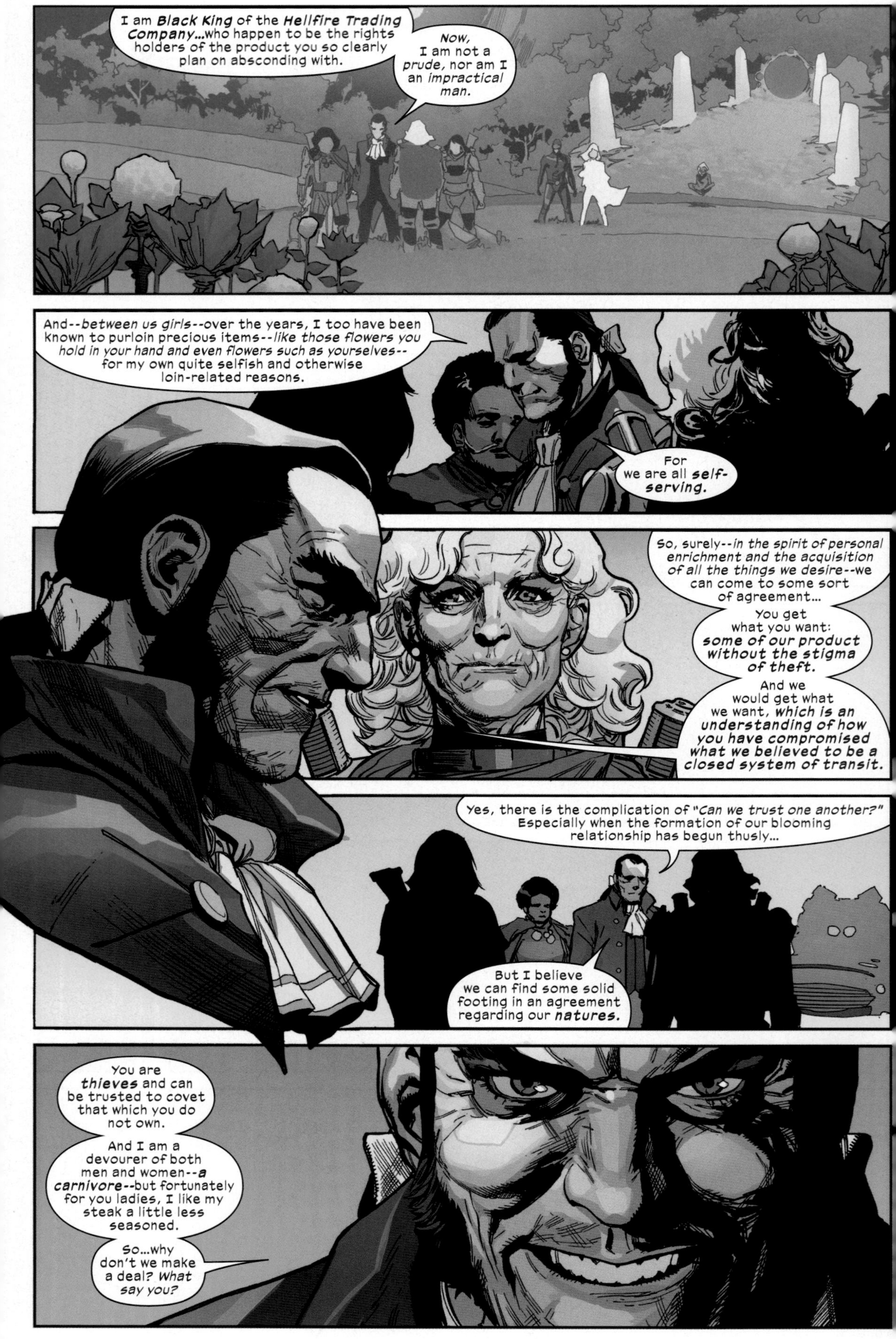

I am Black King of the Hellfire Trading Company...who happen to be the rights holders of the product you so clearly plan on absconding with.
Now, I am not a prude, nor am I an impractical man.
And--between us girls--over the years, I too have been known to purloin precious items--like those flowers you hold in your hand and even flowers such as yourselves--for my own quite selfish and otherwise loin-related reasons.
For we are all self-serving.
So, surely--in the spirit of personal enrichment and the acquisition of all the things we desire--we can come to some sort of agreement...
You get what you want: some of our product without the stigma of theft.
And we would get what we want, which is an understanding of how you have compromised what we believed to be a closed system of transit.
Yes, there is the complication of "Can we trust one another?" Especially when the formation of our blooming relationship has begun thusly...
But I believe we can find some solid footing in an agreement regarding our natures.
You are thieves and can be trusted to covet that which you do not own.
And I am a devourer of both men and women--a carnivore--but fortunately for you ladies, I like my steak a little less seasoned.
So...why don't we make a deal? What say you?

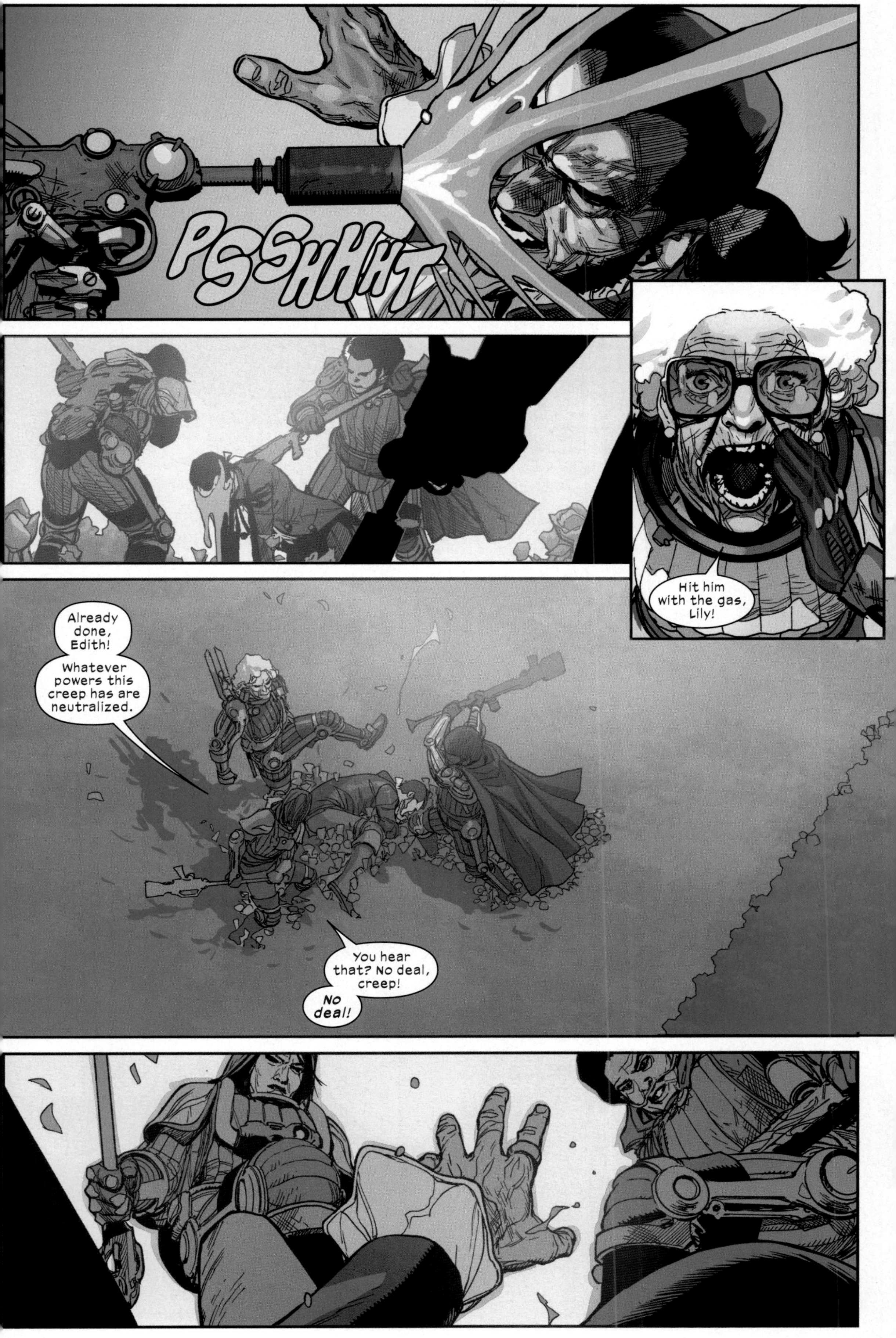
PSSHHHT
Hit him with the gas, Lily!
Already done, Edith!
Whatever powers this creep has are neutralized.
You hear that? No deal, creep!
No deal!

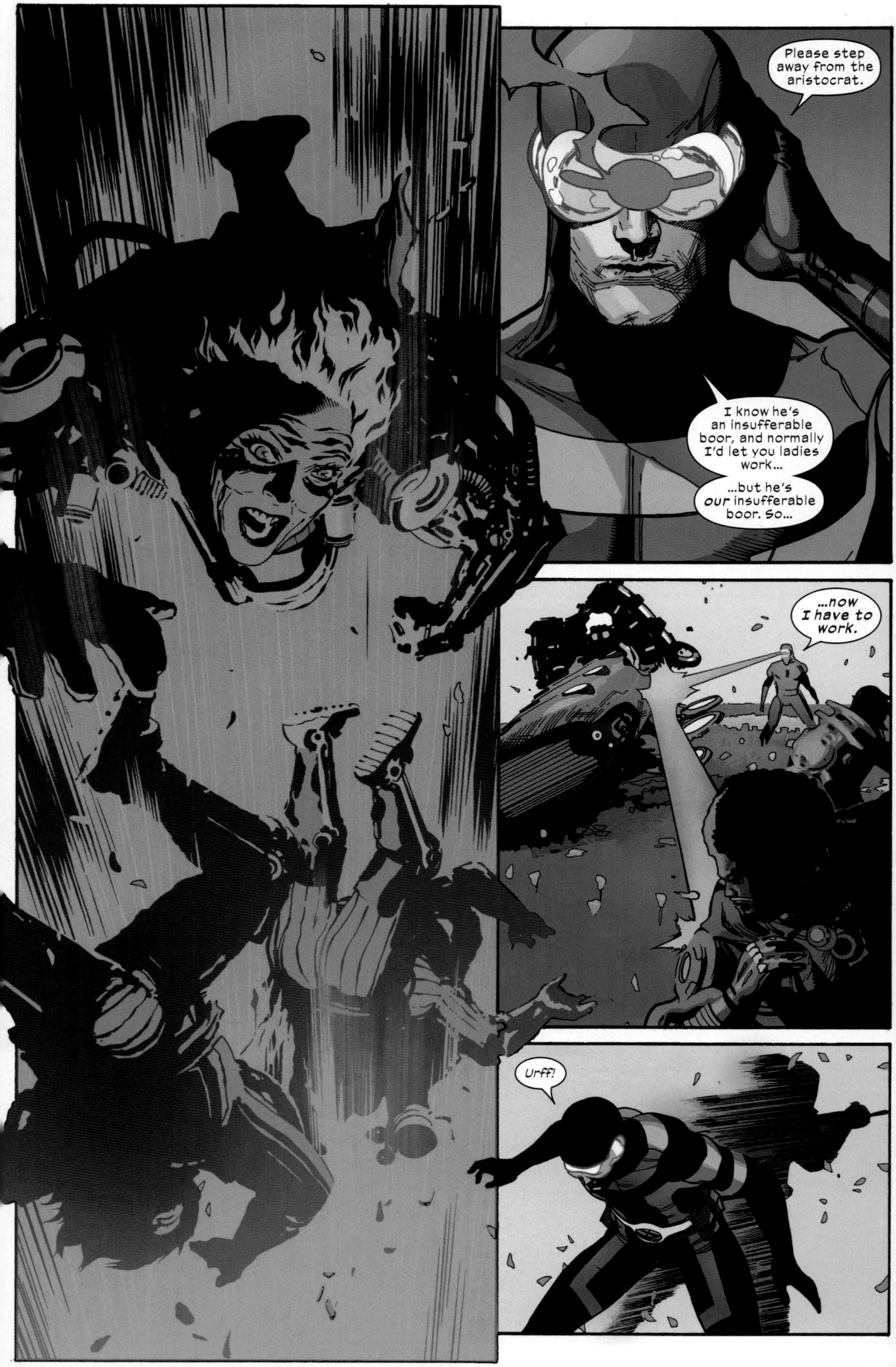
Please step away from the aristocrat.
I know he's an insufferable boor, and normally I'd let you ladies work...
...but he's *our* insufferable boor. So...
...now I have to work.
Urff!

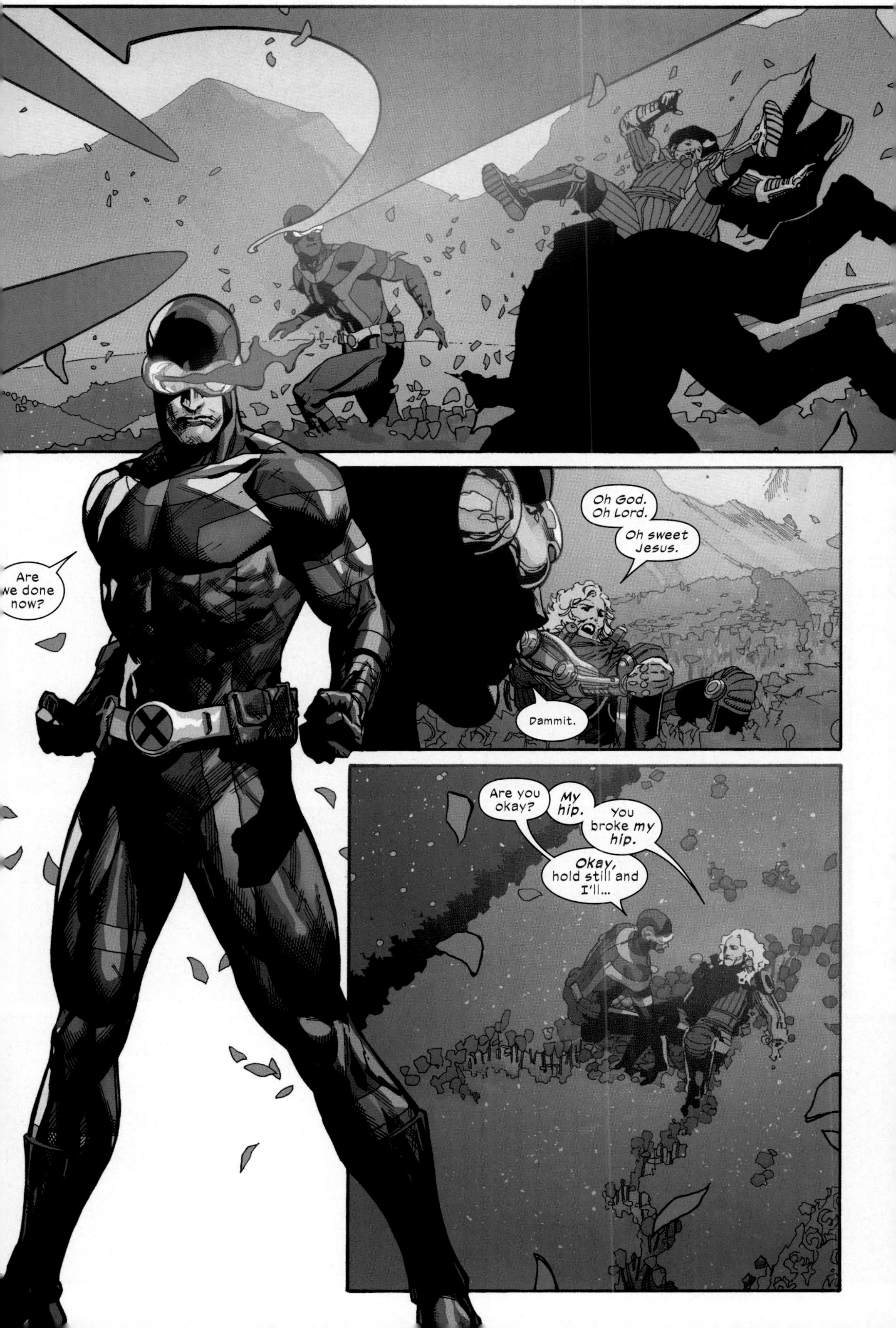
Are we done now?
Oh God. Oh Lord.
Oh sweet Jesus.
Dammit.
Are you okay?
My hip.
You broke my hip.
Okay, hold still and I'll...

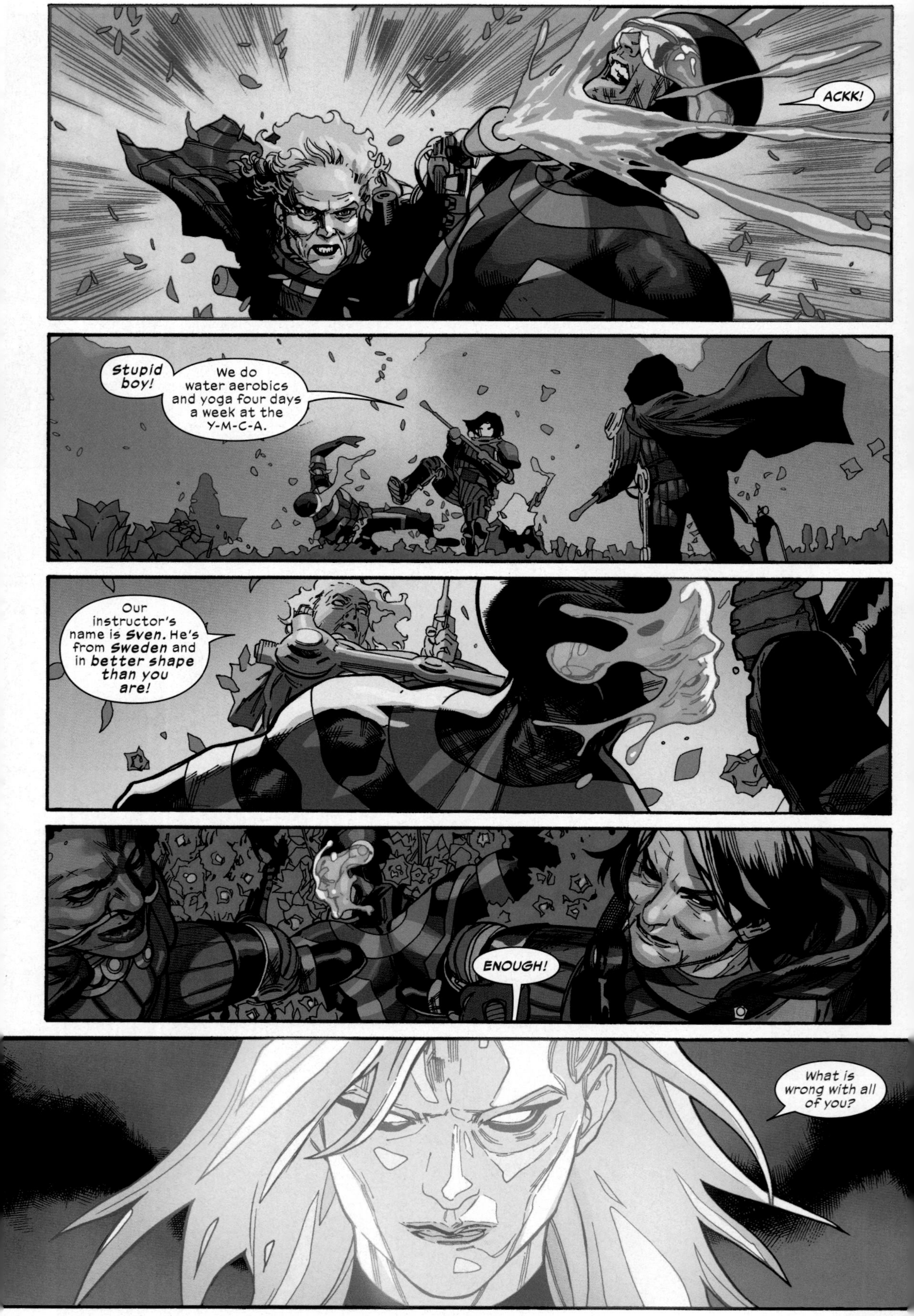
ACKK!
Stupid boy!
We do water aerobics and yoga four days a week at the Y-M-C-A.
Our instructor's name is Sven. He's from Sweden and in better shape than you are!
ENOUGH!
What is wrong with all of you?

Well... You are, girly.

You *mutants* are screwing up our *plan.*

"Even though we are human, Hordeculture--like *you*--has a problem with what mankind has done to this planet.

"We are--all *of us*--radical botanists--gardeners with the *gift of the green thumb*--who are committed to returning this world to its proper state.

"The *four of us* have collectively spent more than *two hundred years* working for the world's best *agrochemical* and *biotech companies.*

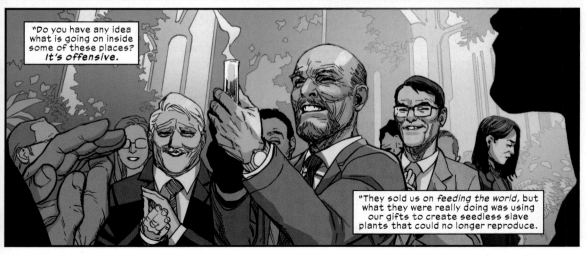

"Do you have any idea what is going on inside some of these places? *It's offensive.*

"They sold us on *feeding the world,* but what they were really doing was using our gifts to create seedless slave plants that could no longer reproduce.

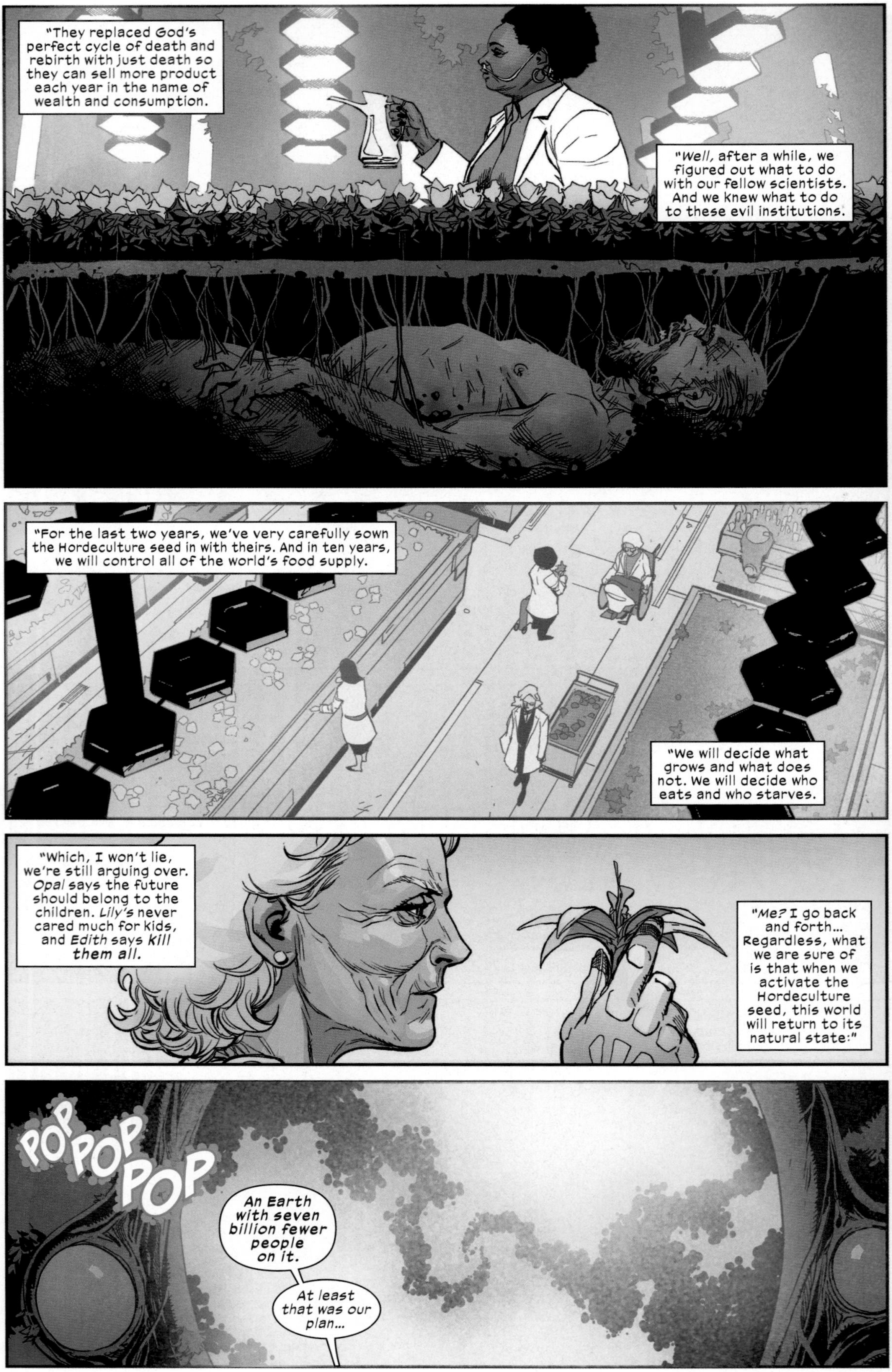
"They replaced God's perfect cycle of death and rebirth with just death so they can sell more product each year in the name of wealth and consumption.
"*Well,* after a while, we figured out what to do with our fellow scientists. And we knew what to do to these evil institutions.
"For the last two years, we've very carefully sown the Hordeculture seed in with theirs. And in ten years, we will control all of the world's food supply.
"We will decide what grows and what does not. We will decide who eats and who starves.
"Which, I won't lie, we're still arguing over. *Opal* says the future should belong to the children. *Lily's* never cared much for kids, and *Edith* says ***kill them all.***
"*Me?* I go back and forth... Regardless, what we are sure of is that when we activate the Hordeculture seed, this world will return to its natural state:"
POP POP POP
An Earth with seven billion fewer people on it.
At least that was our plan...

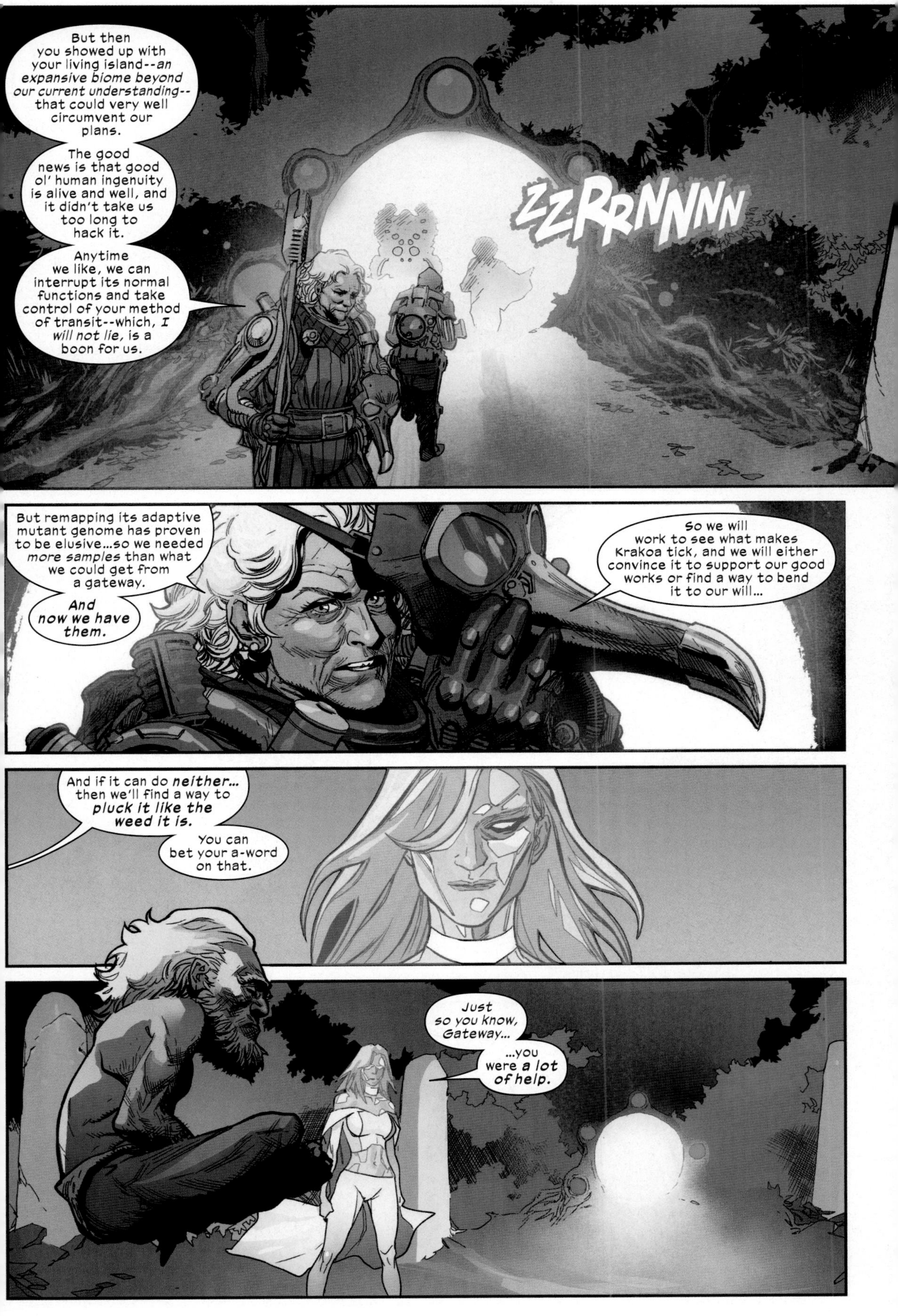
But then you showed up with your living island--*an expansive biome beyond our current understanding*--that could very well circumvent our plans.
The good news is that good ol' human ingenuity is alive and well, and it didn't take us too long to hack it.
Anytime we like, we can interrupt its normal functions and take control of your method of transit--which, *I will not lie,* is a boon for us.
ZZRRNNNN
But remapping its adaptive mutant genome has proven to be elusive...so we needed *more samples* than what we could get from a gateway.
And now we have them.
So we will work to see what makes Krakoa tick, and we will either convince it to support our good works or find a way to bend it to our will...
And if it can do **neither...** then we'll find a way to ***pluck it like the weed it is.***
You can bet your a-word on that.
Just so you know, Gateway...
...you were ***a lot of help.***

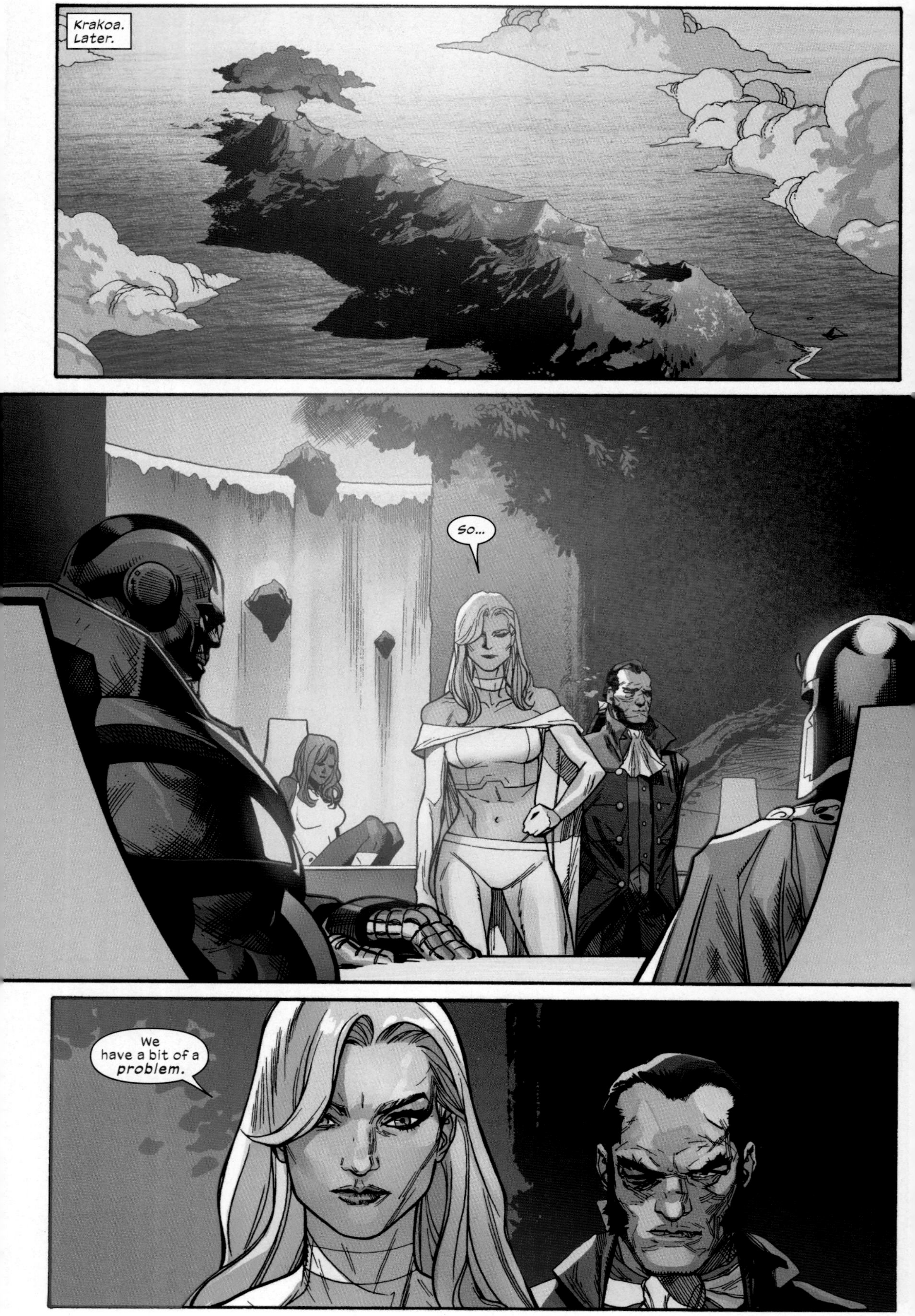

Krakoa. Later.
So...
We have a bit of a problem.

[00.HORDE..........X]
[00................0]

HORDECULTURE IS:

[HORDE]............[000.00]
[CULTR]............[BLD_05]

A collaborative group of like-minded agrochemists, biotechnologists and bioengineers who specialize in the genetic manipulation of -- and propagation of -- all things botanical. Their goal is the radical depopulation of humanity and the return of the planet to what they would consider a more pristine state.

Beyond genetic modifications believed to have been made to themselves [unconfirmed outside of a documented resistance to telepathy], the women of Hordeculture are experts at manipulating the environment to suit their extinction agenda.

While it is unknown if there are more than four members of Hordeculture, the known existing members are:

AUGUSTA BROMES
Agrochemist, 64 years old.
Best friends with Opal.

OPAL VETIVER
Bioengineer, 68 years old.
Best friends with Augusta.

LILY LEYMUS
Geneticist, 71 years old.
Thinks she's best friends with Opal but isn't.

EDITH SCUTCH
Botanical engineer, 81 years old.
Don't need friends, don't want 'em.

—

The Green Thumb is a mobile base of operations designed and built by Edith. It is currently located in Sedona, Arizona, but will move when the current lunar cycle completes.

[AB]..................[OV]
[LL]..................[ES]

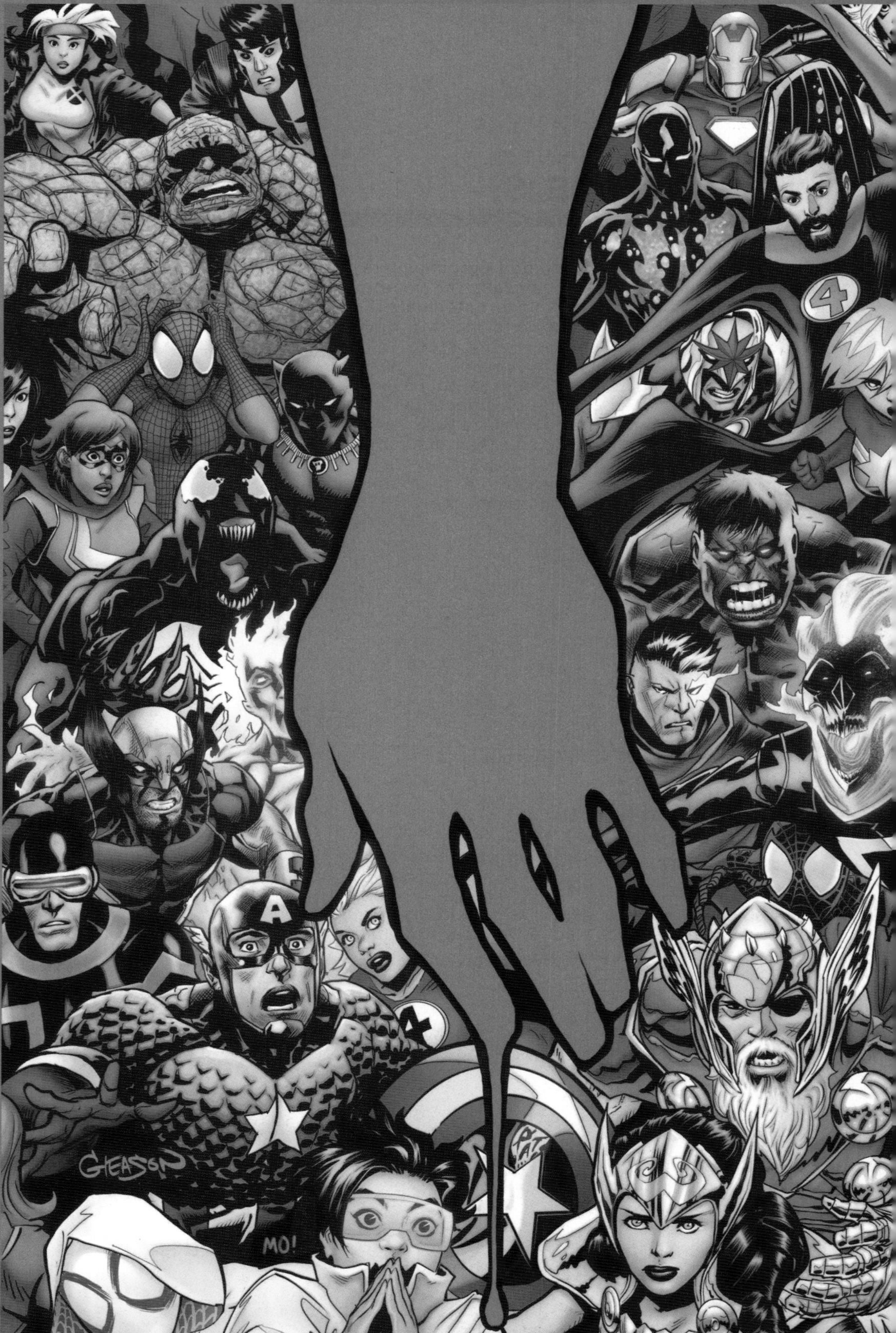
GLEASON
MO!

Incoming

X

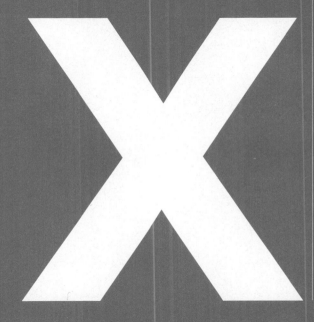

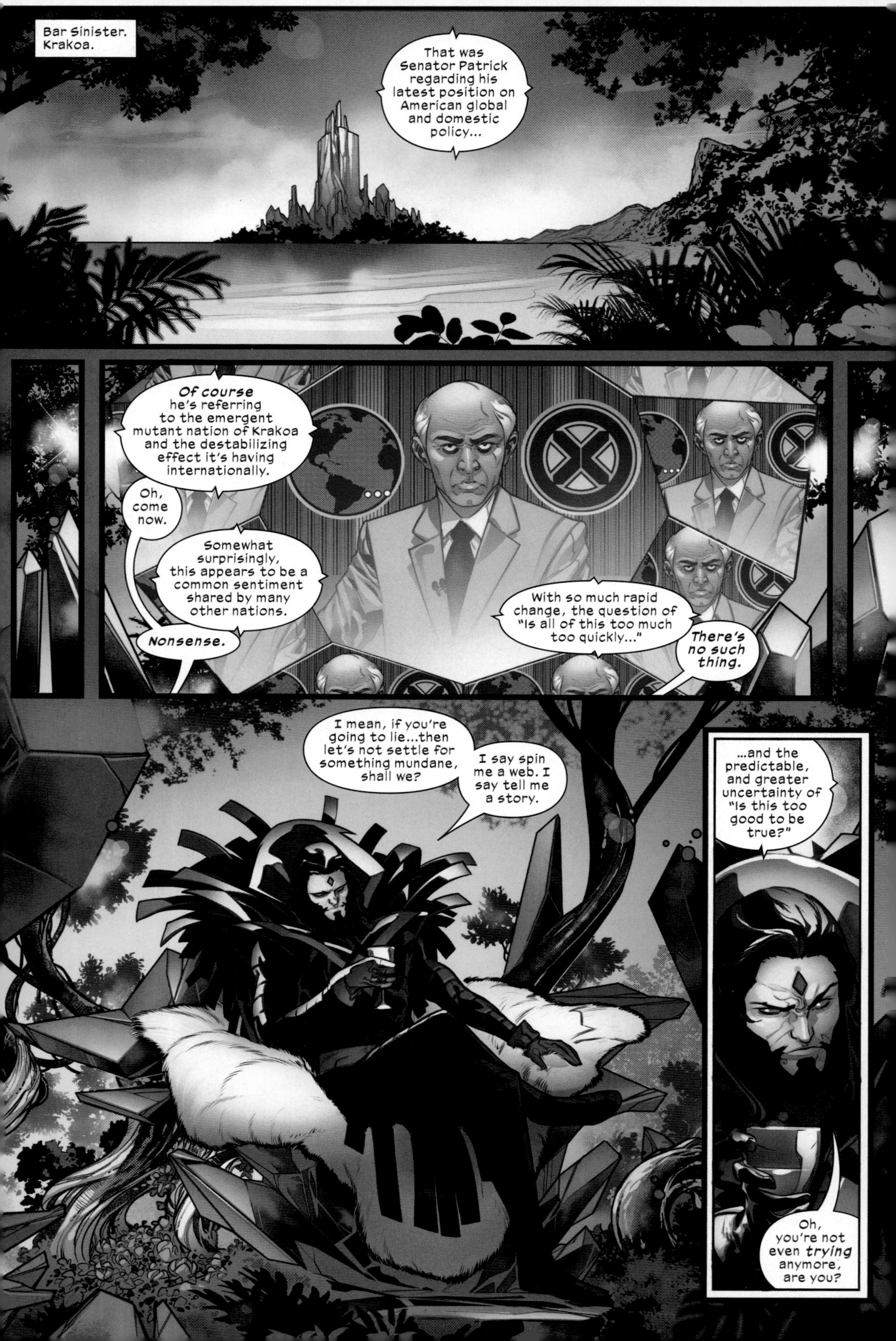
Bar Sinister.
Krakoa.
That was Senator Patrick regarding his latest position on American global and domestic policy...
Of course he's referring to the emergent mutant nation of Krakoa and the destabilizing effect it's having internationally.
Oh, come now.
Somewhat surprisingly, this appears to be a common sentiment shared by many other nations.
Nonsense.
With so much rapid change, the question of "Is all of this too much too quickly..."
There's no such thing.
I mean, if you're going to lie...then let's not settle for something mundane, shall we?
I say spin me a web. I say tell me a story.
...and the predictable, and greater uncertainty of "Is this too good to be true?"
Oh, you're not even *trying* anymore, are you?

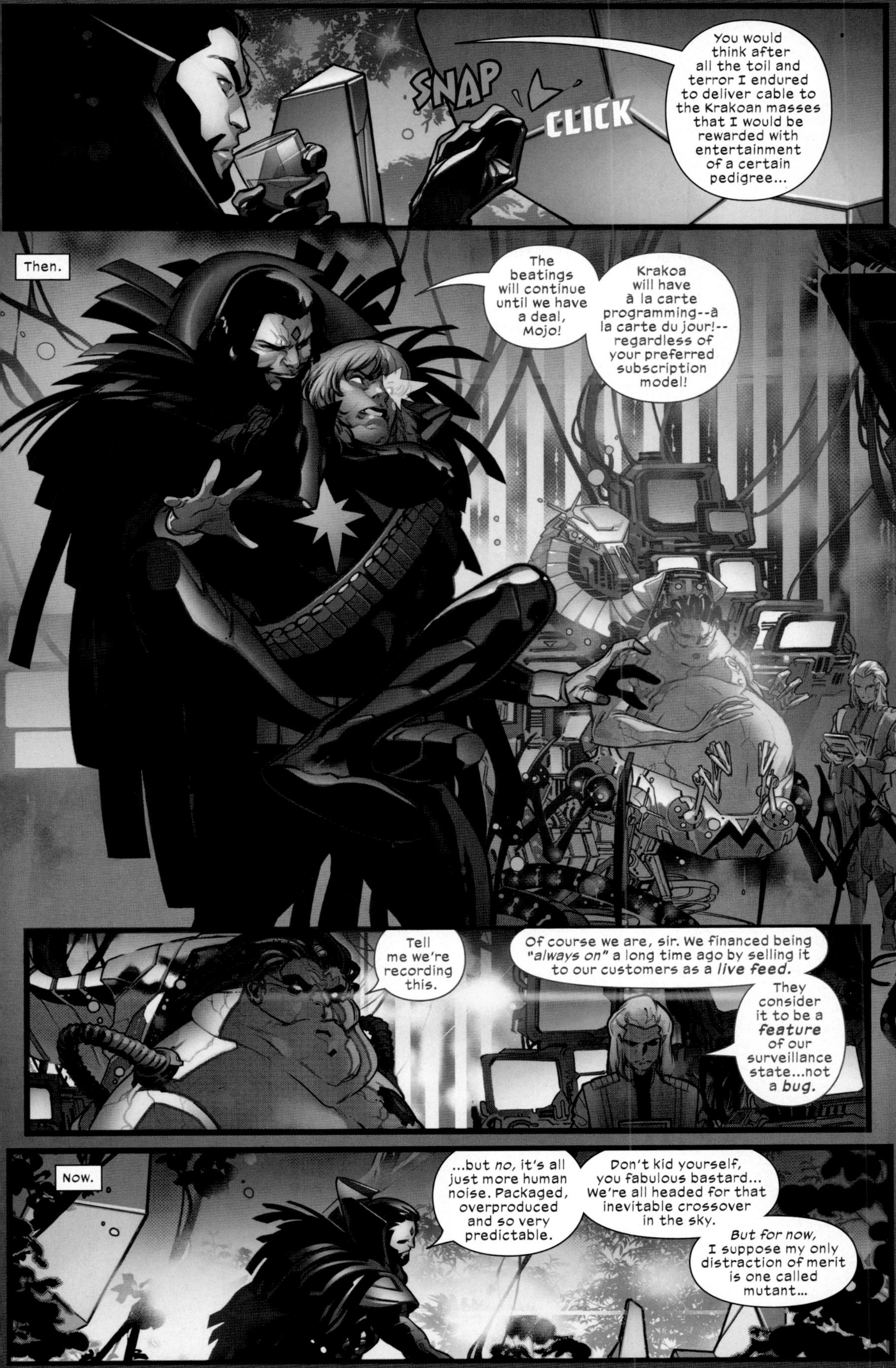
SNAP
CLICK
You would think after all the toil and terror I endured to deliver cable to the Krakoan masses that I would be rewarded with entertainment of a certain pedigree...
Then.
The beatings will continue until we have a deal, Mojo!
Krakoa will have à la carte programming--à la carte du jour!--regardless of your preferred subscription model!
Tell me we're recording this.
Of course we are, sir. We financed being *"always on"* a long time ago by selling it to our customers as a *live feed.*
They consider it to be a ***feature*** of our surveillance state...not a ***bug.***
Now.
...but *no,* it's all just more human noise. Packaged, overproduced and so very predictable.
Don't kid yourself, you fabulous bastard... We're all headed for that inevitable crossover in the sky.
But for now, I suppose my only distraction of merit is one called mutant...

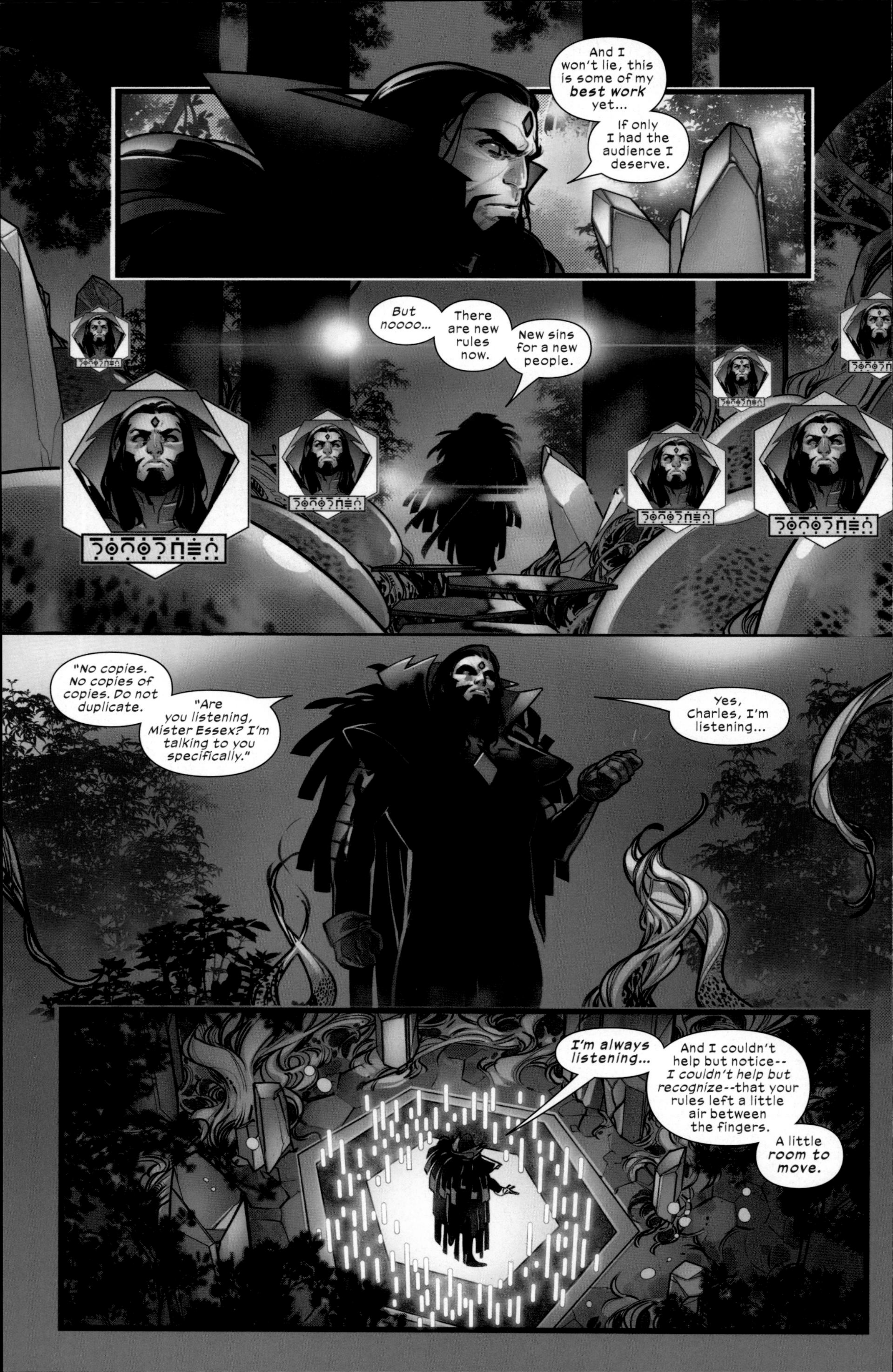
And I won't lie, this is some of my **best work** yet...
If only I had the audience I deserve.
But noooo...
There are new rules now.
New sins for a new people.
"No copies. No copies of copies. Do not duplicate.
"Are you listening, Mister Essex? I'm talking to you specifically."
Yes, Charles, I'm listening...
I'm always listening...
And I couldn't help but notice-- *I couldn't help but recognize*--that your rules left a little air between the fingers.
A little ***room to move.***

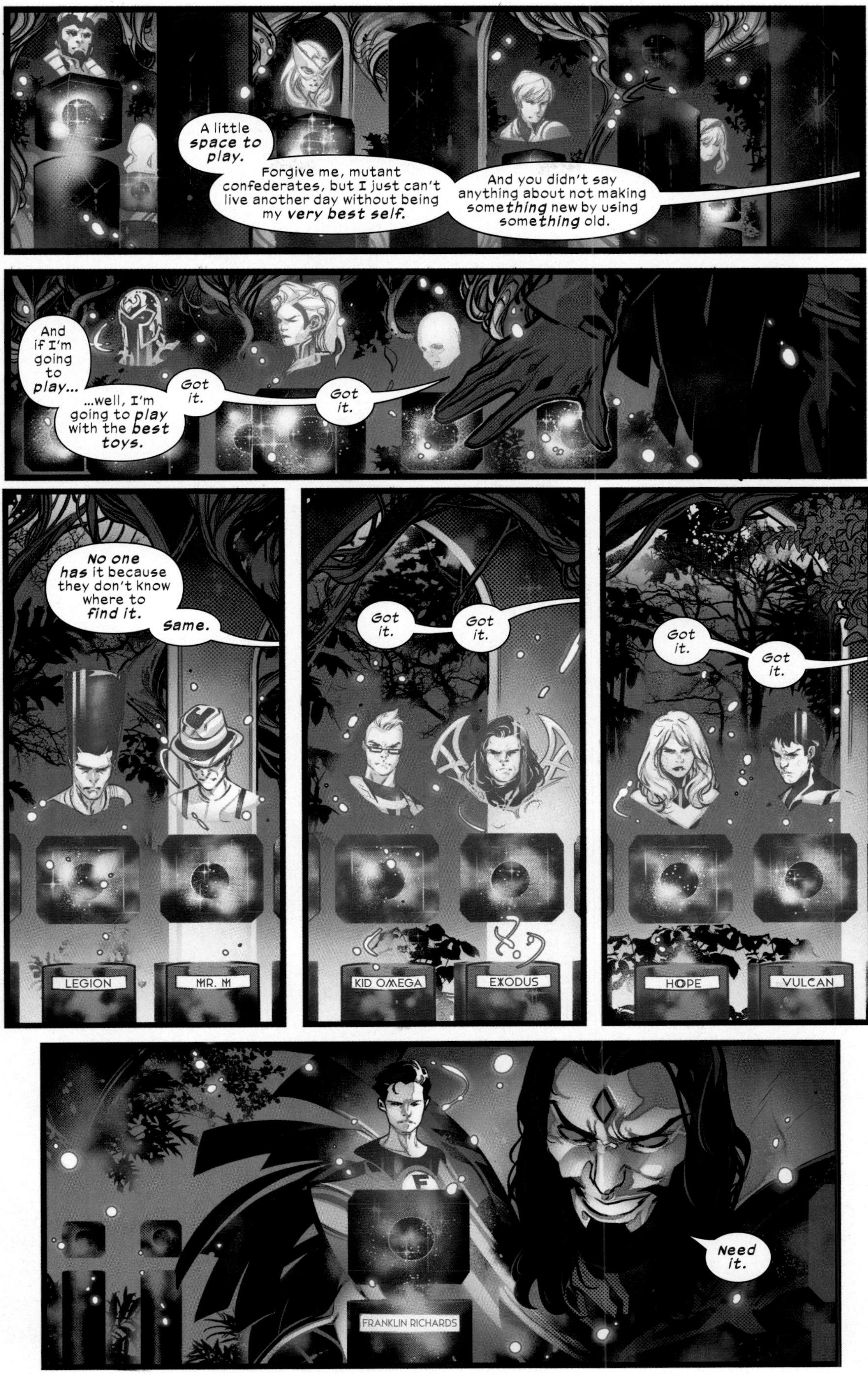

A little space to play.
Forgive me, mutant confederates, but I just can't live another day without being my very best self.
And you didn't say anything about not making something new by using something old.
And if I'm going to play...
...well, I'm going to play with the best toys.
Got it.
Got it.
No one has it because they don't know where to find it.
Same.
Got it.
Got it.
Got it.
Got it.
LEGION
MR. M
KID OMEGA
EXODUS
HOPE
VULCAN
FRANKLIN RICHARDS
Need it.

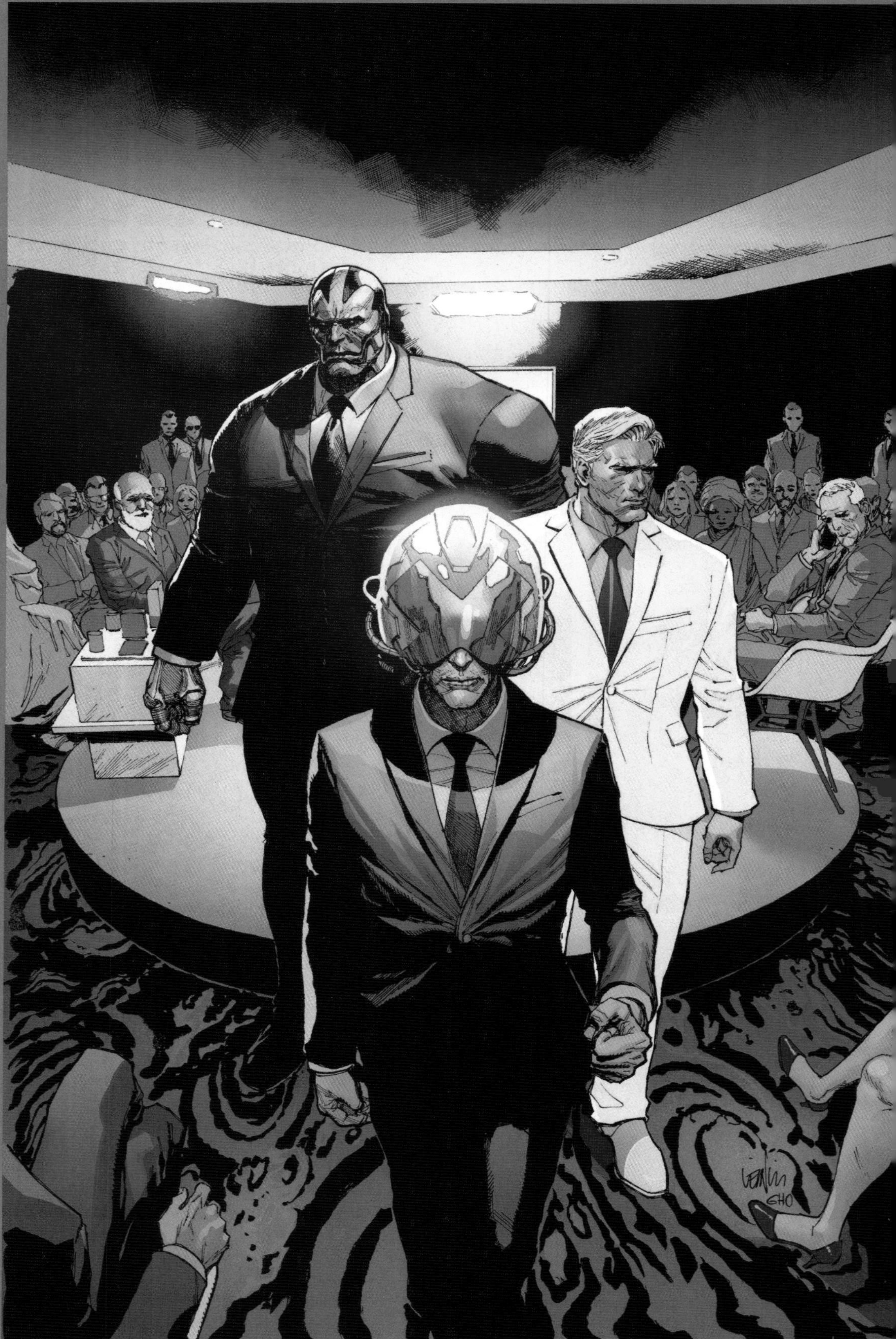

Global Economics

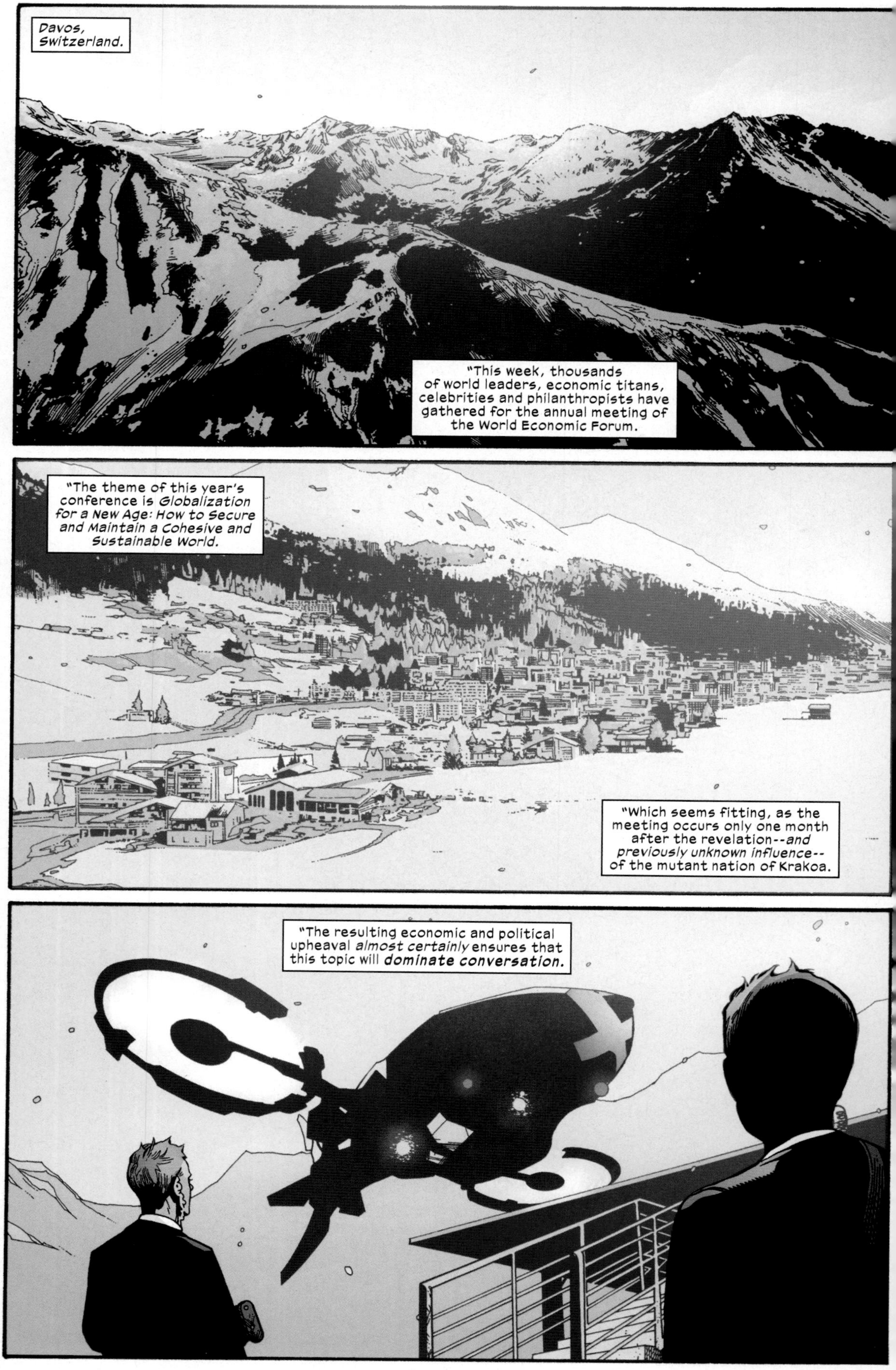
Davos, Switzerland.
"This week, thousands of world leaders, economic titans, celebrities and philanthropists have gathered for the annual meeting of the World Economic Forum.
"The theme of this year's conference is *Globalization for a New Age: How to Secure and Maintain a Cohesive and Sustainable World.*
"Which seems fitting, as the meeting occurs only one month after the revelation--*and previously unknown influence*--of the mutant nation of Krakoa.
"The resulting economic and political upheaval *almost certainly* ensures that this topic will **dominate conversation.**

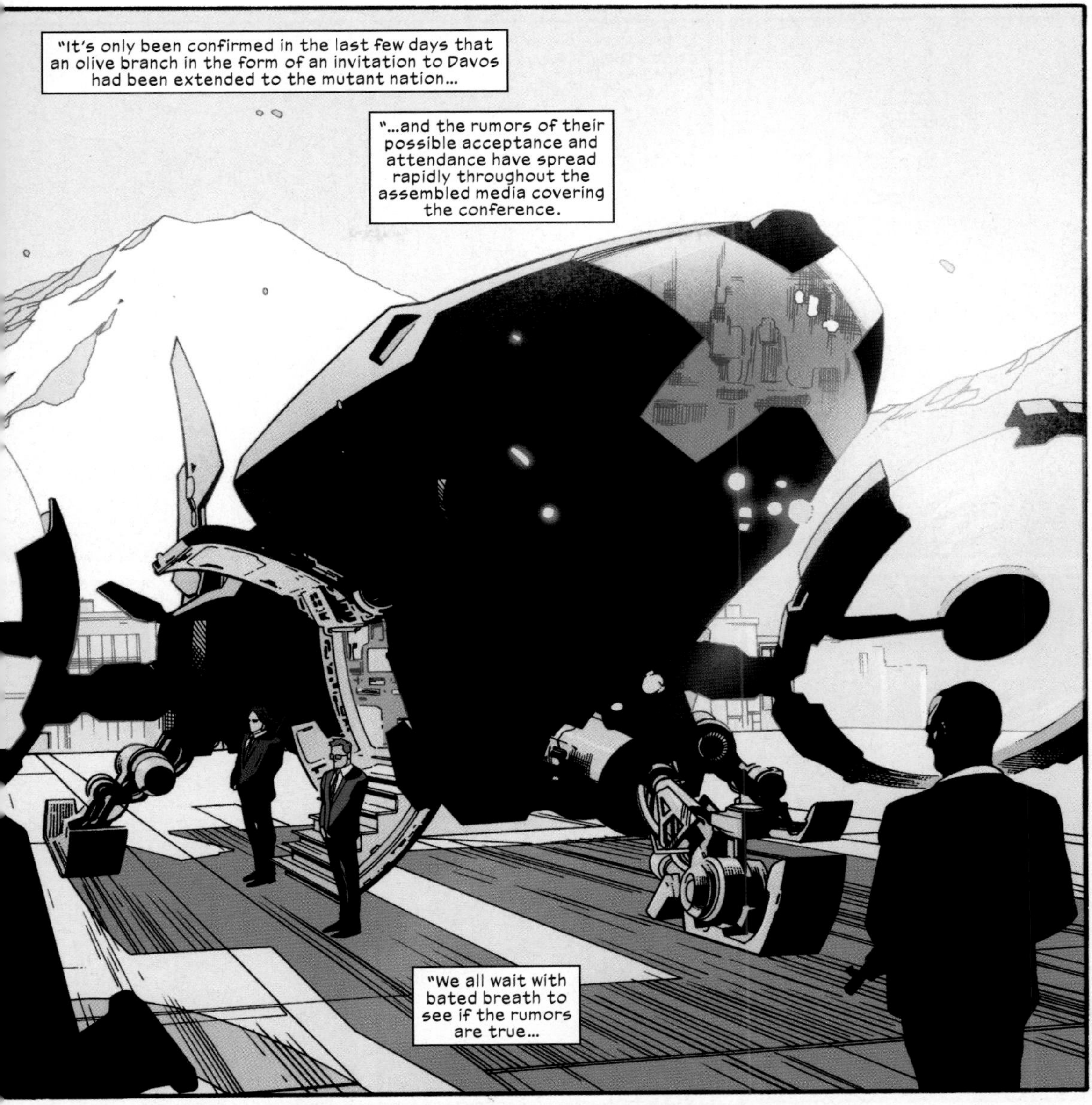
"It's only been confirmed in the last few days that an olive branch in the form of an invitation to Davos had been extended to the mutant nation...
"...and the rumors of their possible acceptance and attendance have spread rapidly throughout the assembled media covering the conference.
"We all wait with bated breath to see if the rumors are true...

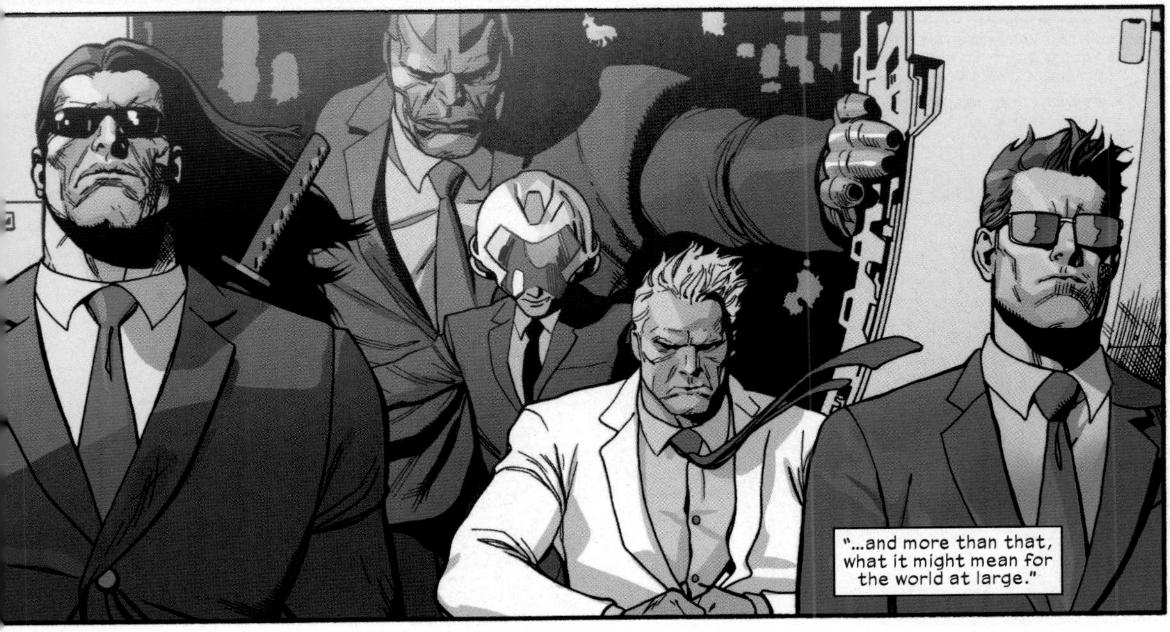
"...and more than that, what it might mean for the world at large."

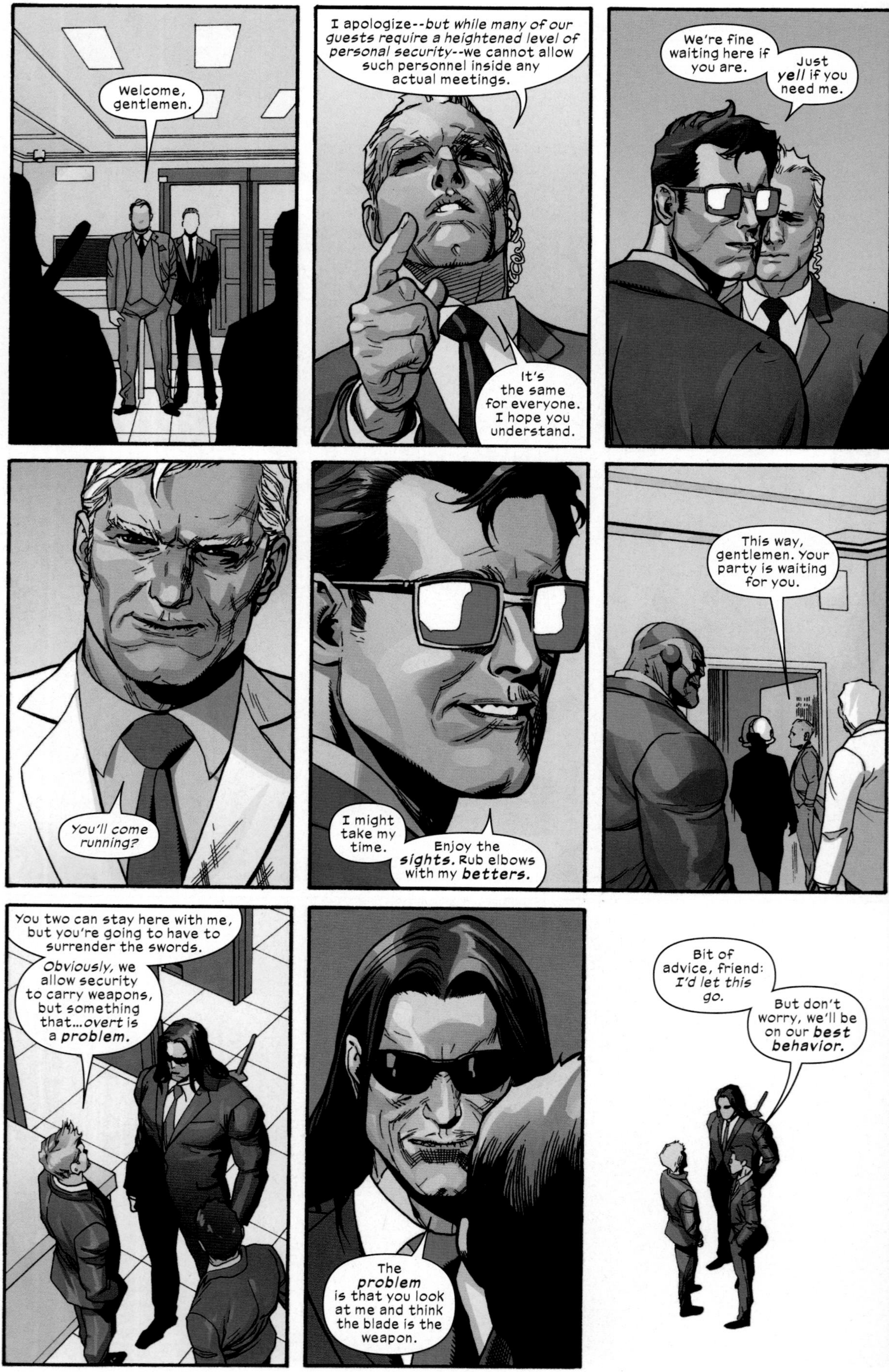
Welcome, gentlemen.
I apologize--but while many of our guests require a heightened level of personal security--we cannot allow such personnel inside any actual meetings.
It's the same for everyone. I hope you understand.
We're fine waiting here if you are.
Just yell if you need me.
You'll come running?
I might take my time.
Enjoy the sights. Rub elbows with my betters.
This way, gentlemen. Your party is waiting for you.
You two can stay here with me, but you're going to have to surrender the swords.
Obviously, we allow security to carry weapons, but something that...overt is a problem.
The problem is that you look at me and think the blade is the weapon.
Bit of advice, friend: I'd let this go.
But don't worry, we'll be on our best behavior.

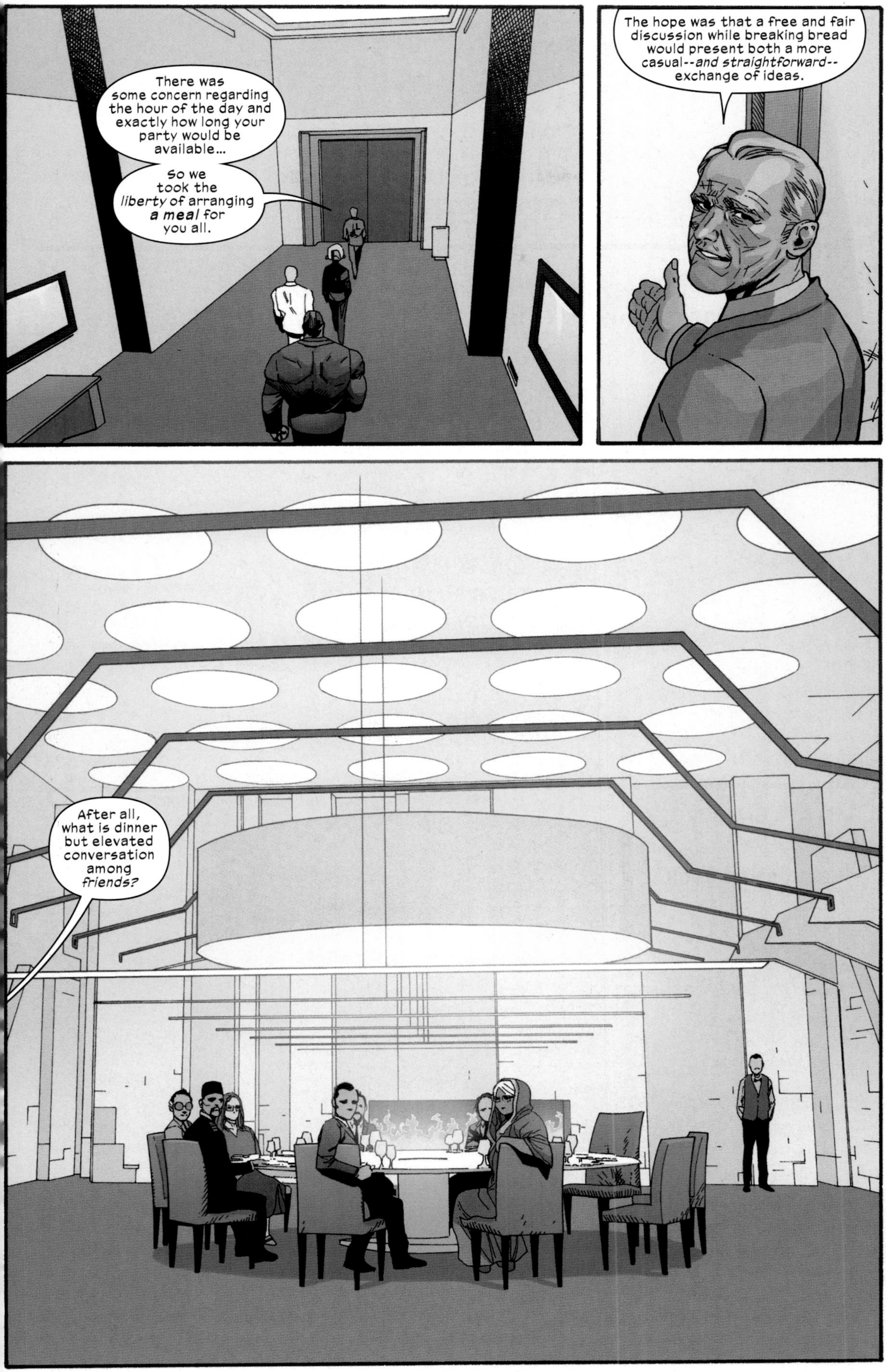

There was some concern regarding the hour of the day and exactly how long your party would be available...
So we took the *liberty* of arranging ***a meal*** for you all.
The hope was that a free and fair discussion while breaking bread would present both a more casual--*and straightforward*--exchange of ideas.
After all, what is dinner but elevated conversation among *friends?*

World Economic Forum
DINNER MENU

Watermelon Gazpacho
Infused with Habanero and Poblano Chiles

+

Shredded Kale,
Mushrooms, Bacon, Parmesan

+

Olive Wagyu
[Kagawa Prefecture]
Colbert Sauce

+

Brioche Tressée de Metz

IN ATTENDANCE:
—

KRAKOAN COUNCIL
```
Charles Xavier...................................Professor X
Erik Lehnsherr...................................Magneto
En Sabah Nur.....................................Apocalypse
```

POLITICAL REPRESENTATIVES
```
Hodari...........................................Wakandan Attaché
Ma Mingyu........................................Chinese Ambassador
Reilly Marshall..................................U.S. Ambassador
```

INTERNATIONAL GUESTS
```
Frederico João de Cézare........................Brazil..........[Academic]
Daniela Gentile.................................Italy...........[Business]
Ludovic von Bergen..............................Switzerland.....[Business]
Banhi Gahlot....................................India...........[Business]
```

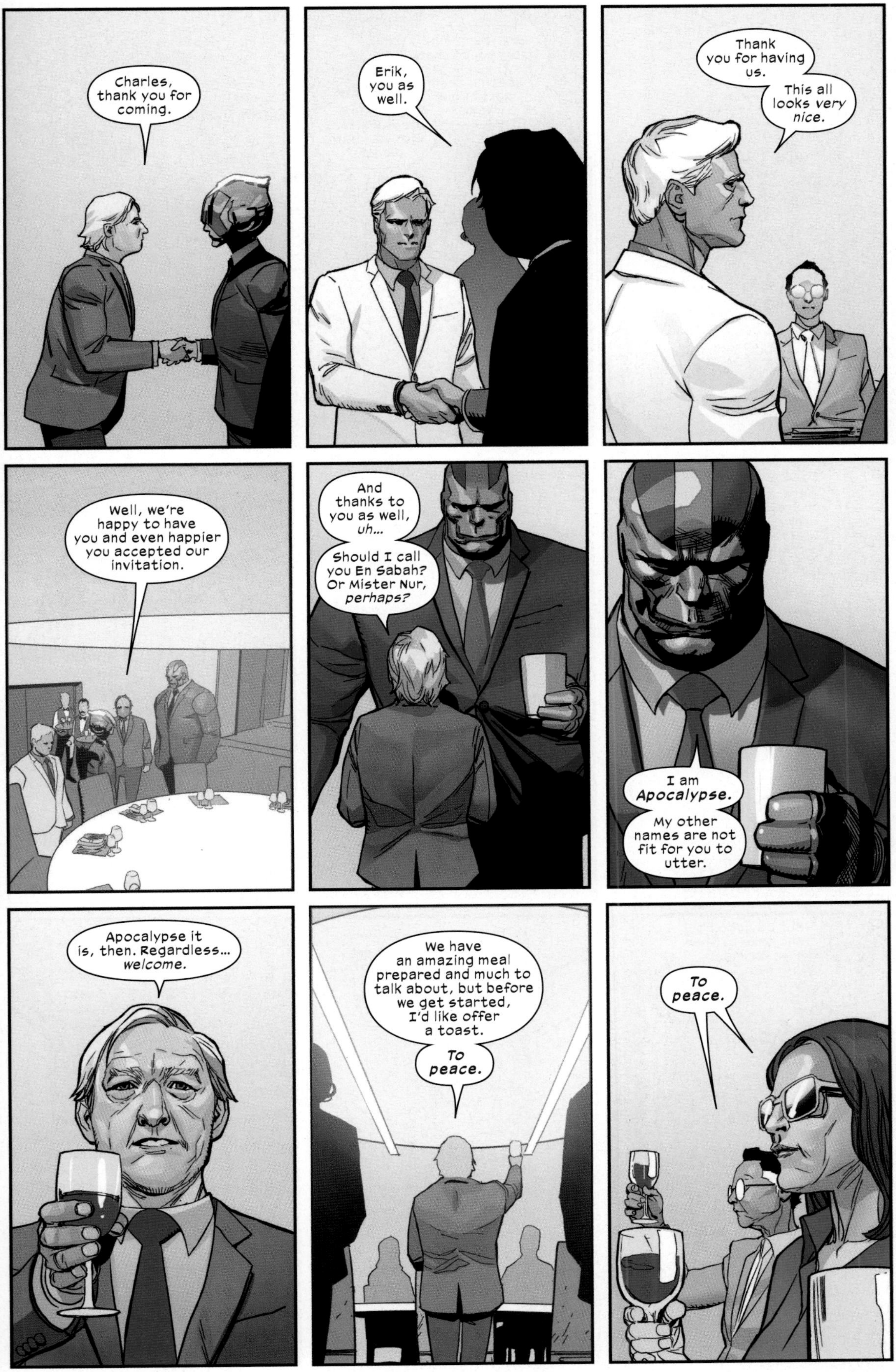
Charles, thank you for coming.
Erik, you as well.
Thank you for having us.
This all looks *very* nice.
Well, we're happy to have you and even happier you accepted our invitation.
And thanks to you as well, *uh...*
Should I call you En Sabah? Or Mister Nur, *perhaps?*
I am *Apocalypse.*
My other names are not fit for you to utter.
Apocalypse it is, then. Regardless... *welcome.*
We have an amazing meal prepared and much to talk about, but before we get started, I'd like offer a toast.
To peace.
To peace.

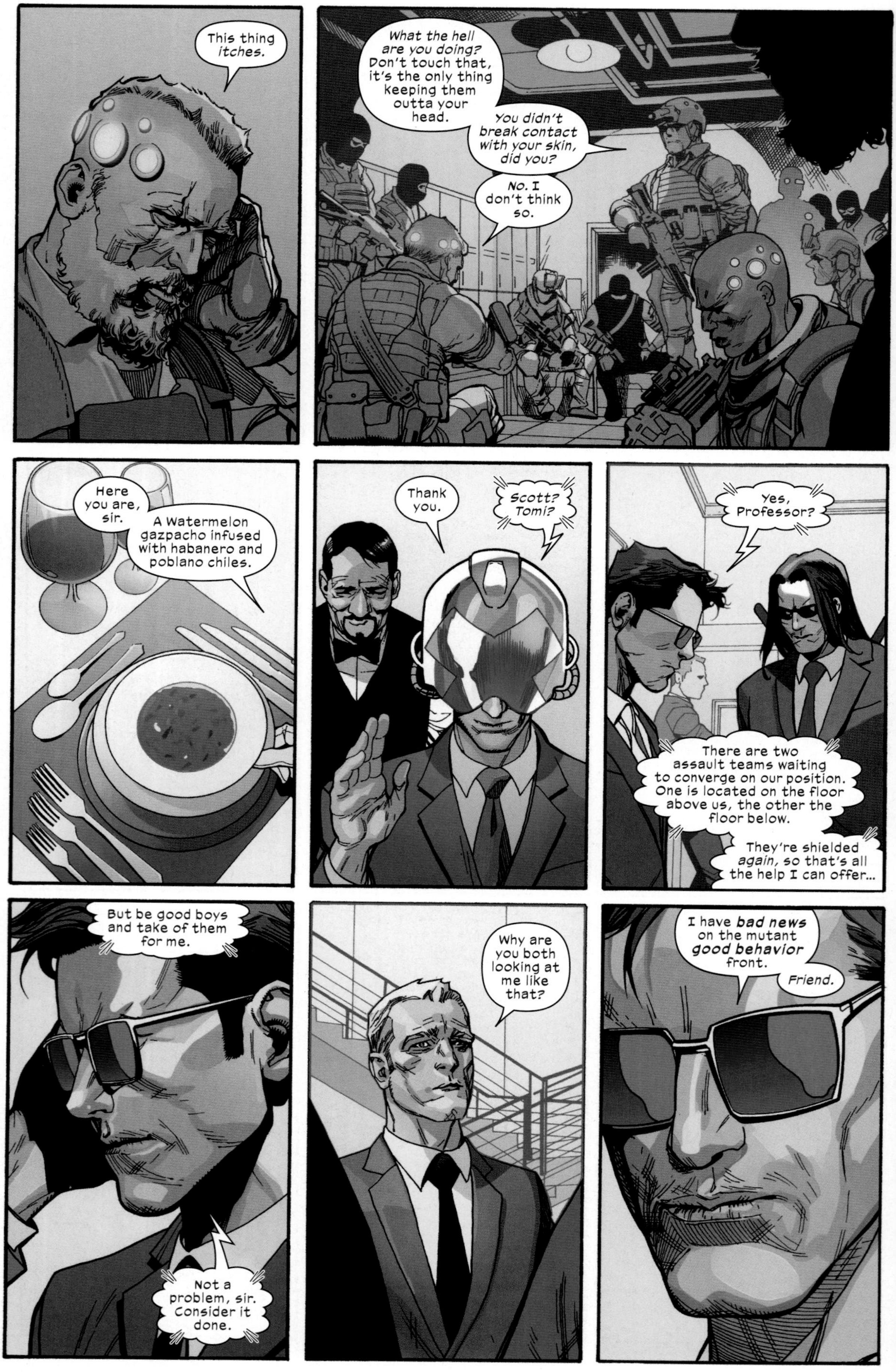

This thing itches.
What the hell are you doing? Don't touch that, it's the only thing keeping them outta your head.
You didn't break contact with your skin, did you?
No. I don't think so.
Here you are, sir.
A watermelon gazpacho infused with habanero and poblano chiles.
Thank you.
Scott? Tomi?
Yes, Professor?
There are two assault teams waiting to converge on our position. One is located on the floor above us, the other the floor below.
They're shielded again, so that's all the help I can offer...
But be good boys and take of them for me.
Not a problem, sir. Consider it done.
Why are you both looking at me like that?
I have bad news on the mutant good behavior front.
Friend.

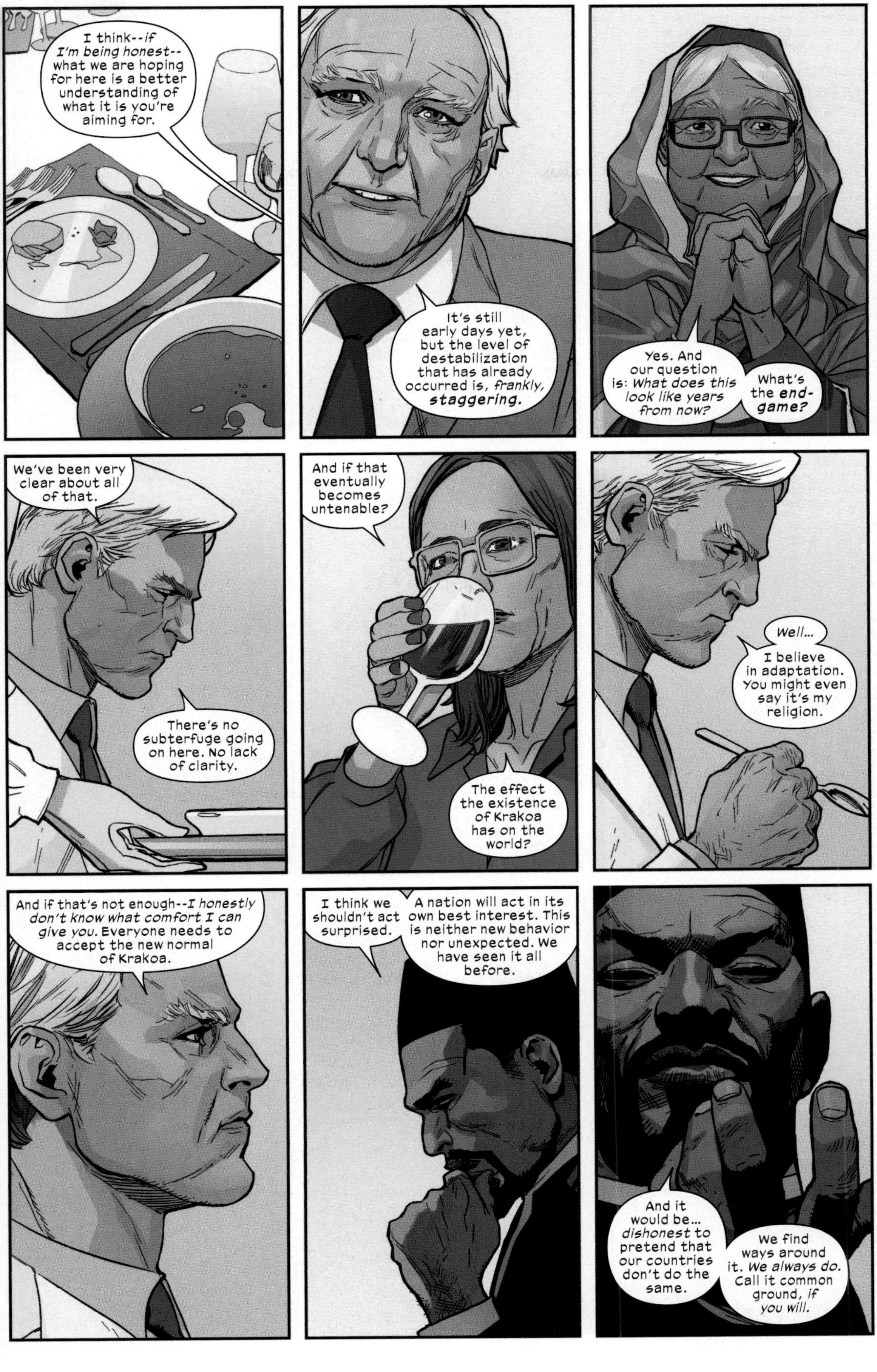
I think--*if I'm being honest*--what we are hoping for here is a better understanding of what it is you're aiming for.
It's still early days yet, but the level of destabilization that has already occurred is, *frankly*, **staggering.**
Yes. And our question is: *What does this look like years from now?*
What's the *end-game?*
We've been very clear about all of that.
There's no subterfuge going on here. No lack of clarity.
And if that eventually becomes untenable?
The effect the existence of Krakoa has on the world?
Well...
I believe in adaptation. You might even say it's my religion.
And if that's not enough--*I honestly don't know what comfort I can give you.* Everyone needs to accept the new normal of Krakoa.
I think we shouldn't act surprised.
A nation will act in its own best interest. This is neither new behavior nor unexpected. We have seen it all before.
And it would be... *dishonest* to pretend that our countries don't do the same.
We find ways around it. *We always do.* Call it common ground, *if you will.*

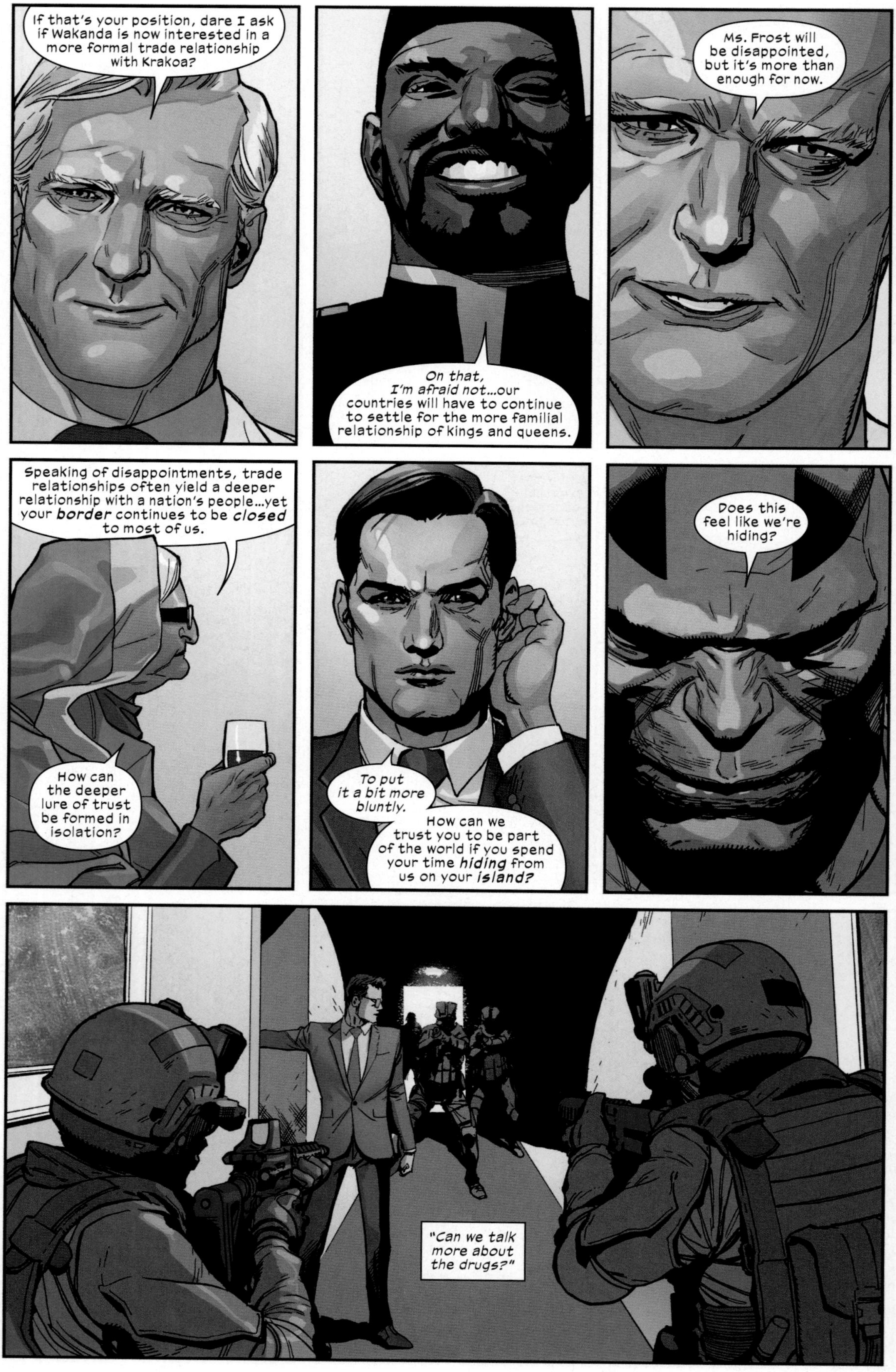
If that's your position, dare I ask if Wakanda is now interested in a more formal trade relationship with Krakoa?
On that, I'm afraid not...our countries will have to continue to settle for the more familial relationship of kings and queens.
Ms. Frost will be disappointed, but it's more than enough for now.
Speaking of disappointments, trade relationships often yield a deeper relationship with a nation's people...yet your border continues to be closed to most of us.
How can the deeper lure of trust be formed in isolation?
To put it a bit more bluntly.
How can we trust you to be part of the world if you spend your time hiding from us on your island?
Does this feel like we're hiding?
"Can we talk more about the drugs?"

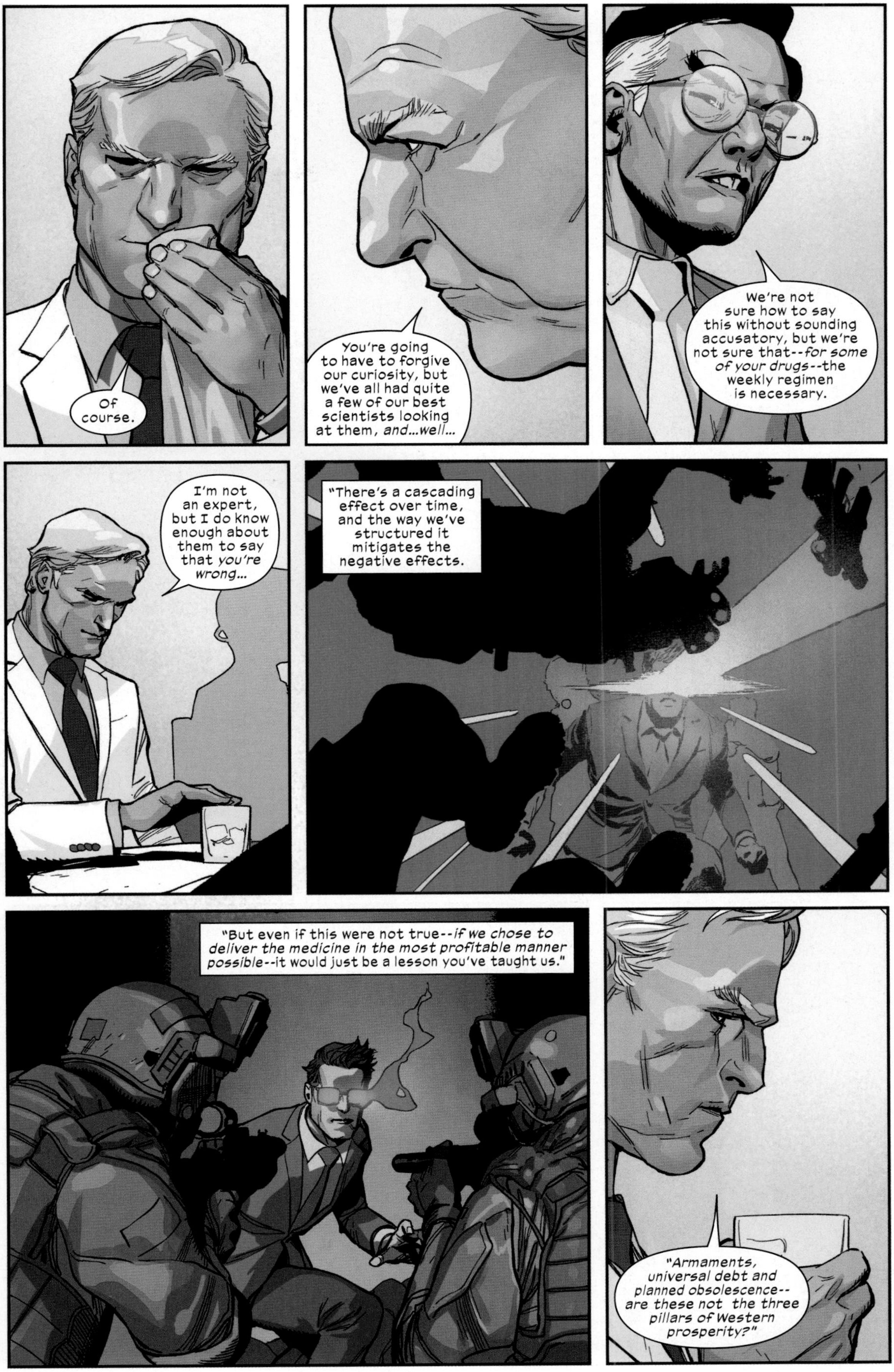

Of course.
You're going to have to forgive our curiosity, but we've all had quite a few of our best scientists looking at them, *and...well...*
We're not sure how to say this without sounding accusatory, but we're not sure that--*for some of your drugs*--the weekly regimen is necessary.
I'm not an expert, but I do know enough about them to say that *you're wrong...*
"There's a cascading effect over time, and the way we've structured it mitigates the negative effects.
"But even if this were not true--*if we chose to deliver the medicine in the most profitable manner possible*--it would just be a lesson you've taught us."
"Armaments, universal debt and planned obsolescence--are these not the three pillars of Western prosperity?"

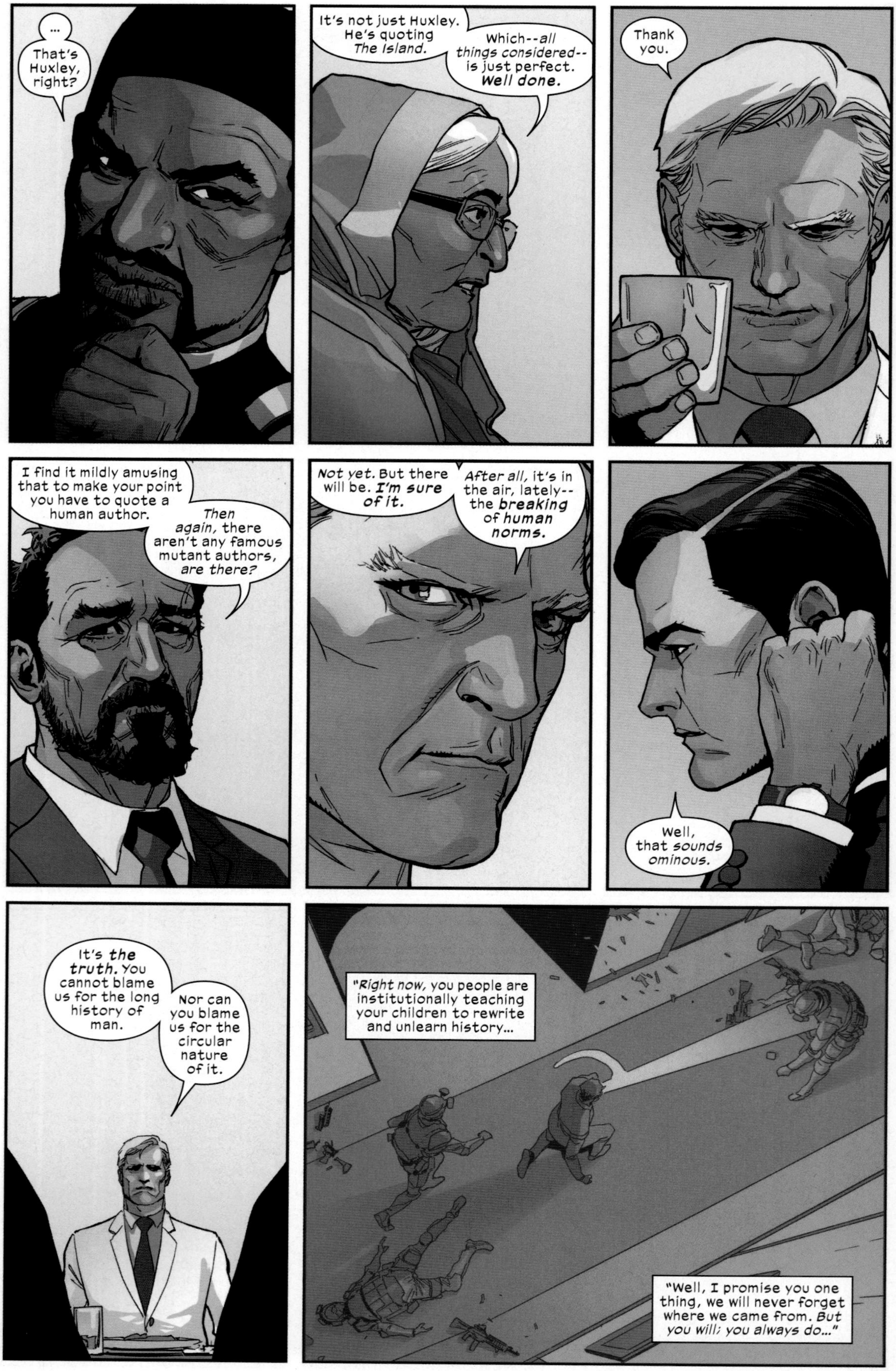

... That's Huxley, right?
It's not just Huxley. He's quoting *The Island.*
Which--*all things considered*--is just perfect. ***Well done.***
Thank you.
I find it mildly amusing that to make your point you have to quote a human author.
Then again, there aren't any famous mutant authors, *are there?*
Not yet. But there will be. ***I'm sure of it.***
After all, it's in the air, lately--the ***breaking*** of ***human norms.***
Well, that *sounds ominous.*
It's ***the truth.*** You cannot blame us for the long history of man.
Nor can you blame us for the circular nature of it.
"*Right now,* you people are institutionally teaching your children to rewrite and unlearn history...
"Well, I promise you one thing, we will never forget where we came from. *But you will; you always do...*"

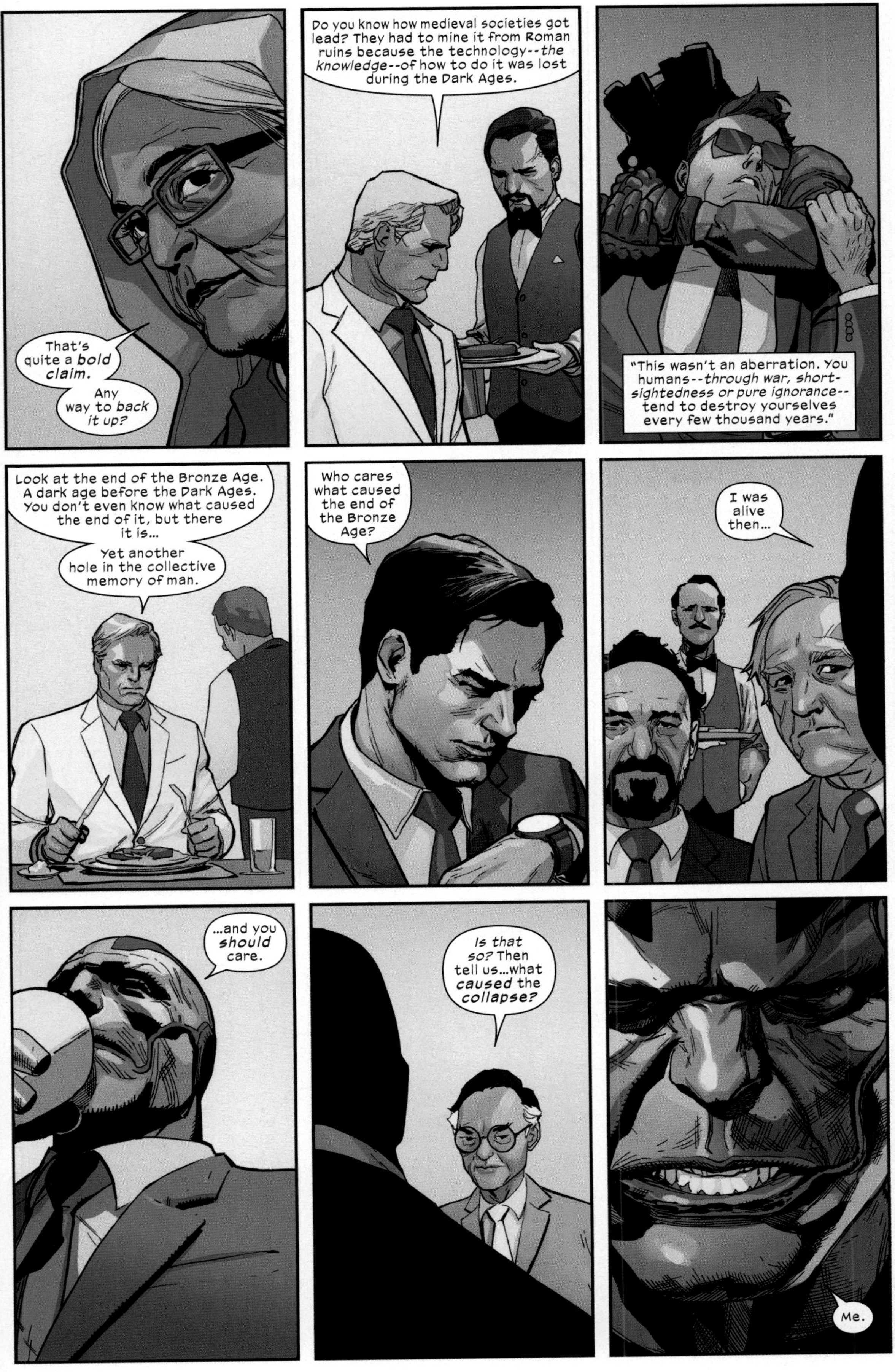
That's quite a *bold claim.*
Any way to *back it up?*
Do you know how medieval societies got lead? They had to mine it from Roman ruins because the technology--*the knowledge*--of how to do it was lost during the Dark Ages.
"This wasn't an aberration. You humans--*through war, short-sightedness or pure ignorance*--tend to destroy yourselves every few thousand years."
Look at the end of the Bronze Age. A dark age before the Dark Ages. You don't even know what caused the end of it, but there it is...
Yet another hole in the collective memory of man.
Who cares what caused the end of the Bronze Age?
I was alive then...
...and you *should* care.
Is that so? Then tell us...what *caused* the *collapse?*
Me.

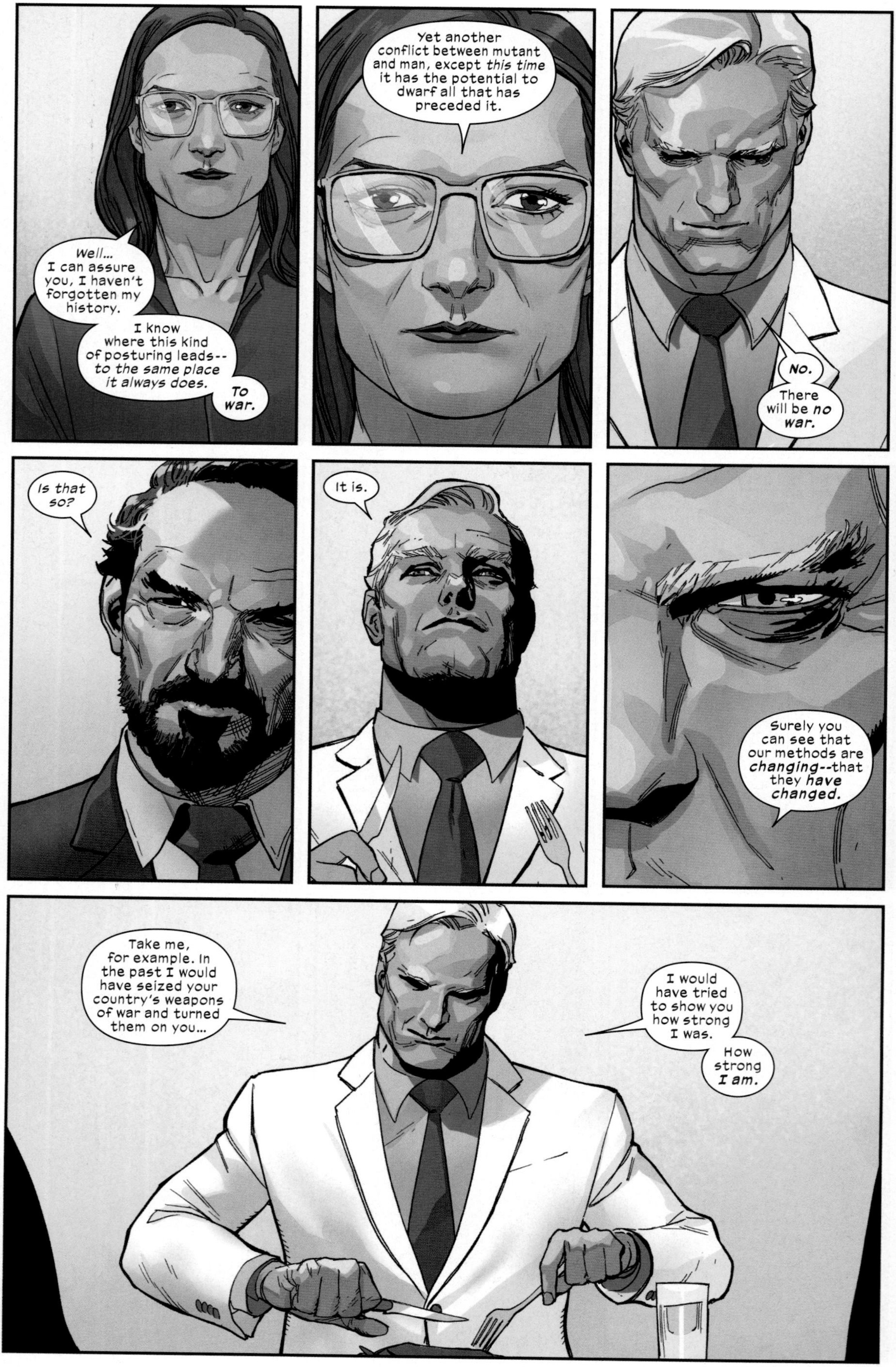
Well... I can assure you, I haven't forgotten my history.
I know where this kind of posturing leads--to the same place it always does.
To war.
Yet another conflict between mutant and man, except this time it has the potential to dwarf all that has preceded it.
No.
There will be no war.
Is that so?
It is.
Surely you can see that our methods are changing--that they have changed.
Take me, for example. In the past I would have seized your country's weapons of war and turned them on you...
I would have tried to show you how strong I was.
How strong I am.

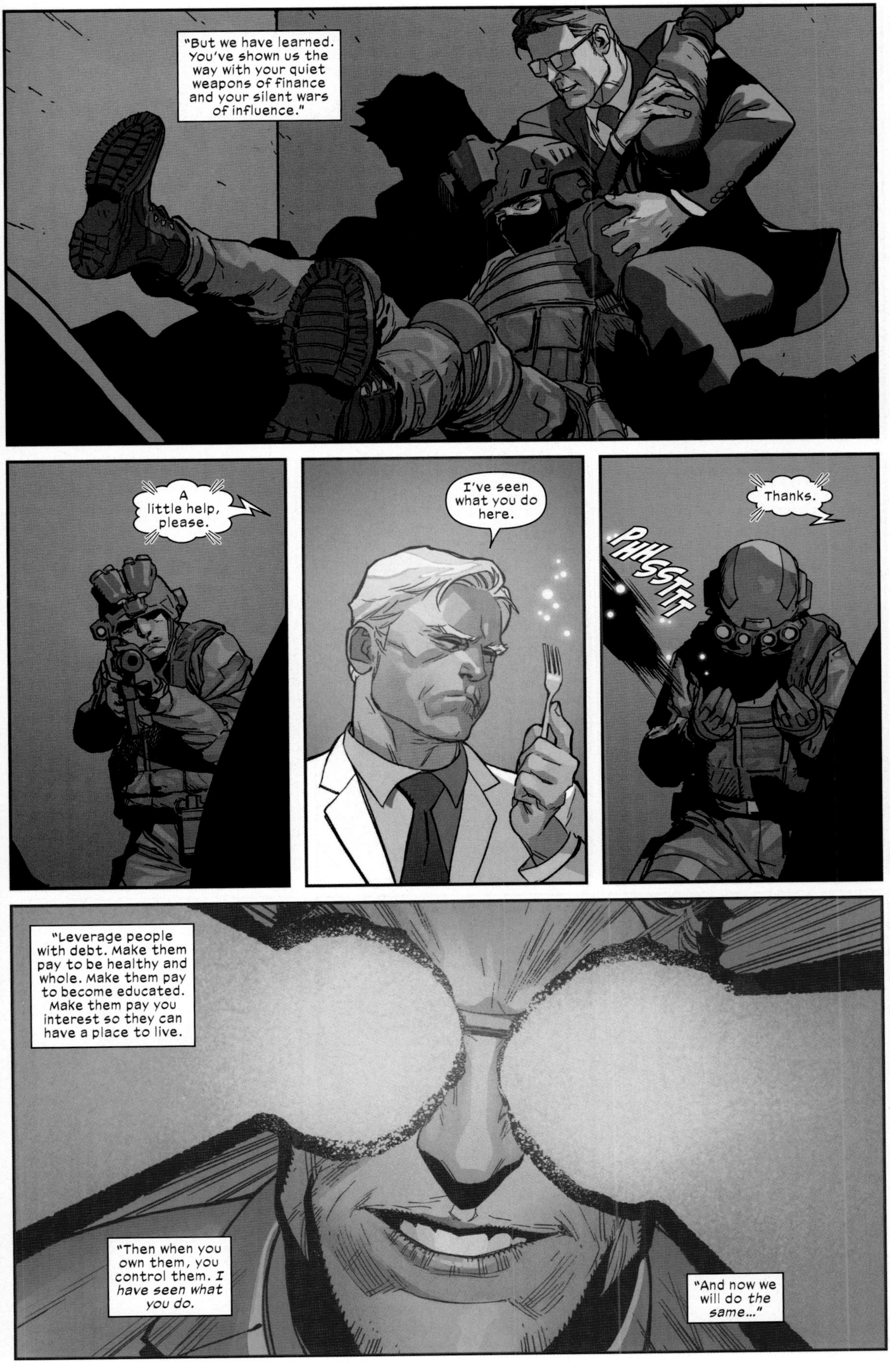
"But we have learned. You've shown us the way with your quiet weapons of finance and your silent wars of influence."
A little help, please.
I've seen what you do here.
Thanks.
PHHSSTTT
"Leverage people with debt. Make them pay to be healthy and whole. Make them pay to become educated. Make them pay you interest so they can have a place to live.
"Then when you own them, you control them. *I have seen what you do.*
"And now we will do *the same*..."

...but better.

Better versions of a better life. Better drugs for a longer, healthier existence.

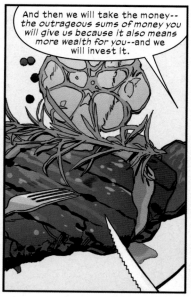

And then we will take the money-- the outrageous sums of money you will give us because it also means more wealth for you--and we will invest it.

We will buy your *banks*. We will buy your *schools*. We will buy your *media*.

We will buy *your* politicians.

And then, when we have bought all the rest, we will buy *you*-- because you have taught us that everything has a price.

And we are *happy to pay*.

Then, when we have this influence-- *we will use it*. We will make sure that the wrong sort of people--*and you know who*--no longer have any economic power.

We will not allow them inside our institutions, because it's important they do not have anywhere to peddle their dangerous, outdated ideas.

And that is how it will end. Like a fire with no oxygen.

Yes, of course, there will still be people who fear and hate us...they just simply won't be able to do anything about it any longer.

So as I said...

There will be *no* war.

Oh, and by the way...

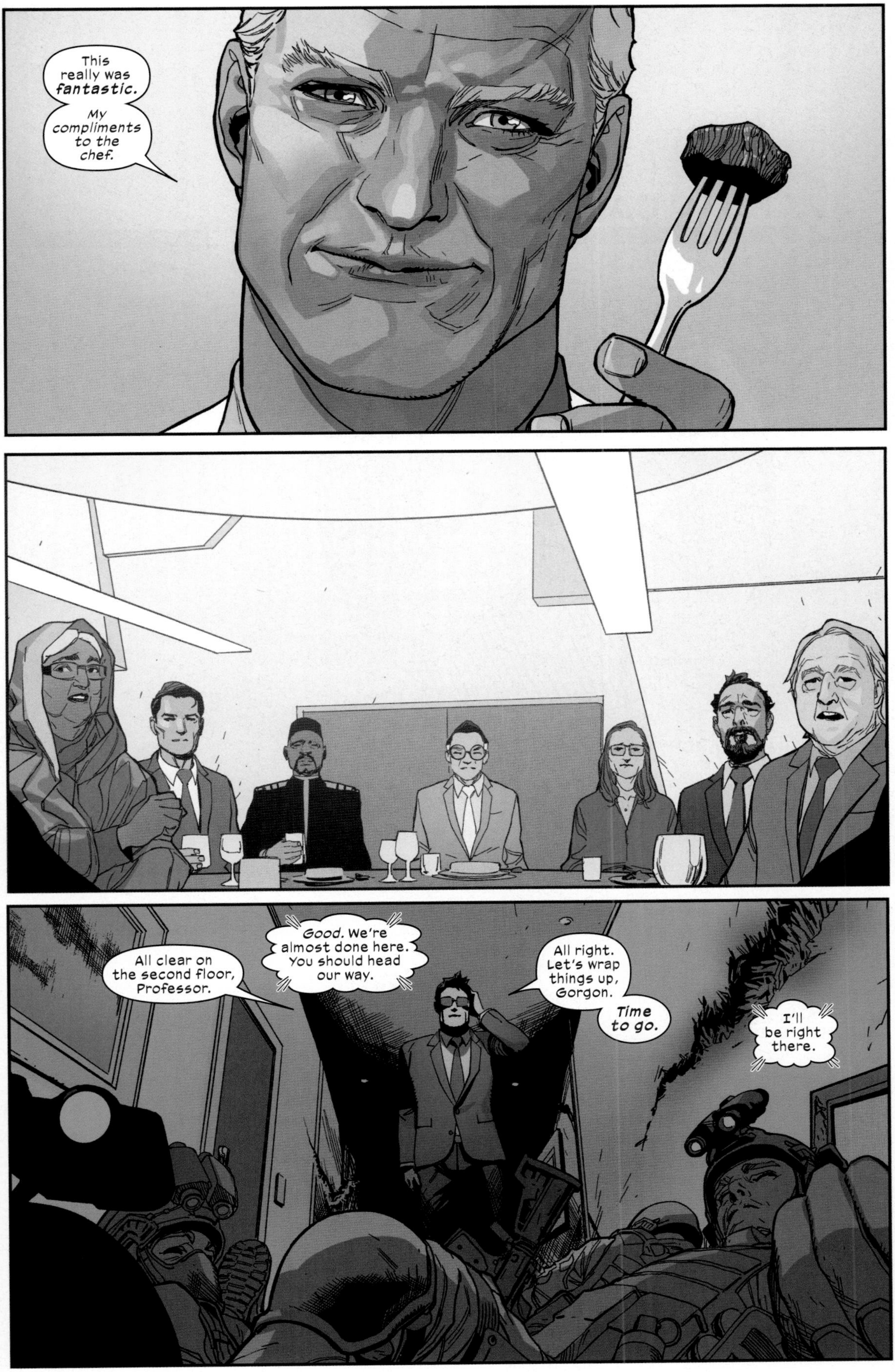
This really was *fantastic.*
My compliments to the chef.
All clear on the second floor, Professor.
Good. We're almost done here. You should head our way.
All right. Let's wrap things up, Gorgon.
Time to go.
I'll be right there.

KRAKOAN CAPTAINS

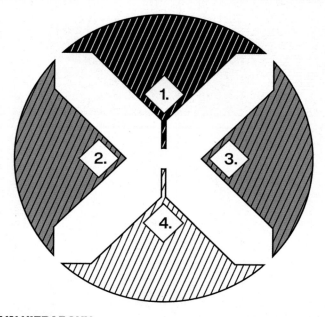

CAPTAIN HIERARCHY

[1]

CYCLOPS..........................
CAPTAIN COMMANDER...............
X-MEN............................

[2]

MAGIK........................
CAPTAIN......................
SEXTANT......................

[3]

BISHOP...........................
CAPTAIN..........................
HELLFIRE TRADING................

[4]

GORGON.......................
CAPTAIN......................
COUNCIL GUARD...............

GORGON

While the other three captains have broader, more extensive jurisdictions, Gorgon has a smaller, more specific one.* As one of the most experienced, and most lethal, mutants on Earth, he was chosen by the Captain Commander [after consultation with Wolverine] to act as the personal protector for members of the Quiet Council [especially when they leave Krakoa].

*After the events surrounding the assassination of Charles Xavier, if an Autumn council member plans to enter a hostile environment, the expectation is that Gorgon will accompany them.

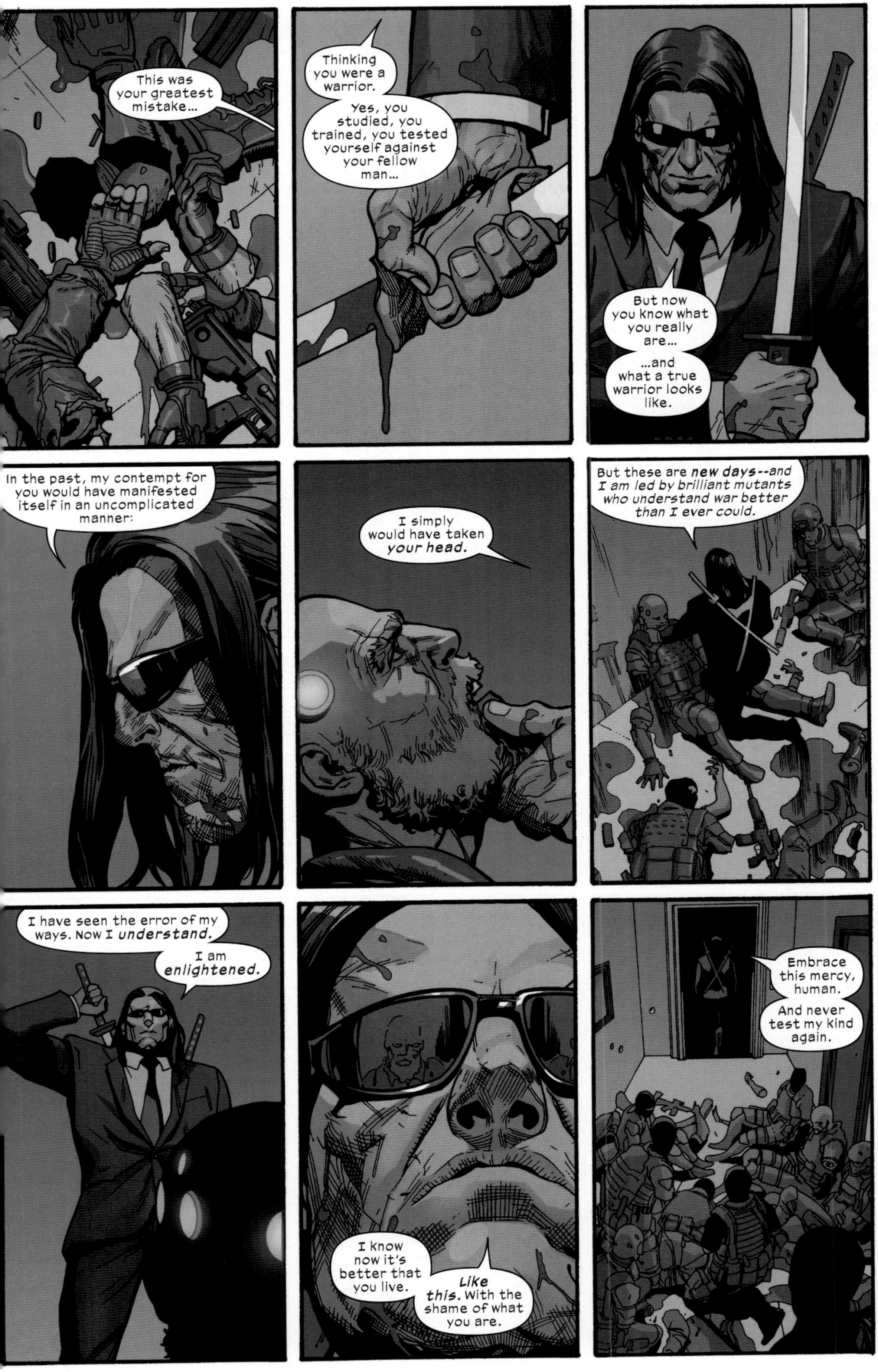

This was your greatest mistake...
Thinking you were a warrior.
Yes, you studied, you trained, you tested yourself against your fellow man...
But now you know what you really are...
...and what a true warrior looks like.
In the past, my contempt for you would have manifested itself in an uncomplicated manner:
I simply would have taken *your head.*
But these are *new days--*and *I am* led by brilliant mutants *who understand war better than I ever could.*
I have seen the error of my ways. Now I *understand.*
I am *enlightened.*
I know now it's better that you live.
Like this. With the shame of what you are.
Embrace this mercy, human.
And never test my kind again.

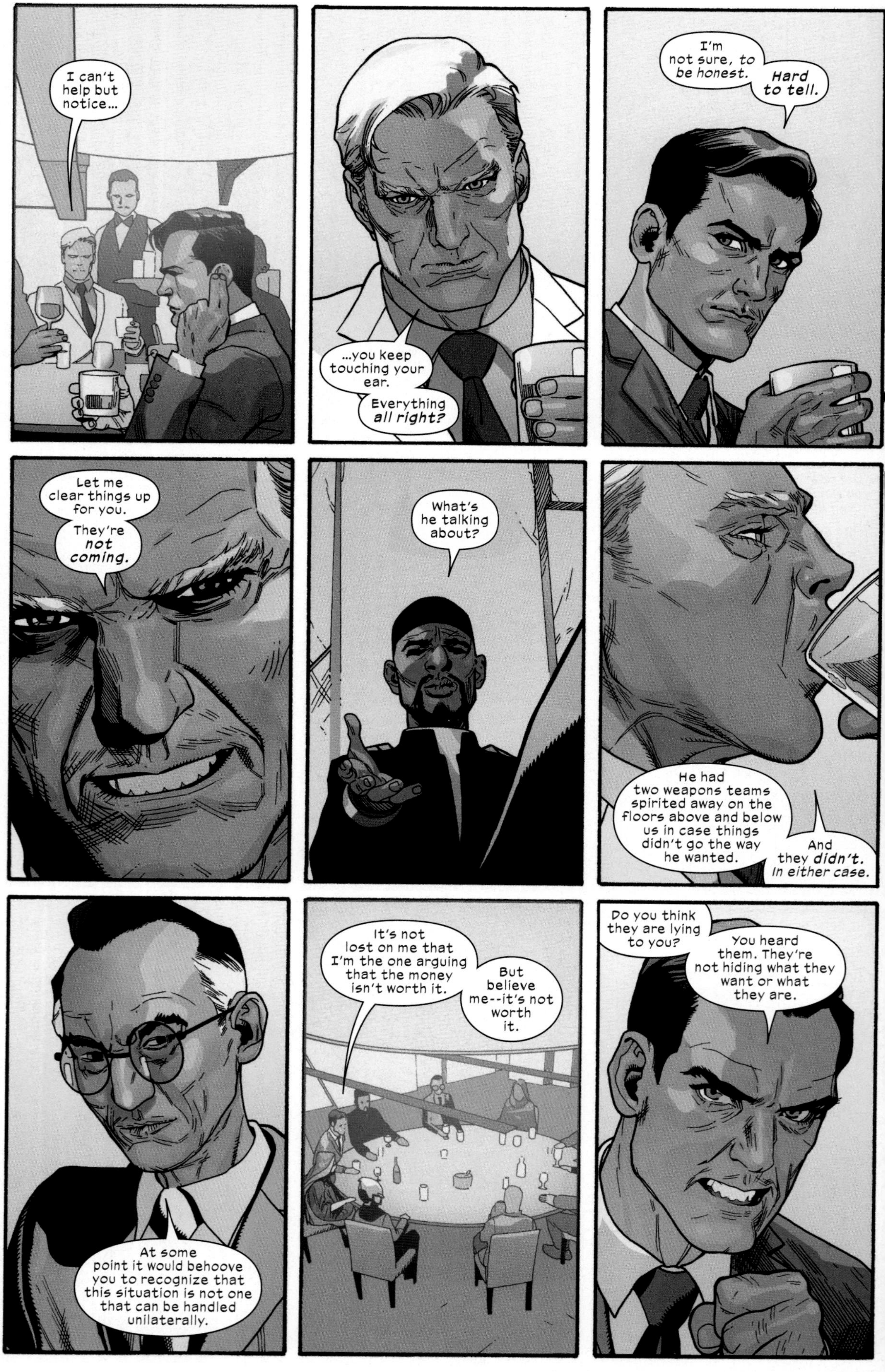

I can't help but notice...
...you keep touching your ear.
Everything *all right?*
I'm not sure, to be honest.
Hard to tell.
Let me clear things up for you.
They're ***not coming.***
What's he talking about?
He had two weapons teams spirited away on the floors above and below us in case things didn't go the way he wanted.
And they ***didn't.*** *In either case.*
At some point it would behoove you to recognize that this situation is not one that can be handled unilaterally.
It's not lost on me that I'm the one arguing that the money isn't worth it.
But believe me--it's not worth it.
Do you think they are lying to you?
You heard them. They're not hiding what they want or what they are.

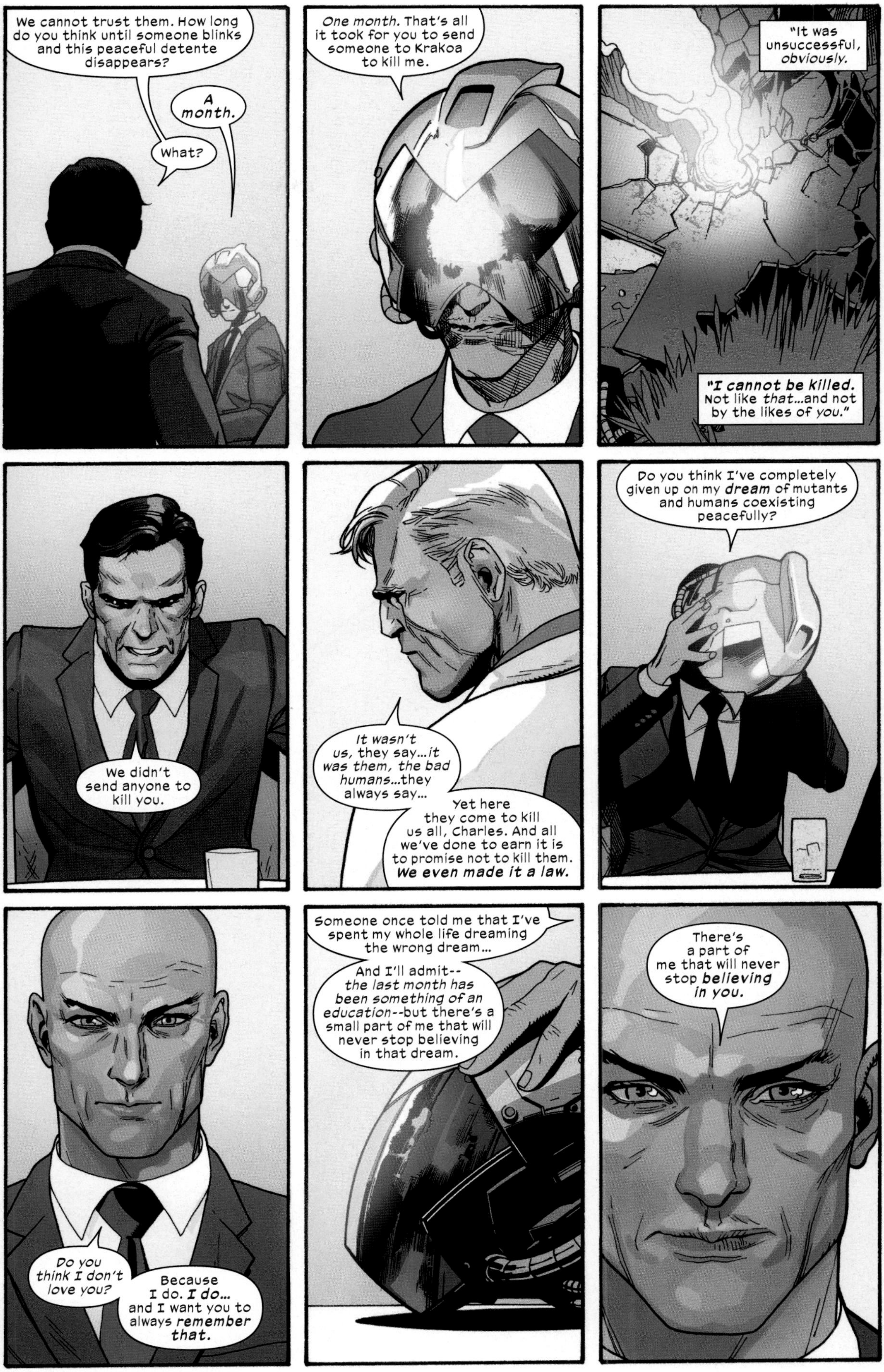
We cannot trust them. How long do you think until someone blinks and this peaceful detente disappears?
A month.
What?
One month. That's all it took for you to send someone to Krakoa to kill me.
"It was unsuccessful, obviously.
"I cannot be killed. Not like that...and not by the likes of you."
We didn't send anyone to kill you.
It wasn't us, they say...it was them, the bad humans...they always say...
Yet here they come to kill us all, Charles. And all we've done to earn it is to promise not to kill them. We even made it a law.
Do you think I've completely given up on my dream of mutants and humans coexisting peacefully?
Do you think I don't love you?
Because I do. I do... and I want you to always remember that.
Someone once told me that I've spent my whole life dreaming the wrong dream...
And I'll admit-- the last month has been something of an education--but there's a small part of me that will never stop believing in that dream.
There's a part of me that will never stop believing in you.

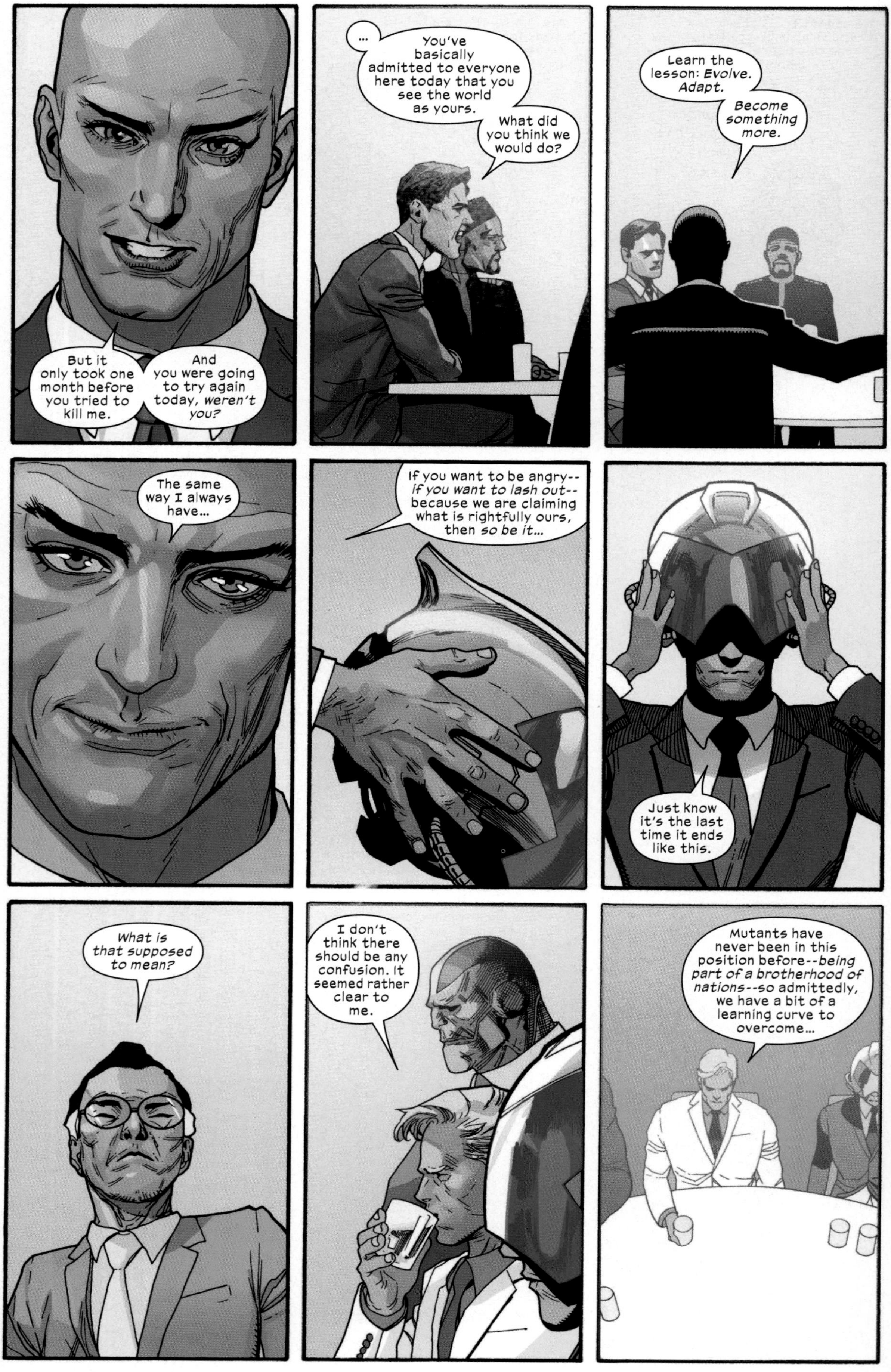
But it only took one month before you tried to kill me.
And you were going to try again today, *weren't you?*
...
You've basically admitted to everyone here today that you see the world as yours.
What did you think we would do?
Learn the lesson: *Evolve. Adapt.*
Become something more.
The same way I always have...
If you want to be angry-- *if you want to lash out*-- because we are claiming what is rightfully ours, then *so be it*...
Just know it's the last time it ends like this.
What is that supposed to mean?
I don't think there should be any confusion. It seemed rather clear to me.
Mutants have never been in this position before--*being part of a brotherhood of nations*--so admittedly, we have a bit of a learning curve to overcome...

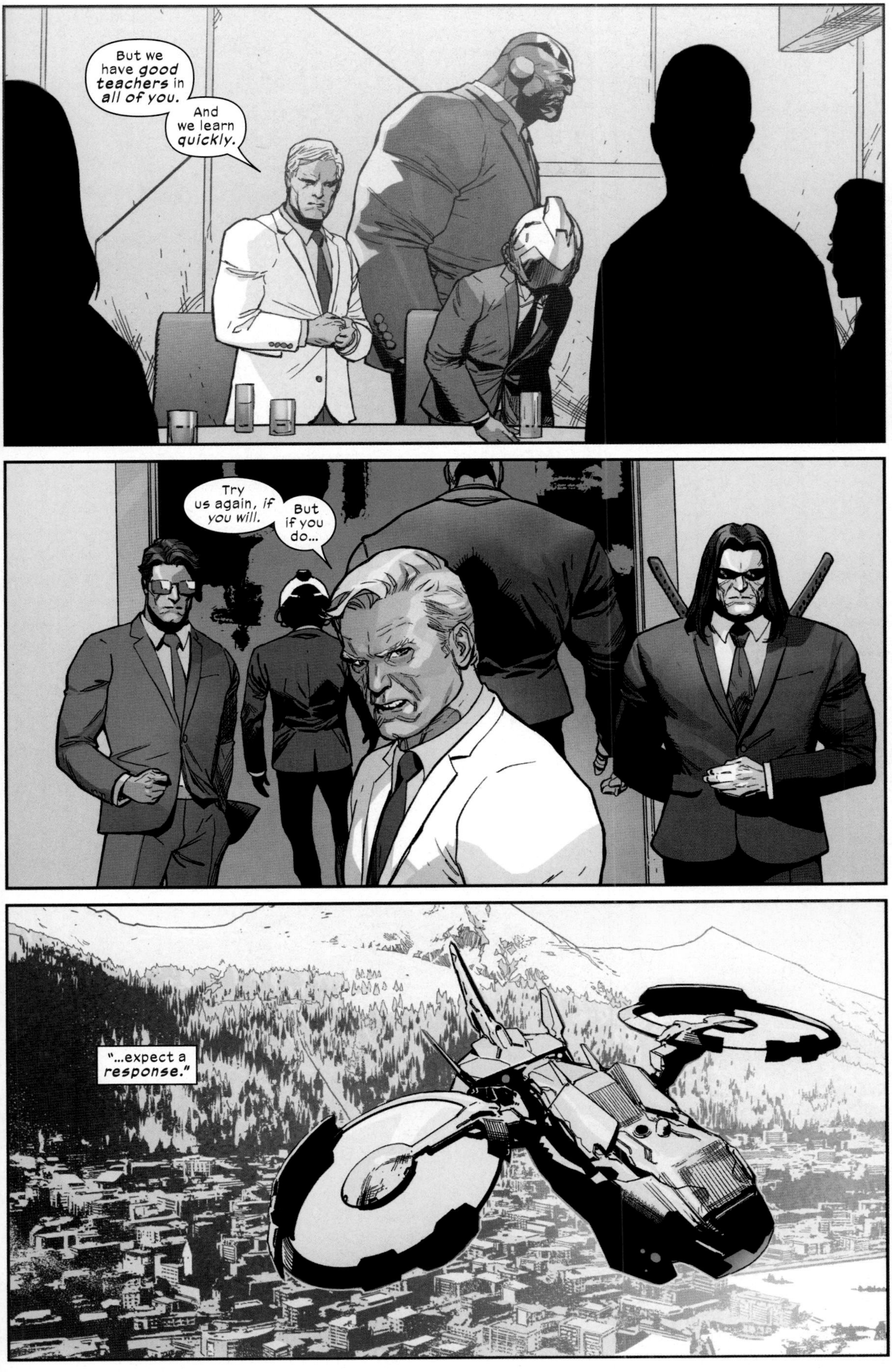
But we have good teachers in all of you.
And we learn quickly.
Try us again, if you will.
But if you do...
"...expect a response."

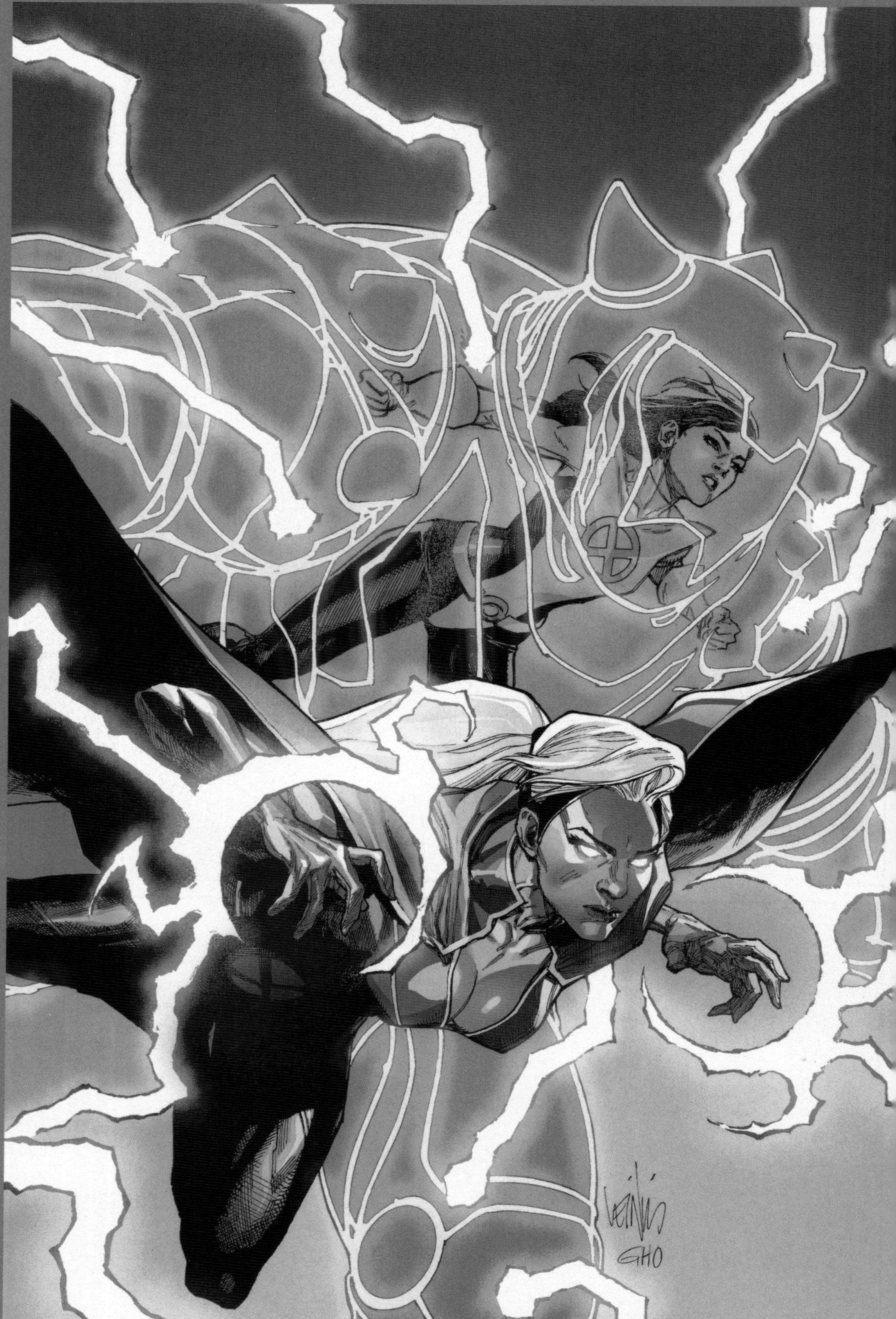

Into the Vault

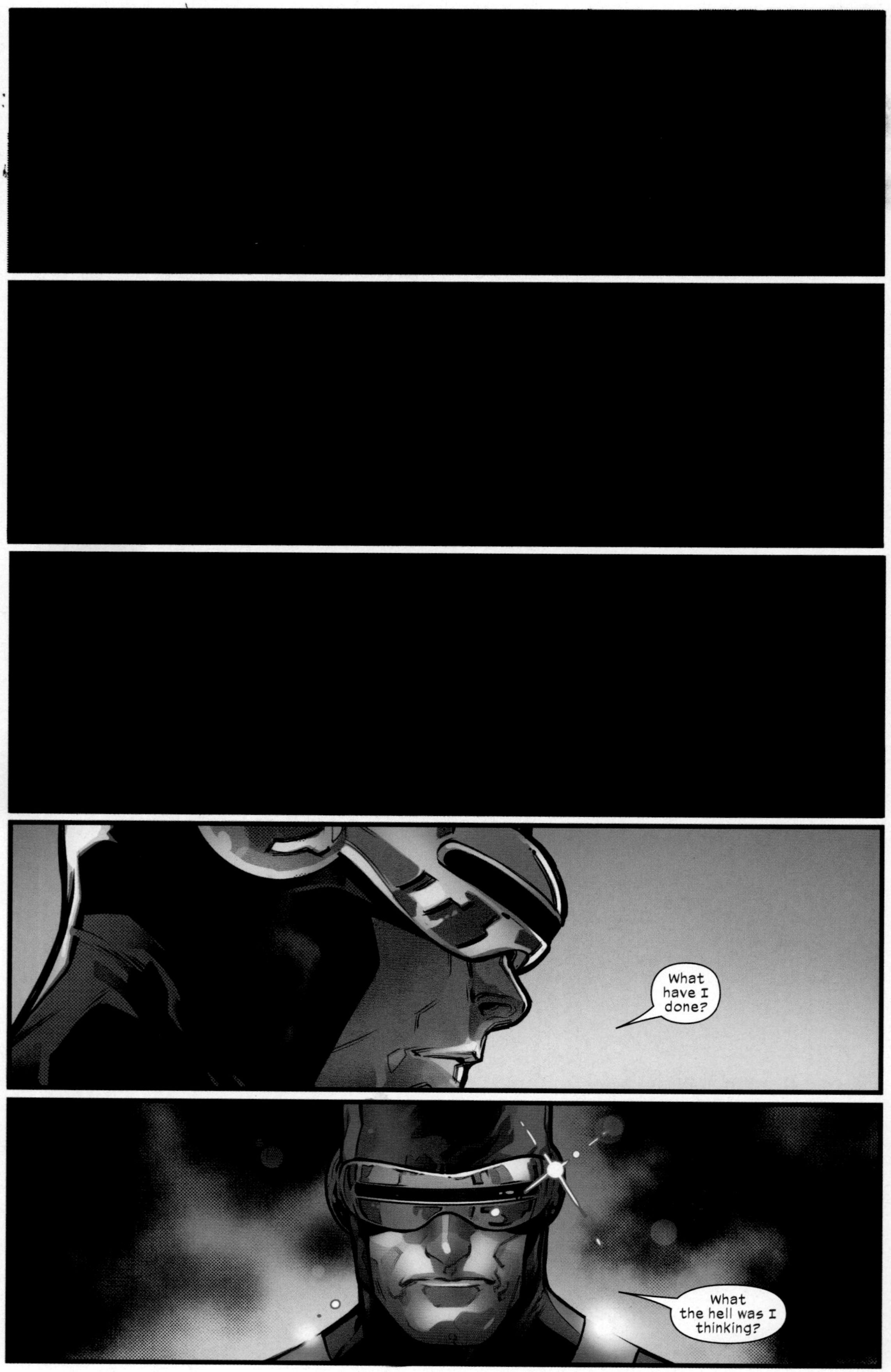
What have I done?
What the hell was I thinking?

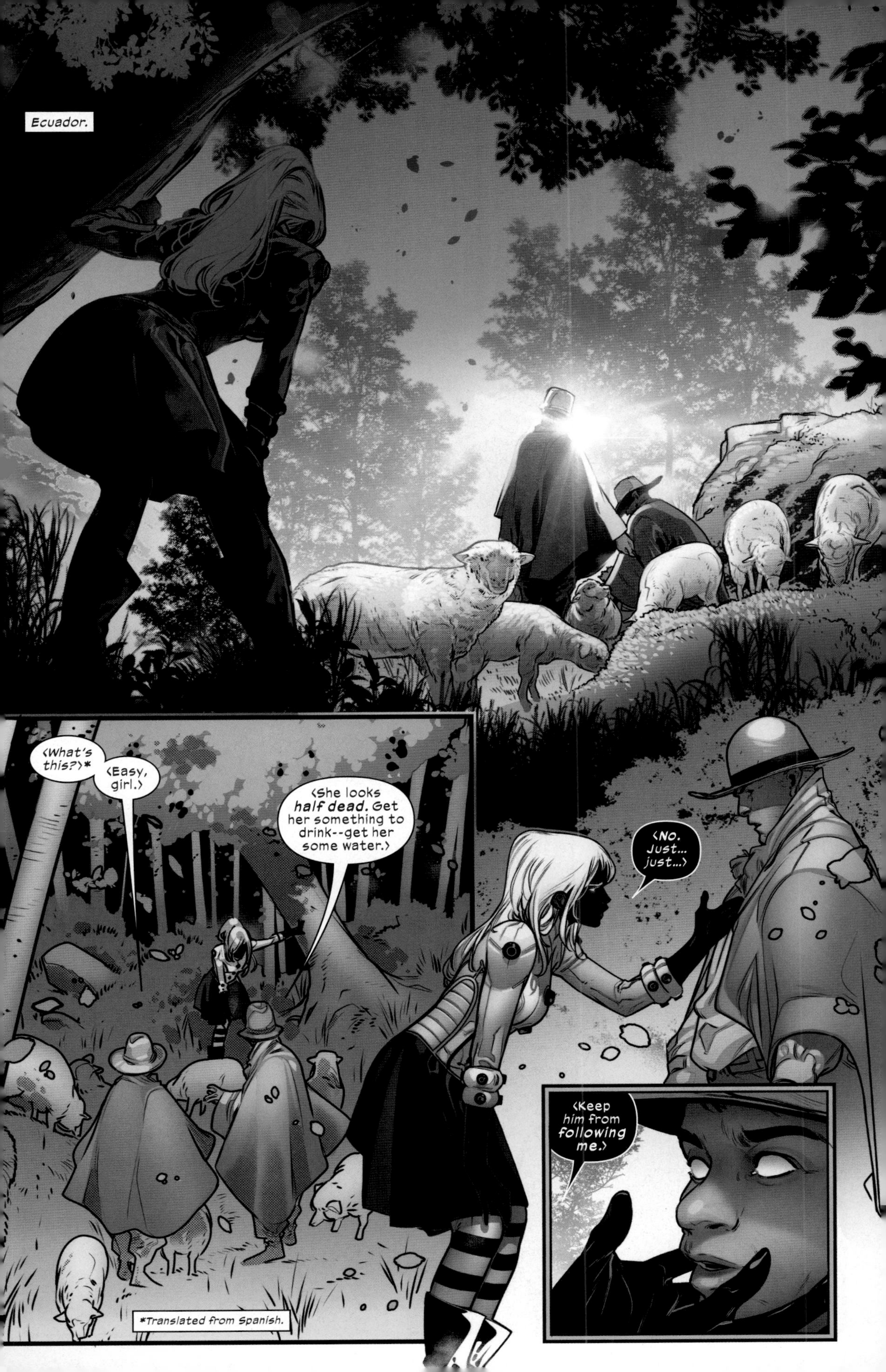
Ecuador.
‹What's this?›*
‹Easy, girl.›
‹She looks half dead. Get her something to drink--get her some water.›
‹No. Just... just...›
‹Keep him from following me.›
*Translated from Spanish.

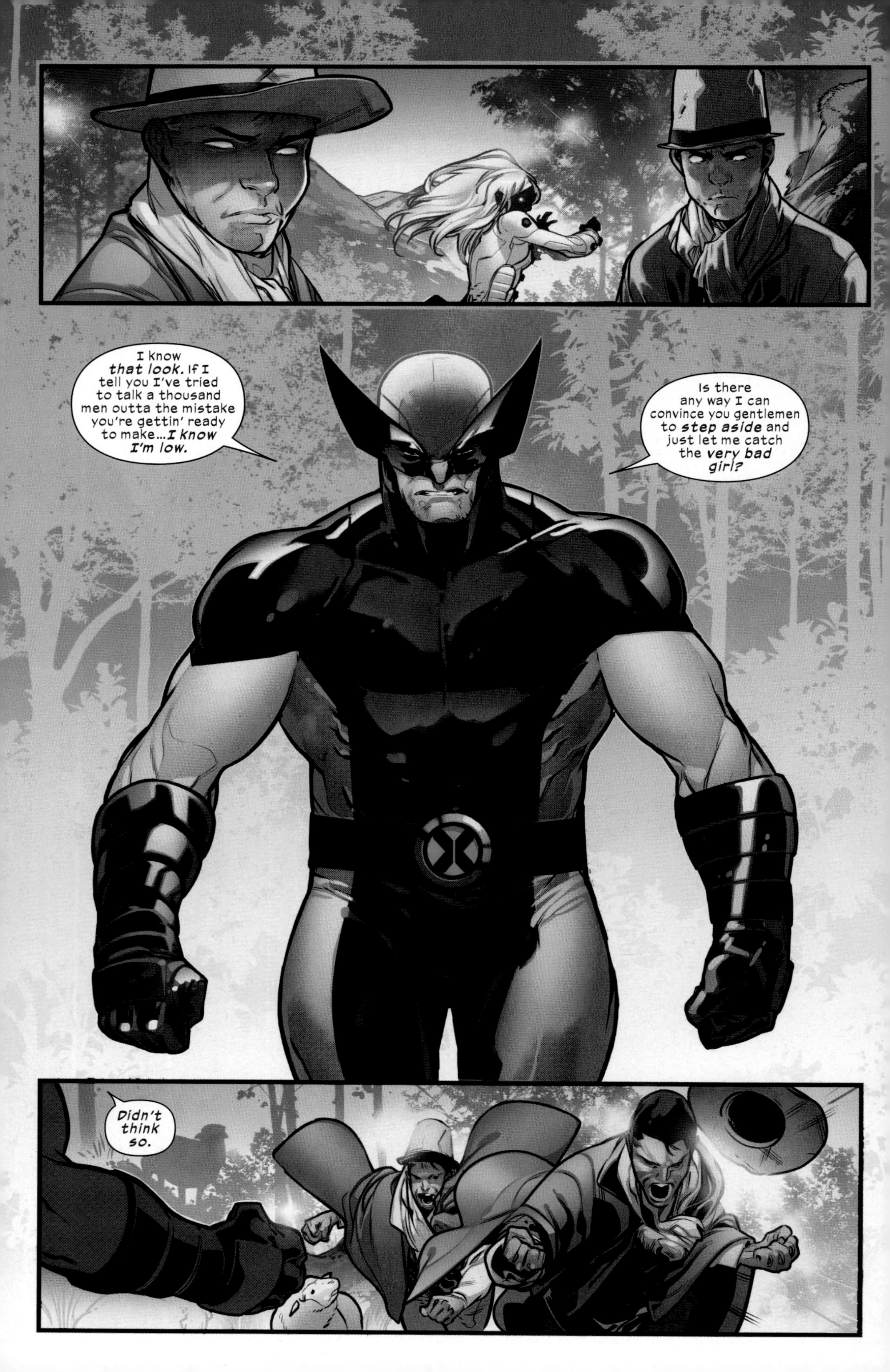
I know *that look.* If I tell you I've tried to talk a thousand men outta the mistake you're gettin' ready to make...*I know I'm low.*
Is there any way I can convince you gentlemen to *step aside* and just let me catch the *very bad girl?*
Didn't think so.

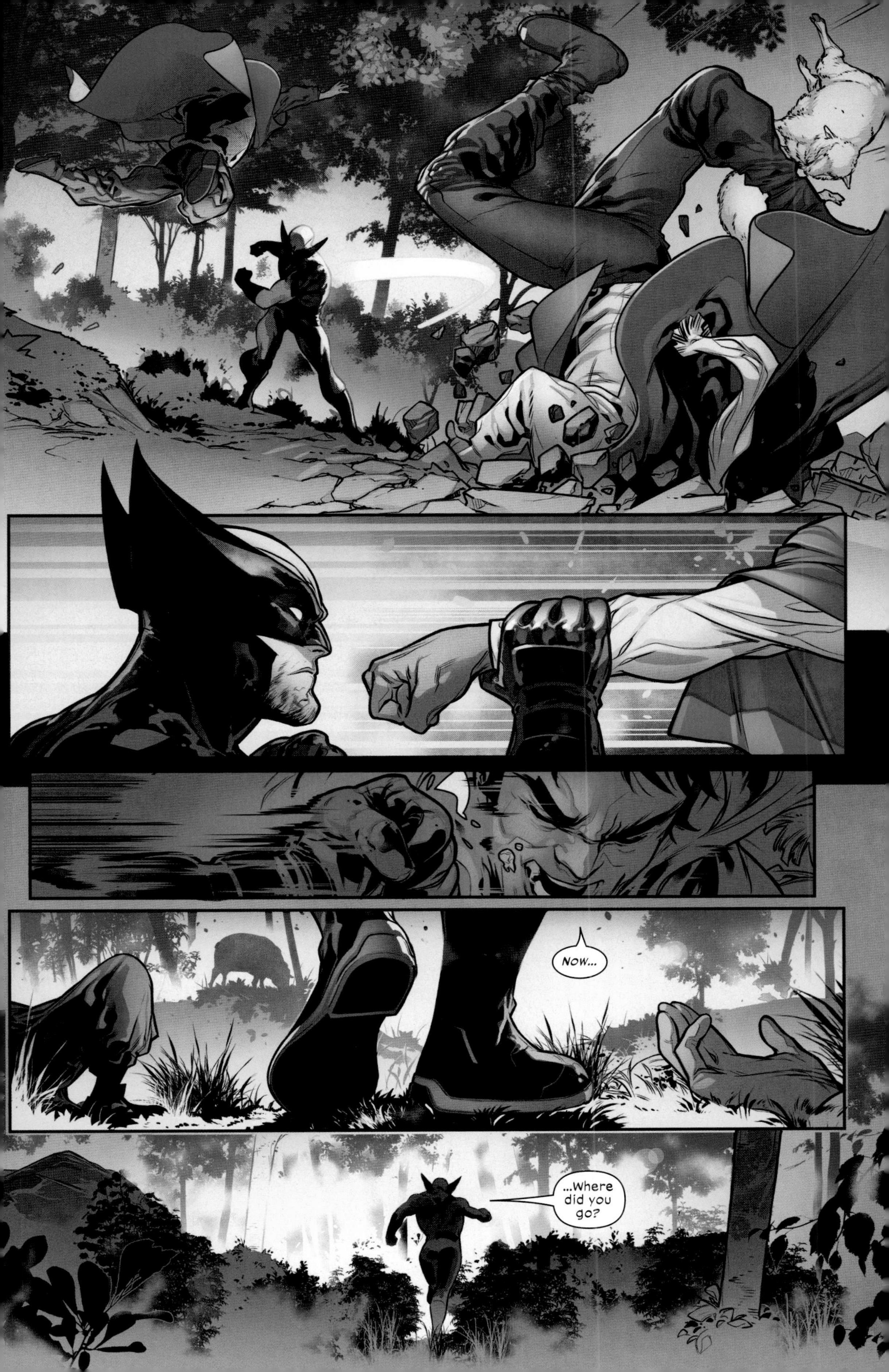
NOW...
...Where did you go?

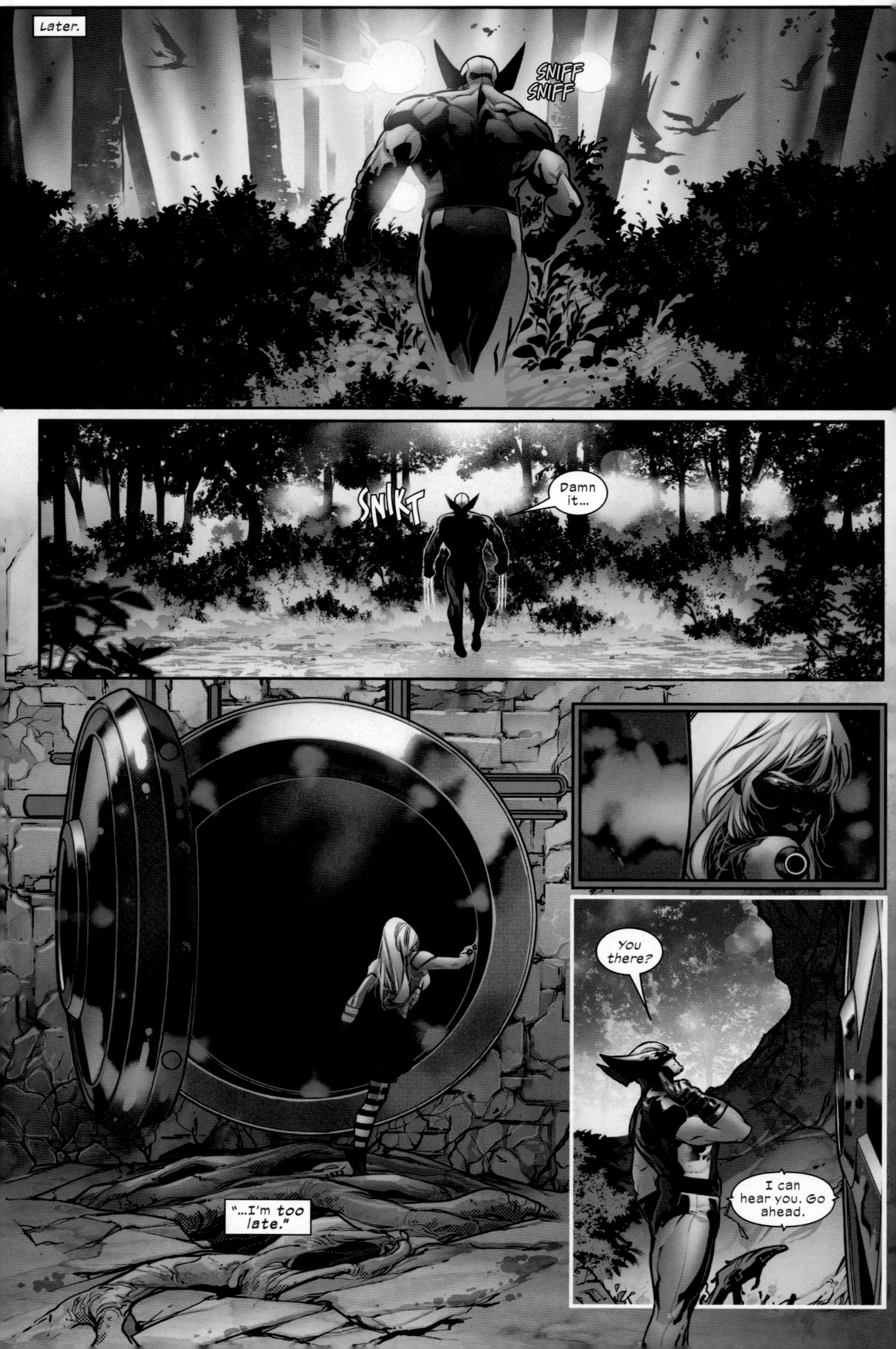
Later.
SNIFF SNIFF
SNIKT
Damn it...
"...I'm too late."
You there?
I can hear you. Go ahead.

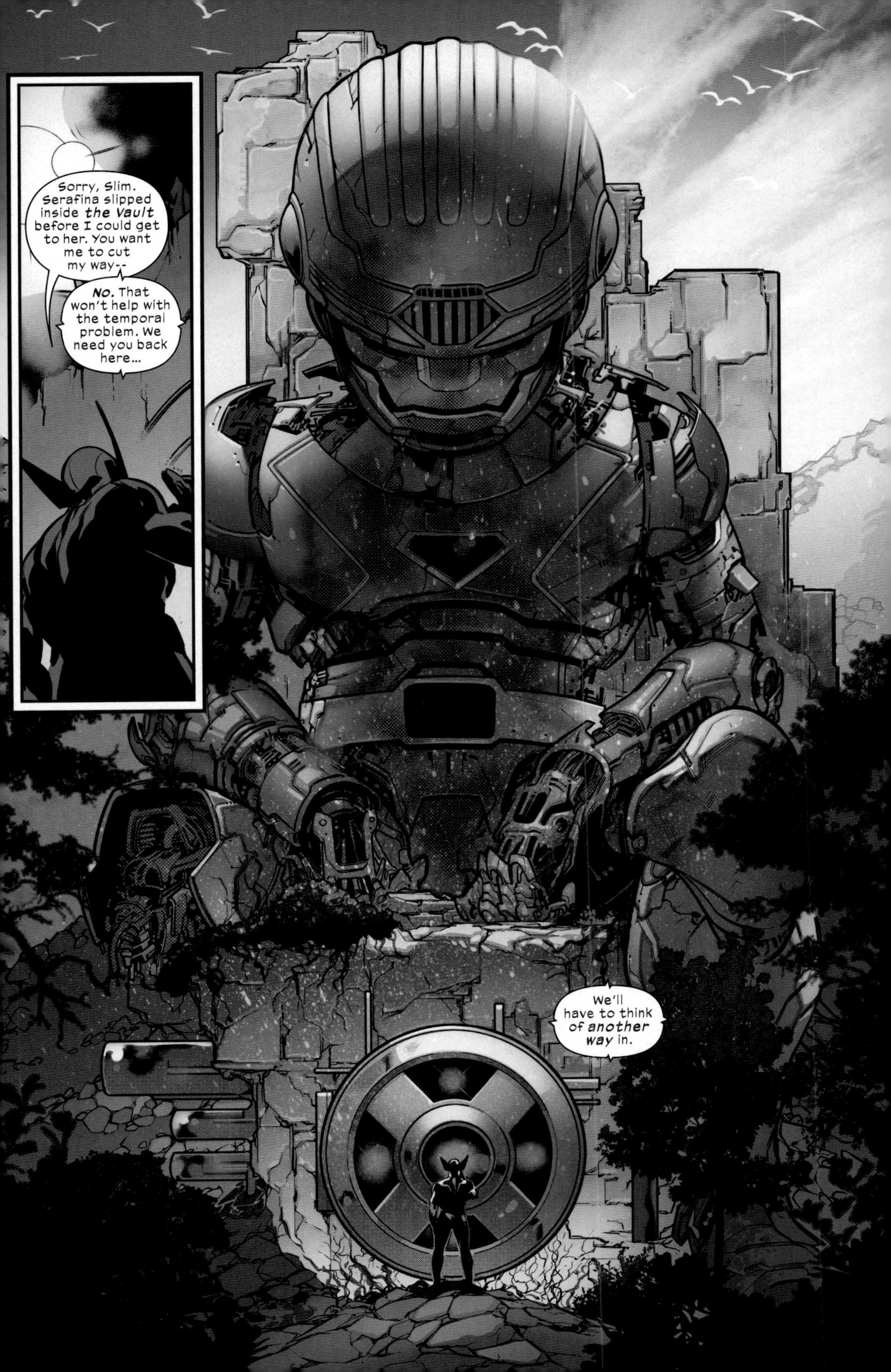
Sorry, Slim. Serafina slipped inside *the Vault* before I could get to her. You want me to cut my way--
No. That won't help with the temporal problem. We need you back here...
We'll have to think of *another way* in.

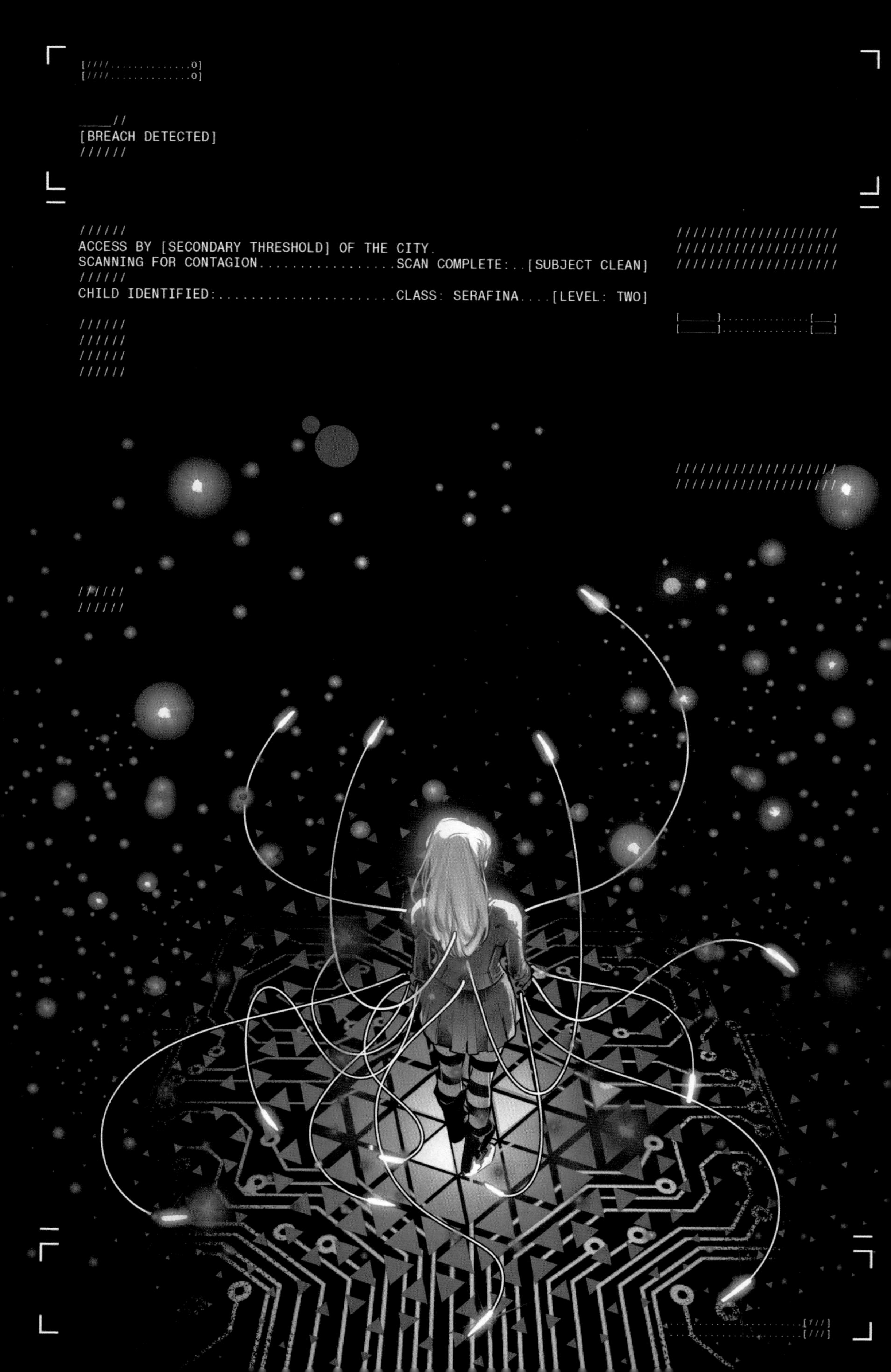
[BREACH DETECTED]
ACCESS BY [SECONDARY THRESHOLD] OF THE CITY.
SCANNING FOR CONTAGION..................SCAN COMPLETE:..[SUBJECT CLEAN]
CHILD IDENTIFIED:......................CLASS: SERAFINA....[LEVEL: TWO]

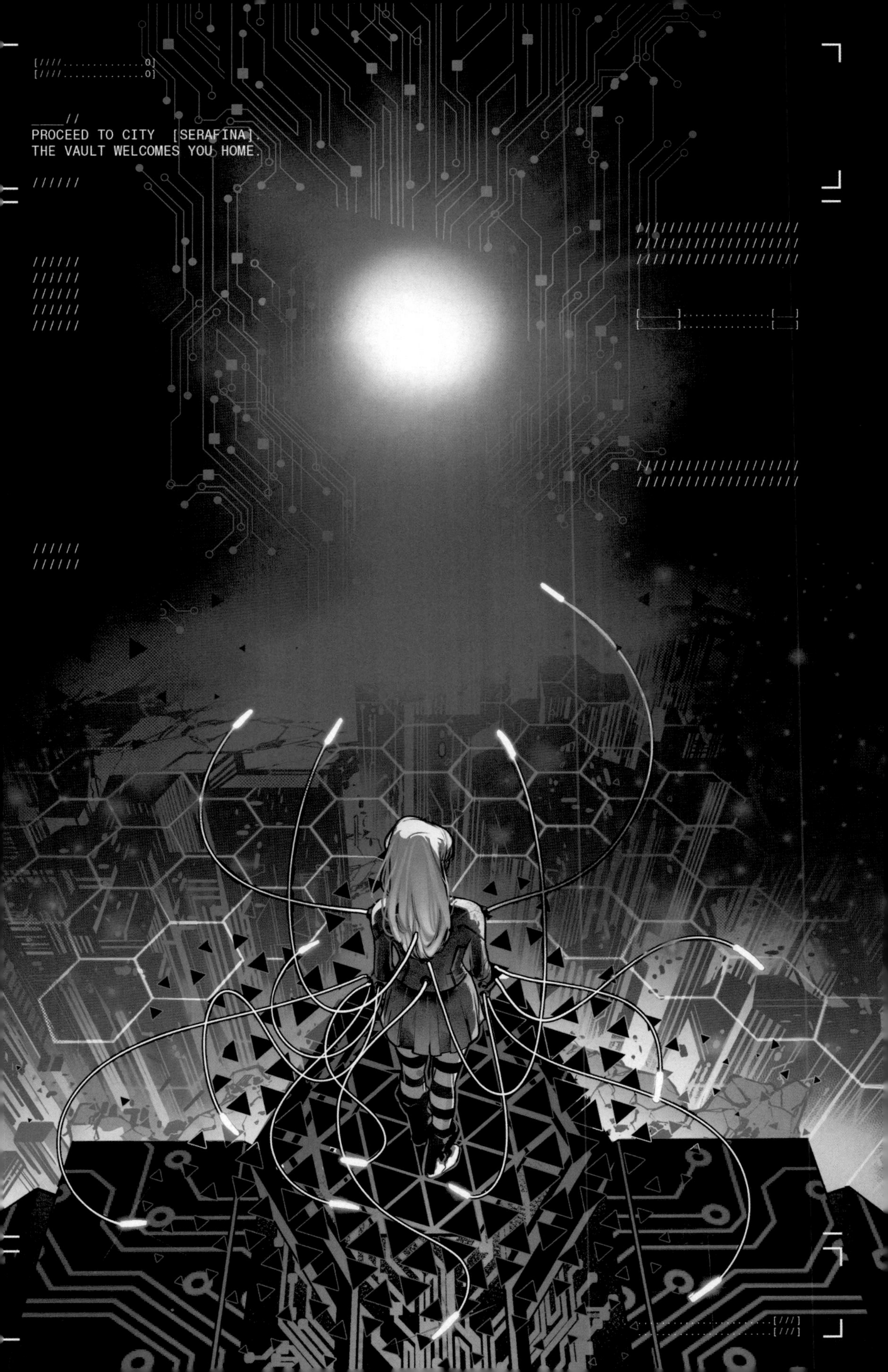

PROCEED TO CITY [SERAFINA].
THE VAULT WELCOMES YOU HOME.

Later.
Krakoa.

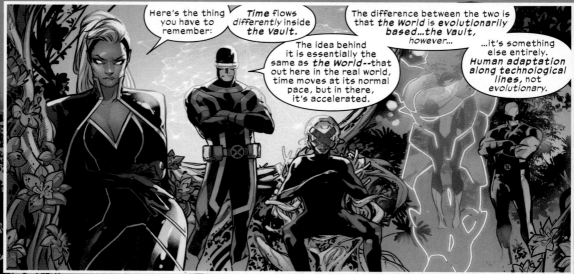

Here's the thing you have to remember:

Time flows differently inside the *Vault.*

The idea behind it is essentially the same as *the World*--that out here in the real world, time moves at its normal pace, but in there, it's accelerated.

The difference between the two is that *the World* is evolutionarily based...the *Vault,* however...

...it's something else entirely. *Human adaptation along technological lines,* not evolutionary.

Sounds like a *problem* in search of a *solution.*

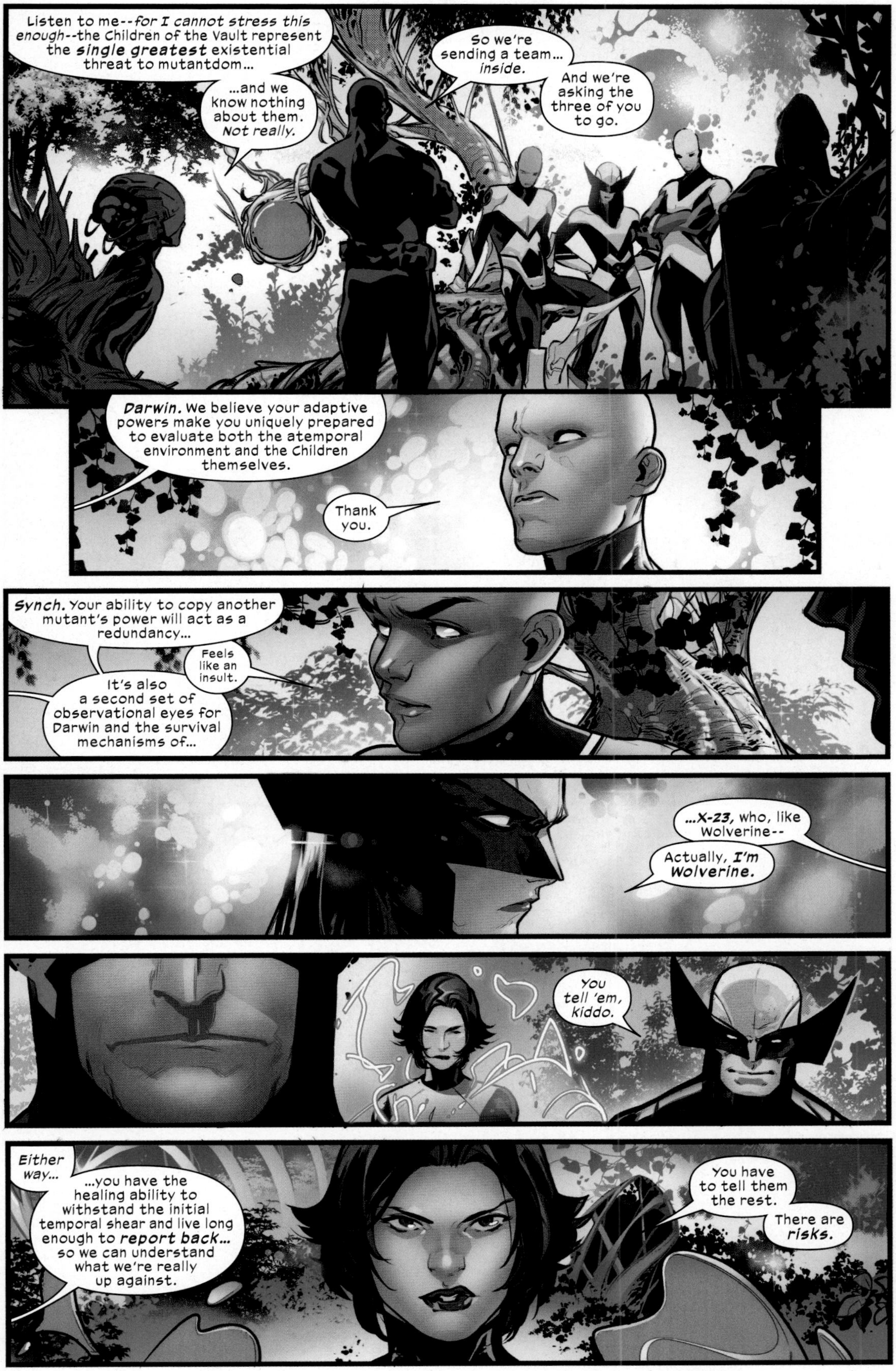
Listen to me--*for I cannot stress this enough*--the Children of the Vault represent the ***single greatest*** existential threat to mutantdom...
...and we know nothing about them. *Not really.*
So we're sending a team... *inside.*
And we're asking the three of you to go.
Darwin. We believe your adaptive powers make you uniquely prepared to evaluate both the atemporal environment and the Children themselves.
Thank you.
Synch. Your ability to copy another mutant's power will act as a redundancy...
Feels like an insult.
It's also a second set of observational eyes for Darwin and the survival mechanisms of...
...X-23, who, like Wolverine--
Actually, ***I'm Wolverine.***
You tell 'em, kiddo.
Either way...
...you have the healing ability to withstand the initial temporal shear and live long enough to ***report back...*** so we can understand what we're really up against.
You have to tell them the rest.
There are ***risks.***

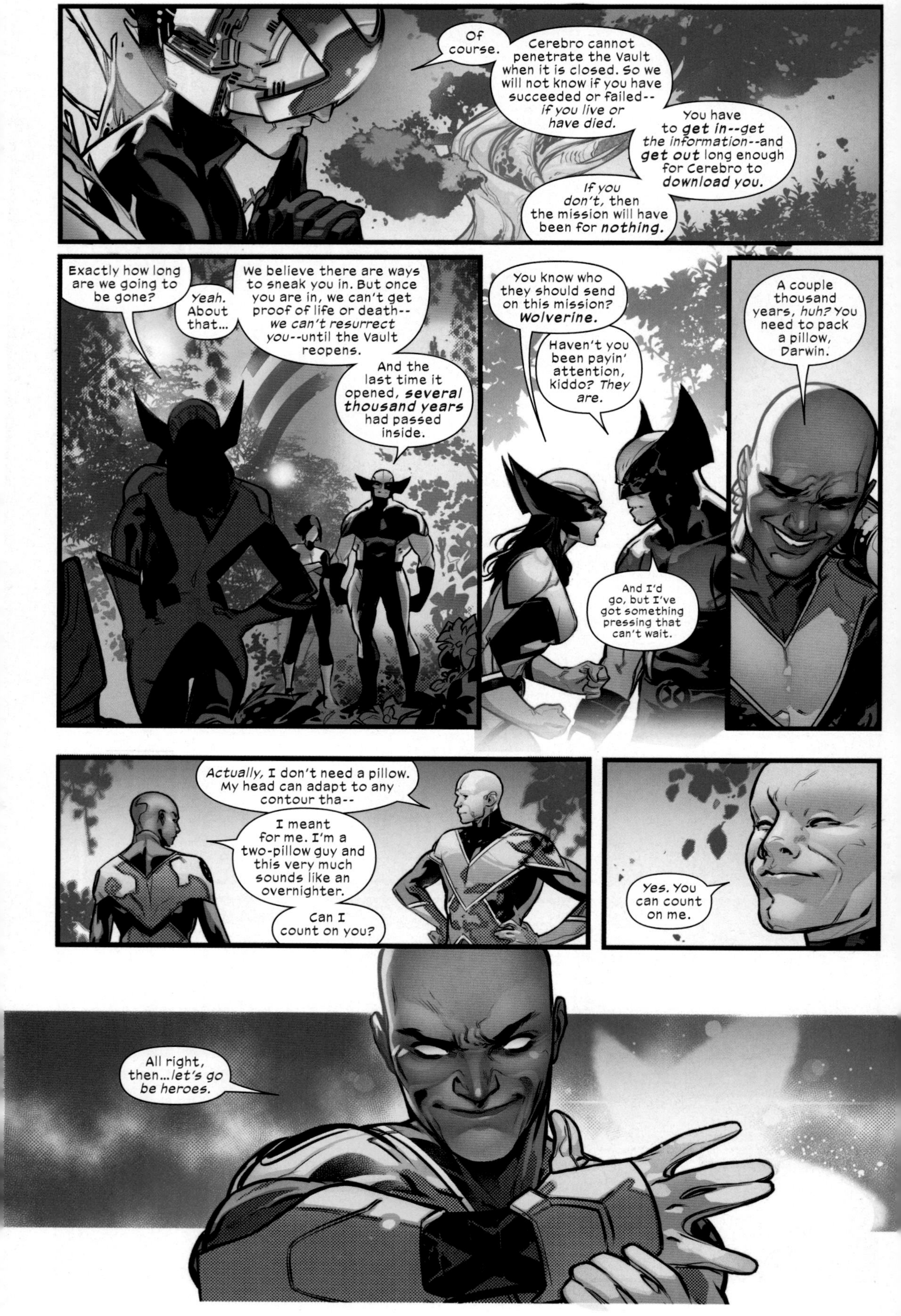
Of course.
Cerebro cannot penetrate the Vault when it is closed. So we will not know if you have succeeded or failed--if you live or have died.
You have to get in--get the information--and get out long enough for Cerebro to download you.
If you don't, then the mission will have been for nothing.
Exactly how long are we going to be gone?
Yeah. About that...
We believe there are ways to sneak you in. But once you are in, we can't get proof of life or death--we can't resurrect you--until the Vault reopens.
And the last time it opened, several thousand years had passed inside.
You know who they should send on this mission? Wolverine.
Haven't you been payin' attention, kiddo? They are.
And I'd go, but I've got something pressing that can't wait.
A couple thousand years, huh? You need to pack a pillow, Darwin.
Actually, I don't need a pillow. My head can adapt to any contour tha--
I meant for me. I'm a two-pillow guy and this very much sounds like an overnighter.
Can I count on you?
Yes. You can count on me.
All right, then...let's go be heroes.

MEDICAL REPORT

PATIENT FILE: #14
RE: Post-resurrection analysis of Synch [Everett Thomas]

PHYSIOLOGY

One week after rebirth, the patient appears to be in good health and excellent physical condition. Testing also indicates there doesn't appear to be a detrimental upper limit to what we are calling "peak physical form." A review of Synch's training sessions from his time at the Massachusetts Academy shows that he is now operating at a four percent increase in natural physical ability. The Five, it seems, are correcting [possibly unconsciously] the minor imperfections of each mutant they resurrect.

[NOTE: Synch was one of the earliest resurrected mutants because it was believed that his powers could enable him to act as a substitute for any of the Five who might need one. And while this proved to be the case, it was unknown at the time that resurrection isn't taxing for the Five but restorative.]

PSYCHOLOGY

Unfortunately, while the patient appears to be physically fine, the same cannot be said for his psychological condition. I would stop short of saying Everett is in denial, but he is clearly putting on a brave face regarding his current situation.

There is no escaping the fact that he looks around and sees a world that has changed in ways that he doesn't fully comprehend. And while this is burdensome enough, to see other mutants who were once fellow students of his having changed and in some ways passed him by has proven to be incredibly difficult for him.

So much so that I cannot currently recommend the further resurrection of similar mutants in Everett's situation unless a less harmful solution presents itself.*

- Dr. Cecilia Reyes

*[NOTE: Because of this experience, the idea of clustering mutants together from similar backgrounds and time periods was tested by resurrecting the mutant Skin [Angelo Espinosa] ahead of [his scheduled] time to serve as a companion for Synch. The success of this served to adapt our early resurrection protocols to better serve mutant society.]

[////..............0]
[////..............0]

____//
FIELD DOWNLOAD:
CLASS: SERAFINA [LEVEL: TWO]

//////
REPORT FOR CHILD POD 5/600 [RECONNAISSANCE]

////////////////////
////////////////////
////////////////////

...........................CHILD: SANGRE.........DECEASED [_]
...........................CHILD: PERRO..........DECEASED [_]
...........................CHILD: SERAFINA.......CAPTURED [/]
...........................CHILD: AGUJA..........DECEASED [_]
...........................CHILD: FUEGO..........DECEASED [_]

[______]...............[___]
[______]...............[___]

//////
//////

PRIMARY ANALYSIS:
Mission failure.

SECONDARY ANALYSIS:
Increased threat activity level of non-augmented, naturally occurring human population
[Non-posthuman resistance expected. Threat level: secondary.]

////////////////////
////////////////////

Increased threat activity level of *Homo superior*
[Mutant resistance expected. Threat level: primary.]

CONCLUSION:
Vault opening delayed. Child level: Three necessary for successful occupation/subjugation of external environment [World].

//////
//////
//////
//////

//////
//////

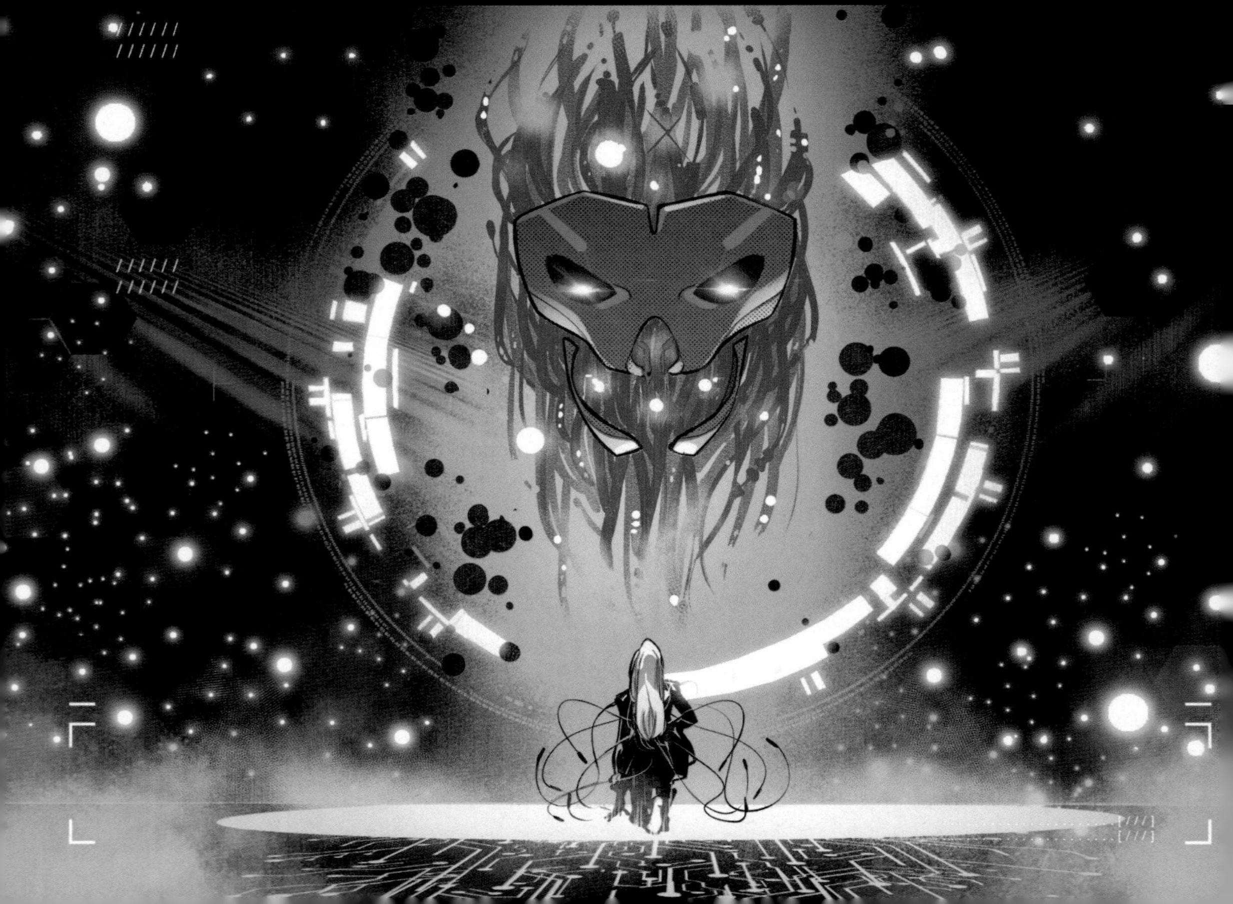

.......RESTORE CHILD: CLASS: SANGRE...............LEVEL: ONE [RESTORE]
.......RESTORE CHILD: CLASS: PERRO................LEVEL: ONE [RESTORE]
.......UPGRADE CHILD: CLASS: SERAFINA.............LEVEL: TWO [UPGRADE]
.......RESTORE CHILD: CLASS: AGUJA................LEVEL: ONE [RESTORE]
.......RESTORE CHILD: CLASS: FUEGO................LEVEL: ONE [RESTORE]

////////////////////
////////////////////

//////
POD 6/600 [KNIFE].............................LEVEL: TWO [UPGRADE]
POD 7/600 [FLIGHT]............................LEVEL: TWO [UPGRADE]
POD 8/600 [COMMUNICATION].....................LEVEL: TWO [UPGRADE]
POD 9/600 [TEACHER]...........................LEVEL: TWO [UPGRADE]
POD 10/600 [SOLDIER]...........................LEVEL: ONE [UPGRADE]
POD 11/600 [SOLDIER]...........................LEVEL: TWO [UPGRADE]
POD 12/600 [SOLDIER]...........................LEVEL: TWO [UPGRADE]
POD 13/600 [SOLDIER]...........................LEVEL: ONE [UPGRADE]
POD 14/600 [SOLDIER]...........................LEVEL: ONE [UPGRADE]
POD 15/600 [ENVOY]..........

//////

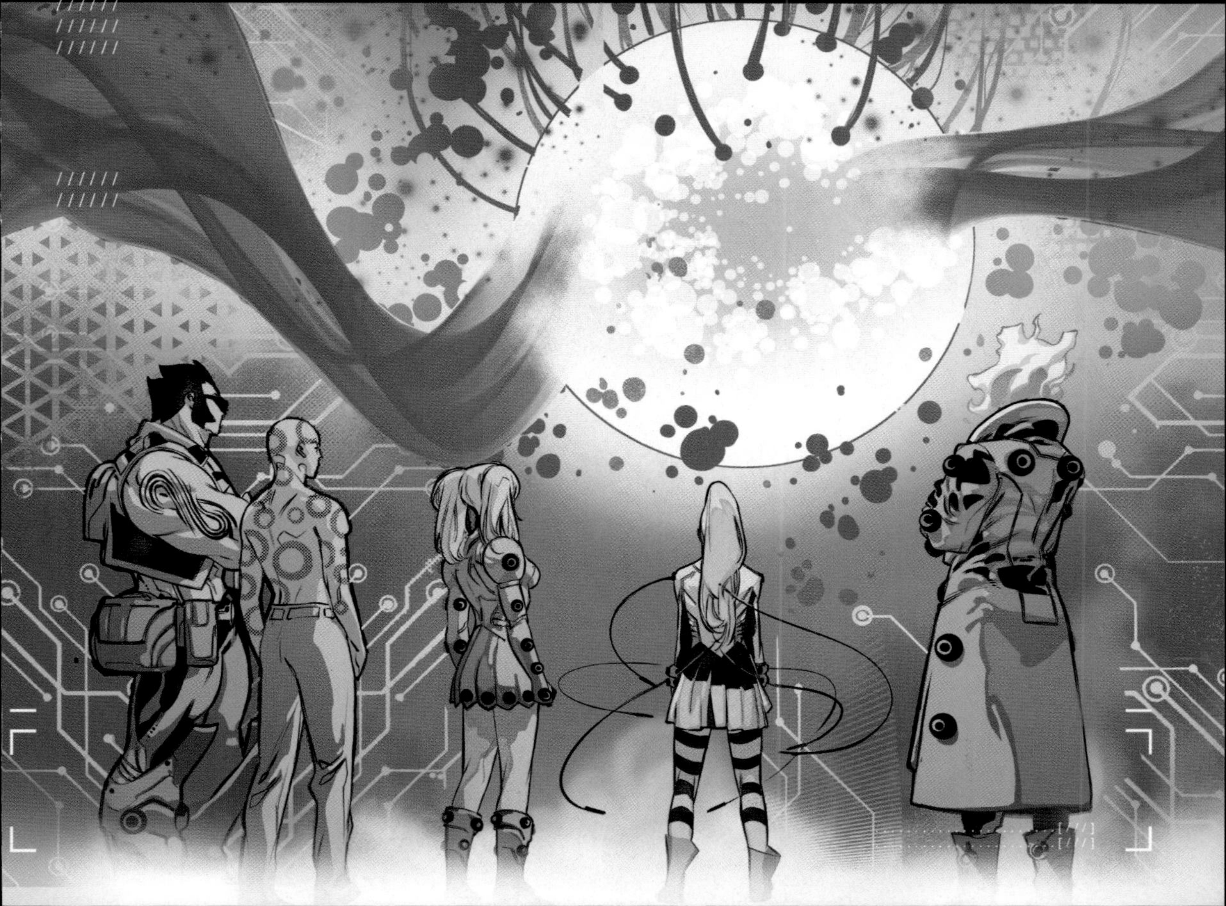
//////
//////
//////
//////
//////

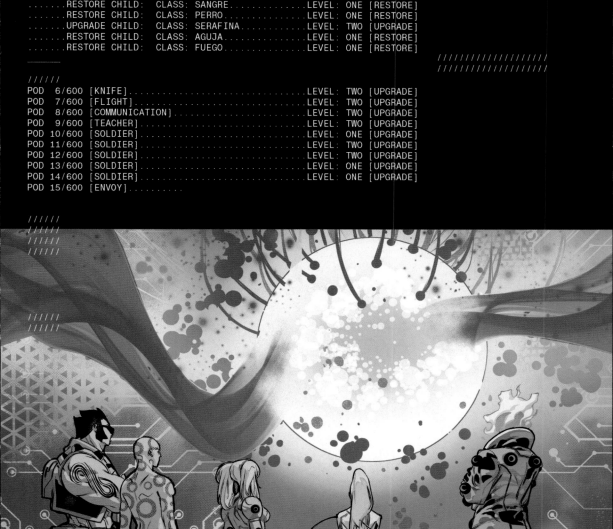

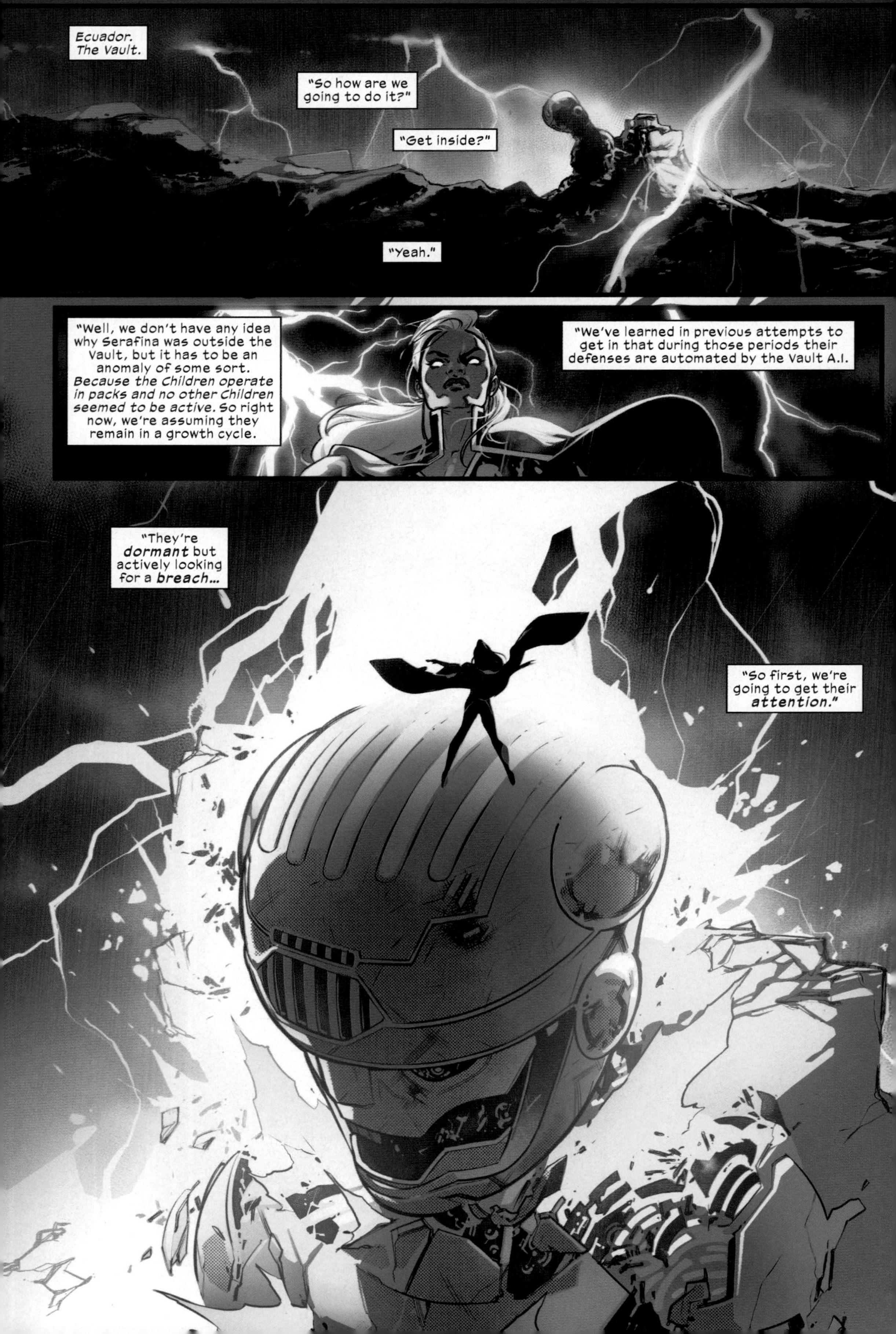
Ecuador.
The Vault.
"So how are we going to do it?"
"Get inside?"
"Yeah."
"Well, we don't have any idea why Serafina was outside the Vault, but it has to be an anomaly of some sort. Because the Children operate in packs and no other Children seemed to be active. So right now, we're assuming they remain in a growth cycle.
"We've learned in previous attempts to get in that during those periods their defenses are automated by the Vault A.I.
"They're dormant but actively looking for a breach...
"So first, we're going to get their attention."

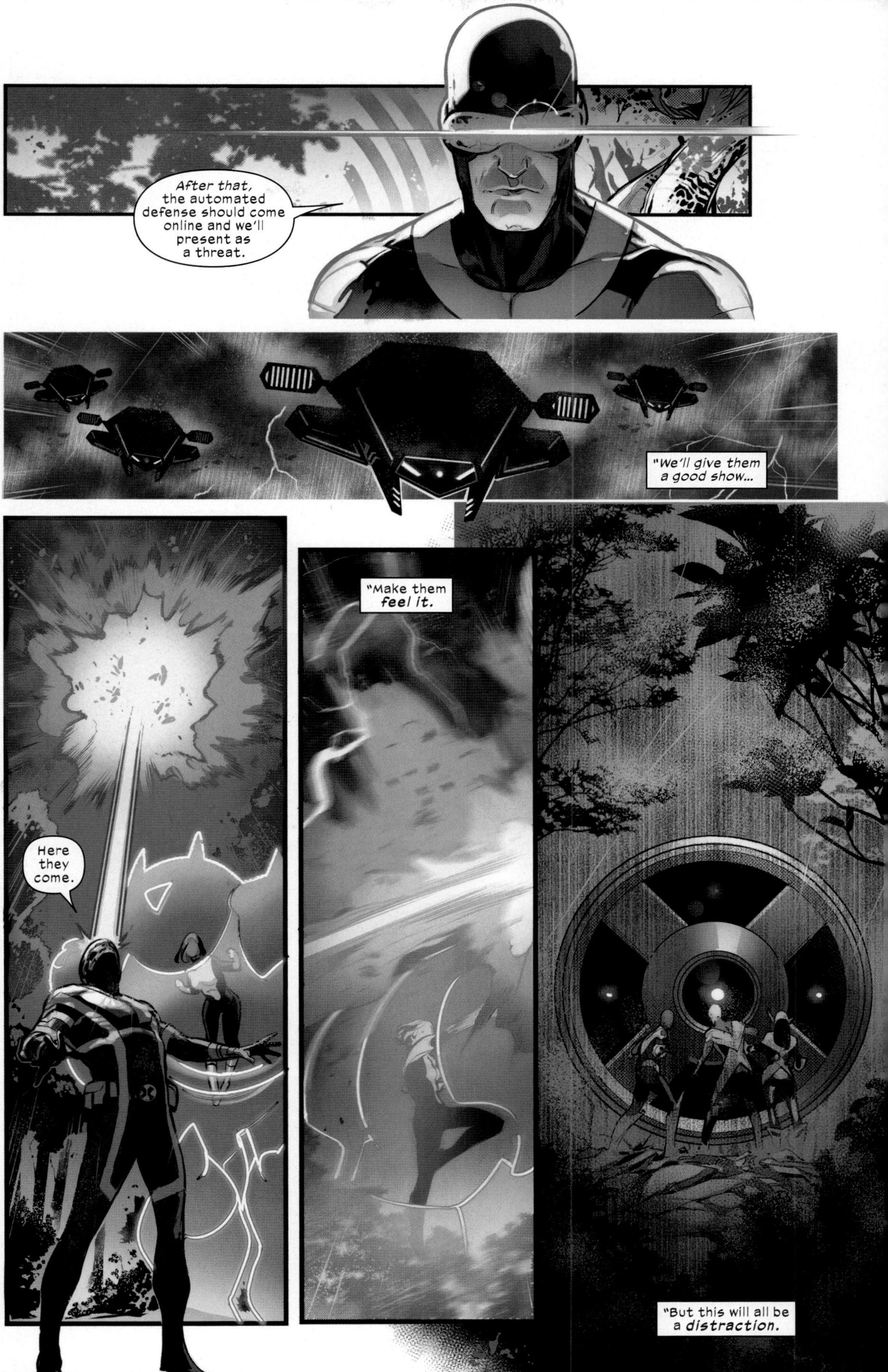
After that, the automated defense should come online and we'll present as a threat.
"We'll give them a good show...
Here they come.
"Make them feel it.
"But this will all be a distraction.

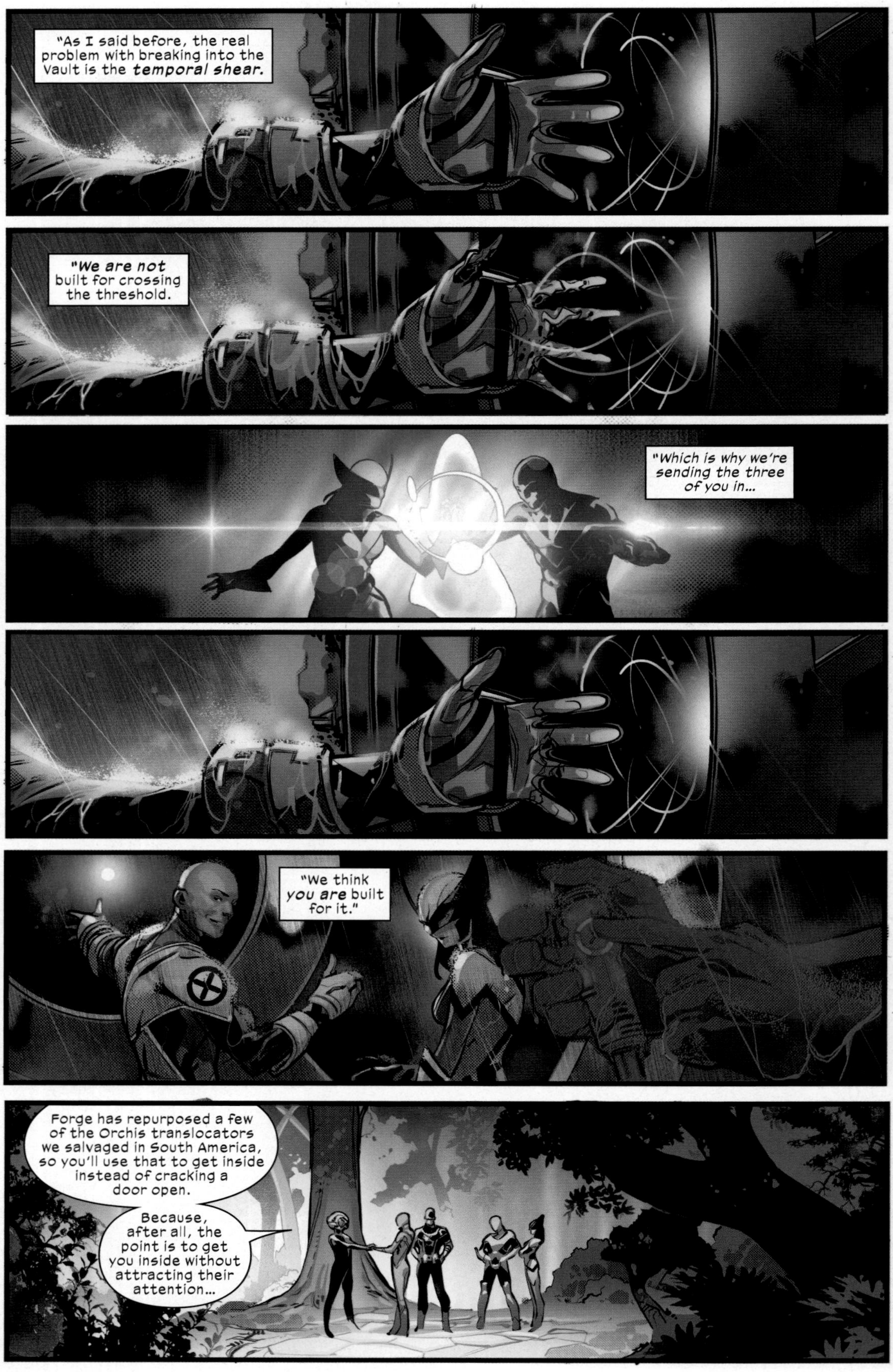
"As I said before, the real problem with breaking into the Vault is the *temporal shear.*
"*We are not* built for crossing the threshold.
"*Which is why we're sending the three of you in...*
"We think *you are* built for it."
Forge has repurposed a few of the Orchis translocators we salvaged in South America, so you'll use that to get inside instead of cracking a door open.
Because, after all, the point is to get you inside without attracting their attention...

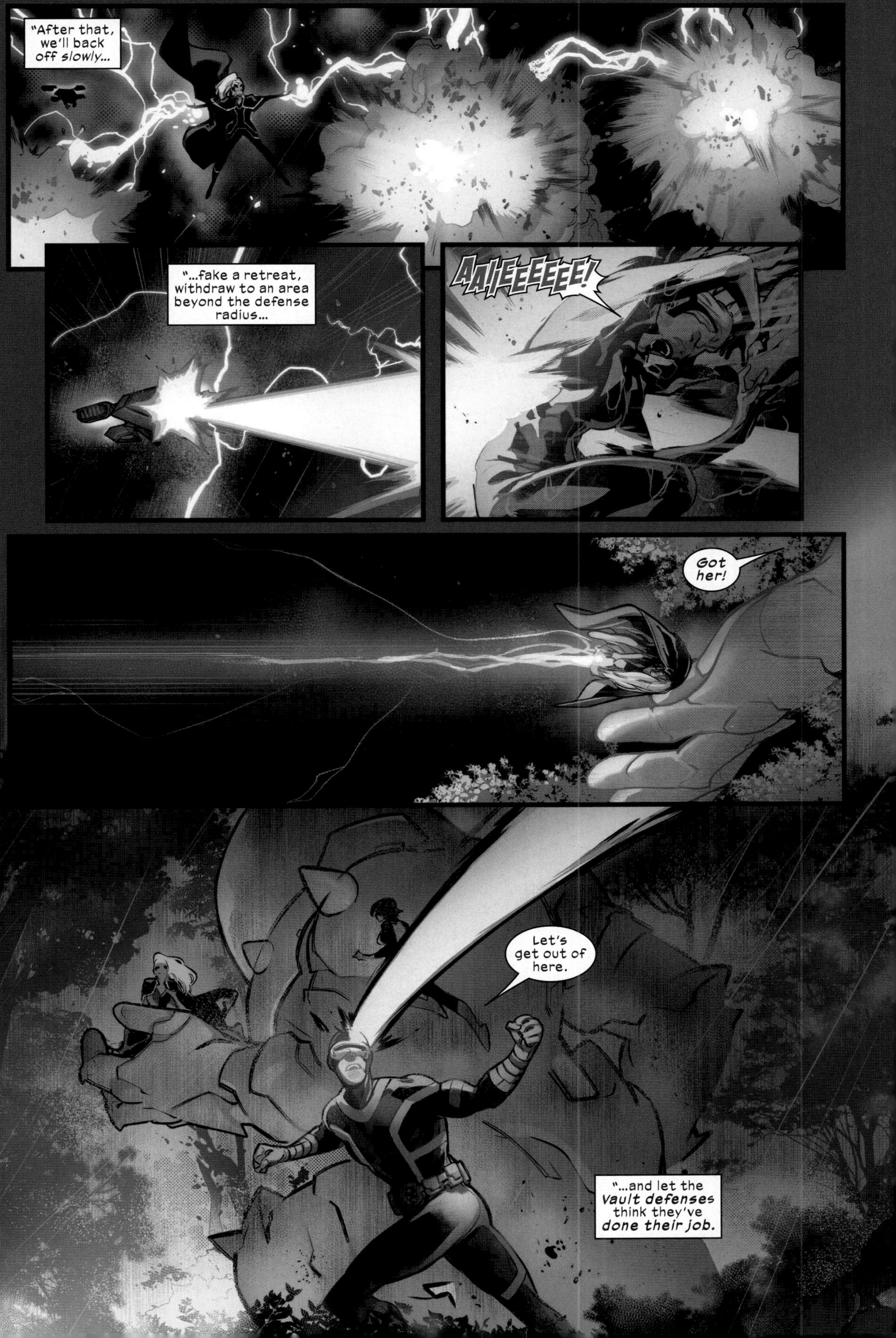
"After that, we'll back off *slowly*...
"...fake a retreat, withdraw to an area beyond the defense radius...
AAIIEEEEEE!
Got her!
Let's get out of here.
"...and let the *Vault defenses* think they've *done their job.*

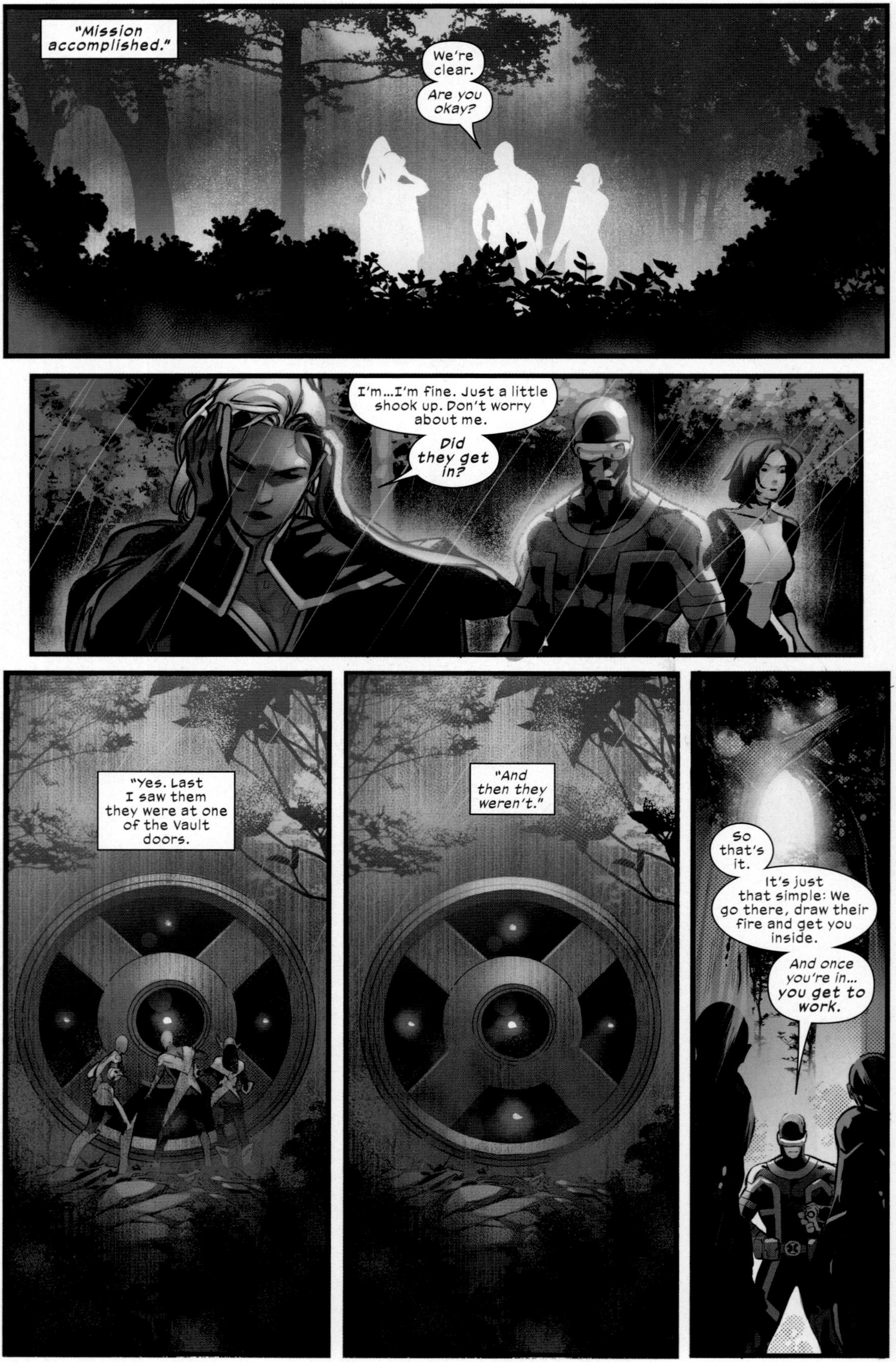
"Mission accomplished."
We're clear.
Are you okay?
I'm...I'm fine. Just a little shook up. Don't worry about me.
Did they get in?
"Yes. Last I saw them they were at one of the Vault doors.
"And then they weren't."
So that's it.
It's just that simple: We go there, draw their fire and get you inside.
And once you're in... you get to work.

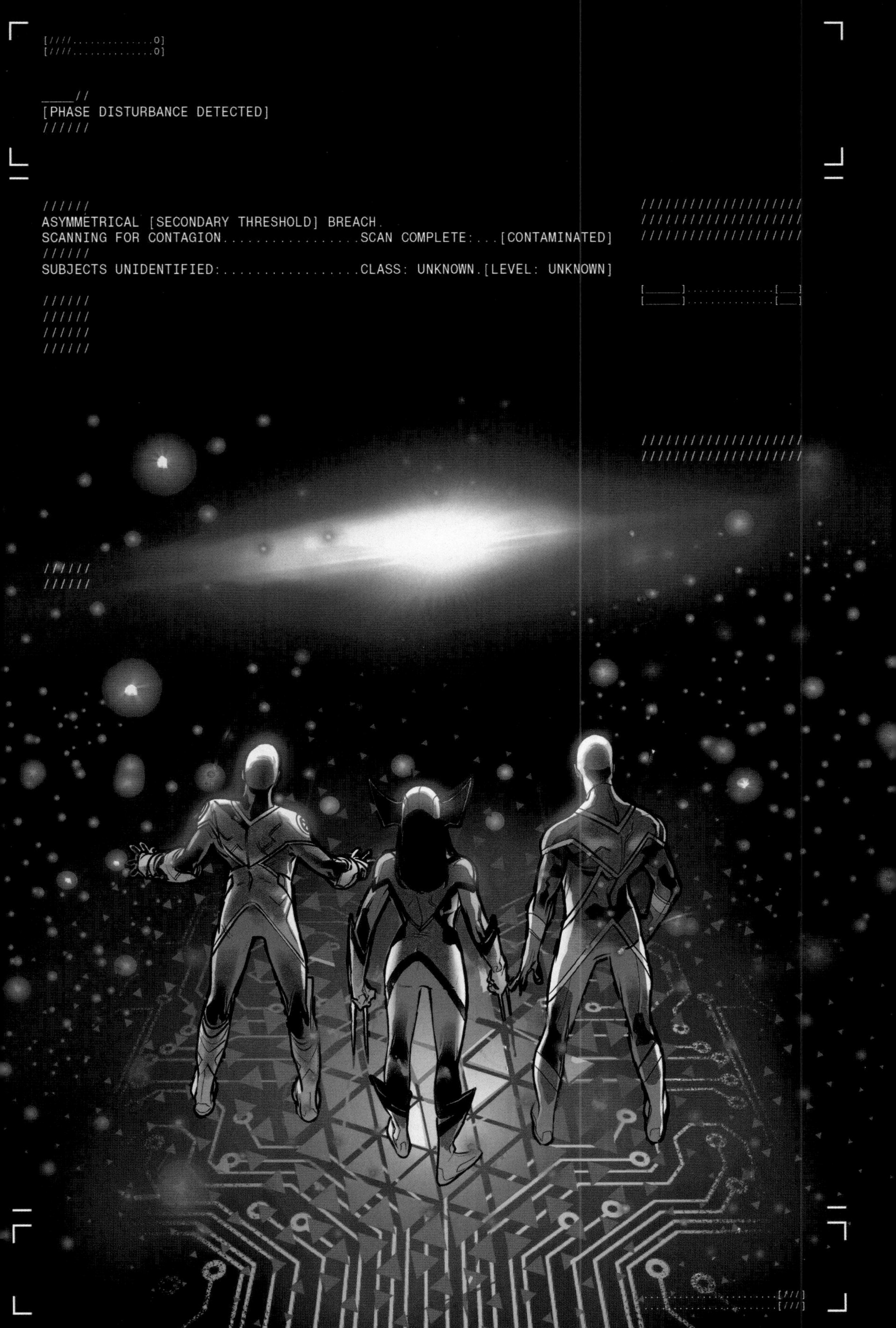
[PHASE DISTURBANCE DETECTED]
ASYMMETRICAL [SECONDARY THRESHOLD] BREACH.
SCANNING FOR CONTAGION..................SCAN COMPLETE:...[CONTAMINATED]
SUBJECTS UNIDENTIFIED:..................CLASS: UNKNOWN.[LEVEL: UNKNOWN]

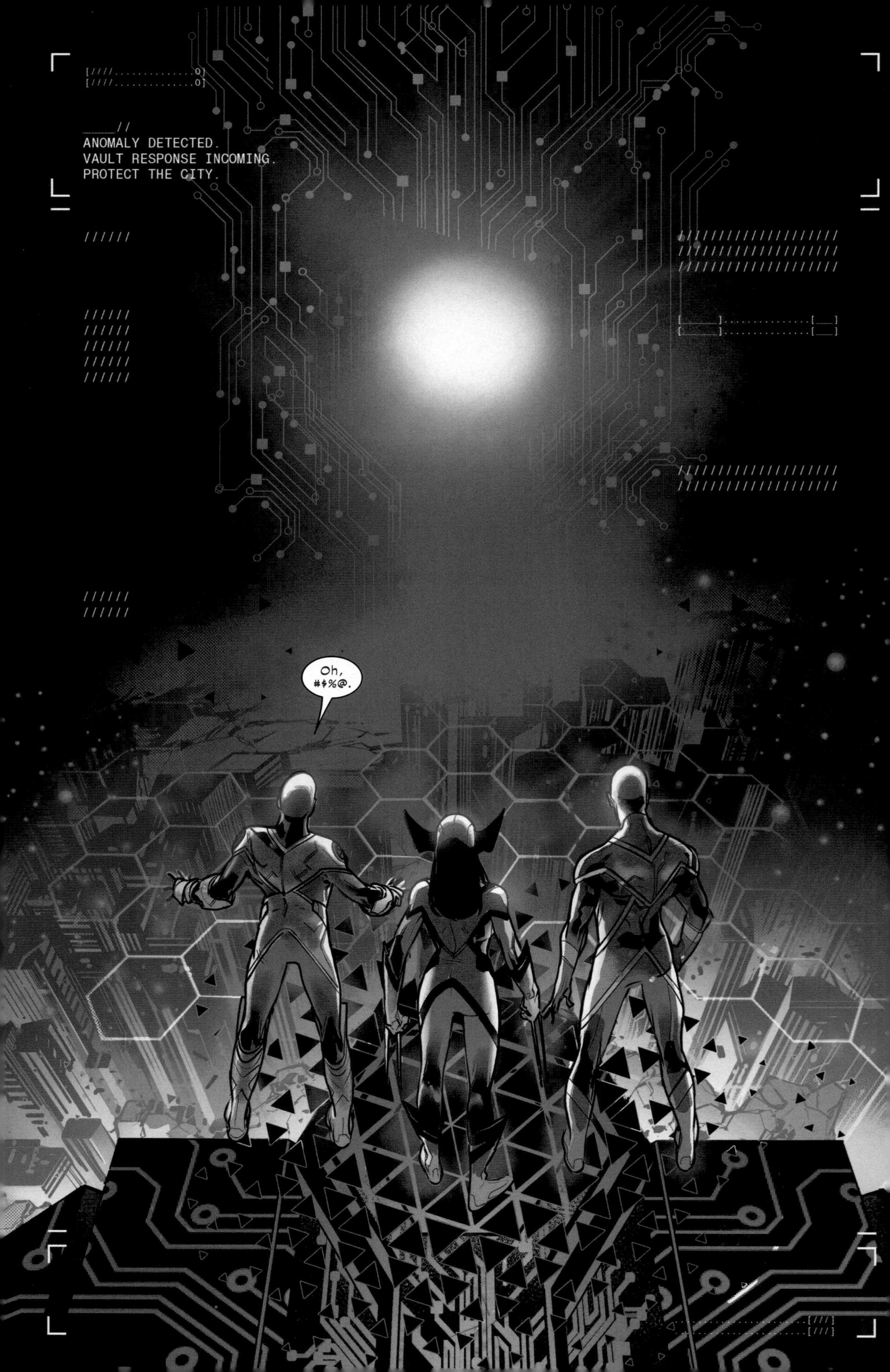

[////..............0]
[////..............0]
_____//
ANOMALY DETECTED.
VAULT RESPONSE INCOMING.
PROTECT THE CITY.
Oh, #$%@.

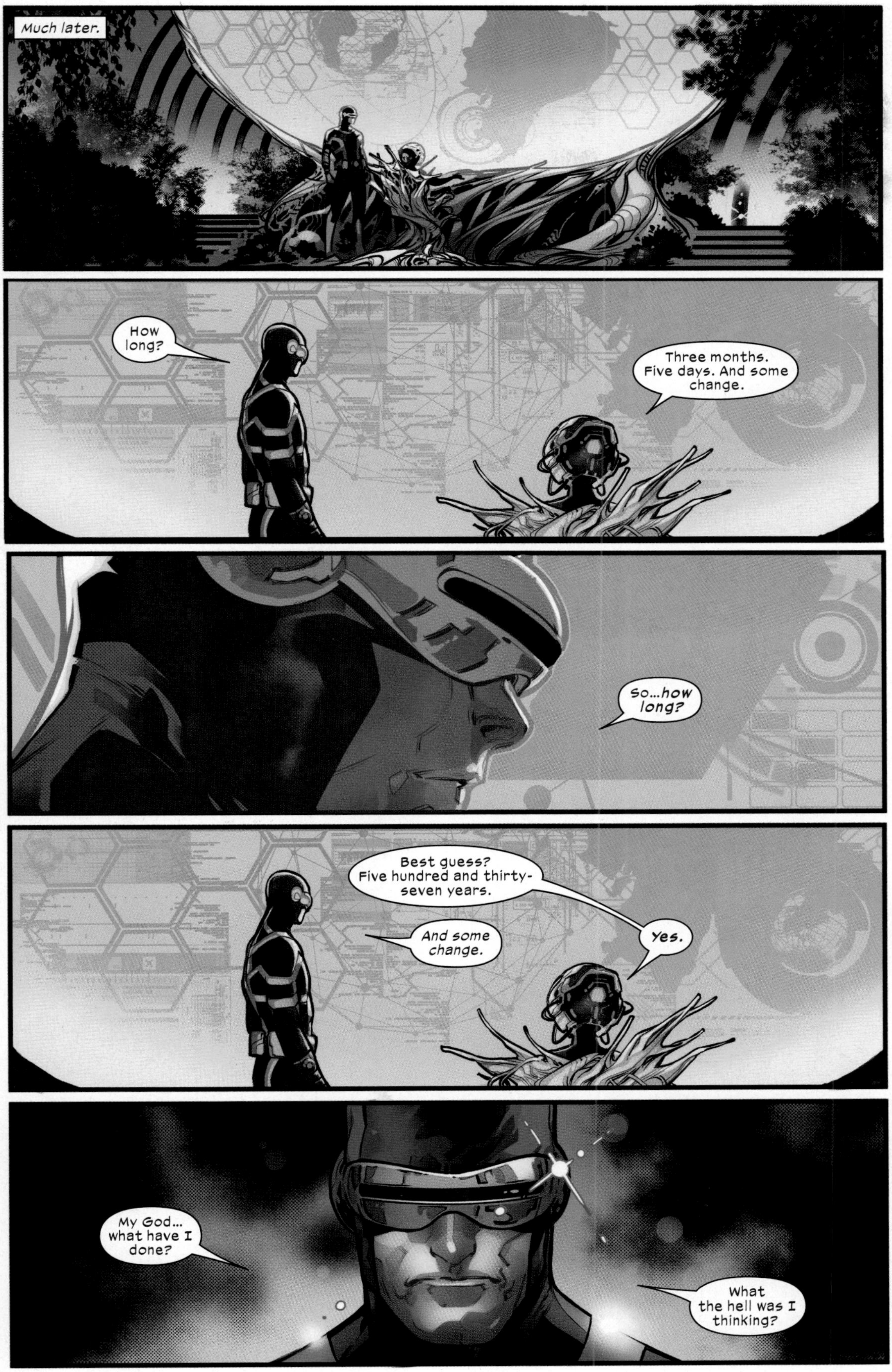
Much later.
How long?
Three months. Five days. And some change.
So...how long?
Best guess? Five hundred and thirty-seven years.
And some change.
Yes.
My God... what have I done?
What the hell was I thinking?

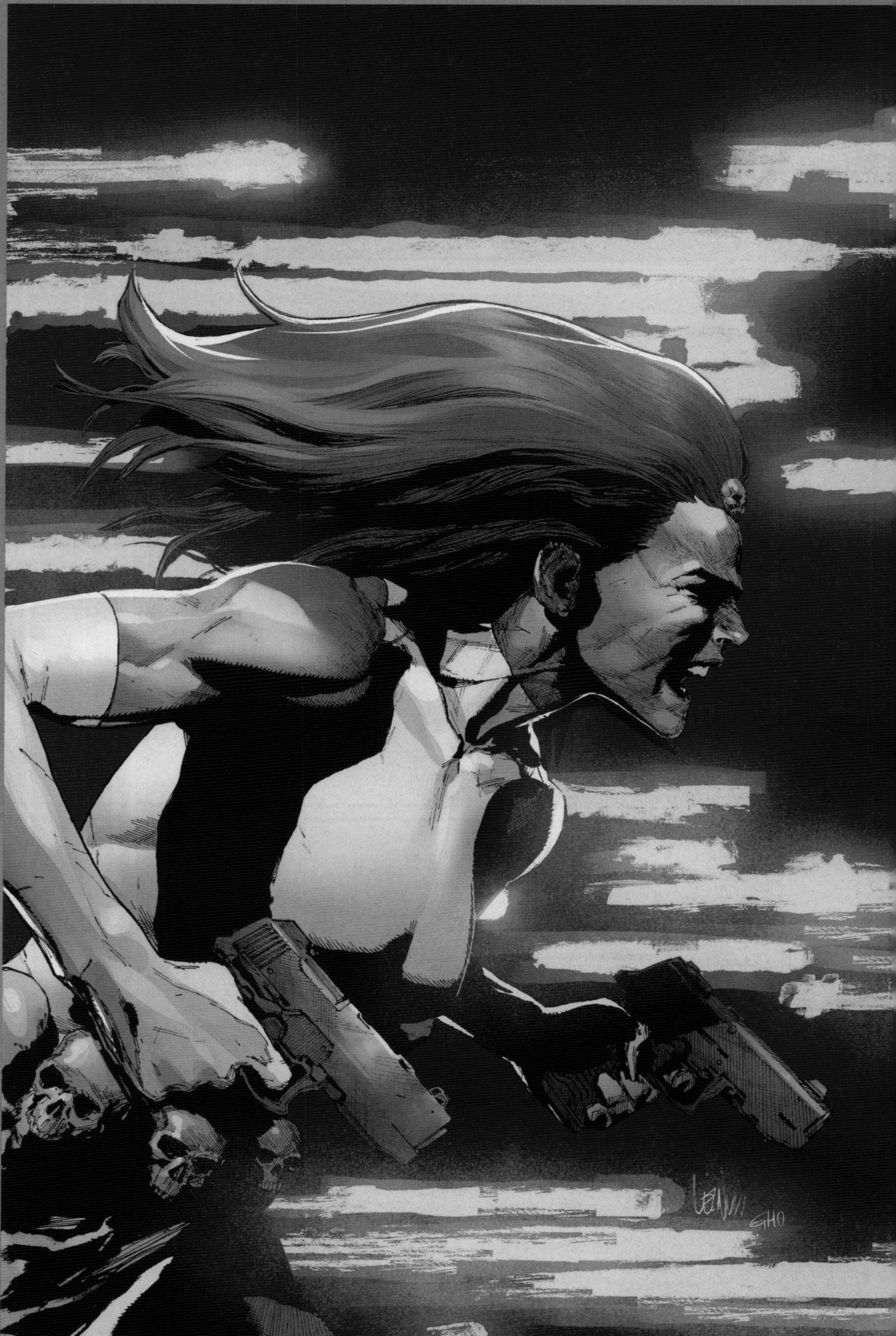

The Oracle

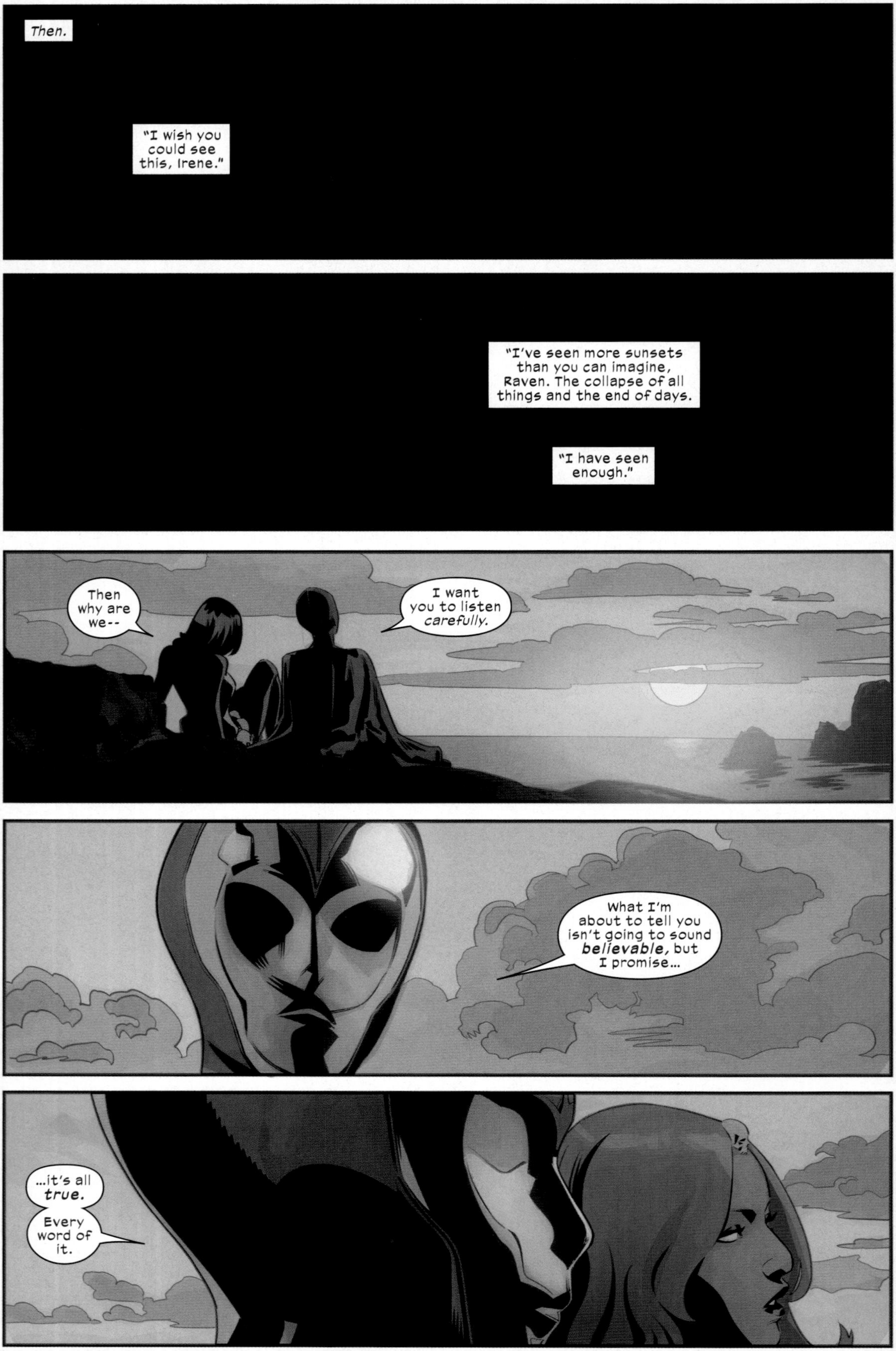
Then.
"I wish you could see this, Irene."
"I've seen more sunsets than you can imagine, Raven. The collapse of all things and the end of days.
"I have seen enough."
Then why are we--
I want you to listen carefully.
What I'm about to tell you isn't going to sound believable, but I promise...
...it's all true.
Every word of it.

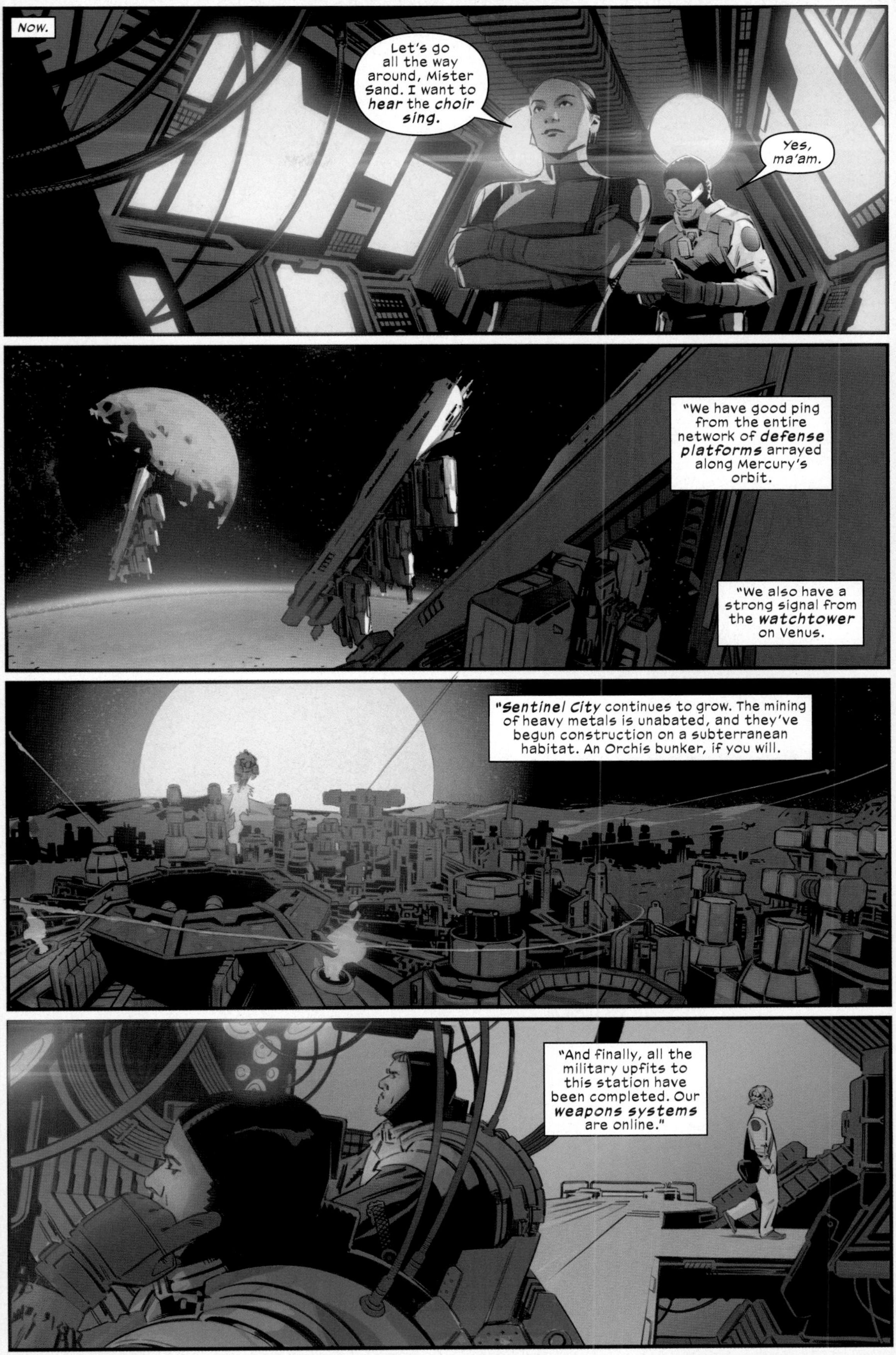
Now.
Let's go all the way around, Mister Sand. I want to hear the choir sing.
Yes, ma'am.
"We have good ping from the entire network of defense platforms arrayed along Mercury's orbit.
"We also have a strong signal from the watchtower on Venus.
"Sentinel City continues to grow. The mining of heavy metals is unabated, and they've begun construction on a subterranean habitat. An Orchis bunker, if you will.
"And finally, all the military upfits to this station have been completed. Our weapons systems are online."

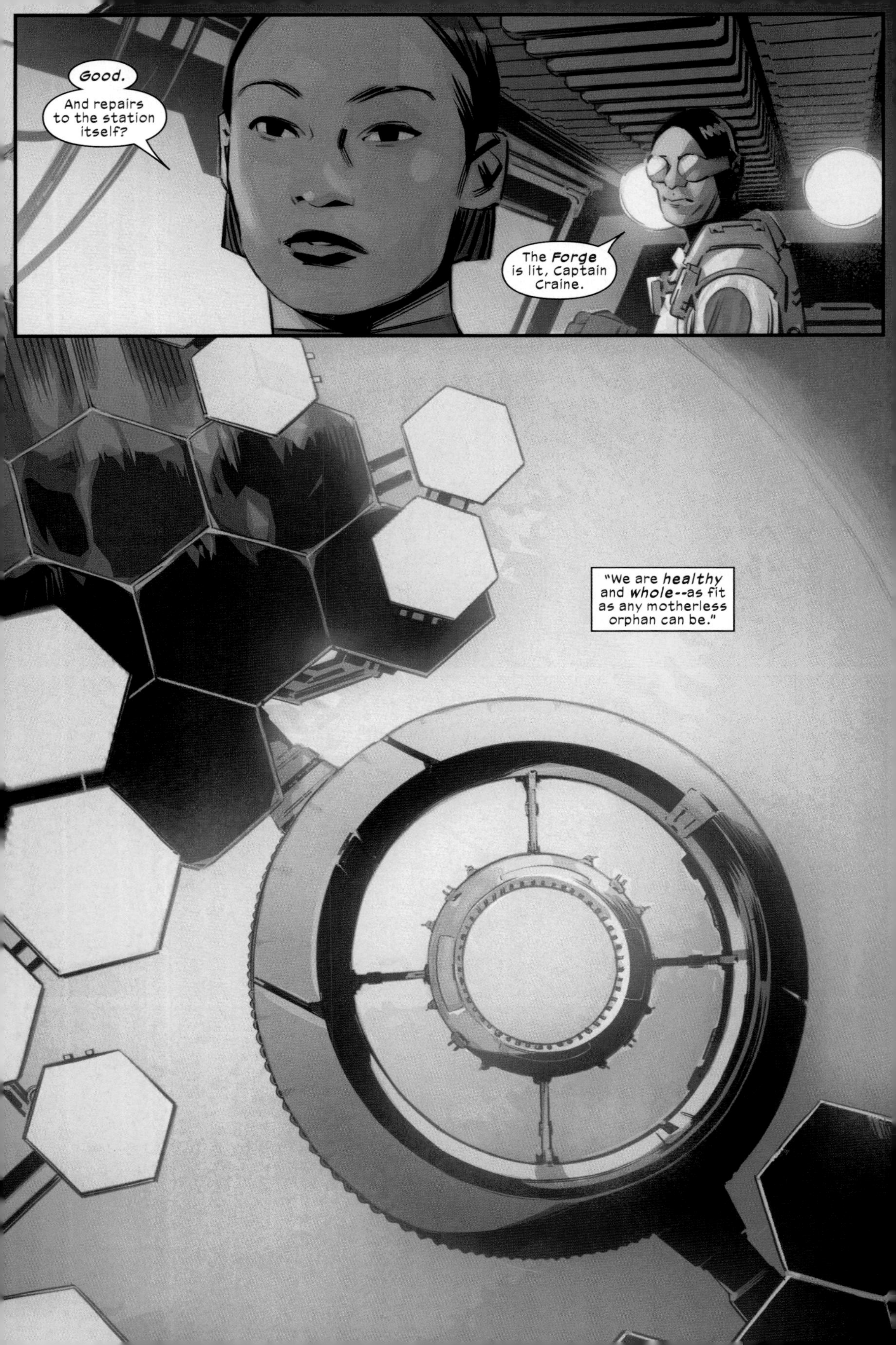
Good.
And repairs to the station itself?
The *Forge* is lit, Captain Craine.
"We are *healthy* and *whole*--as fit as any motherless orphan can be."

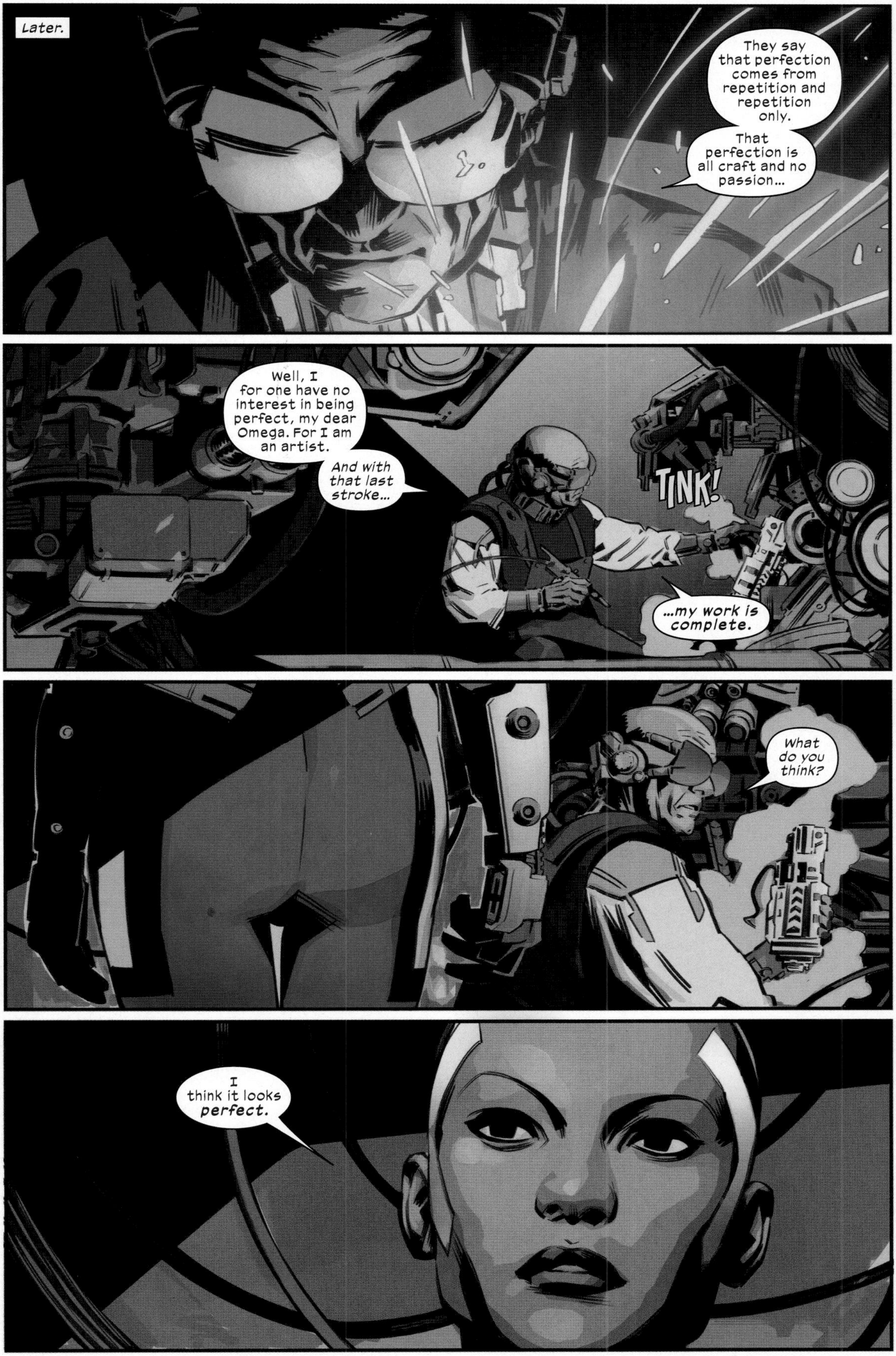

Later.
They say that perfection comes from repetition and repetition only.
That perfection is all craft and no passion...
Well, I for one have no interest in being perfect, my dear Omega. For I am an artist.
And with that last stroke...
TINK!
...my work is complete.
What do you think?
I think it looks perfect.

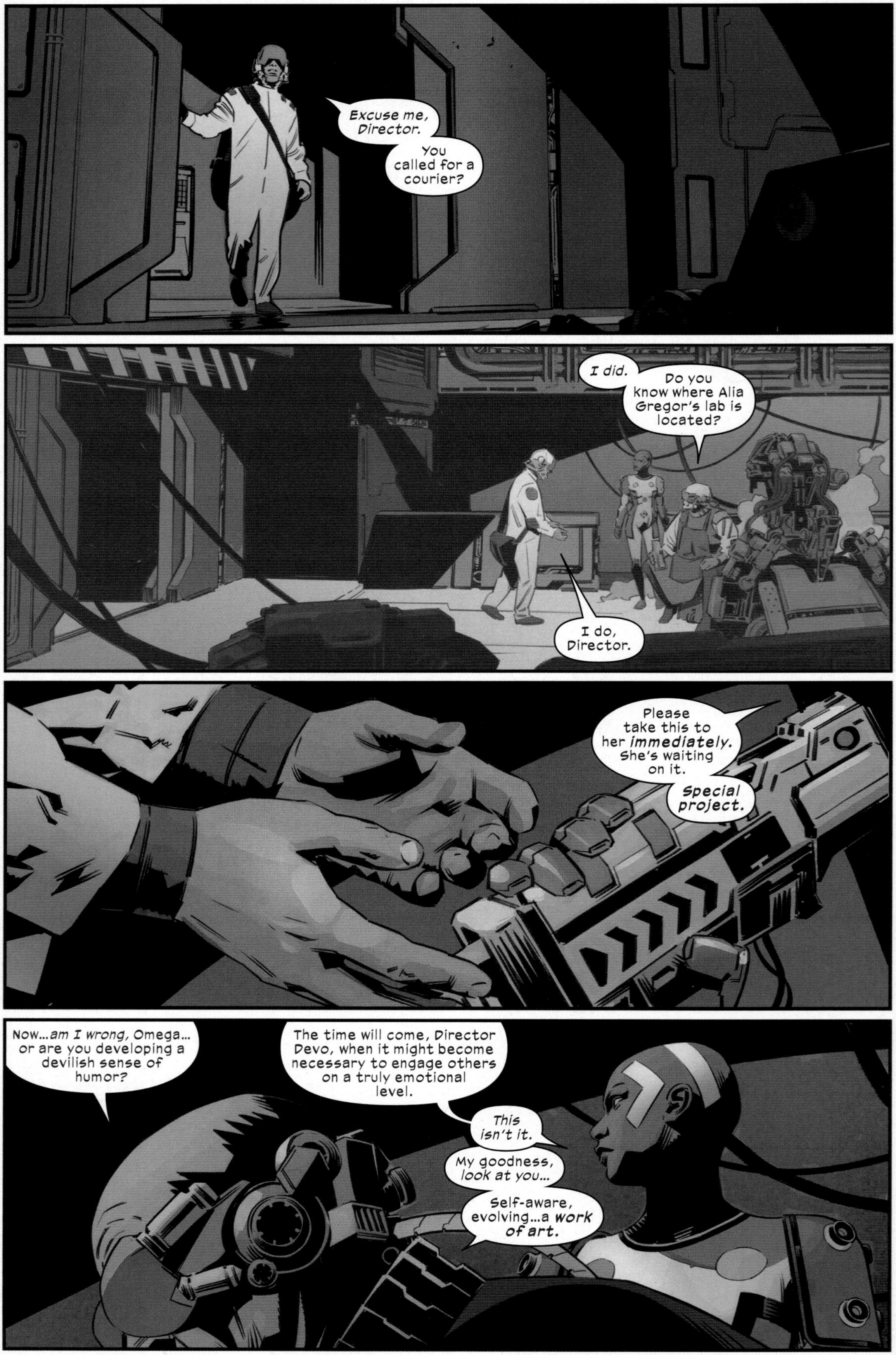
Excuse me, Director.
You called for a courier?
I did.
Do you know where Alia Gregor's lab is located?
I do, Director.
Please take this to her *immediately*. She's waiting on it.
Special project.
Now...*am I wrong,* Omega... or are you developing a devilish sense of humor?
The time will come, Director Devo, when it might become necessary to engage others on a truly emotional level.
This isn't it.
My goodness, look at you...
Self-aware, evolving...a *work of art.*

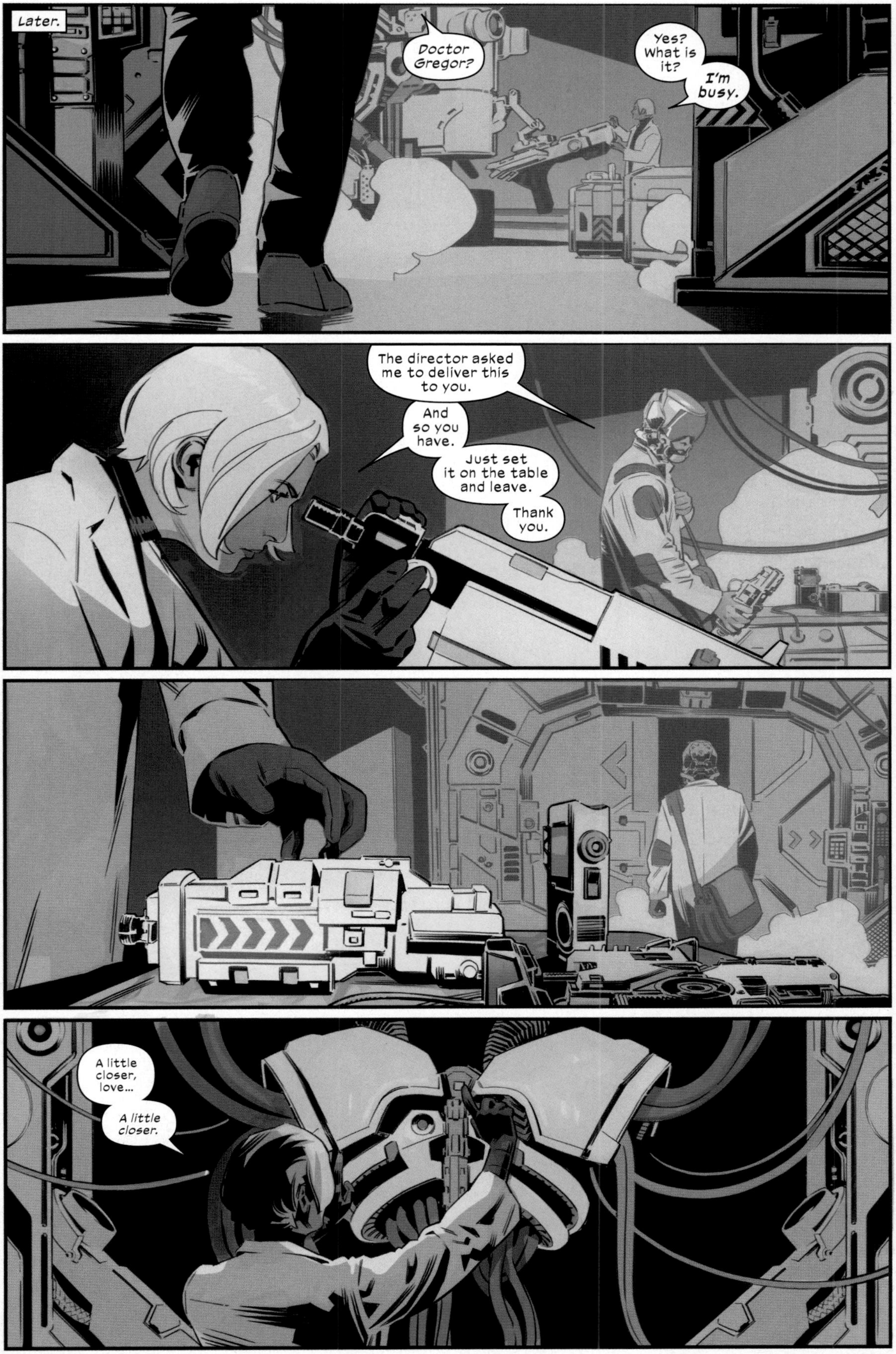
Later.
Doctor Gregor?
Yes? What is it?
I'm busy.
The director asked me to deliver this to you.
And so you have.
Just set it on the table and leave.
Thank you.
A little closer, love...
A little closer.

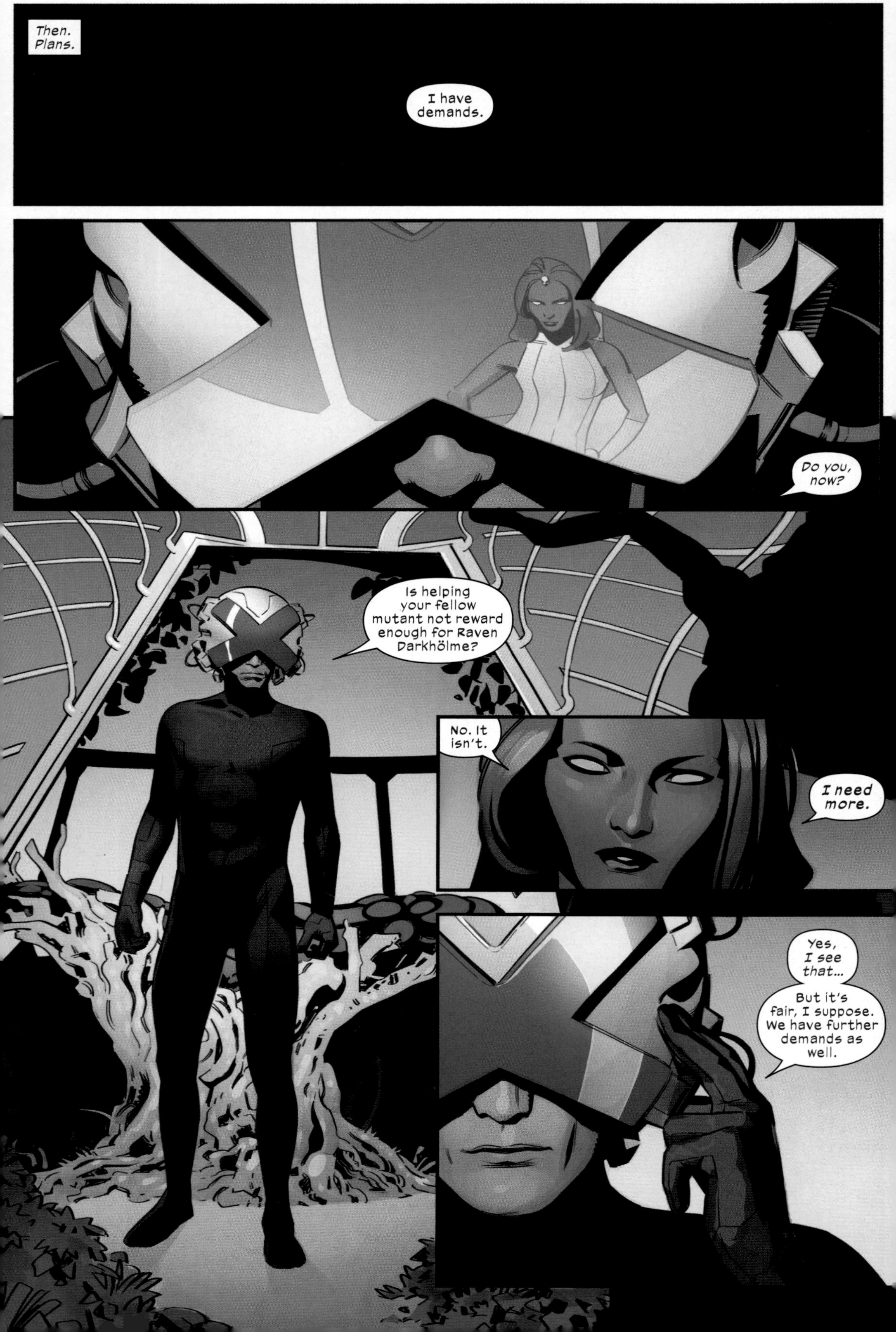

Then. Plans.
I have demands.
Do you, now?
Is helping your fellow mutant not reward enough for Raven Darkhölme?
No. It isn't.
I need more.
Yes, I see that...
But it's fair, I suppose. We have further demands as well.

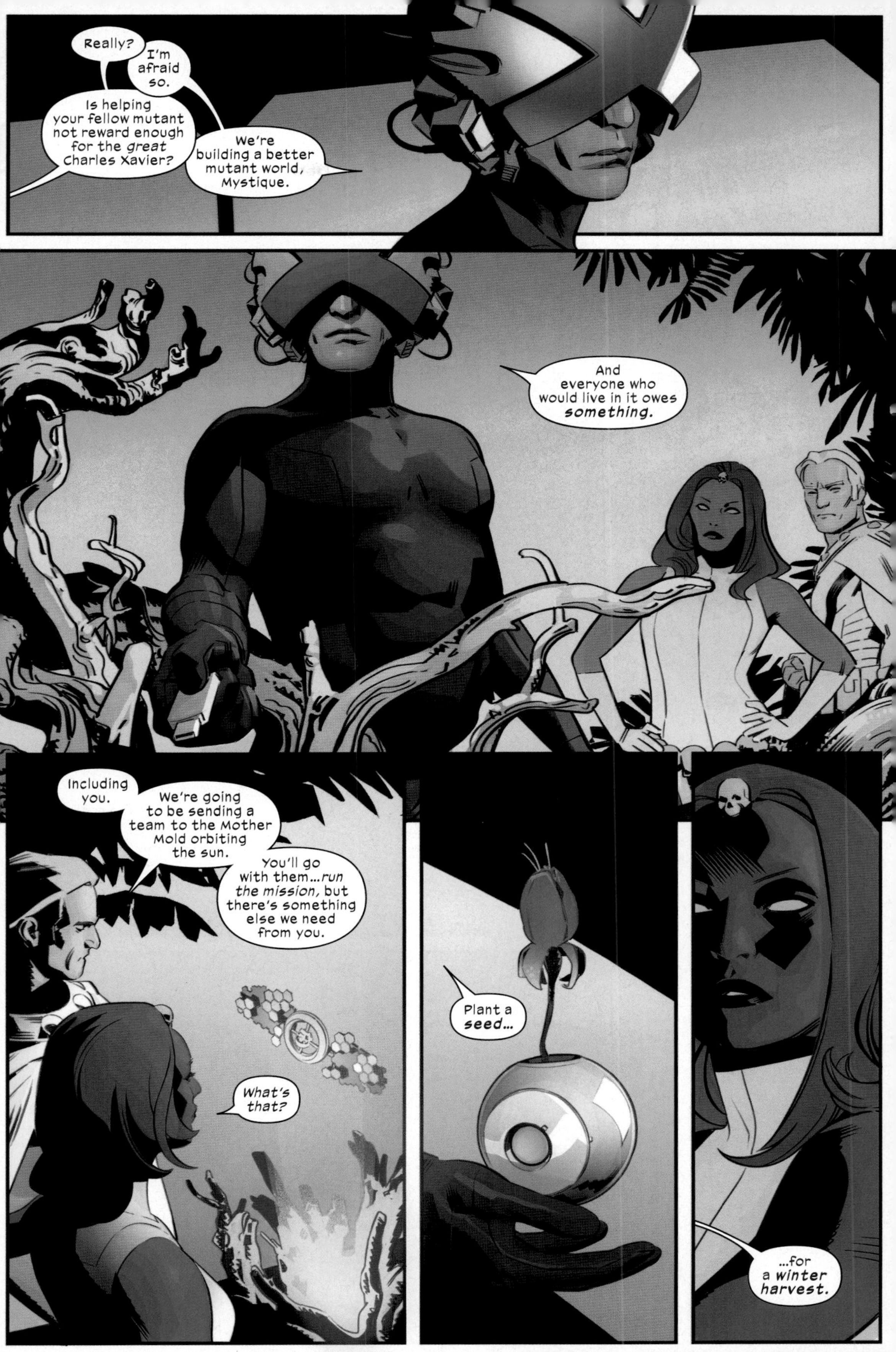

Really?
I'm afraid so.
Is helping your fellow mutant not reward enough for the *great* Charles Xavier?
We're building a better mutant world, Mystique.
And everyone who would live in it owes *something.*
Including you.
We're going to be sending a team to the Mother Mold orbiting the sun.
You'll go with them... *run the mission,* but there's something else we need from you.
What's that?
Plant a *seed...*
...for a *winter harvest.*

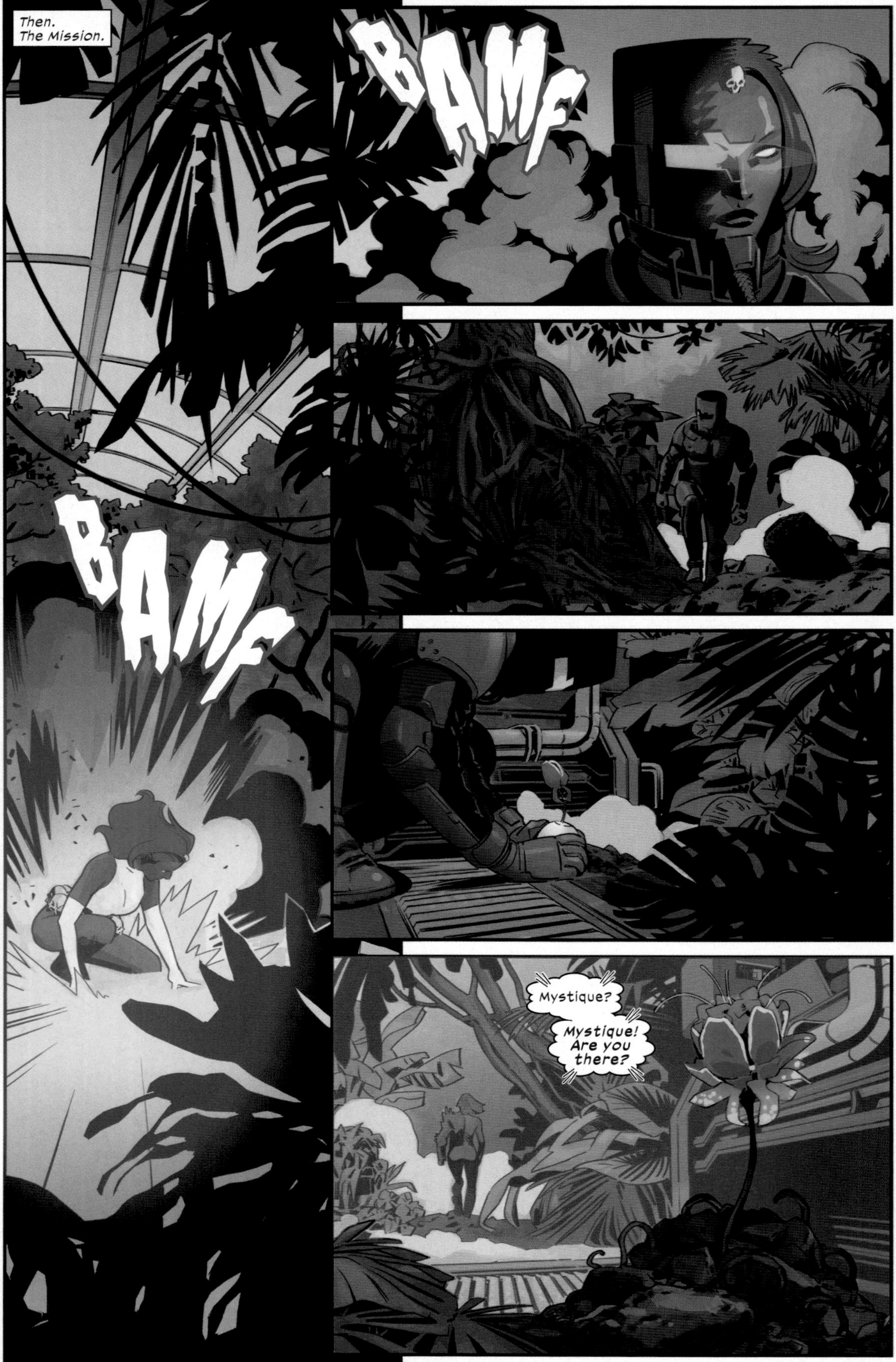

Then.
The Mission.
BAMF
BAMF
Mystique?
Mystique! Are you there?

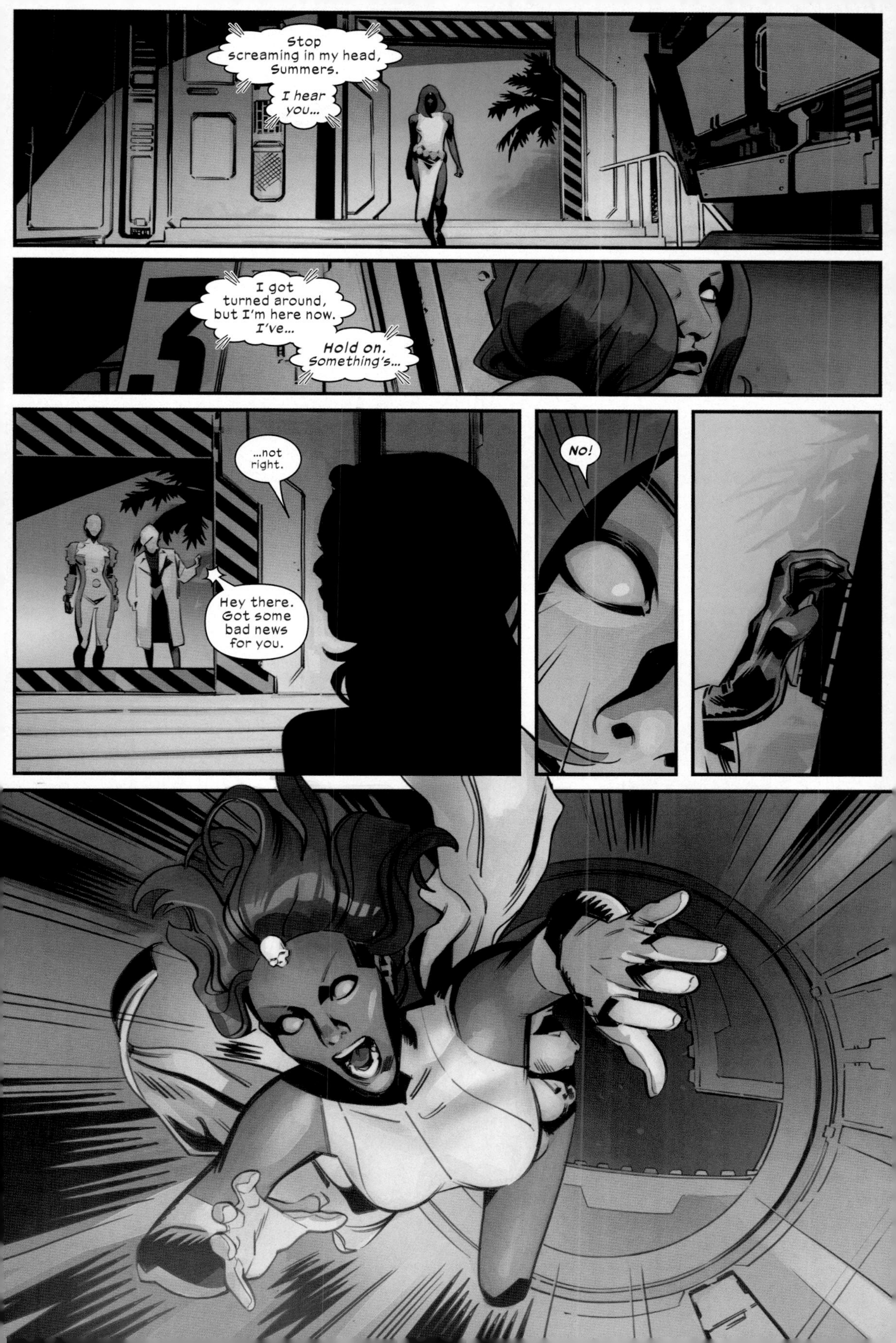
Stop screaming in my head, Summers.
I hear you...
I got turned around, but I'm here now. I've...
Hold on. Something's...
...not right.
Hey there. Got some bad news for you.
NO!

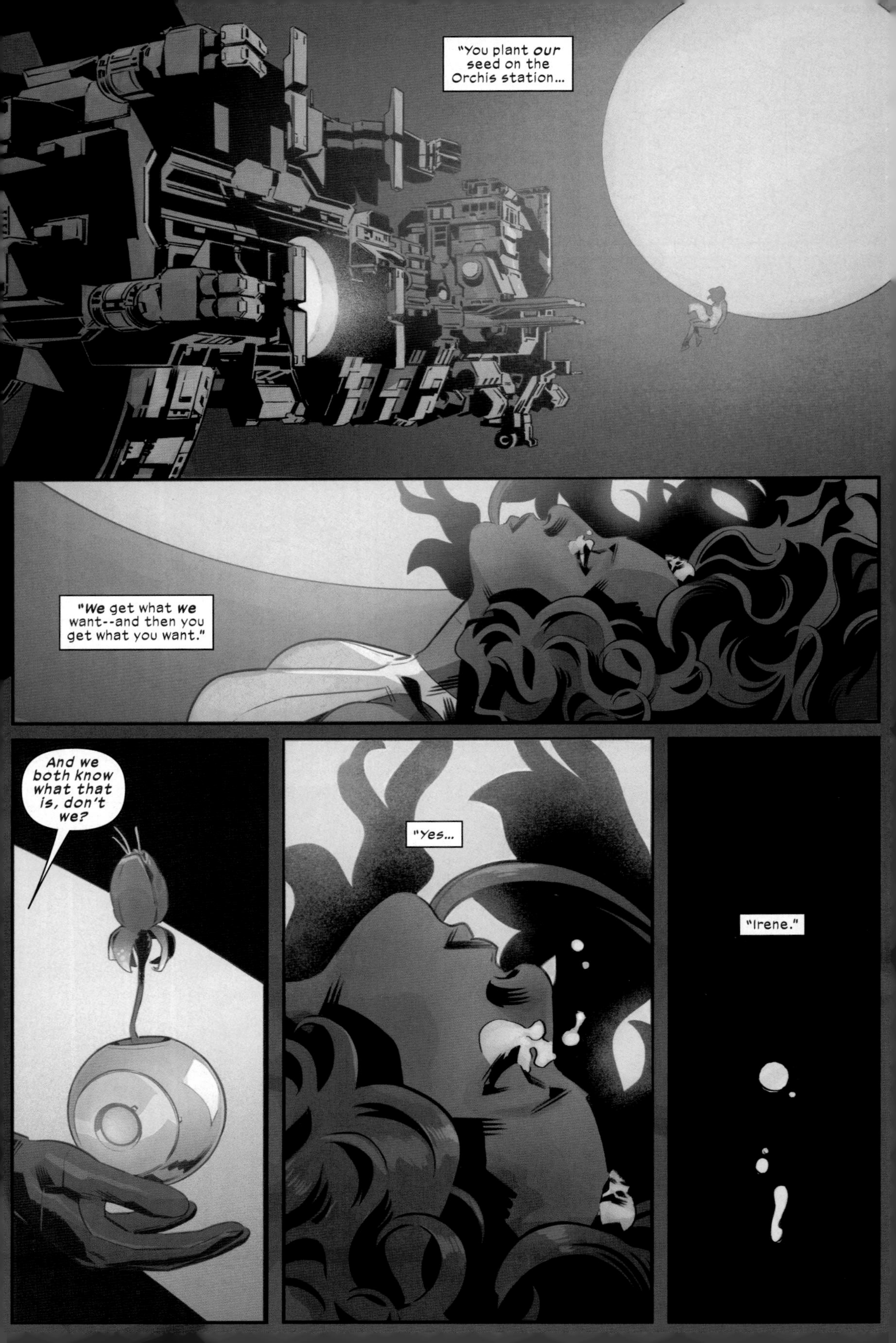
"You plant *our* seed on the Orchis station...
"*We* get what *we* want--and then you get what you want."
And we both know what that is, don't we?
"Yes...
"Irene."

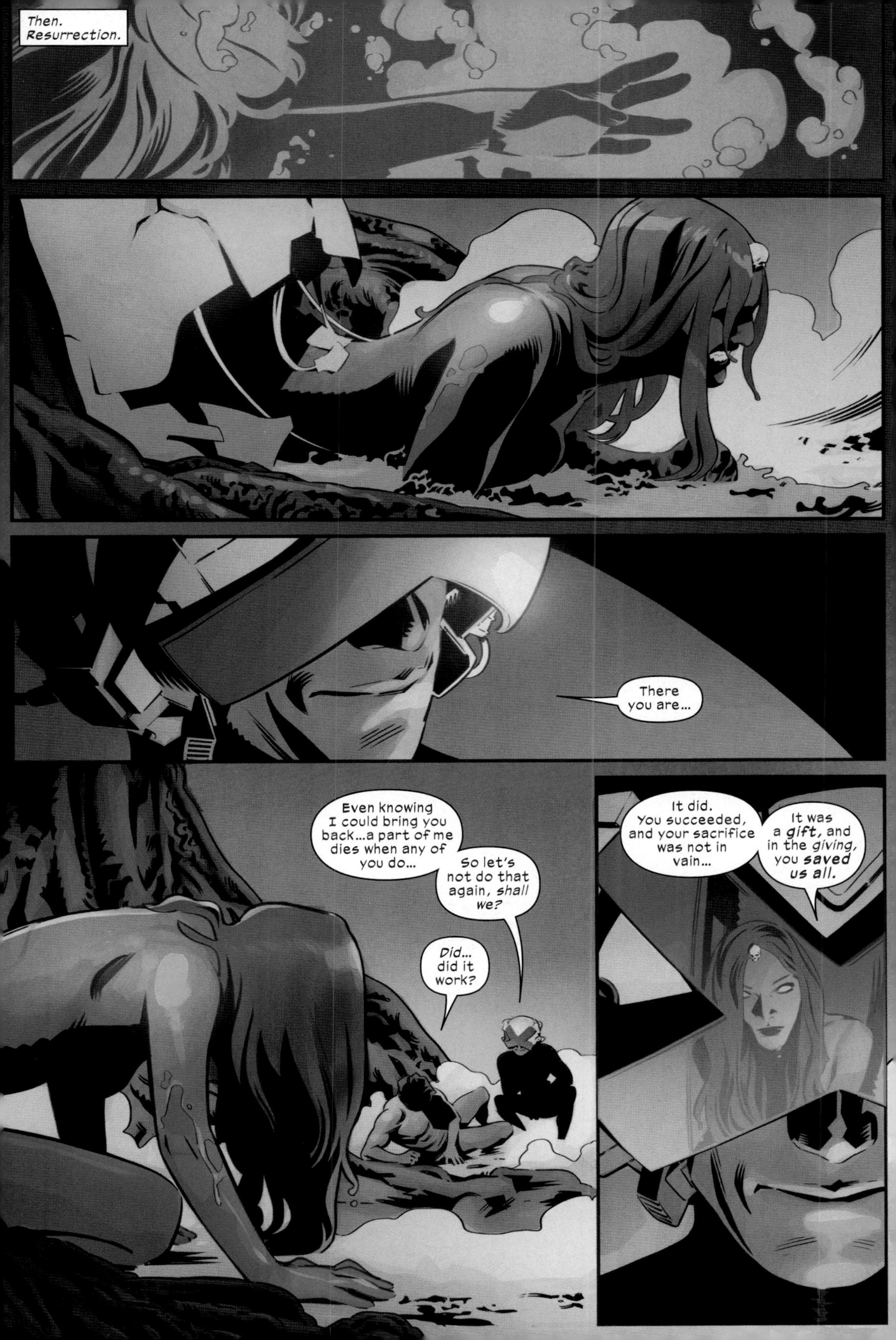
Then. Resurrection.
There you are...
Even knowing I could bring you back...a part of me dies when any of you do...
So let's not do that again, *shall* we?
Did... did it work?
It did. You succeeded, and your sacrifice was not in vain...
It was a ***gift***, and in the *giving*, you ***saved*** ***us all.***

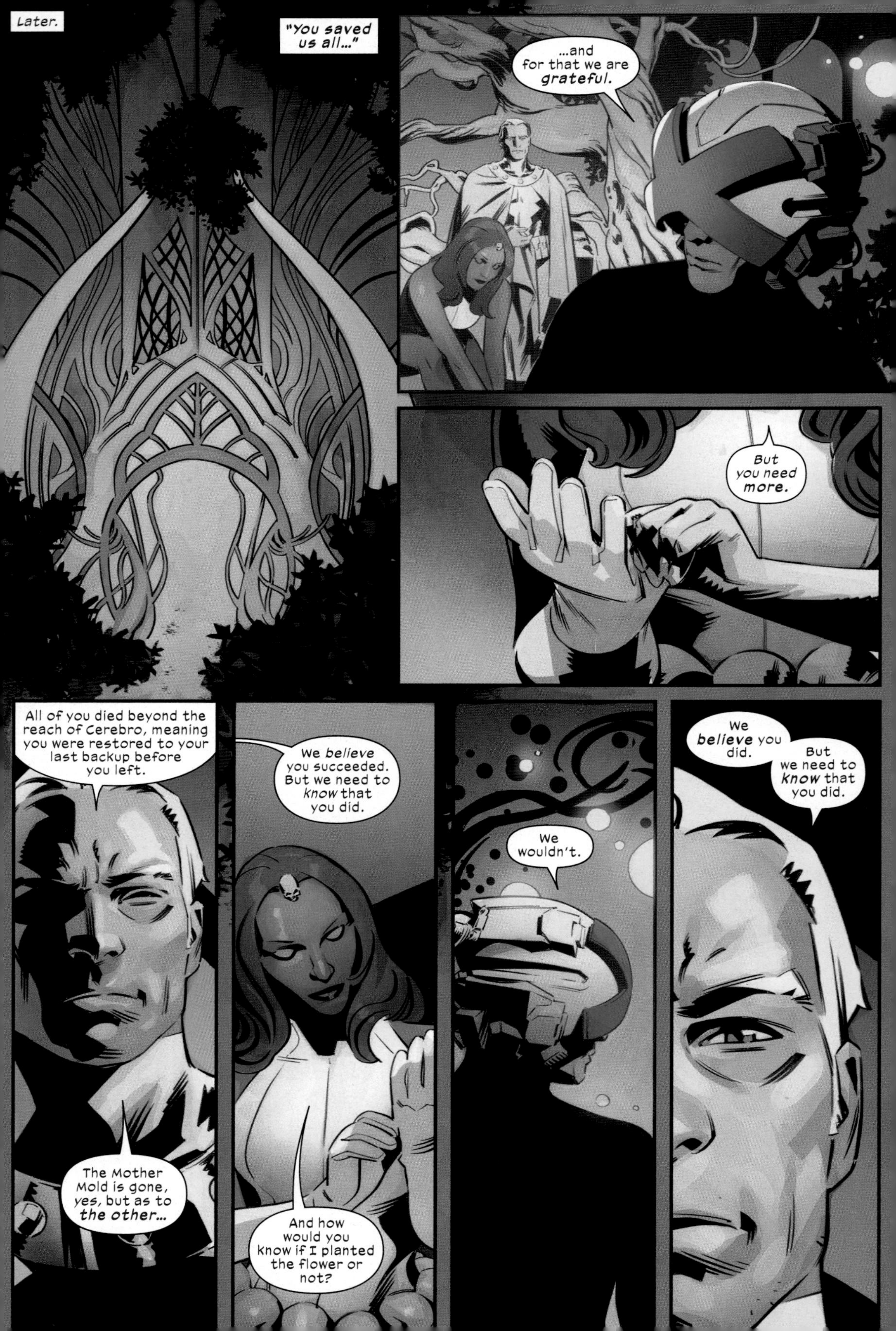
Later.
"You saved us all..."
...and for that we are grateful.
But you need more.
All of you died beyond the reach of Cerebro, meaning you were restored to your last backup before you left.
The Mother Mold is gone, yes, but as to the other...
We believe you succeeded. But we need to know that you did.
And how would you know if I planted the flower or not?
We wouldn't.
We believe you did.
But we need to know that you did.

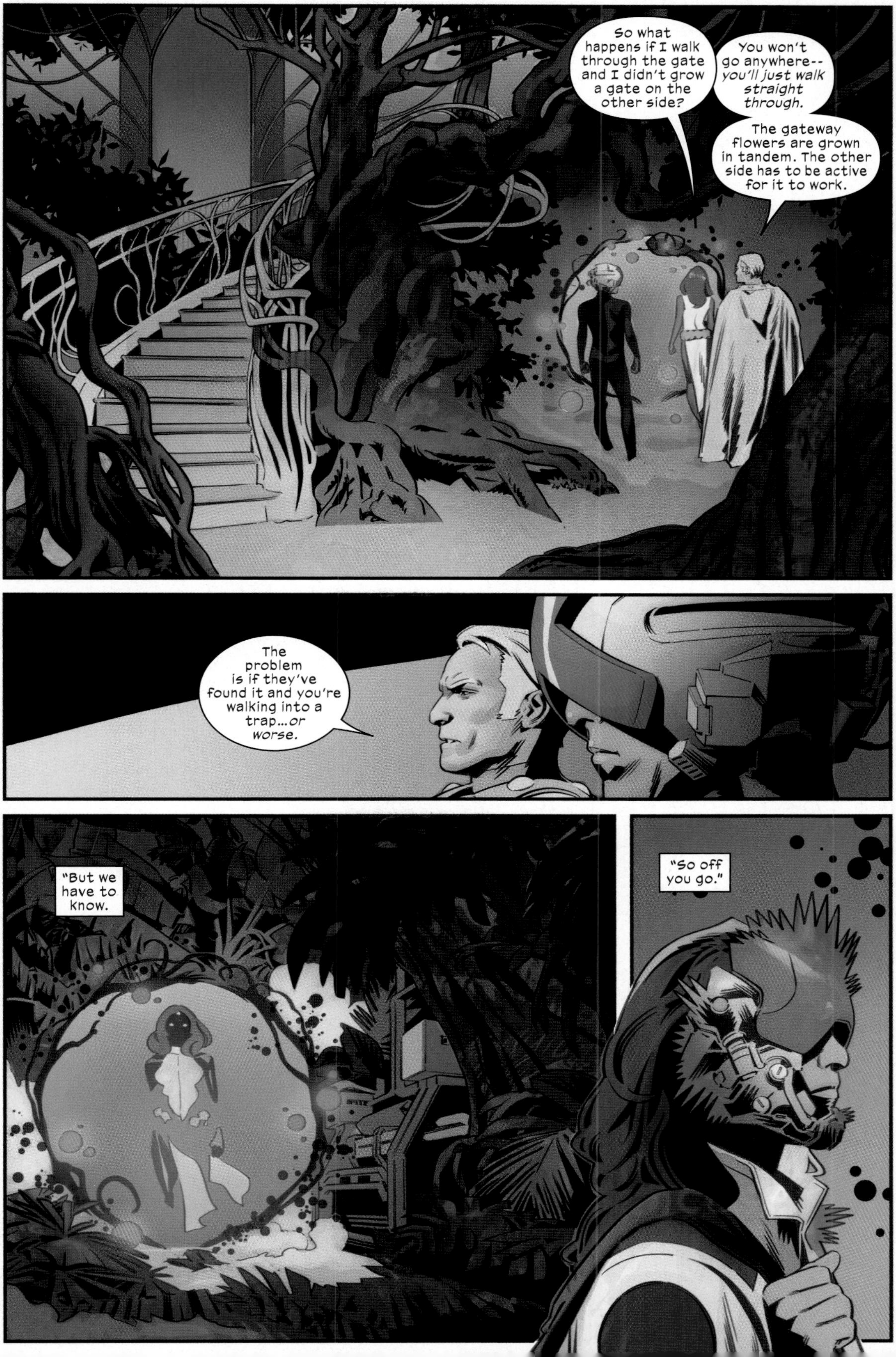
So what happens if I walk through the gate and I didn't grow a gate on the other side?
You won't go anywhere-- *you'll just walk straight through.*
The gateway flowers are grown in tandem. The other side has to be active for it to work.
The problem is if they've found it and you're walking into a trap... *or worse.*
"But we have to know.
"So off you go."

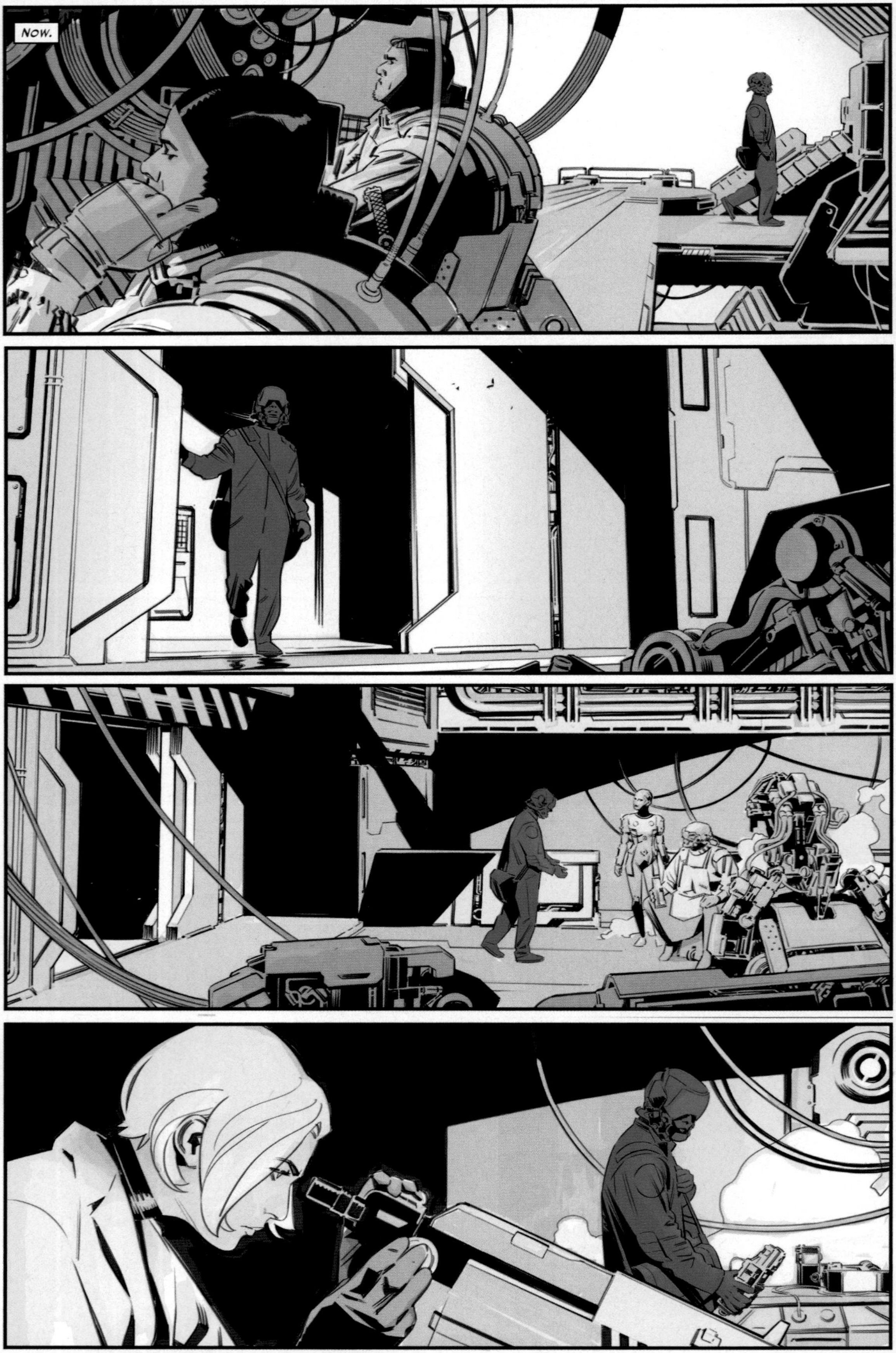
NOW.

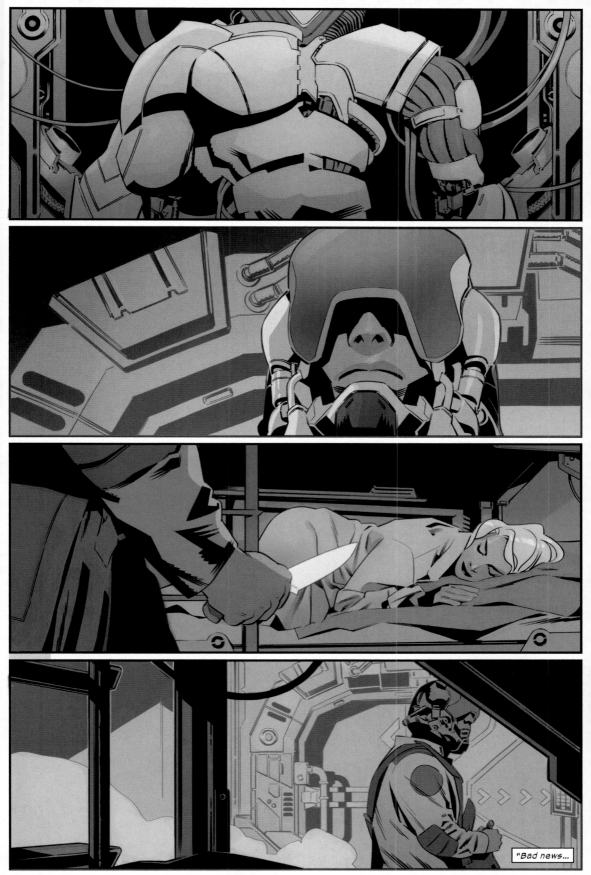

"Bad news...

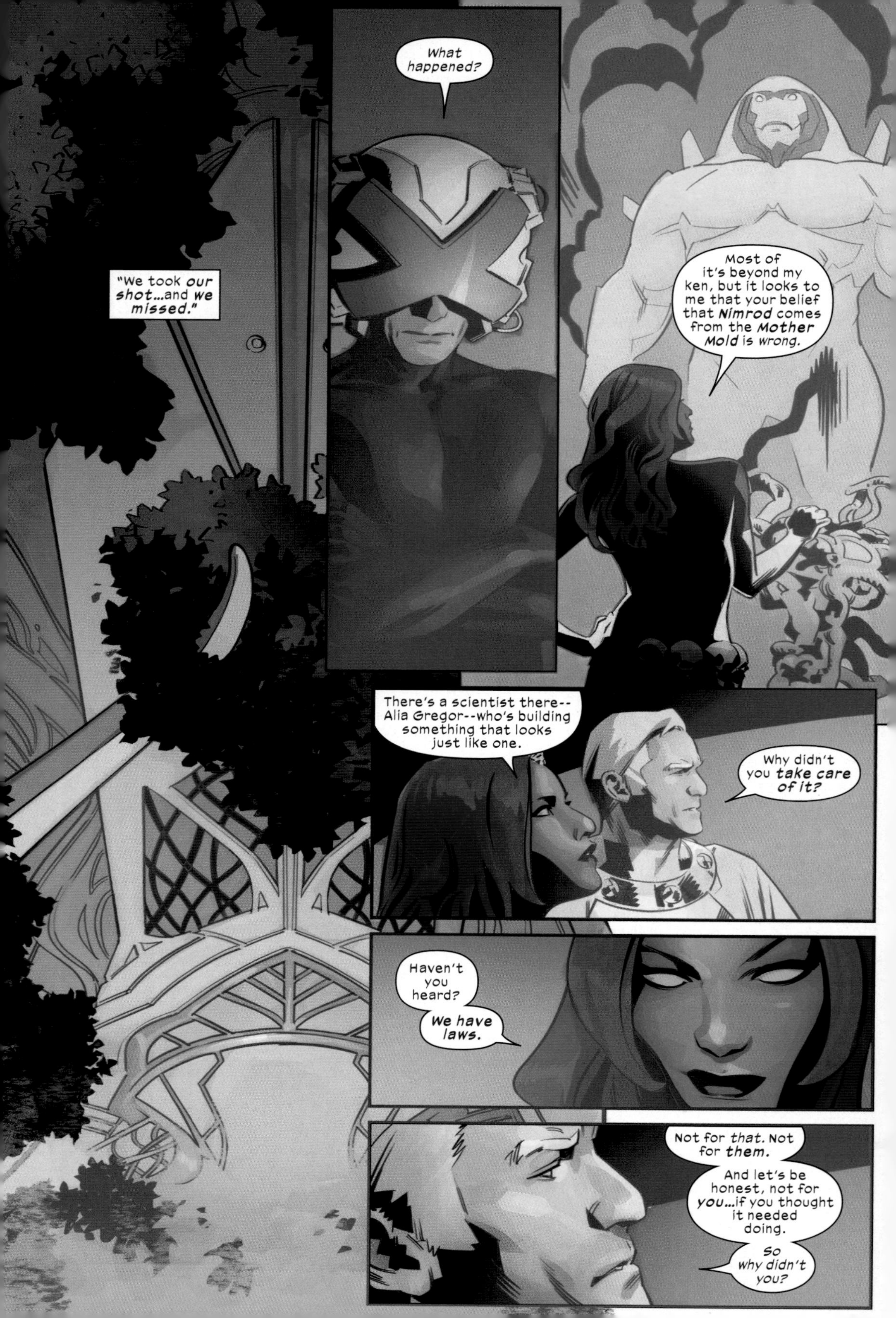

"We took *our* *shot*...and *we* *missed*."
What happened?
Most of it's beyond my ken, but it looks to me that your belief that ***Nimrod*** comes from the ***Mother Mold*** is *wrong*.
There's a scientist there--Alia Gregor--who's building something that looks just like one.
Why didn't you ***take care of it?***
Haven't you heard?
We have laws.
Not for *that*. Not for ***them***.
And let's be honest, not for ***you***...if you thought it needed doing.
So why didn't you?

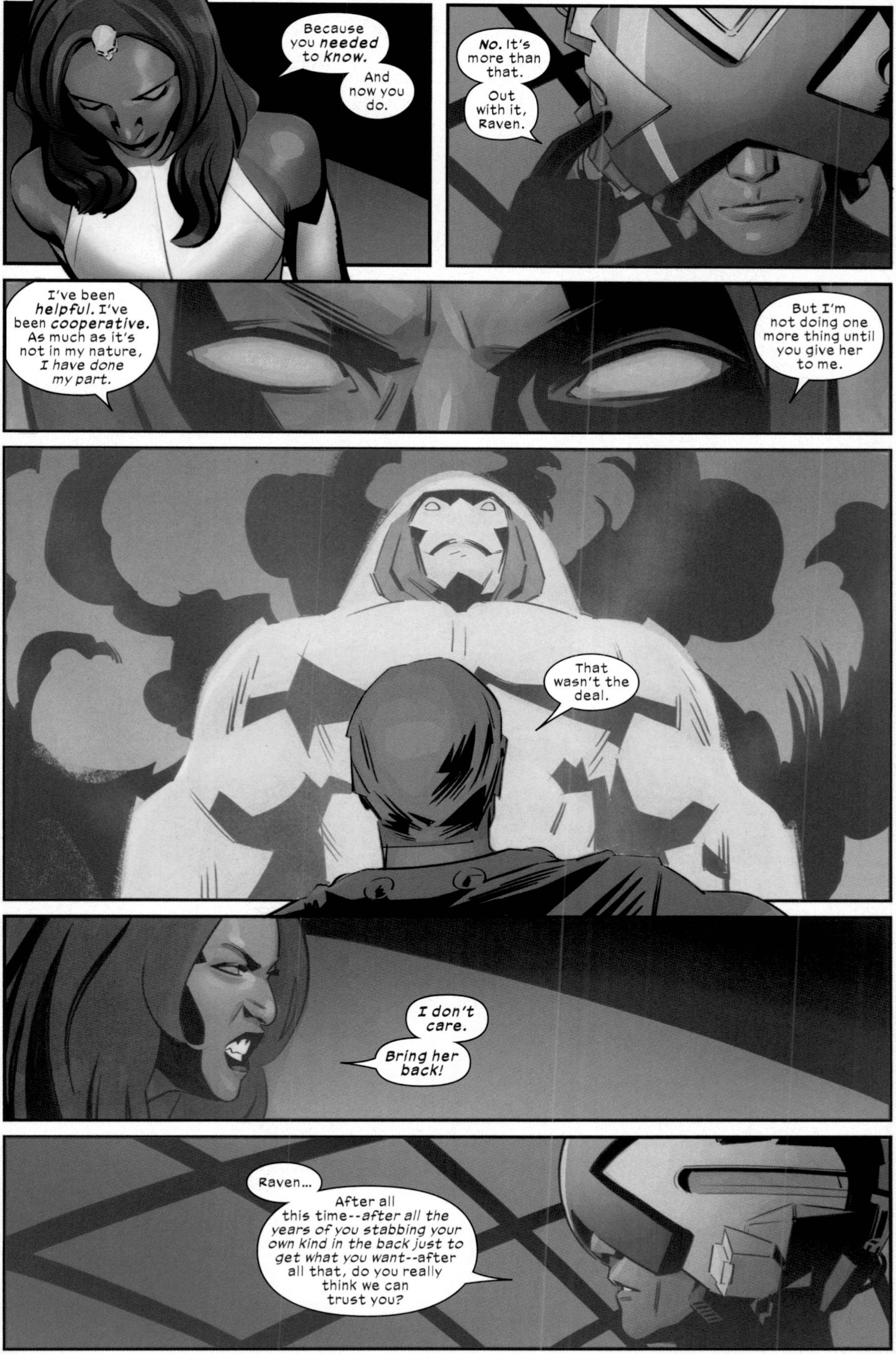
Because you needed to know.
And now you do.
No. It's more than that.
Out with it, Raven.
I've been helpful. I've been cooperative. As much as it's not in my nature, I have done my part.
But I'm not doing one more thing until you give her to me.
That wasn't the deal.
I don't care.
Bring her back!
Raven...
After all this time--after all the years of you stabbing your own kind in the back just to get what you want--after all that, do you really think we can trust you?

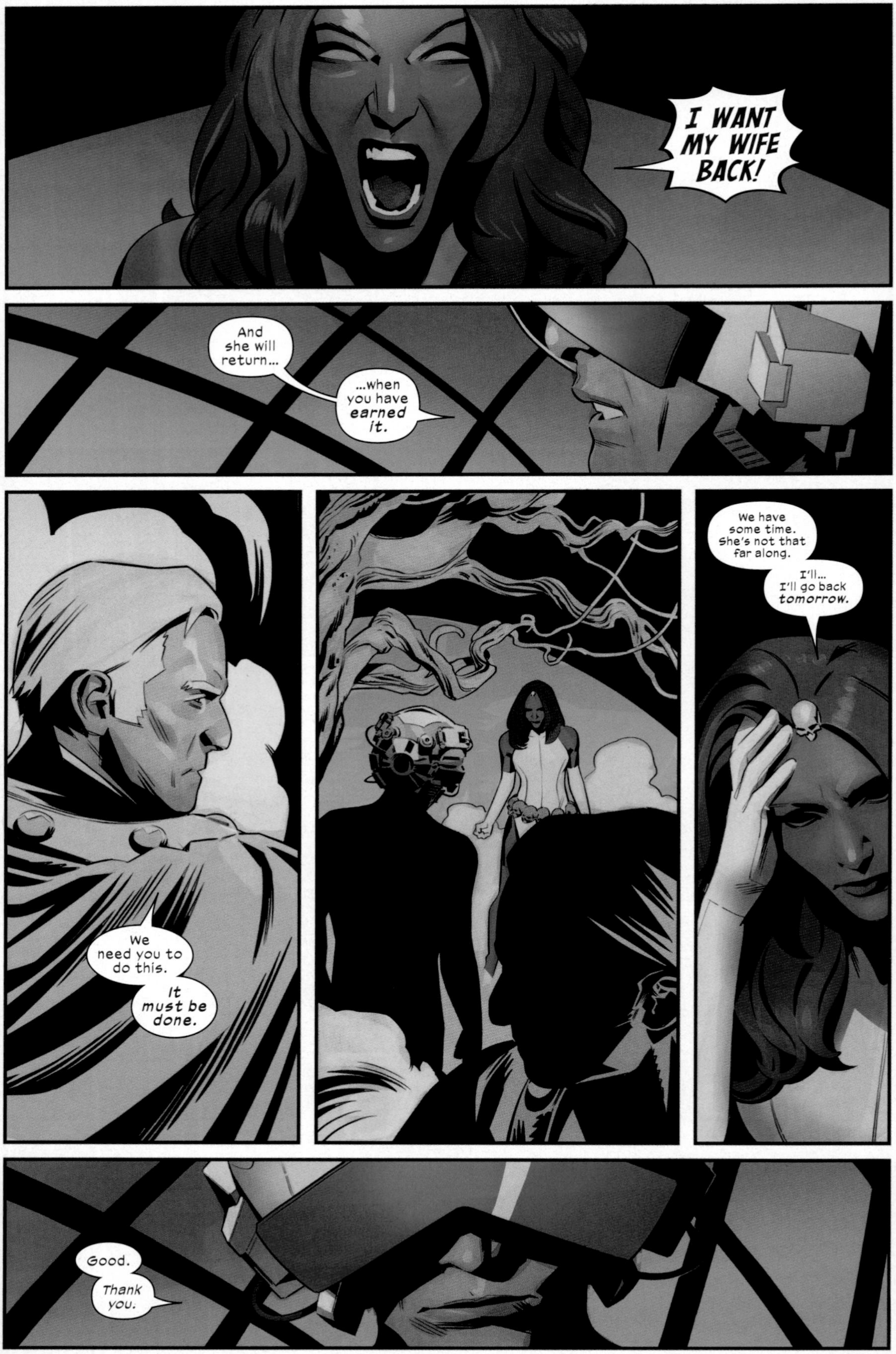
I WANT MY WIFE BACK!
And she will return...
...when you have *earned* it.
We need you to do this.
It must be done.
We have some time. She's not that far along.
I'll... I'll go back *tomorrow.*
Good.
Thank you.

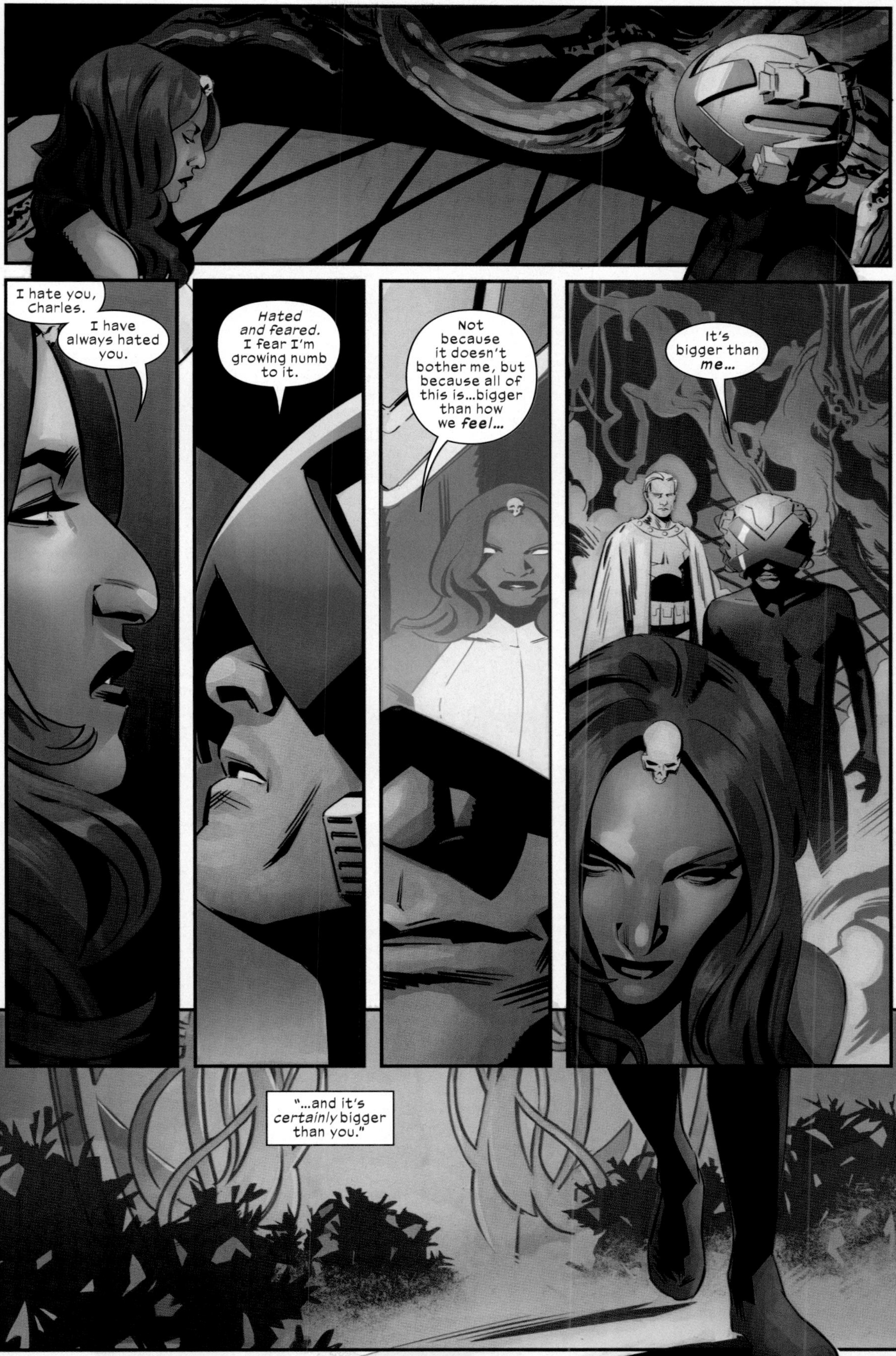
I hate you, Charles.
I have always hated you.
Hated and feared. I fear I'm growing numb to it.
Not because it doesn't bother me, but because all of this is...bigger than how we ***feel...***
It's bigger than ***me...***
"...and it's *certainly* bigger than you."

The Oracle.

"What I'm about to tell you isn't going to sound *believable*, but I promise, it's all *true*.

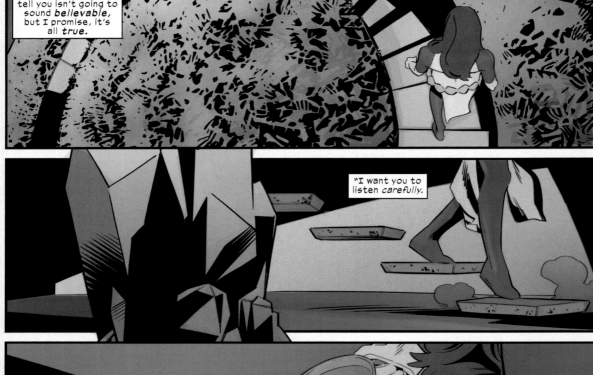

"I want you to listen *carefully*.

"Every word of it."

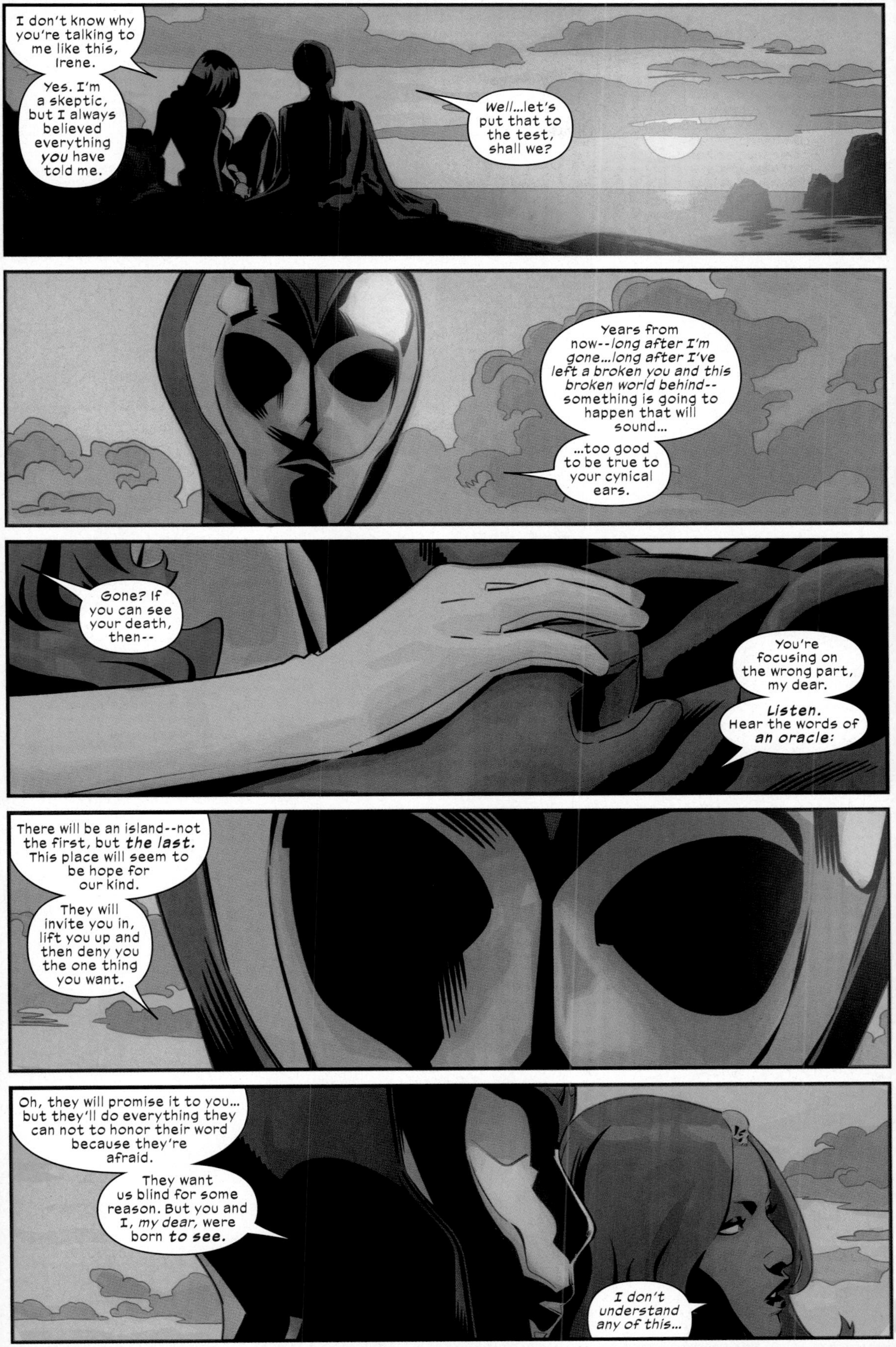
I don't know why you're talking to me like this, Irene.
Yes. I'm a skeptic, but I always believed everything *you* have told me.
Well...let's put that to the test, shall we?
Years from now--*long after I'm gone...long after I've left a broken you and this broken world behind*--something is going to happen that will sound...
...too good to be true to your cynical ears.
Gone? If you can see your death, then--
You're focusing on the wrong part, my dear.
Listen. Hear the words of ***an oracle:***
There will be an island--not the first, but ***the last.*** This place will seem to be hope for our kind.
They will invite you in, lift you up and then deny you the one thing you want.
Oh, they will promise it to you... but they'll do everything they can not to honor their word because they're afraid.
They want us blind for some reason. But you and I, *my dear,* were born ***to see.***
I don't understand any of this...

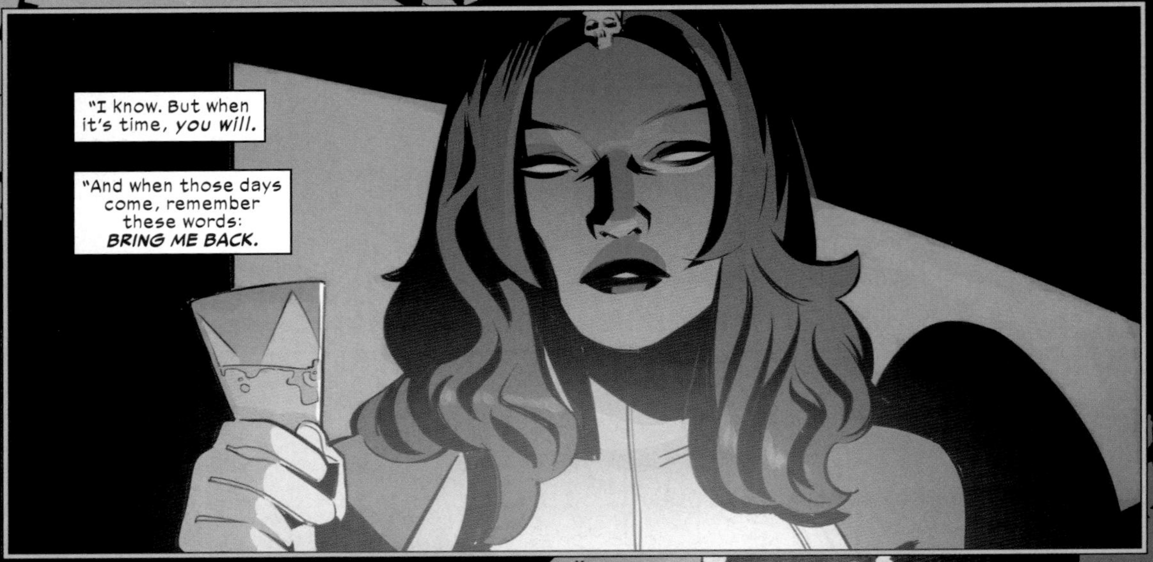
"I know. But when it's time, *you will.*
"And when those days come, remember these words: ***BRING ME BACK.***
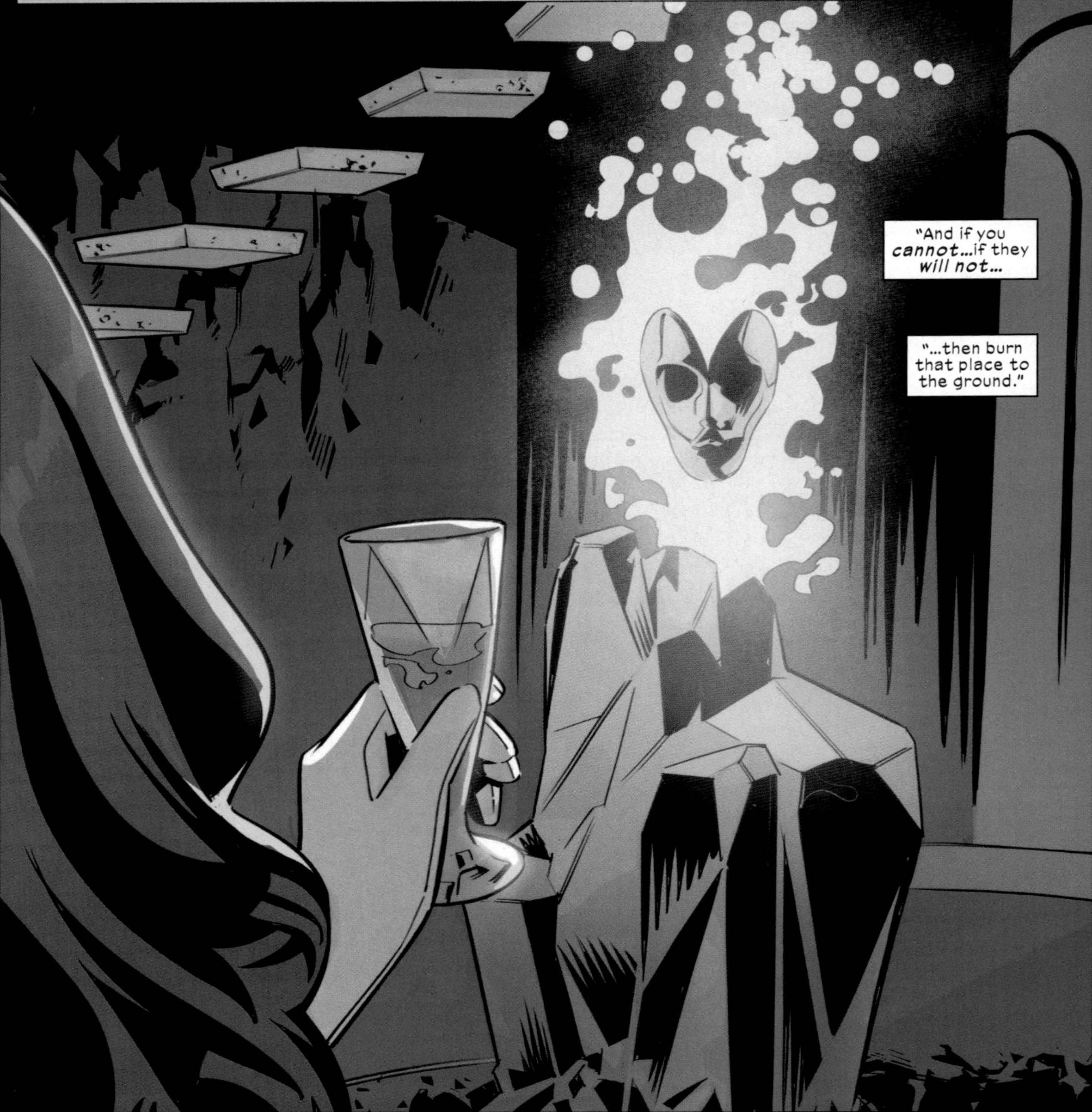
"And if you *cannot*...if they *will not*...
"...then burn that place to the ground."

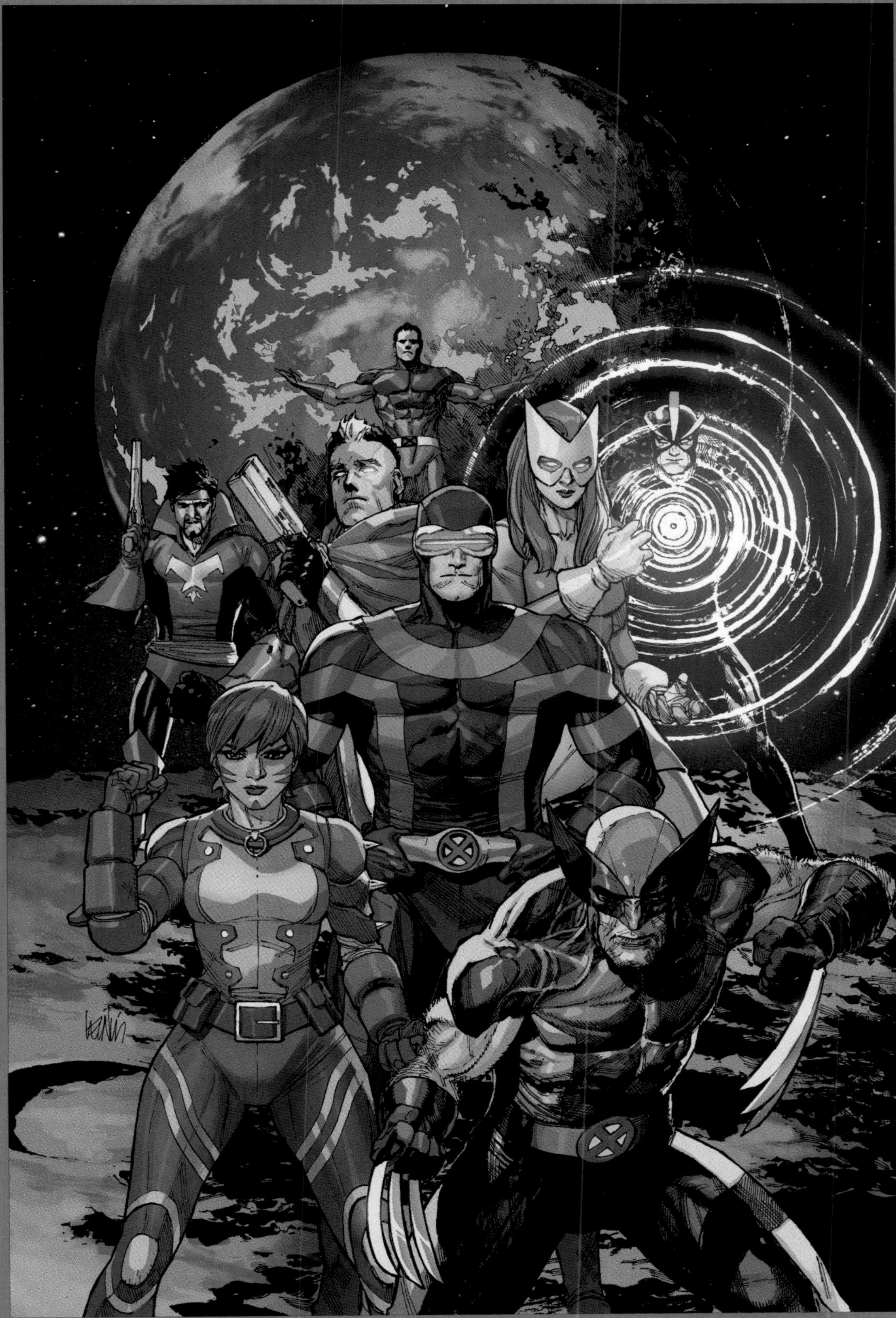

X-Men #1 by Leinil Francis Yu & Sunny Gho

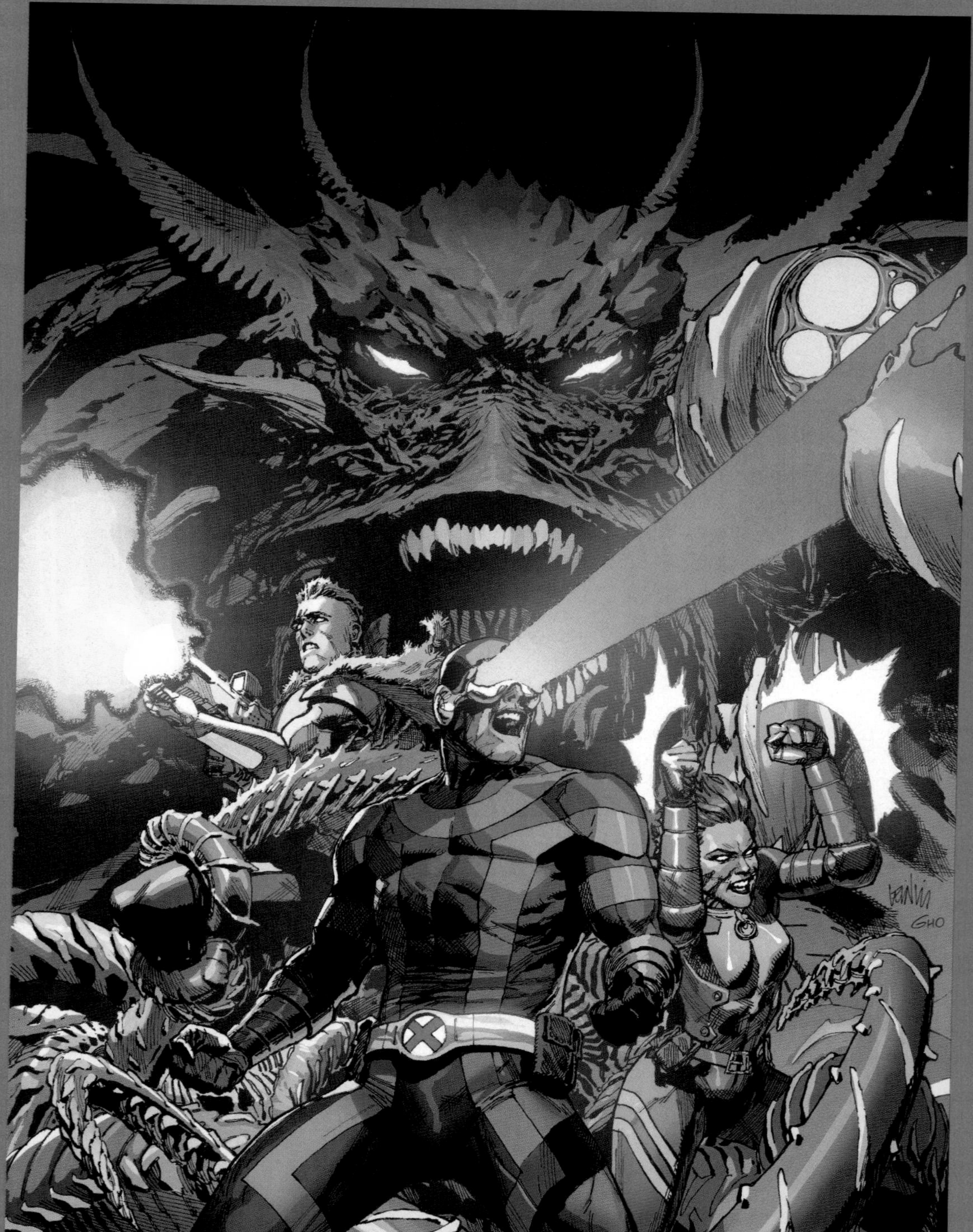

X-Men #2

by Leinil Francis Yu & Sunny Gho

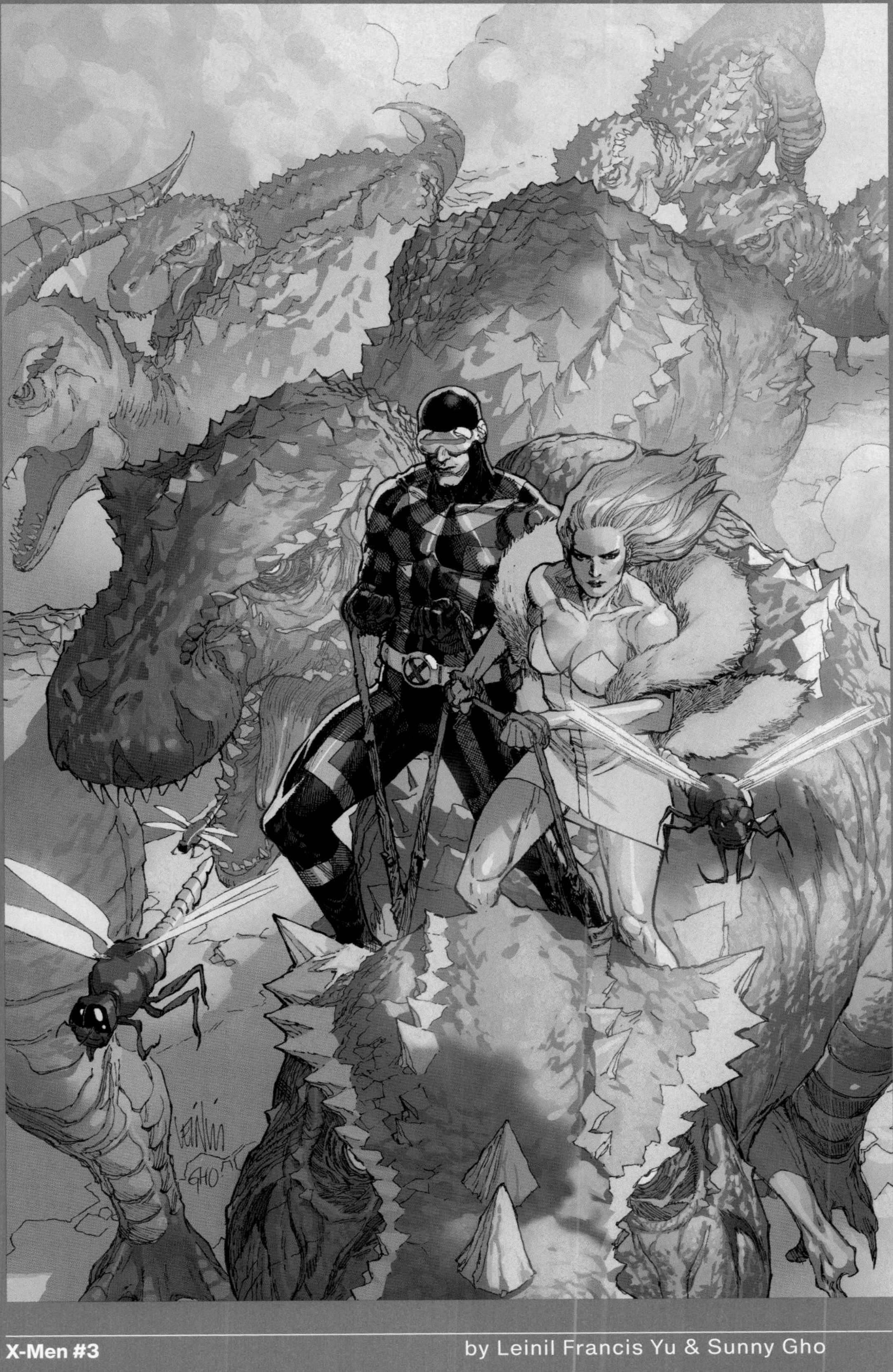
LEINIL
GHO

X-Men #3 by Leinil Francis Yu & Sunny Gho

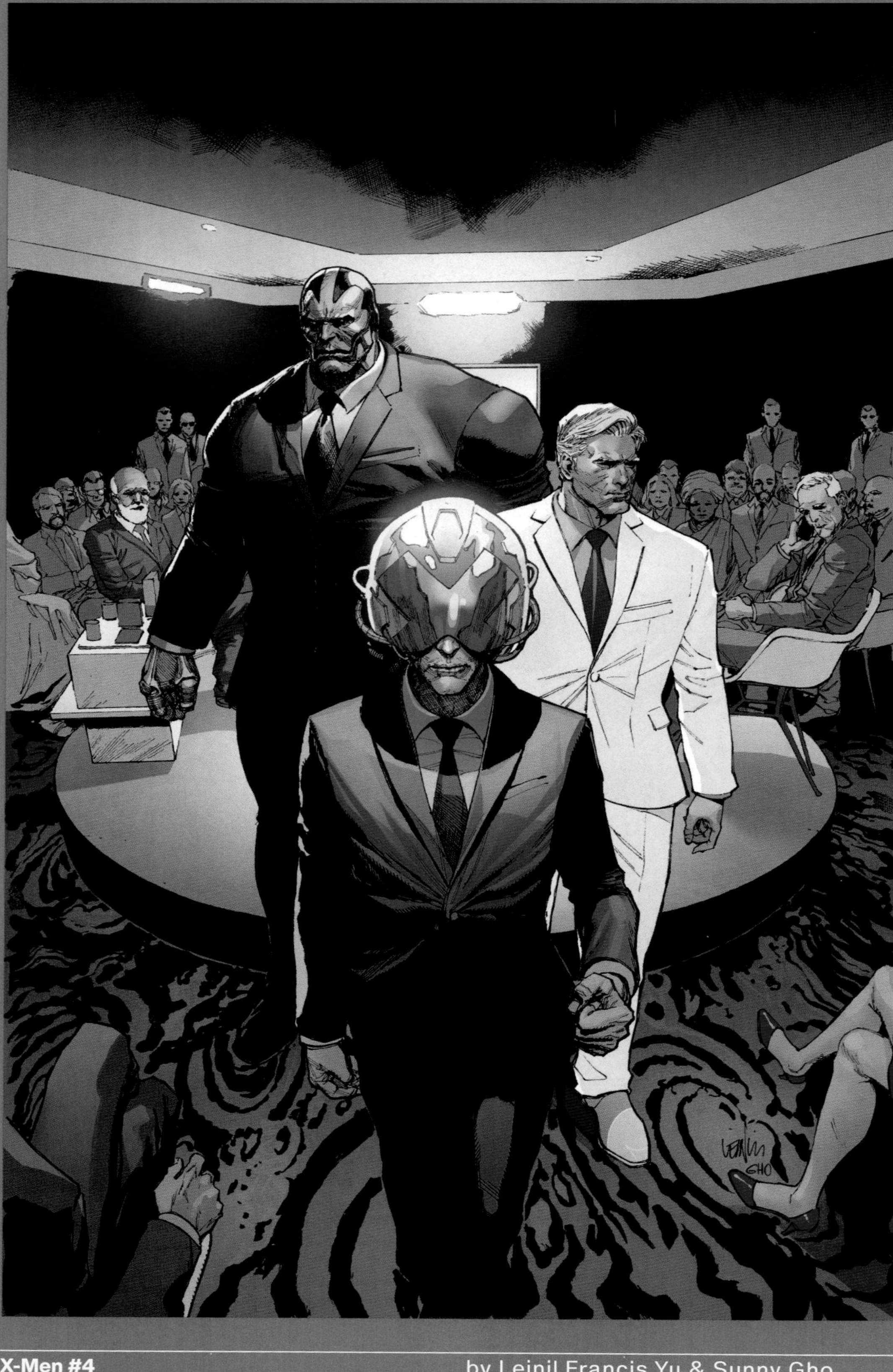
LEINIL
GHO

X-Men #4 by Leinil Francis Yu & Sunny Gho

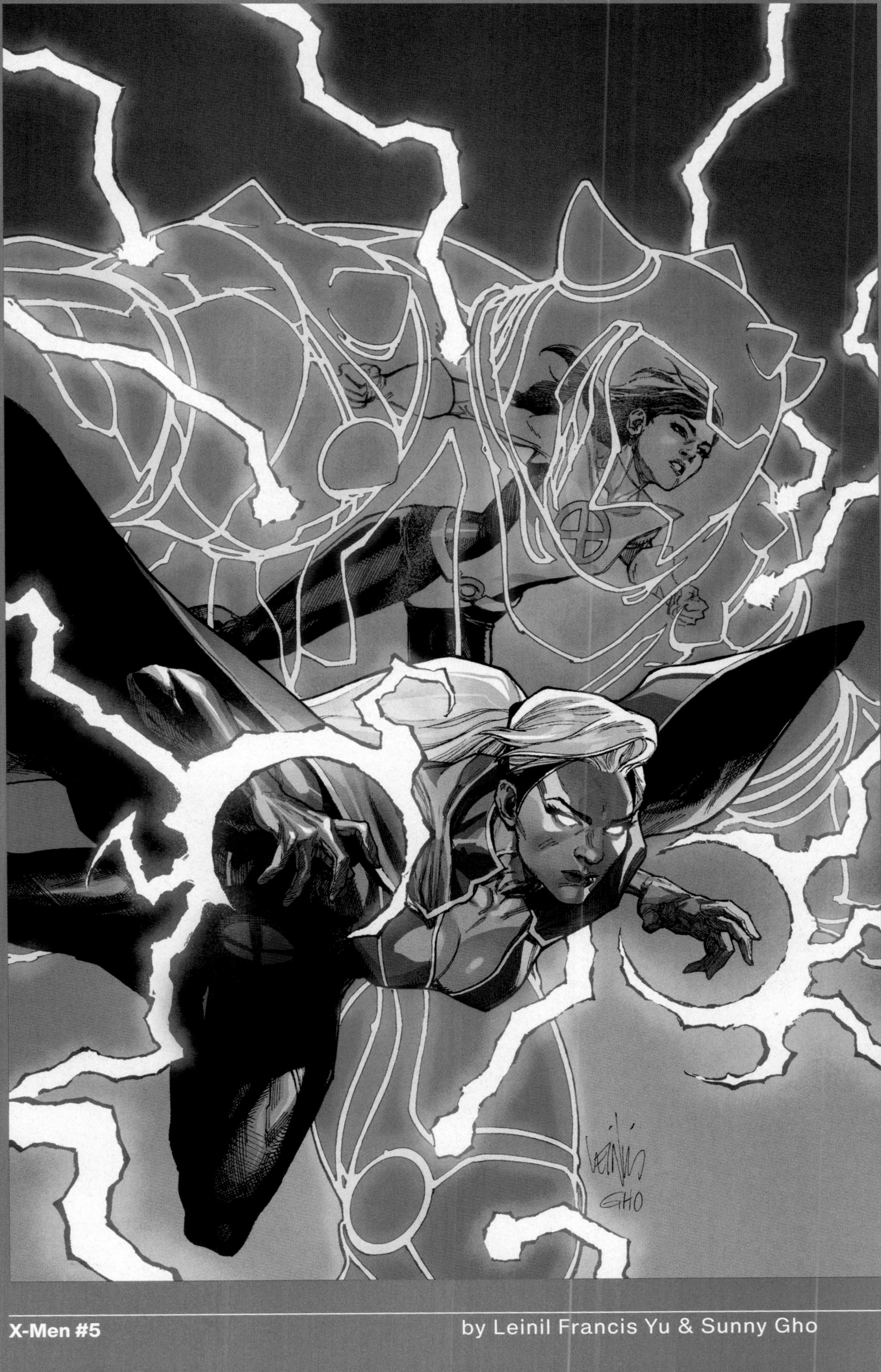
LEINIL
GHO

X-Men #5

by Leinil Francis Yu & Sunny Gho

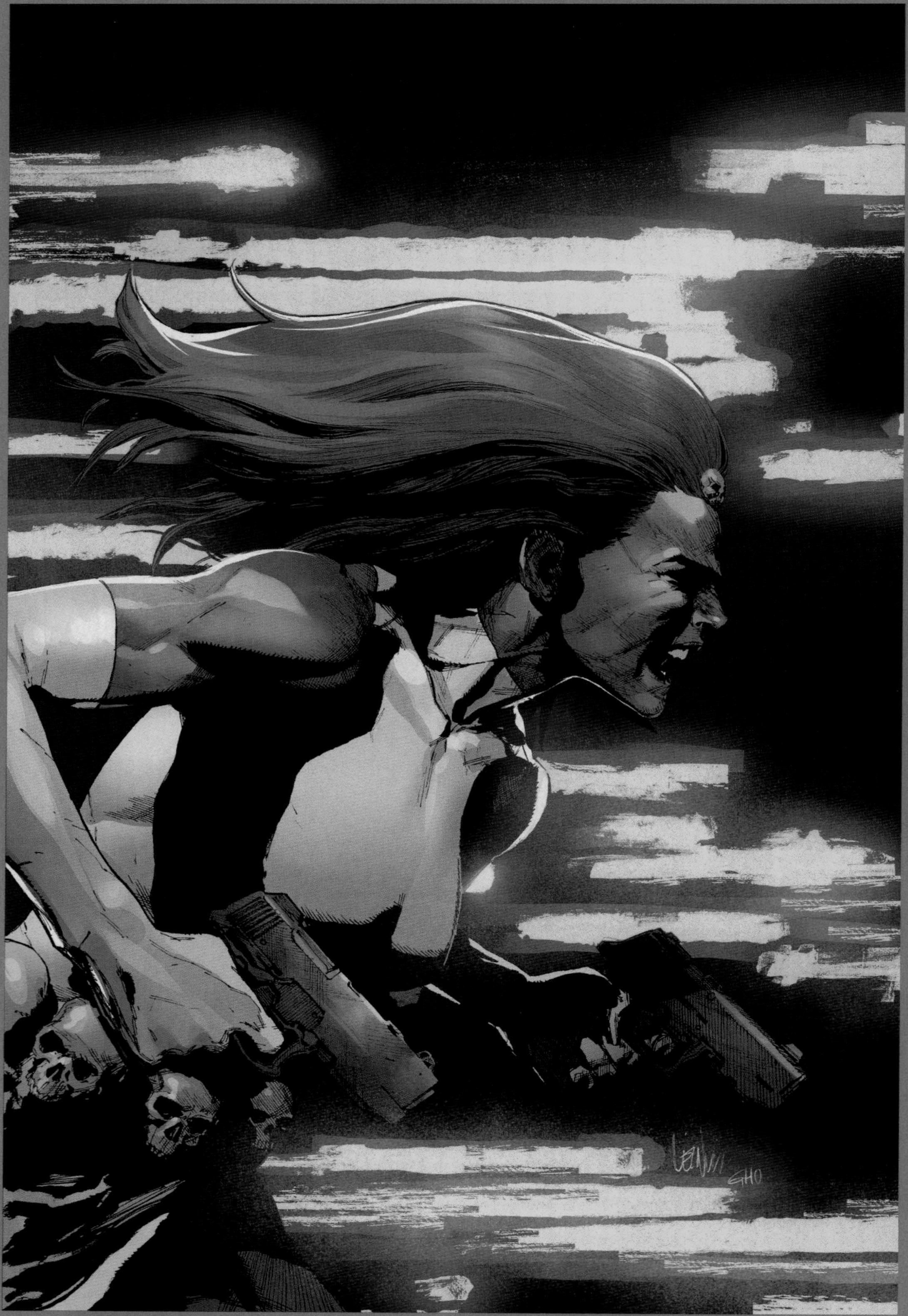

X-Men #6 by Leinil Francis Yu & Sunny Gho

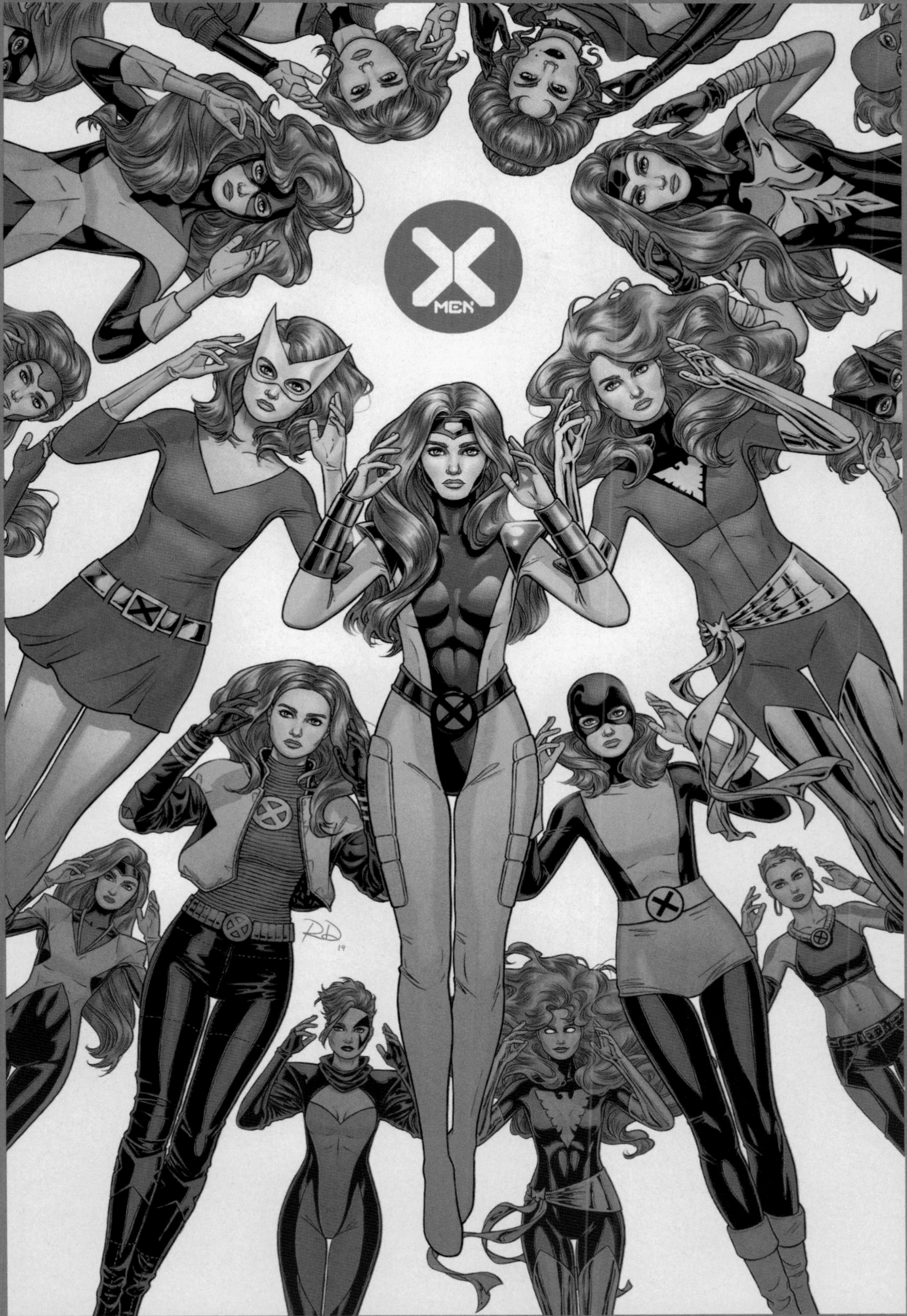
X
MEN

X-Men #1 Variant by Russell Dauterman

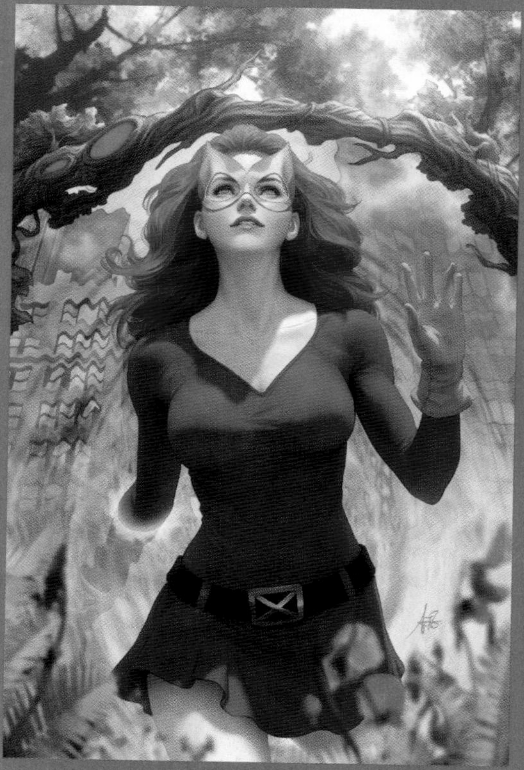

X-Men #1 Variant
by Stanley "Artgerm" Lau

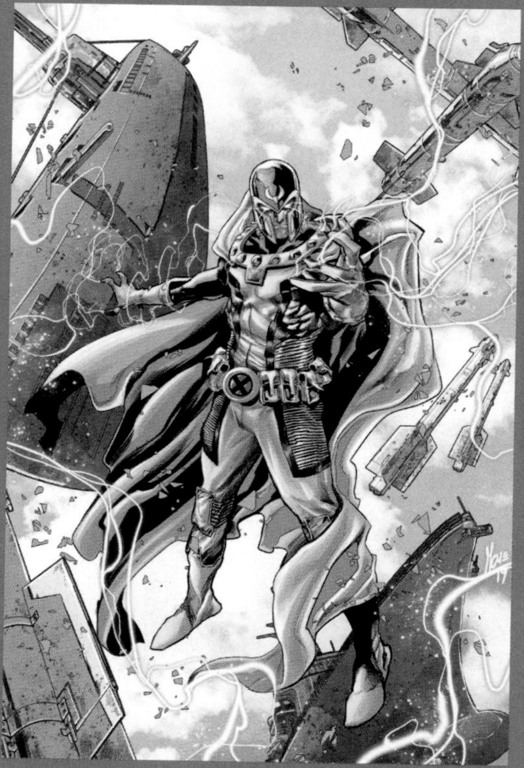

X-Men Young Guns #1 Variant
by Marco Checchetto

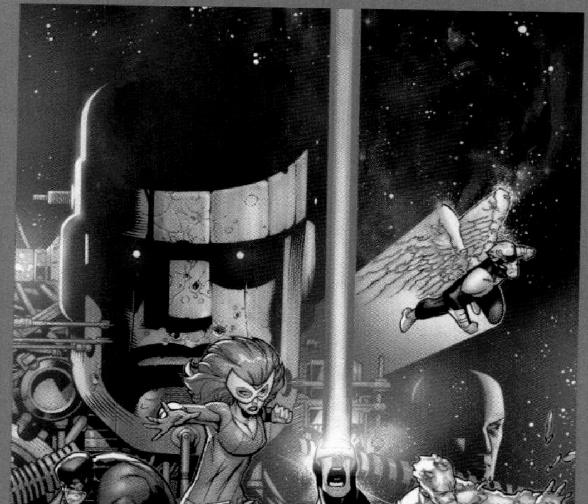

X-Men #1 Hidden Gem Variant
by Chris Bachalo, Tim Townsend & Edgar Delgado

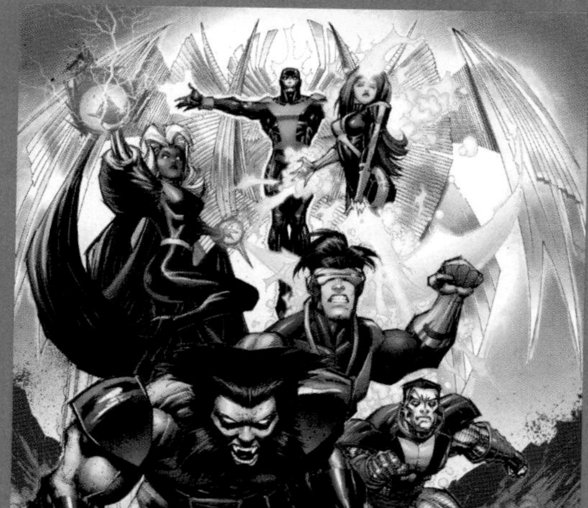

X-Men #1 Variant
by Whilce Portacio & Chris Sotomayor

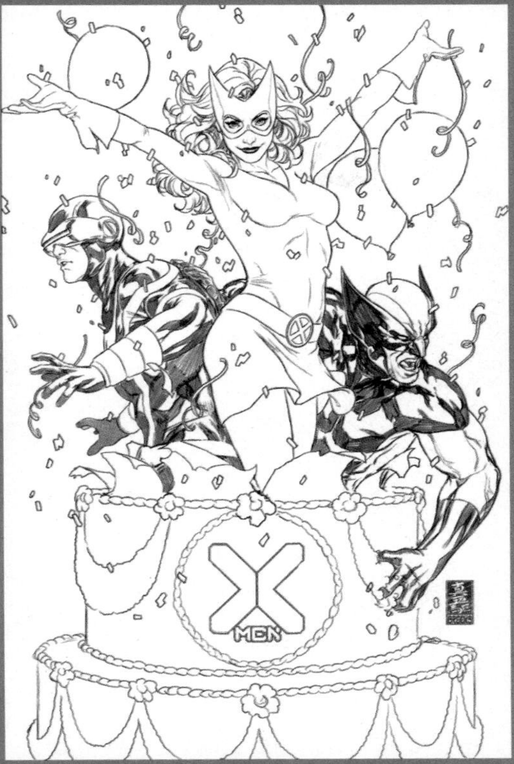
X
MEN

X-Men #1 Party Sketch Variant
by Mark Brooks

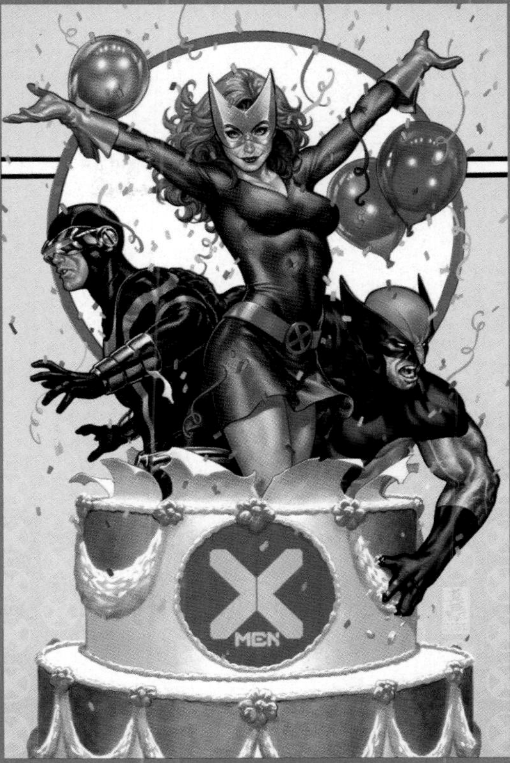
X
MEN

X-Men #1 Party Variant
by Mark Brooks

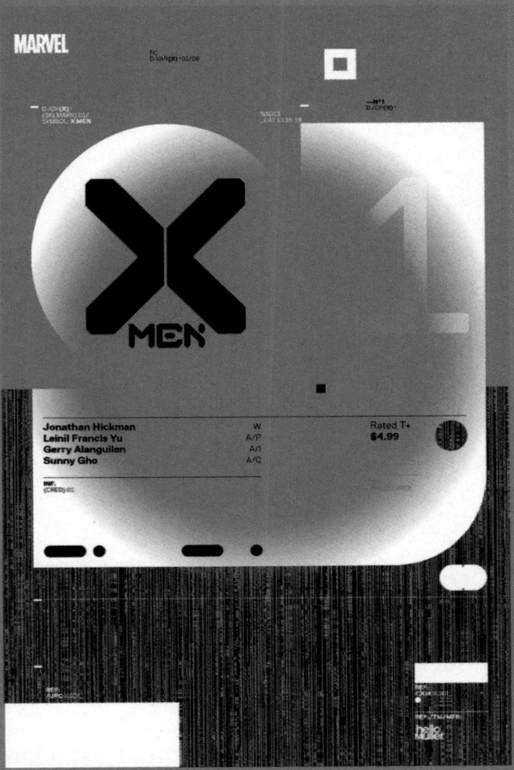
MARVEL
X
MEN
1
Jonathan Hickman W
Leinil Francis Yu A/P
Gerry Alanguilan A/I
Sunny Gho A/C
Rated T+
$4.99
hello
Muller

X-Men #1 Design Variant
by Tom Muller

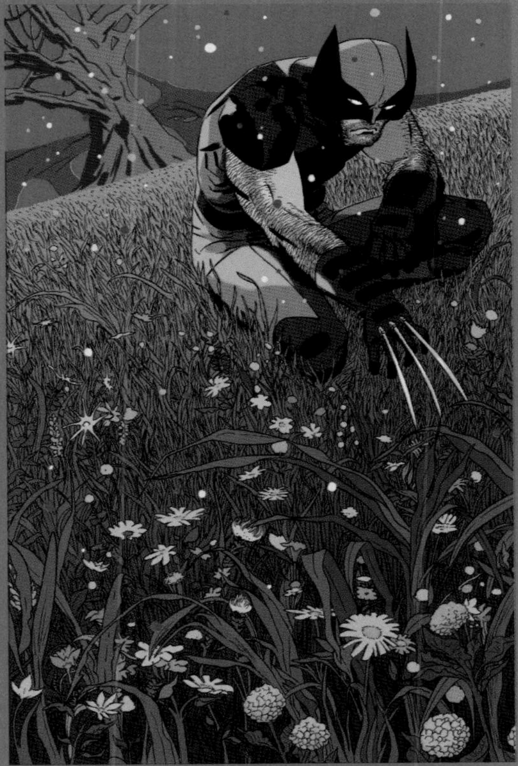

X-Men #2 Variant
by Marcos Martin

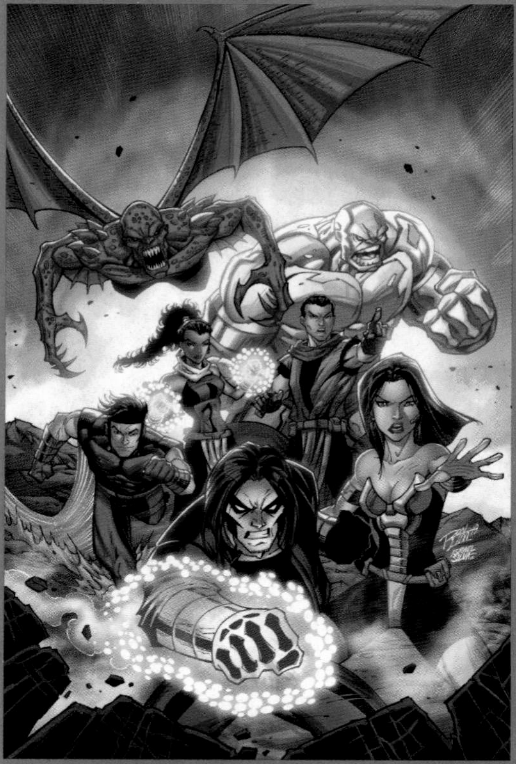

X-Men #2 2099 Variant
by Ron Lim & Israel Silva

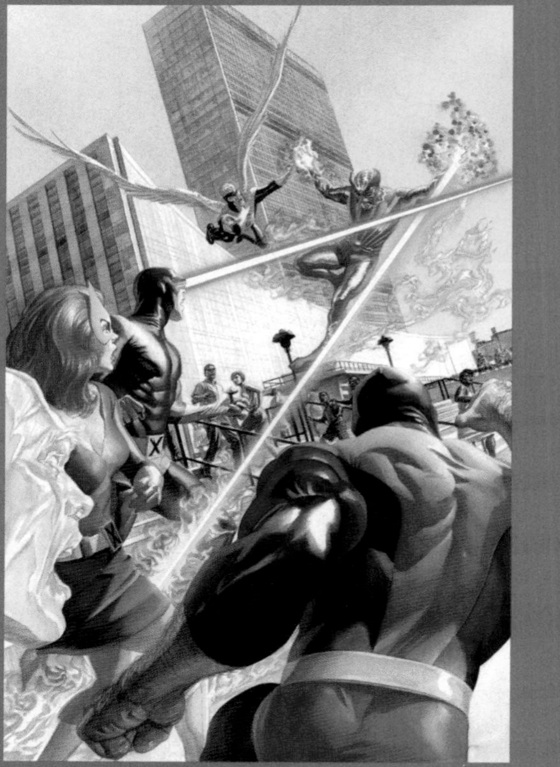

X-Men #3 Marvels 25th Anniversary Variant
by Alex Ross

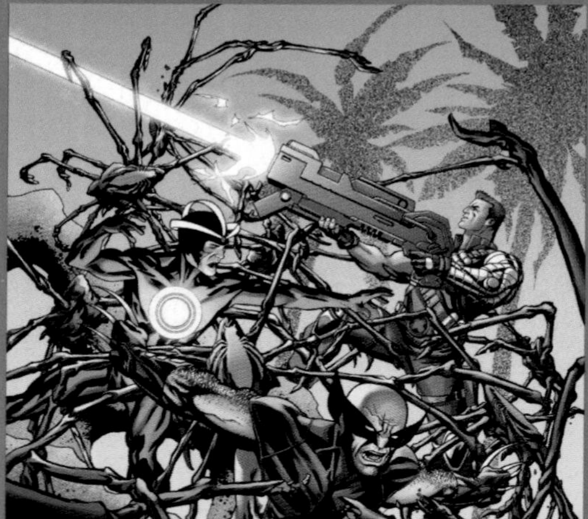

X-Men #3 Venom Island Variant
by Mike McKone & Rachelle Rosenberg

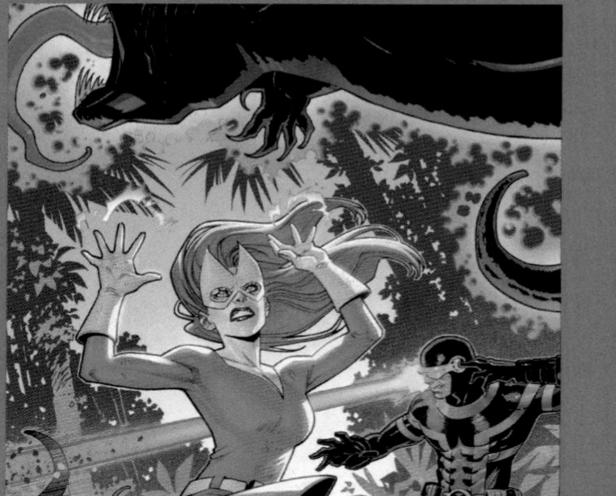

X-Men #4 Venom Island Variant
by Belén Ortega & Jesus Aburtov

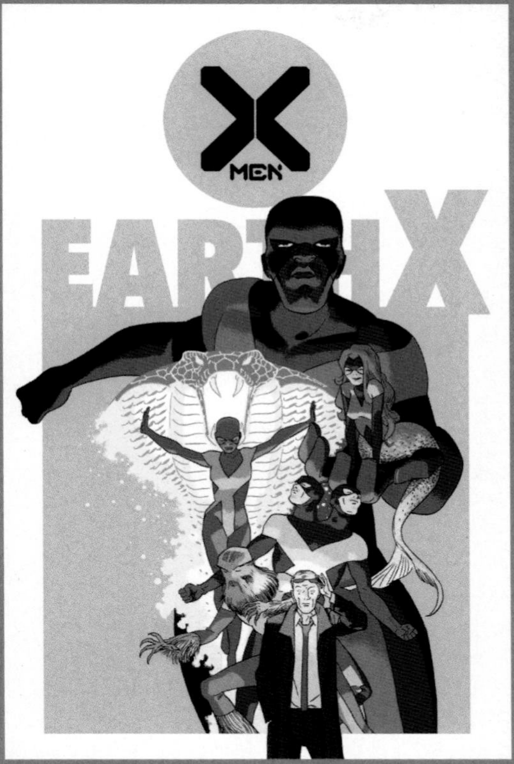
X
MEN

X-Men #5 Marvels X Variant
by Marcos Martin

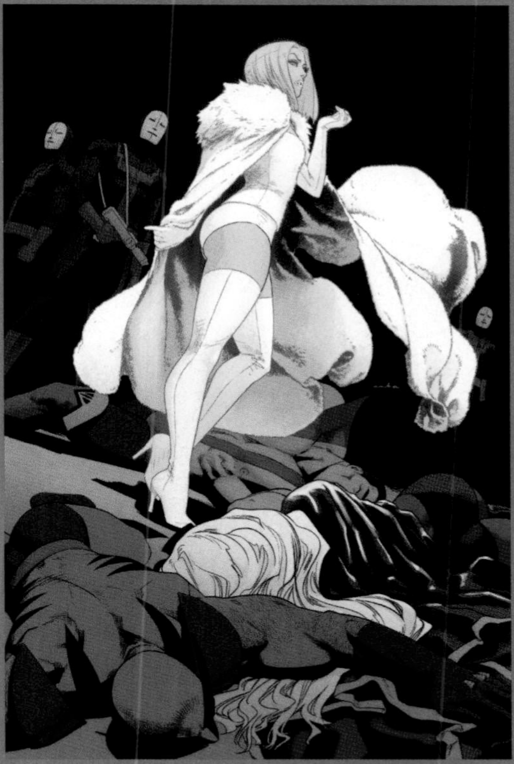

X-Men #5 Dark Phoenix Saga 40th Anniversary Variant by Kris Anka

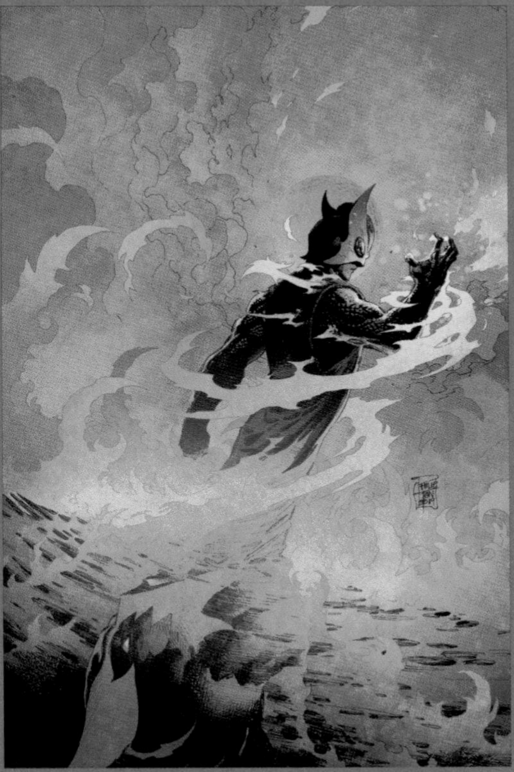

X-Men #6 Marvels X Variant
by Philip Tan & Dave McCaig

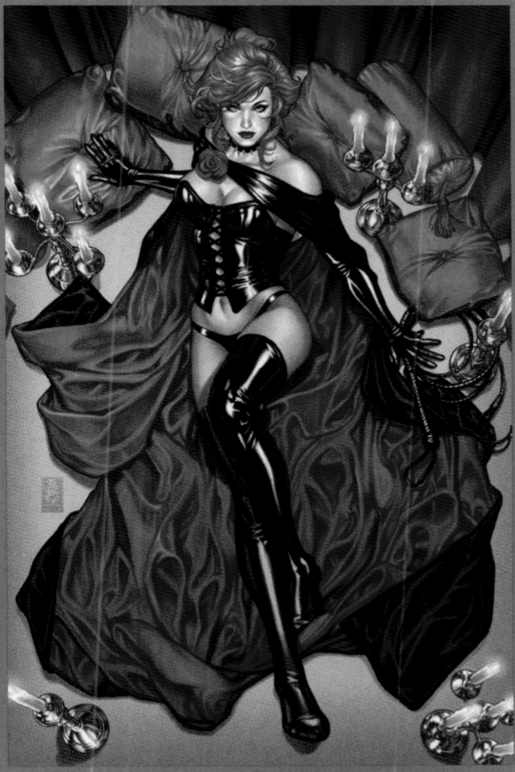

X-Men #6 Dark Phoenix Saga 40th Anniversary Variant by Mark Brooks